AF594534

DRAW ANYTHING

ARTHUR ZAIDENBERG

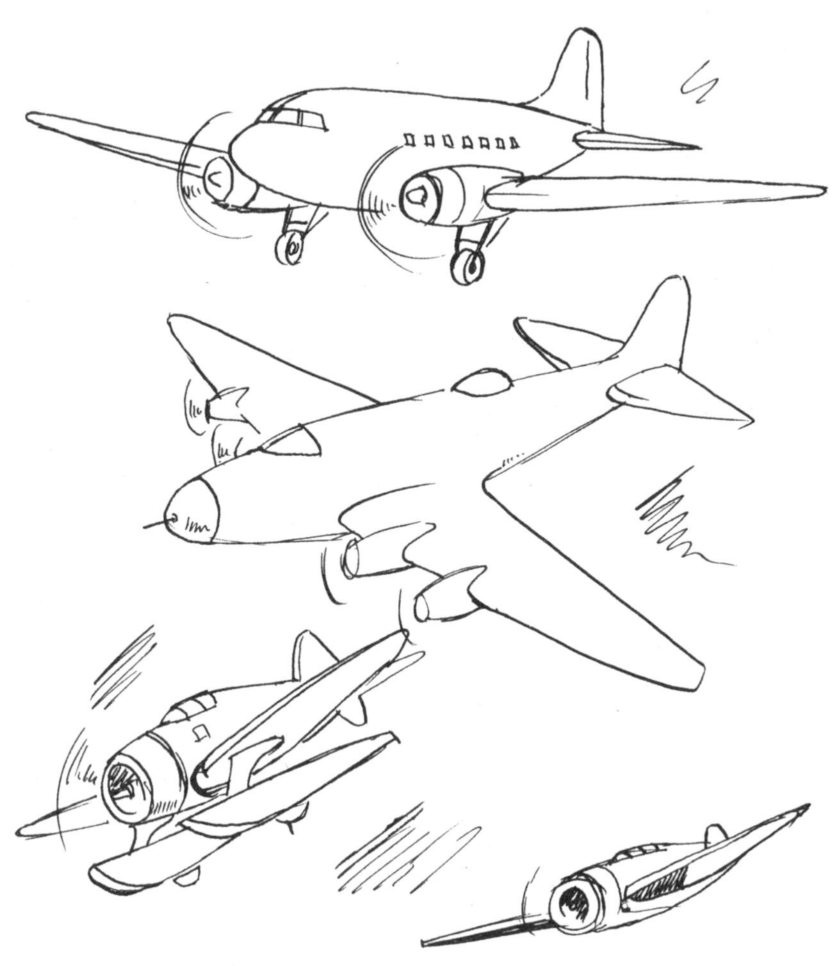

DOVER PUBLICATIONS, INC.
Mineola, New York

Bibliographical Note

This Dover edition, first published in 2009, is an unabridged republication of *The Draw Anything Book*, originally published in 1950 by Harper & Brothers, New York.

Library of Congress Cataloging-in-Publication Data

Zaidenberg, Arthur, 1908–1990.
[Draw anything book]
Draw anything / Arthur Zaidenberg. — Dover ed.
p. cm.
Originally published: The draw anything book. New York : Harper & Brothers, 1950.
ISBN-13: 978-0-486-47400-7
ISBN-10: 0-486-47400-3
1. Drawing—Study and teaching. I. Title.

NC730.Z35 2009
741.2—dc22

2009009002

Printed in Canada
47400305 2025
www.doverpublications.com

Introduction

The extraordinary growth of interest in drawing and painting and the large number of students of art testify to the fact that the graphic arts need not be restricted to "professionals" as was the case until comparatively recent times. The amateur—and the word is used in its best sense, i.e., "one who loves"—has come into his own with the stimulating advent of what is loosely called "modern art." Because of the greater call upon the intuitive and less stress upon highly developed technical skills which were the indispensable preamble to the practice of "academic art," students of modern art are able to approach the creative stages of drawing and painting without a long apprenticeship in the somber halls of the old art institutes.

It is not implied here that modern art is "easy" or that the creation of good drawings and paintings does not call for as serious and intense an approach as did the works of previous eras. Respect for the tools and techniques of the craft and mental and emotional integrity are still basic requirements. However, the path is clearer and the means of expression are more direct for the modern student.

As the study of drawing and painting becomes less a highly technical craft and more a direct means of free expression, the teaching methods have become less and less intrusive upon the personality of the student, and the teacher has in most cases become the guide to simplification and an advisor in the search for essentials.

The title of this book, *The Draw Anything Book*, is not intended to convey the impression that the student, in learning how to draw all things in the same manner as indicated here, no longer needs to study drawing. Nor is it claimed that the methods and systems employed here are the sole or best ones. One can no more translate drawing into set, immutable methodology, its linear and tonal variations bounded by rules, than one can limit the explorative possibilities of the eye and the imaginative vistas of the mind. Drawing, like speech, encompasses the range of human statement, its power and subtlety dictated only by the co-ordinative aptitude of the mental and physical. Like a language, one may learn its grammar and conventions of terminology. A primer for approach may be acquired and, with practice, a dexterity of manual and visual analysis may be evolved to aid the beginner in his early stages of development. Beyond this stage, again as in the use of spoken language, the highly personal equation of the individual enters and the departures from restricting styles and methods are as innumerable and variable in quality and strength as are the spoken statements of individuals.

Without a basic primer a student of the drawing language may stammer and struggle with drawing idioms. With it, while carefully avoiding clichés, he may establish a firm point from which to make his own art statements.

In this dictionary of drawing most of the objects dealt with are of a generic nature in that they are the basic forms of the most common species of each form of life, still life or manufactured object.

The instruction method used here is to reduce each object to its simplest structural essence and build from that point a simulation of the three dimensional in terms of the flat, two dimensional graphic and thereby symbolize the "real" object. A simulation or a symbolization are all that the artist can hope for and all that he should desire to accomplish.

The "realist" in art is, at best, one who evolves a facsimile, a representational image, one which conveys most of the physical surface truths of the object drawn. Beyond a certain point even the most expert realist must trust to symbols and suggestion, and that is where art begins and the creative elements enter.

Arthur Zaidenberg

July, 1950

How to Use This Book

There are in this book several thousand drawings of figures, animals, and objects in various positions and in various actions.

In most cases the drawing was made with the intent to show the basic structure in its simplest elements. In many other cases a relatively "finished" drawing is used as a base for display of a costume or to demonstrate a game or a form of work.

The two major purposes of this book are each served by the above two types of drawings. The first purpose is to demonstrate how to construct, in drawing, the figure or object desired, utilizing as a working drawing the "scaffold" forms shown here. These scaffold forms are the essential shapes, reduced to their salient elements, firm bases upon which may be added the details and techniques desired by, and peculiar to each artist.

It is not suggested that the method of reduction to basic structures herein employed is the only possible approach to analysis of a figure or object to be drawn. It is merely suggested here that these basic forms are those which this author has found adequate upon which to build and that the student may employ a similar method without jeopardizing his individual viewpoint or compromising his originality.

The second purpose of this book is to serve as a source of information and research, inasmuch as an attempt has been made to assemble drawing data on virtually every species of figure, animal, and object which the art student may be called upon to draw and which may not be available to him in the original, or if available, not in a position to be drawn.

Many students and professional illustrators collect a voluminous "morgue," a file of clippings from magazines, newspapers, etc., as a source of research for details needed, at various times, for their special drawing problems.

Though this book does not entirely obviate the necessity for such a file, it may well serve as an adjunct, since, within it, the details of the sought object have been broken down to their basic component parts, predigested as it were, and the student is not confronted with the difficult job of reducing complicated photos or highly detailed drawings to simple terms upon which he may build his own art statement.

In choosing subjects to be included in this book and deciding on the space allotment for each, the author was guided by more personal considerations than a set division of equal space and choice of all the commonplace things mentioned in the dictionary.

First, in choosing, out of the vast number of "things" in the world, he chose such objects as would constitute basic generalizations, from which departures and variations could be made by the user of this book. The second consideration, that of deciding the amount of space to be allotted to a particular subject, was based on the author's personal experience with the problems of drawing one thing as compared with another. The "hard to draw" things were given more space than the "easy" ones.

In using this book the student may have recourse to several categories of the drawings in order to meet his own need. For instance, he might use the classifications marked "figure," "action," and "costume" to produce a period figure in the position and clothes he desires. In addition he might refer to the various strips showing details of hands, arms, hair, etc.

For secondary details of his picture there are the innumerable data drawings available for incorporation into his composition. These are all listed in alphabetic order and cross-indexed for easy correlation.

DRAW ANYTHING

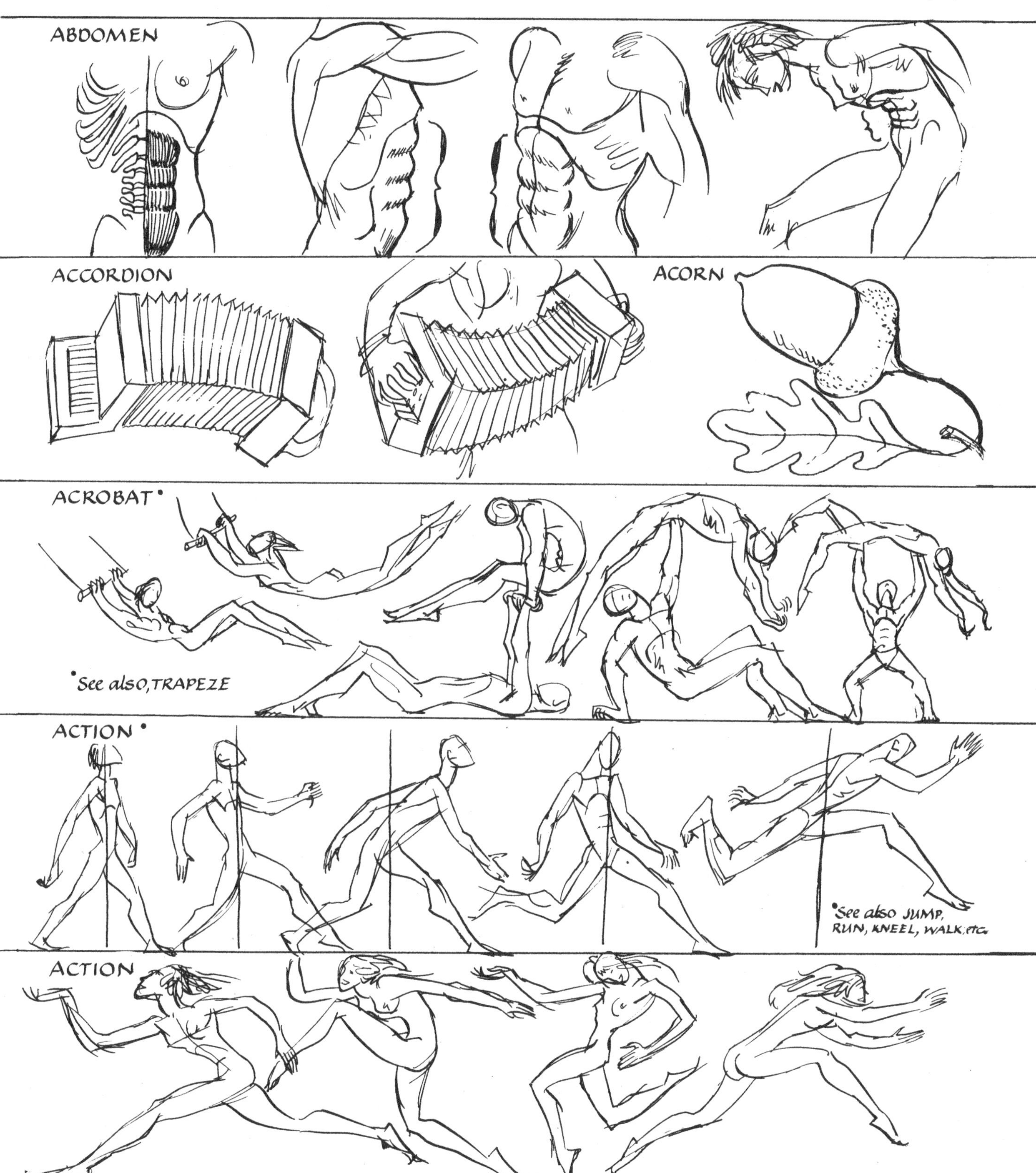
ABDOMEN
ACCORDION
ACORN
ACROBAT•
•See also, TRAPEZE
ACTION•
•See also JUMP, RUN, KNEEL, WALK, etc.
ACTION

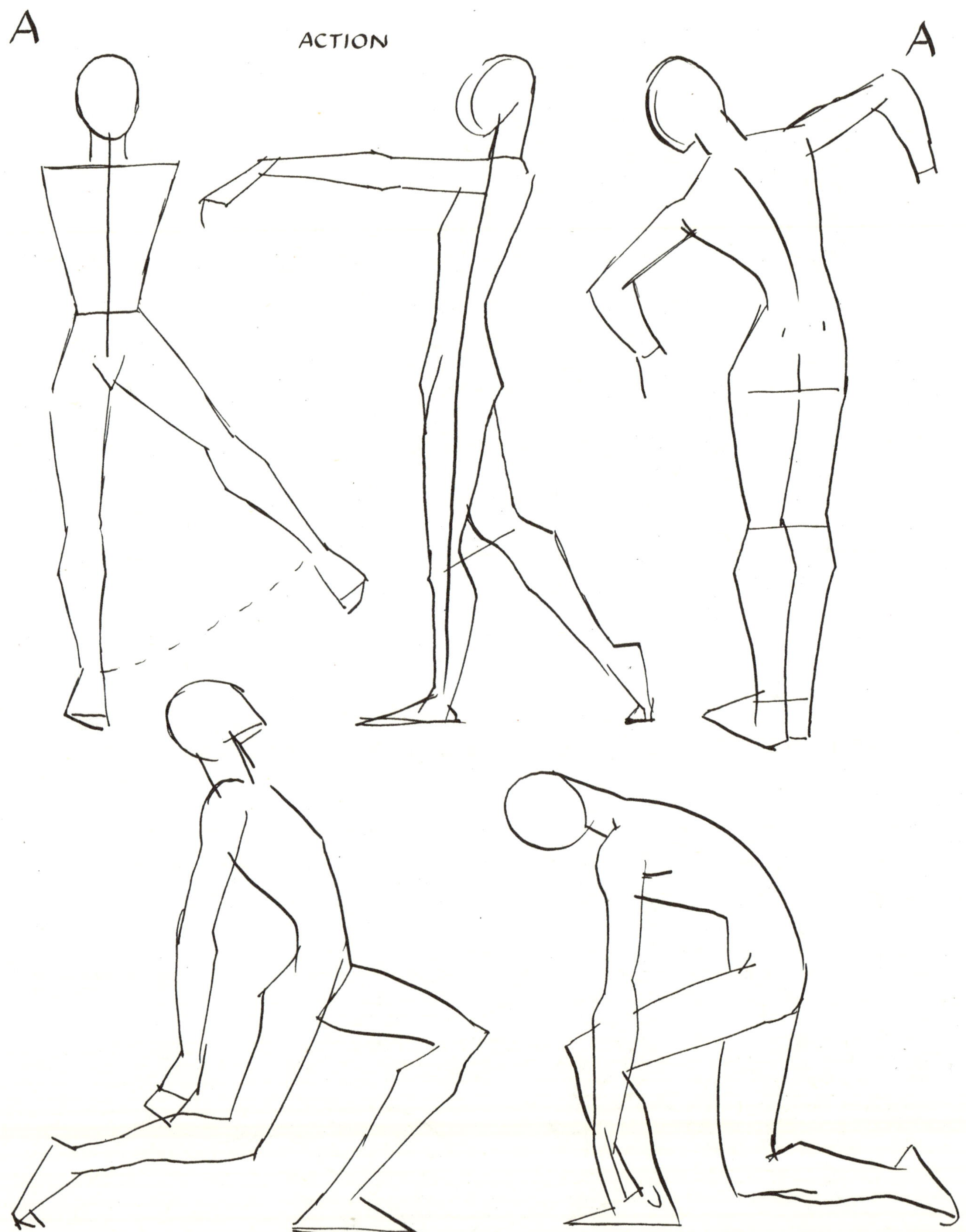
A
ACTION
A

ACTION

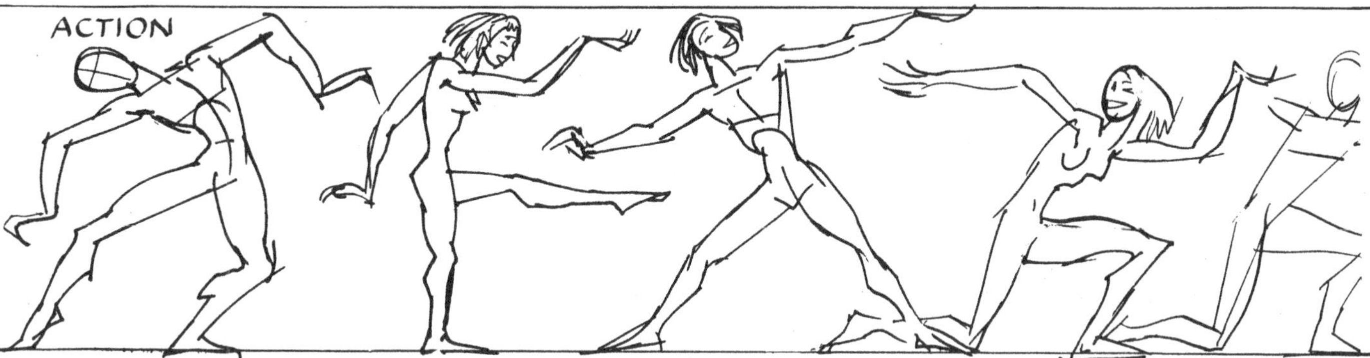

ACTION

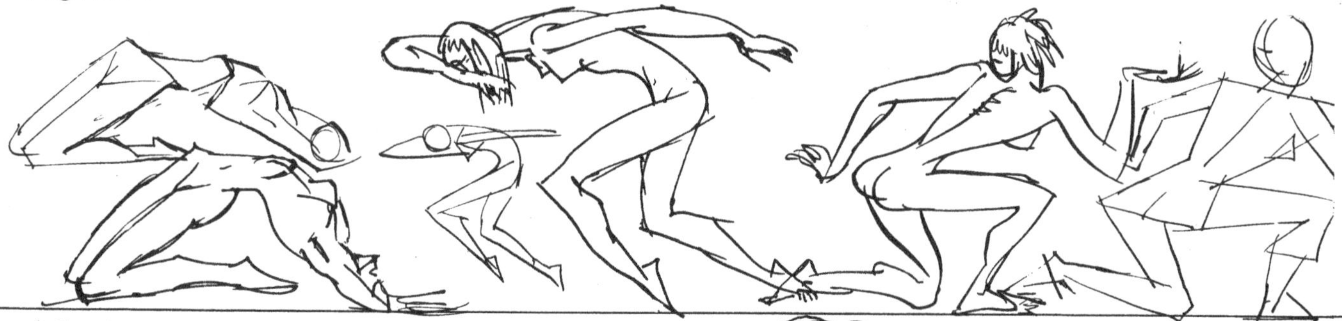

ACTION

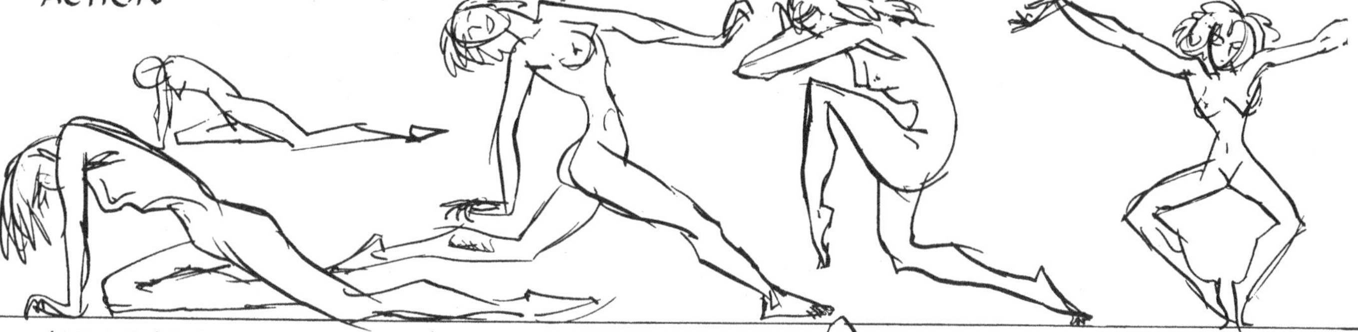

AIRCRAFT

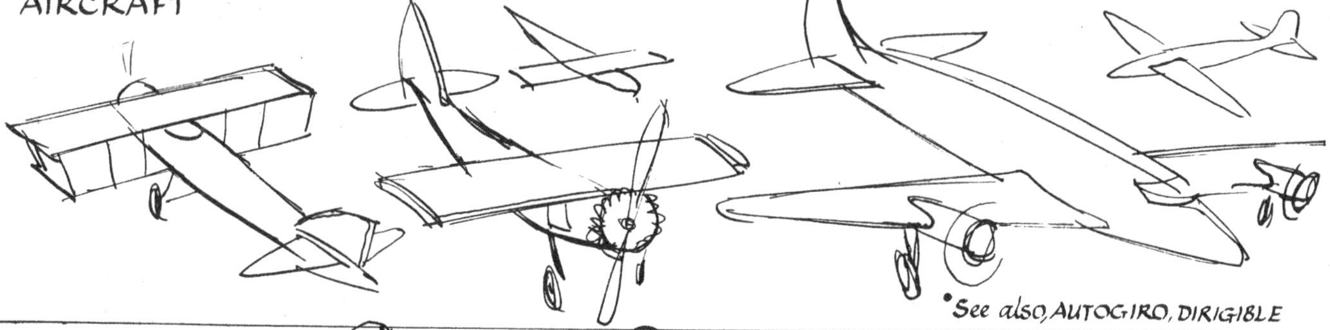

*See also, AUTOGIRO, DIRIGIBLE

AIRCRAFT

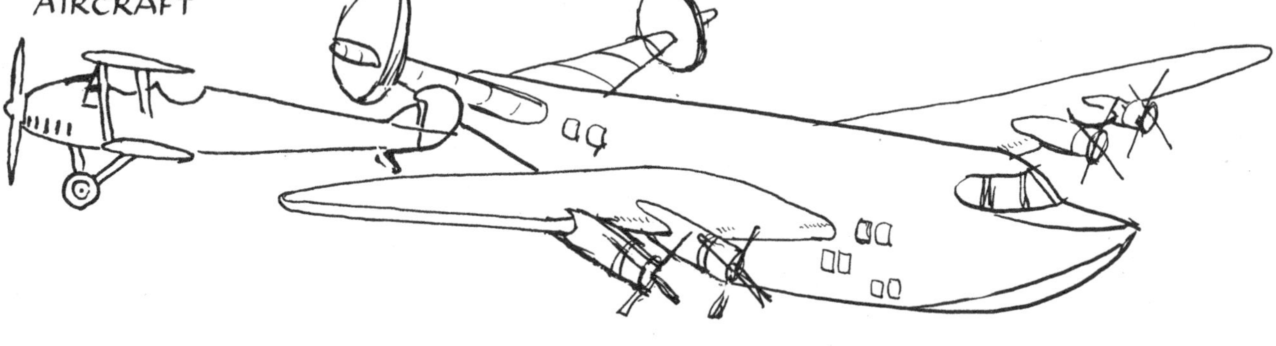

AIRCRAFT

A

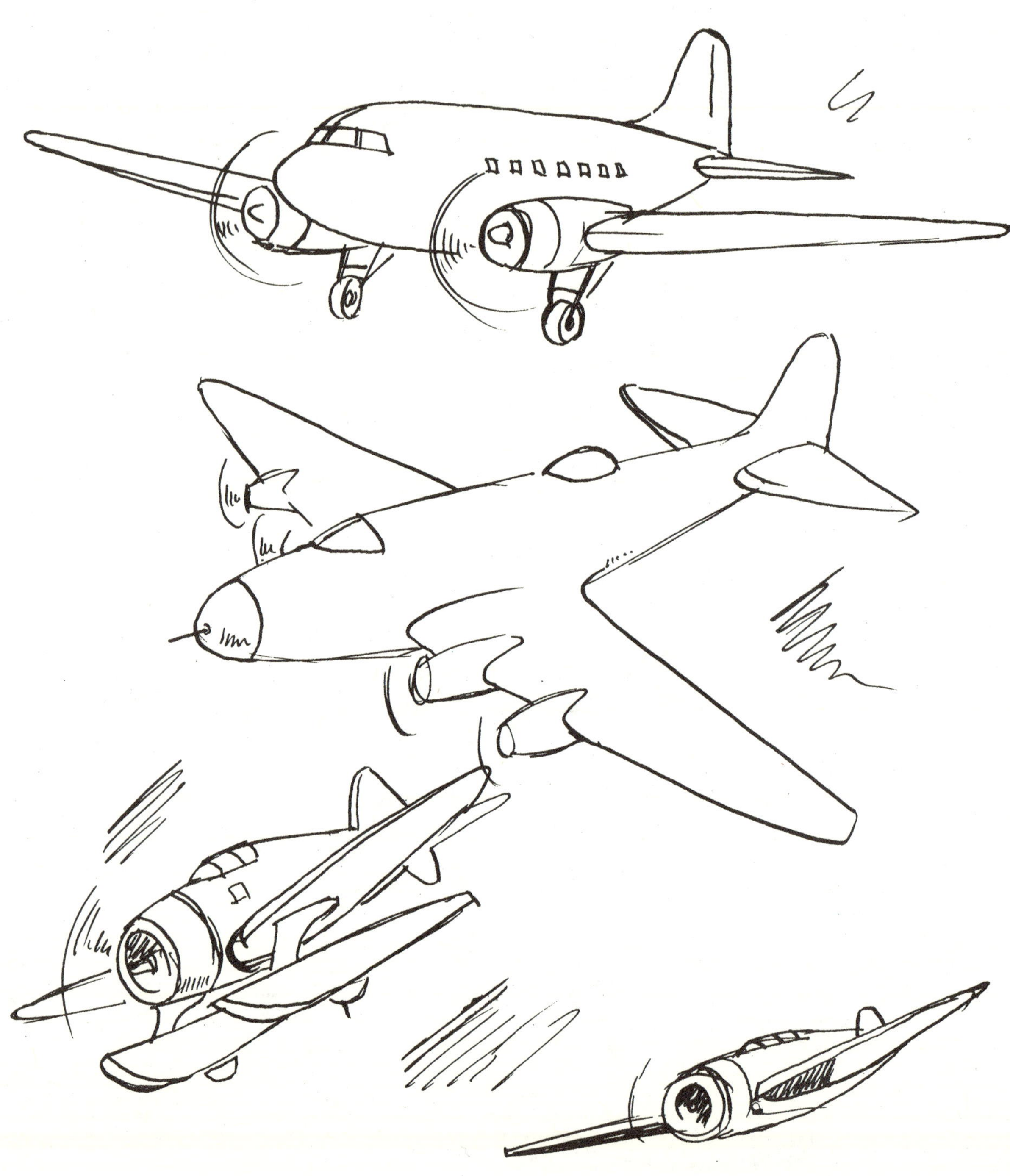

AIRCRAFT

AIRCRAFT

AIRCRAFT

ALLIGATOR

ALBATROSS

ALPACA

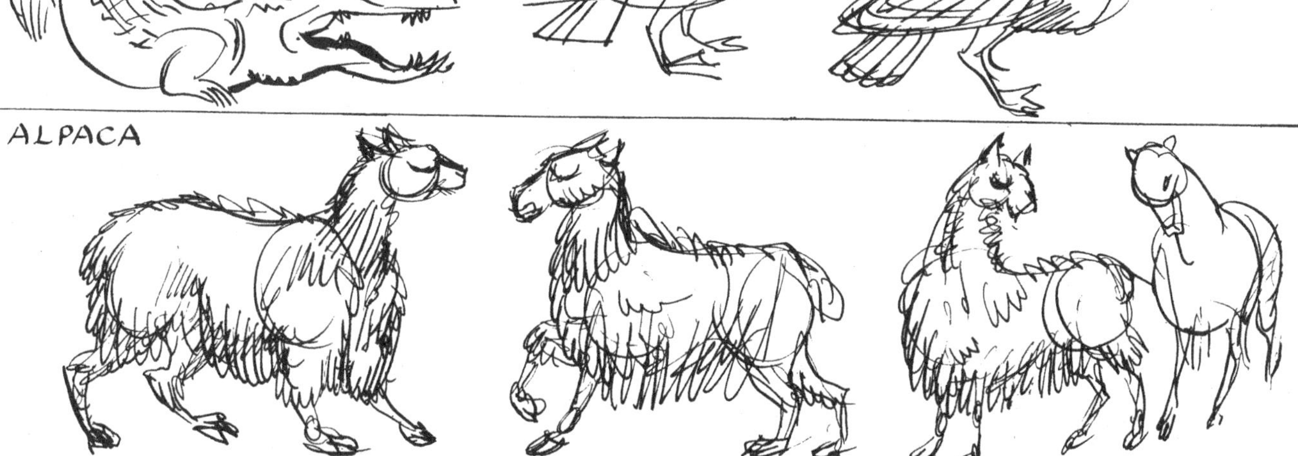

ANATOMY•

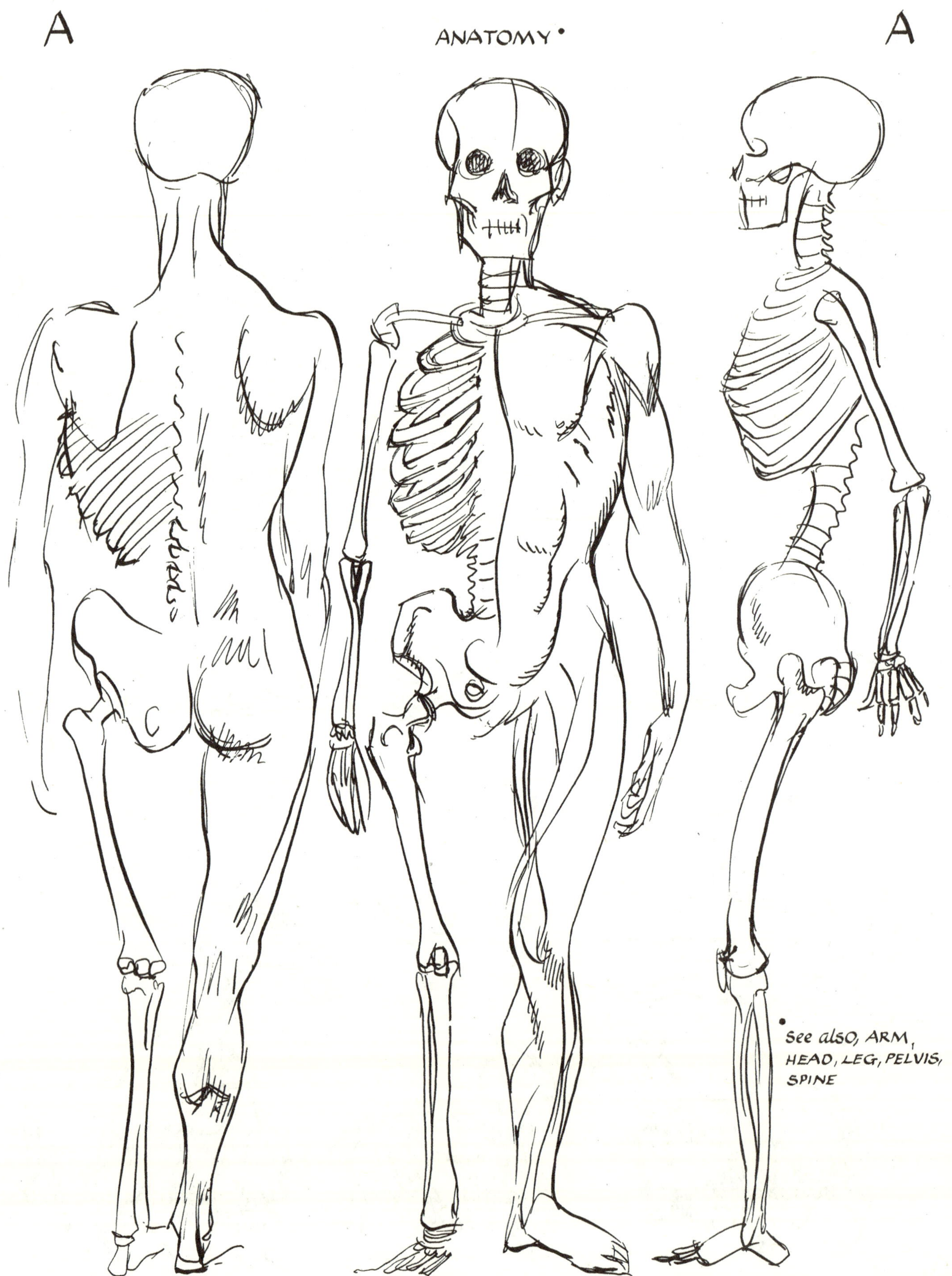

• See also, ARM, HEAD, LEG, PELVIS, SPINE

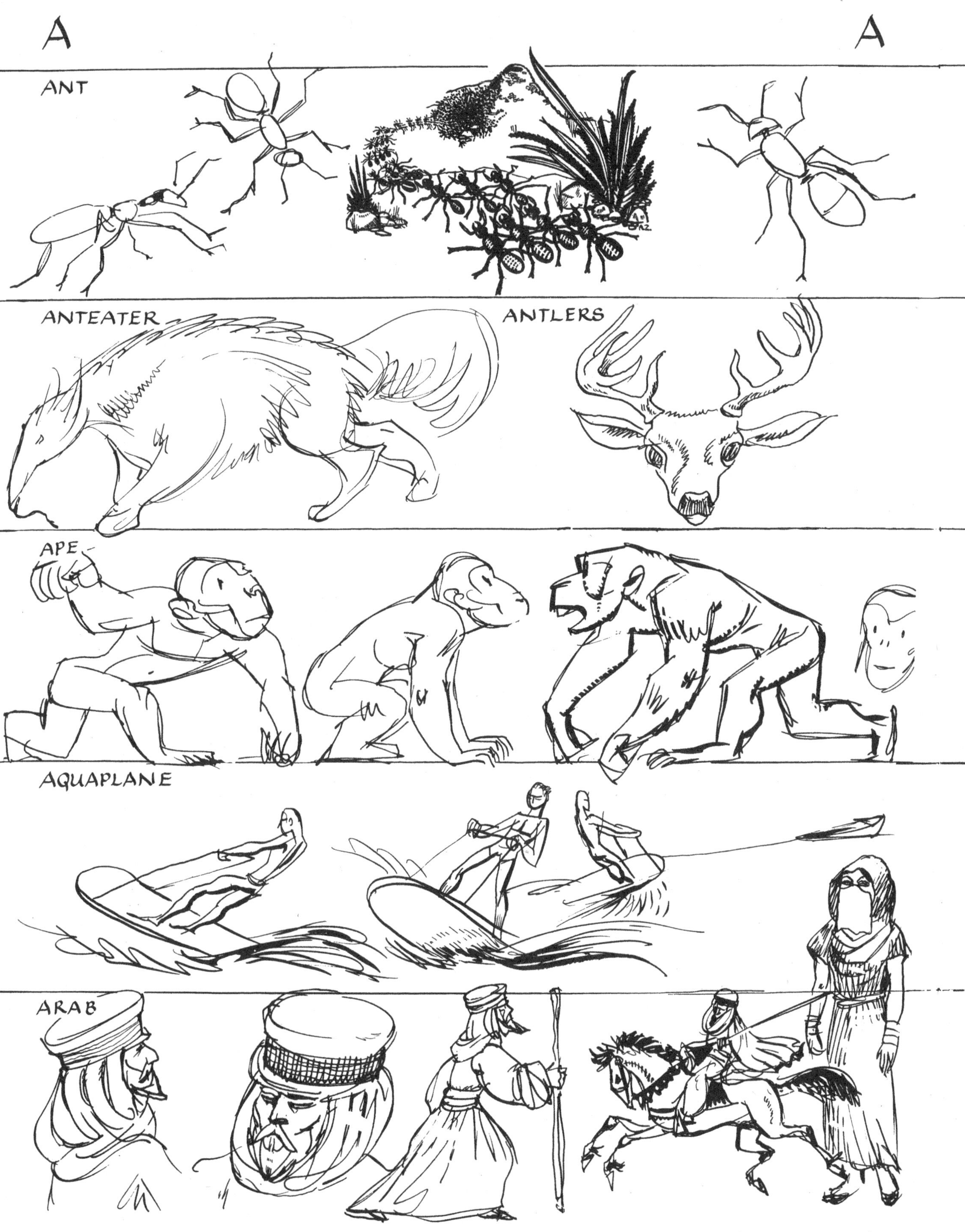
ANT
ANTEATER
ANTLERS
APE
AQUAPLANE
ARAB

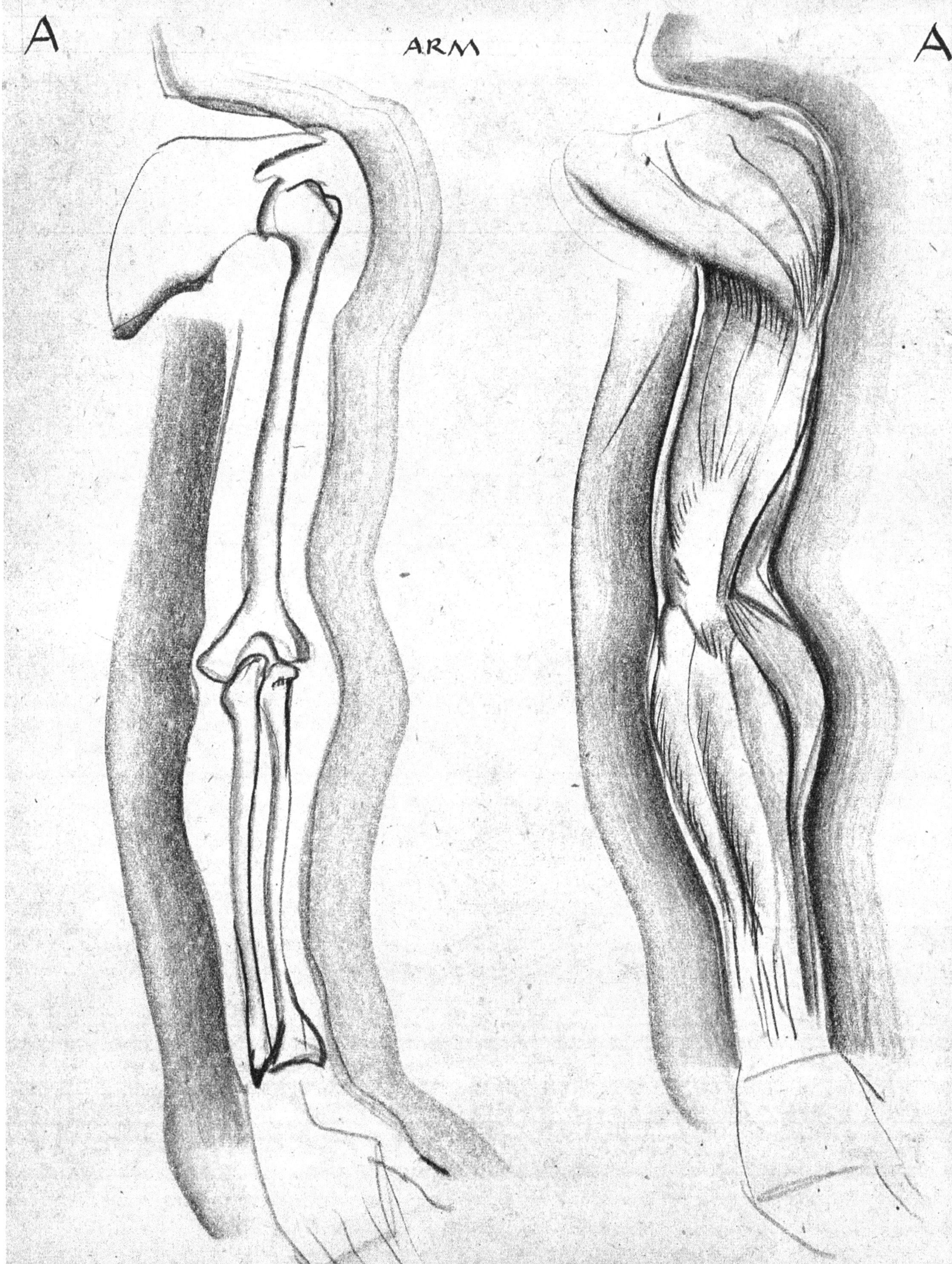
A
ARM
A

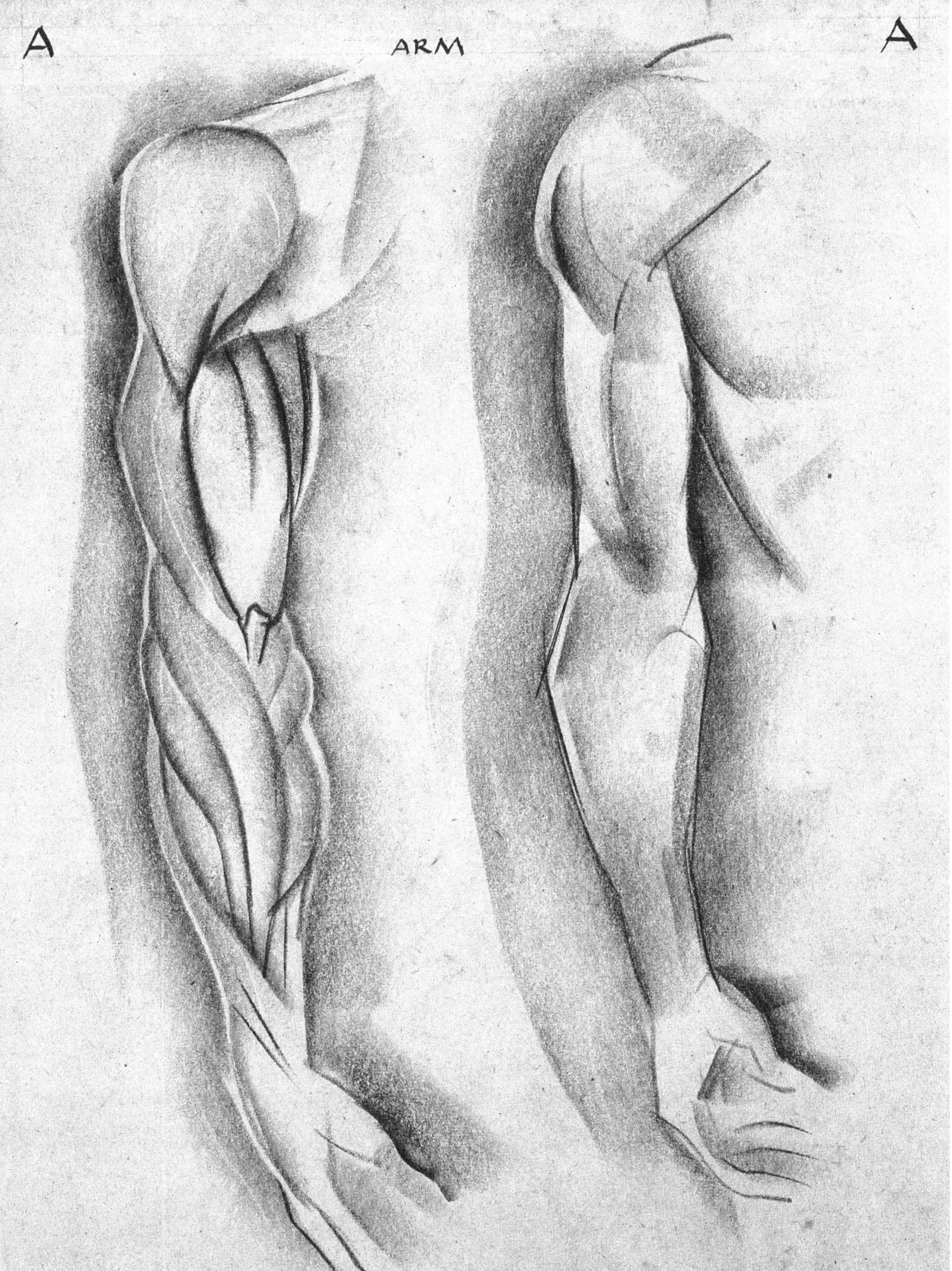
A
ARM
A

ARM

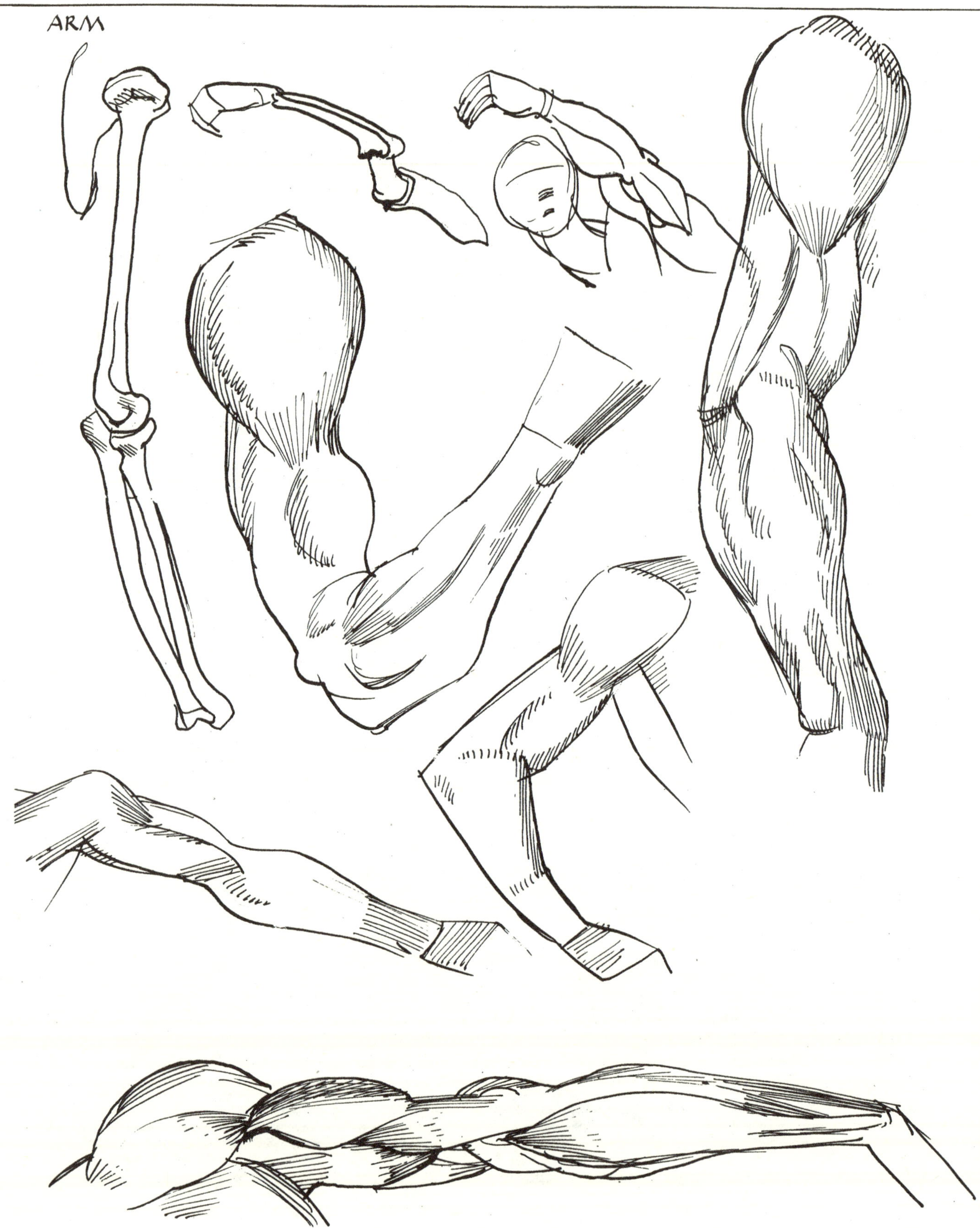

ARM•

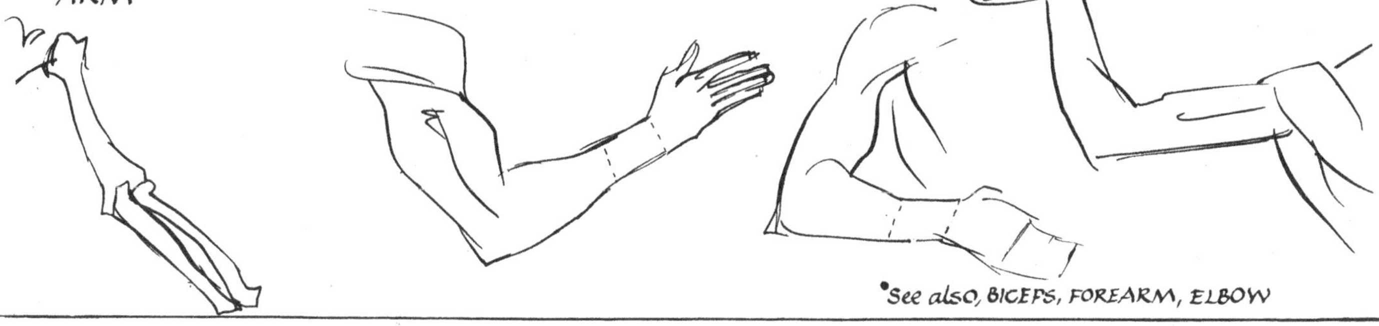

•See also, BICEPS, FOREARM, ELBOW

ARM

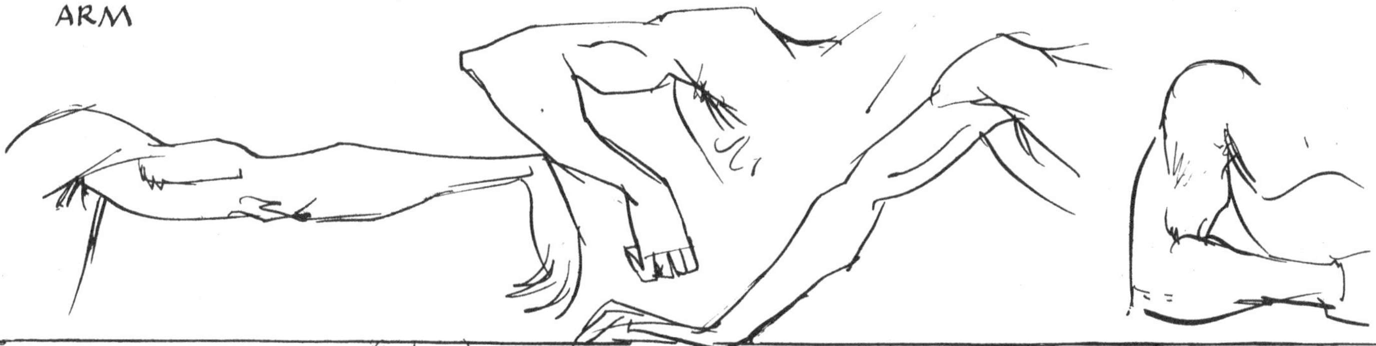

ARM

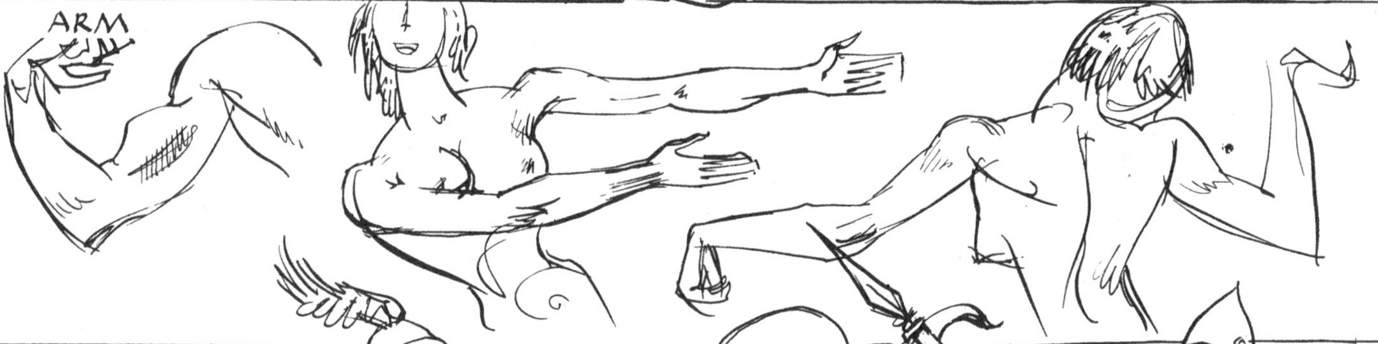

ARMOR•

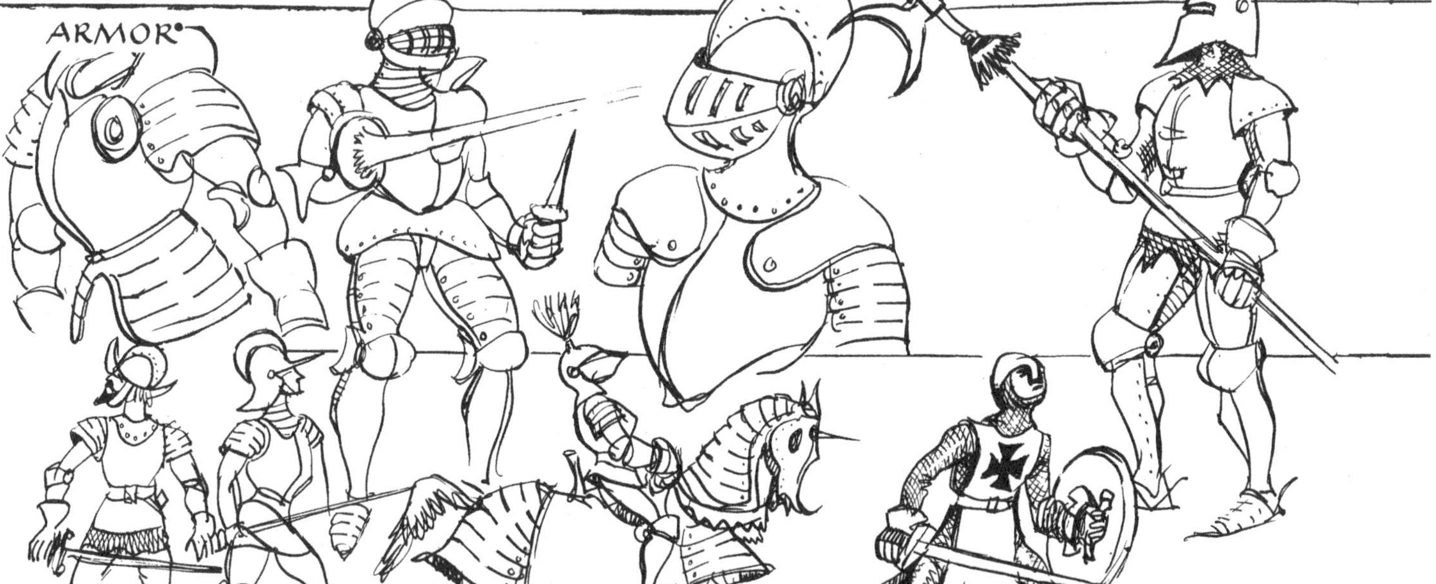

•See also JOUST
BREAST PLATE

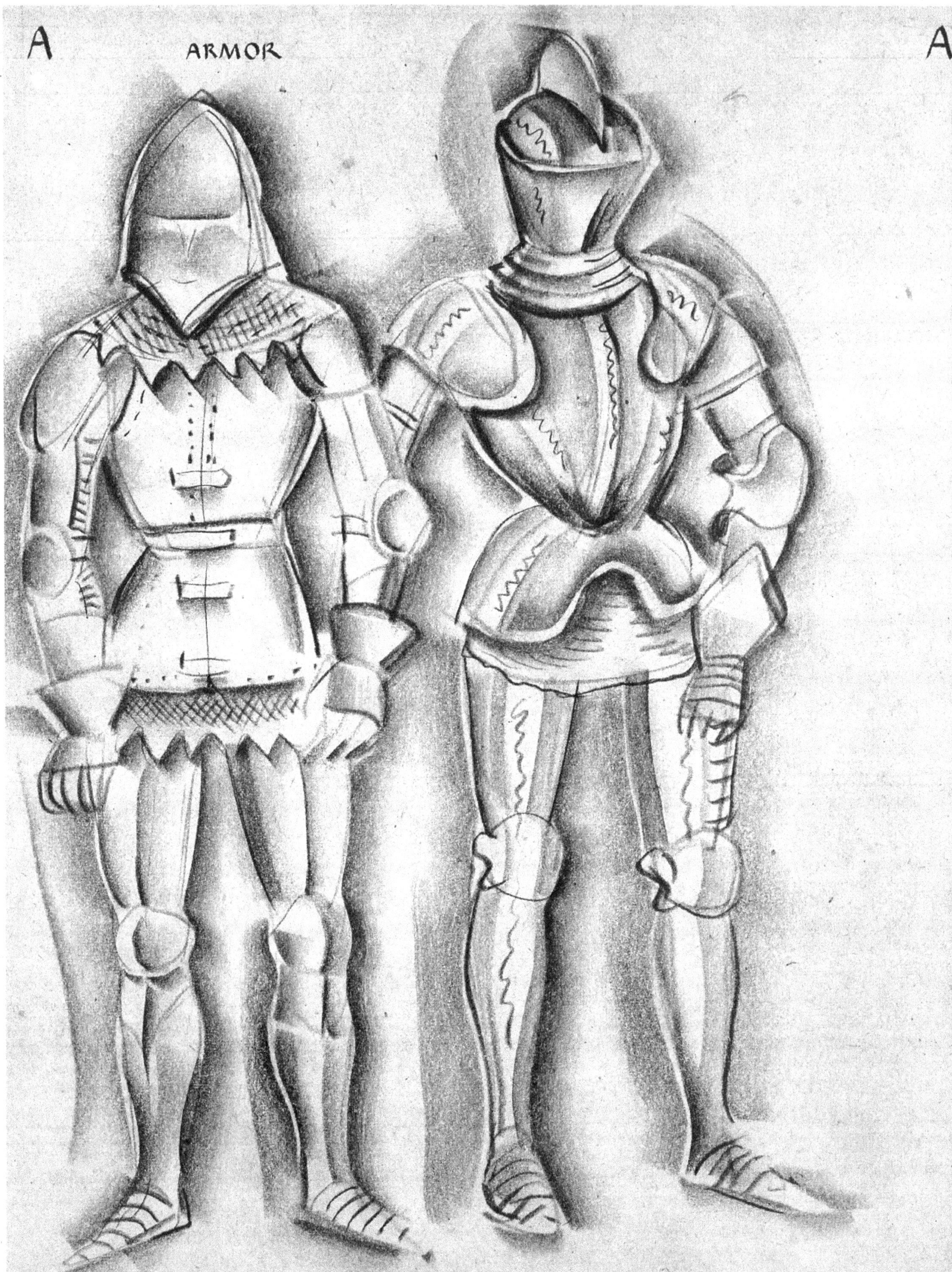
A
ARMOR
A

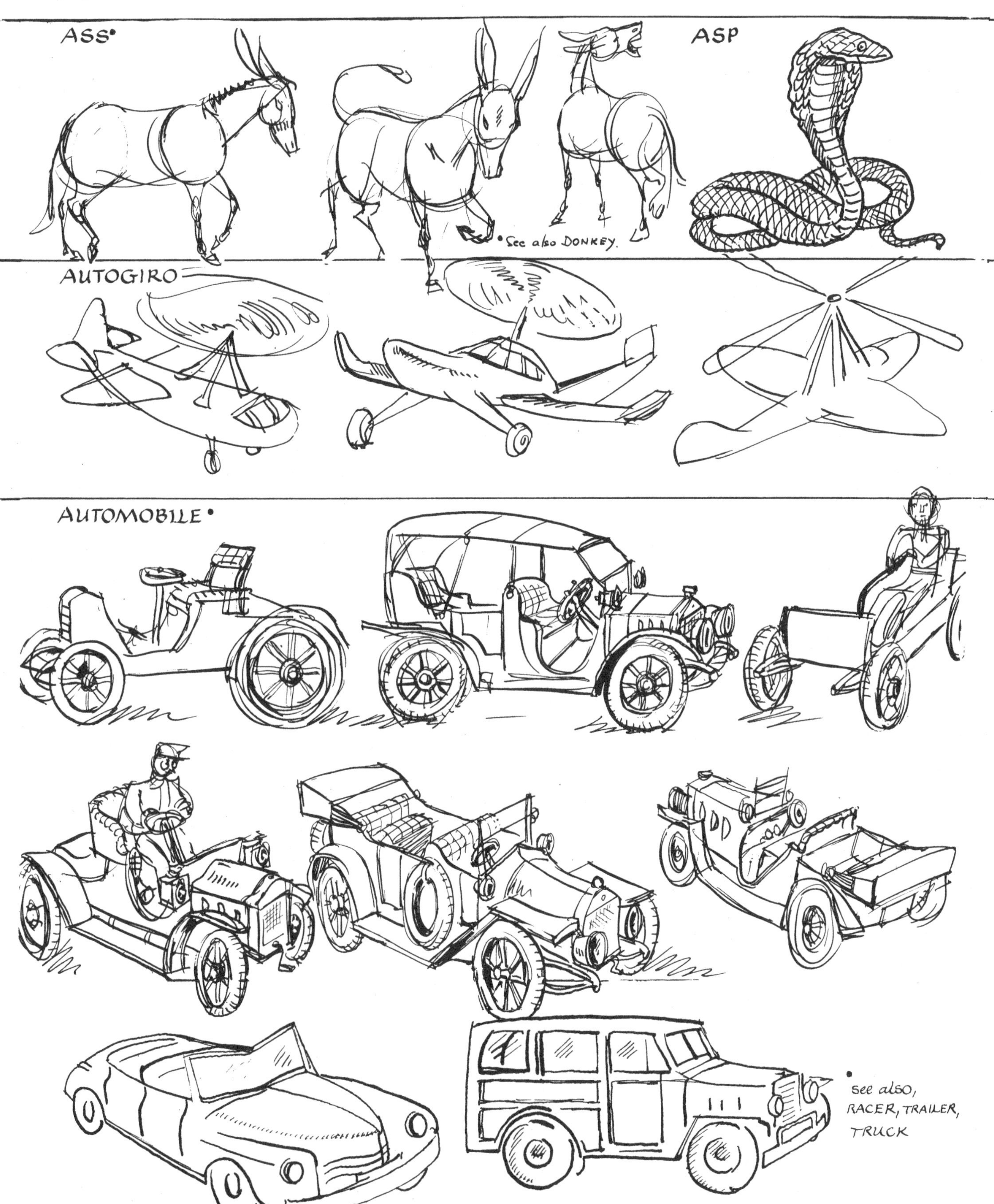
ASS•
ASP
•See also DONKEY.
AUTOGIRO
AUTOMOBILE•
•see also, RACER, TRAILER, TRUCK

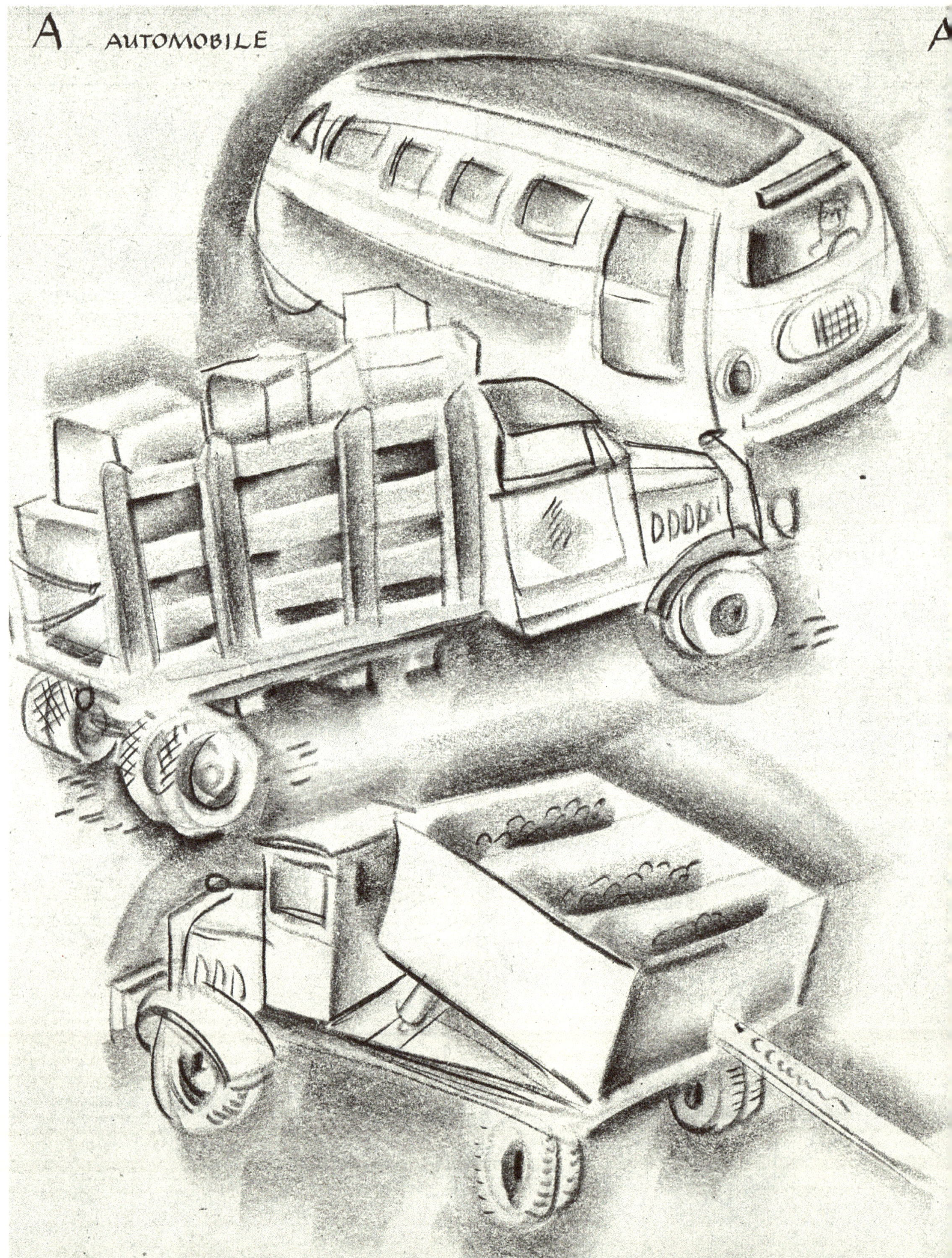
A
AUTOMOBILE
A

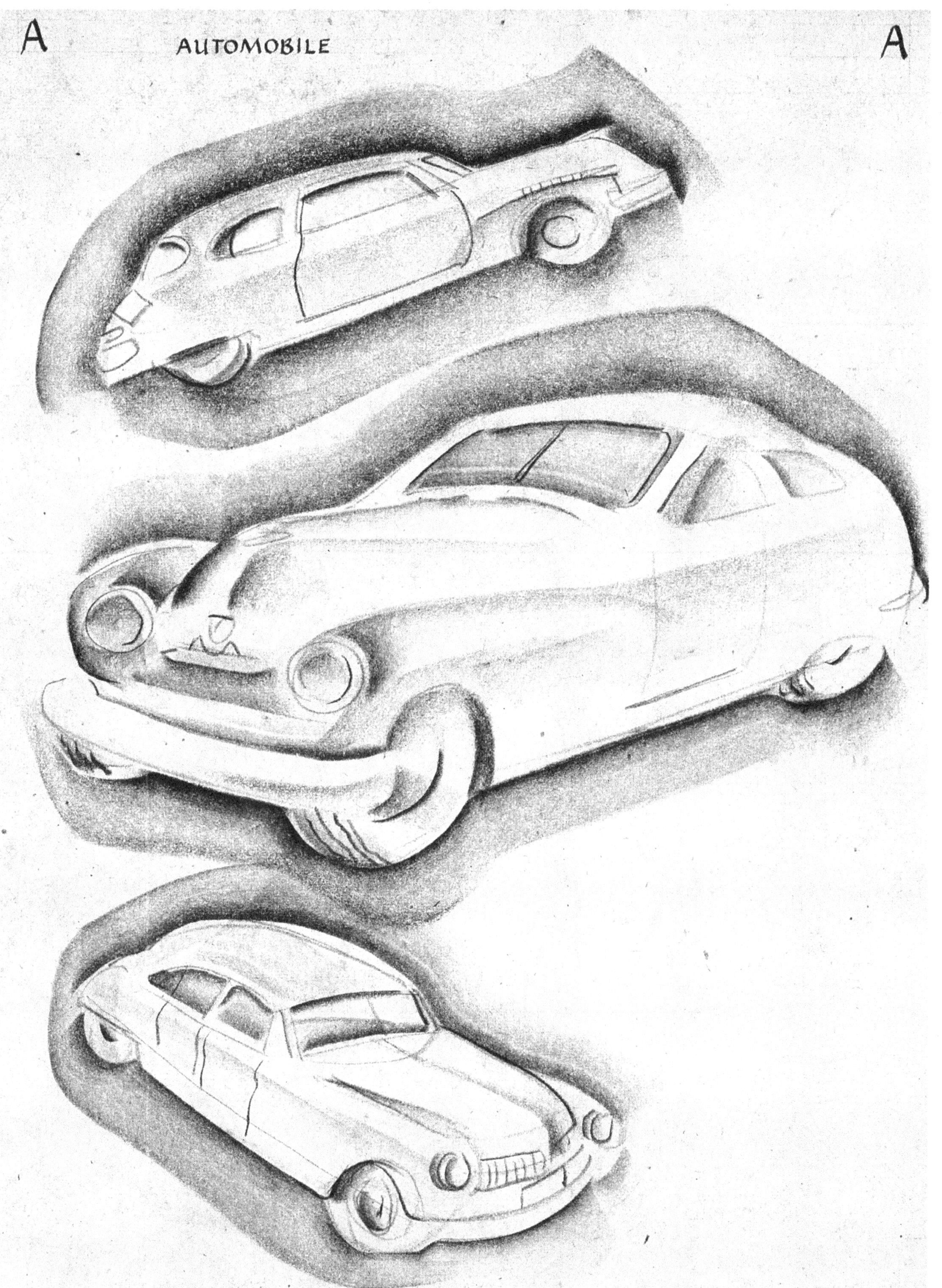
A
AUTOMOBILE
A

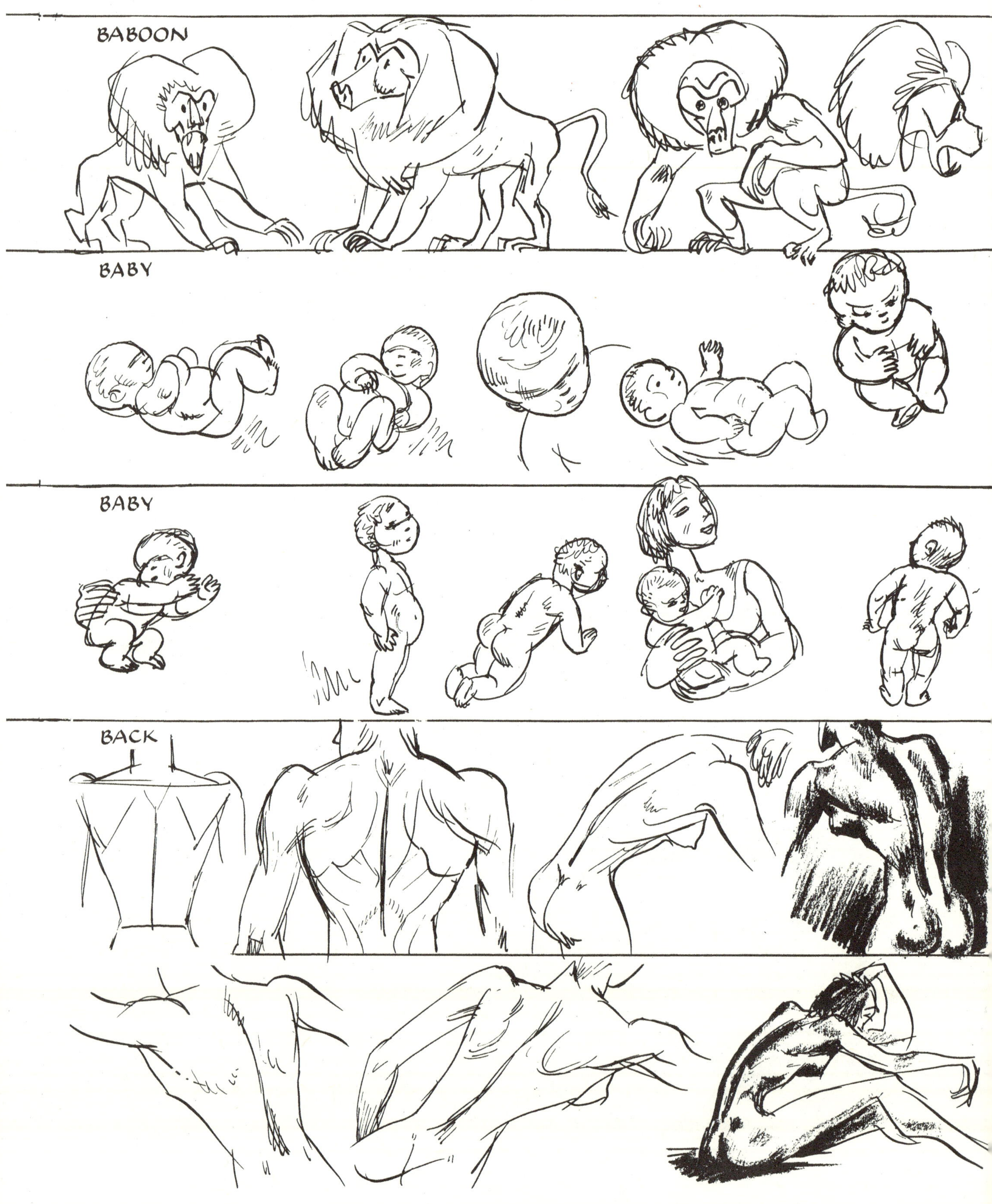
BABOON
BABY
BABY
BACK

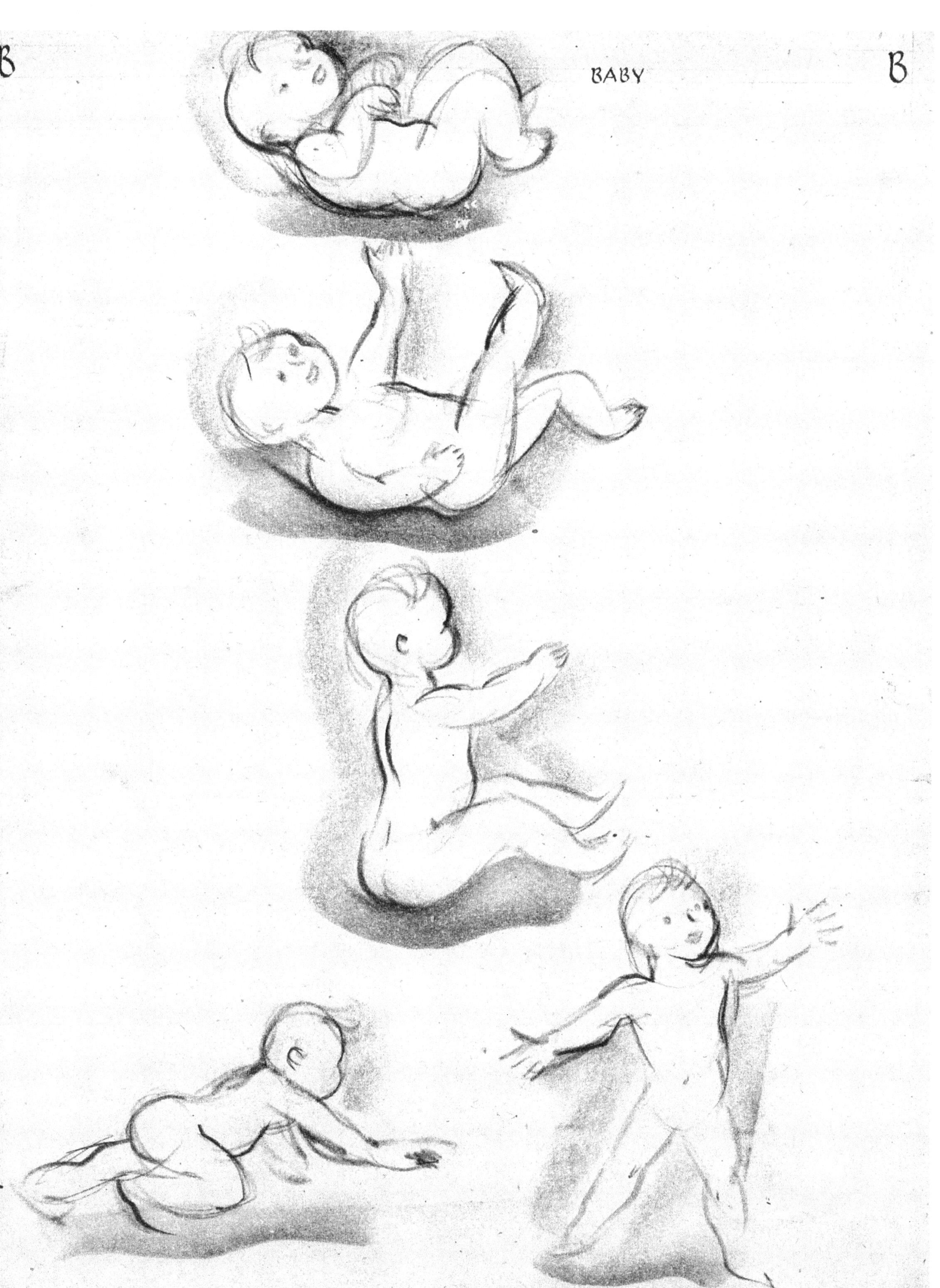

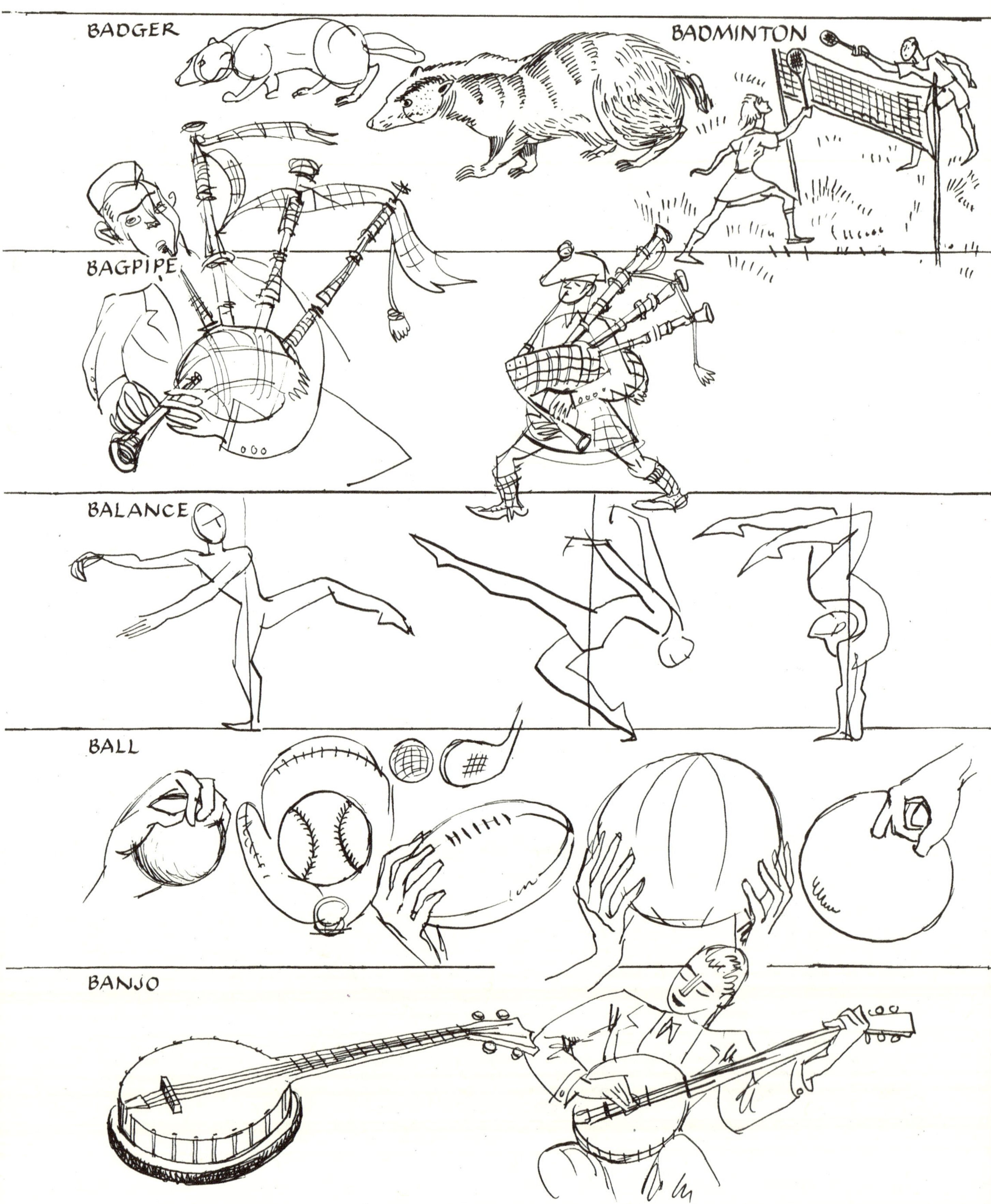
BADGER
BADMINTON
BAGPIPE
BALANCE
BALL
BANJO

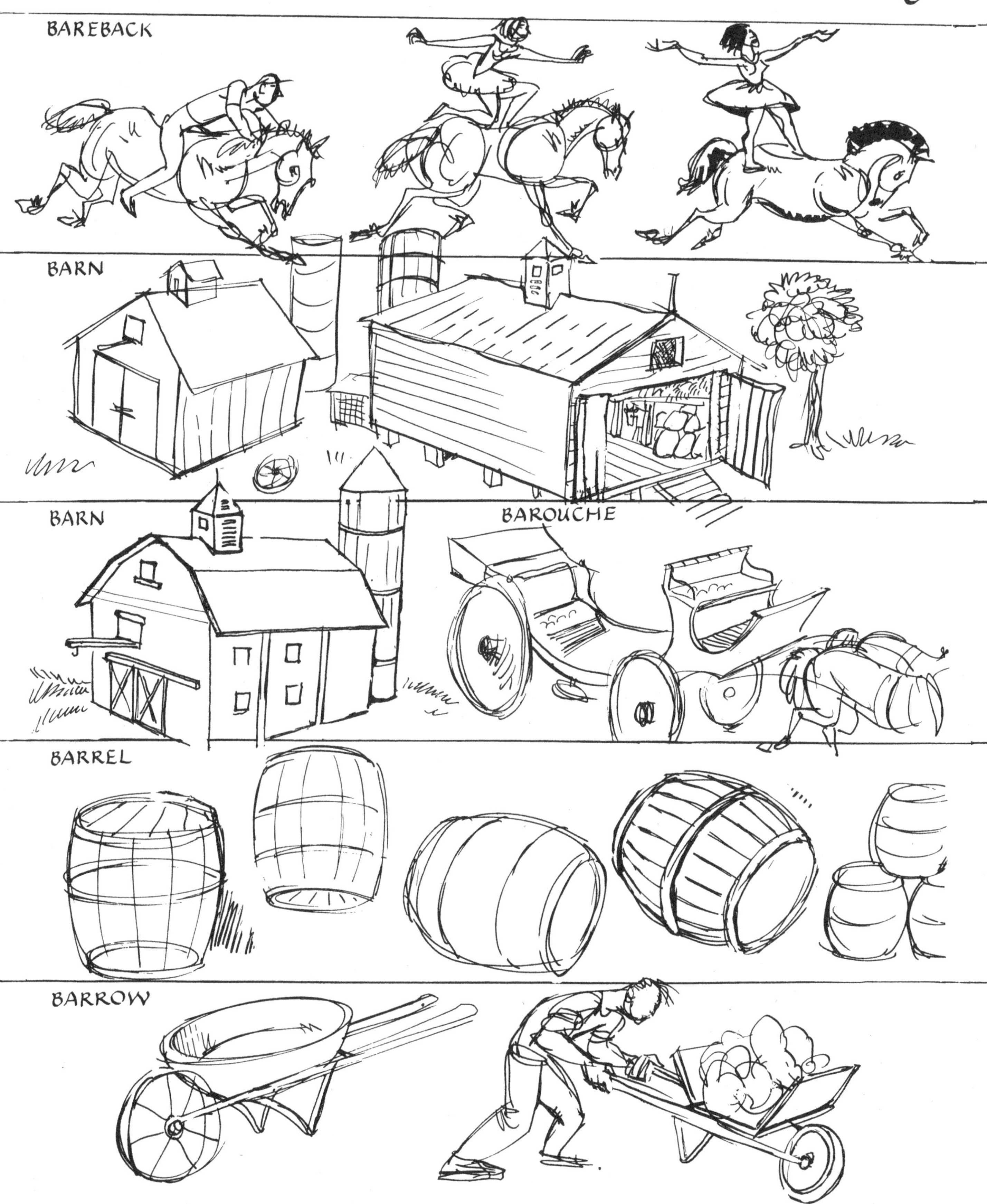
BAREBACK
BARN
BARN
BAROUCHE
BARREL
BARROW

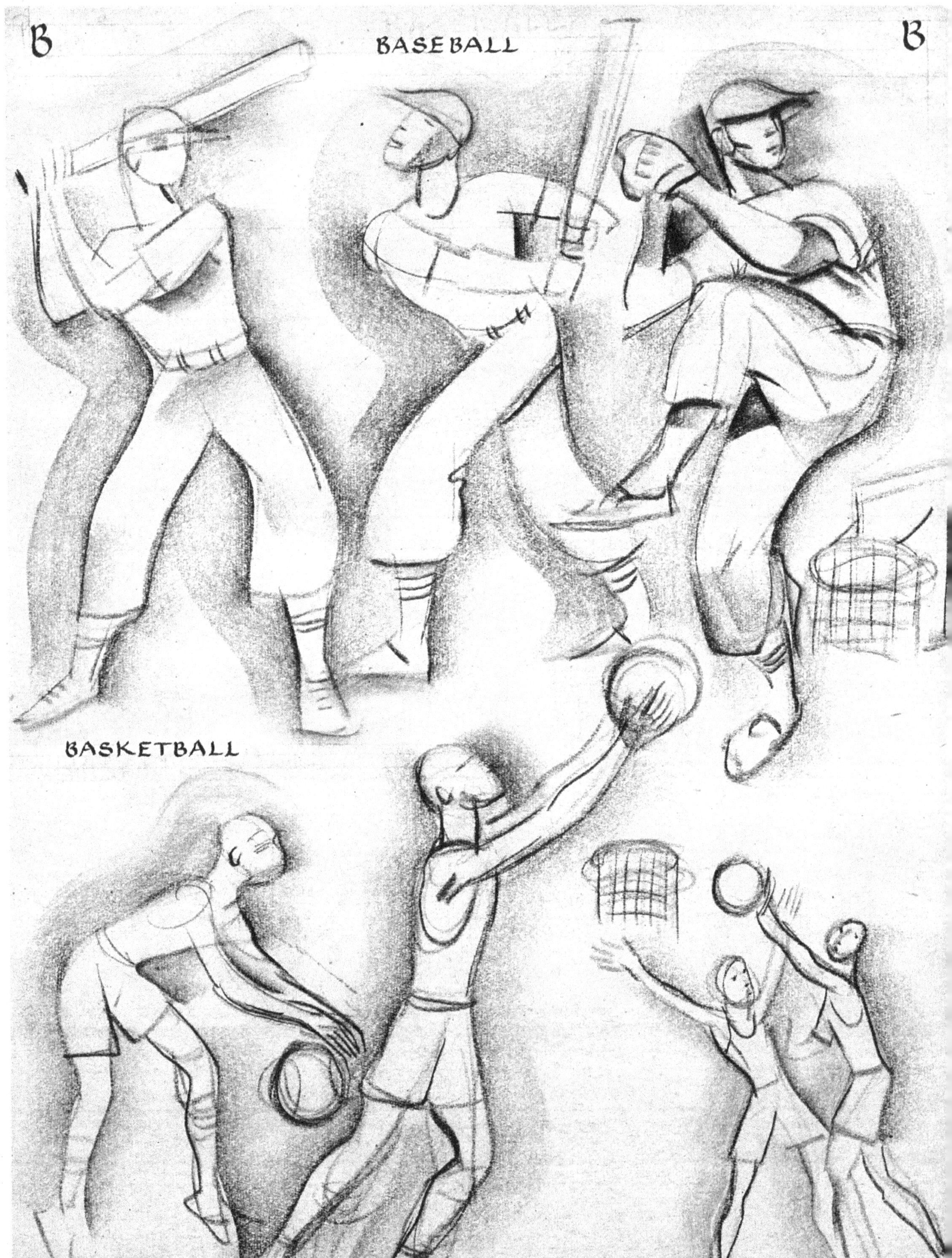
B
BASEBALL
B
BASKETBALL

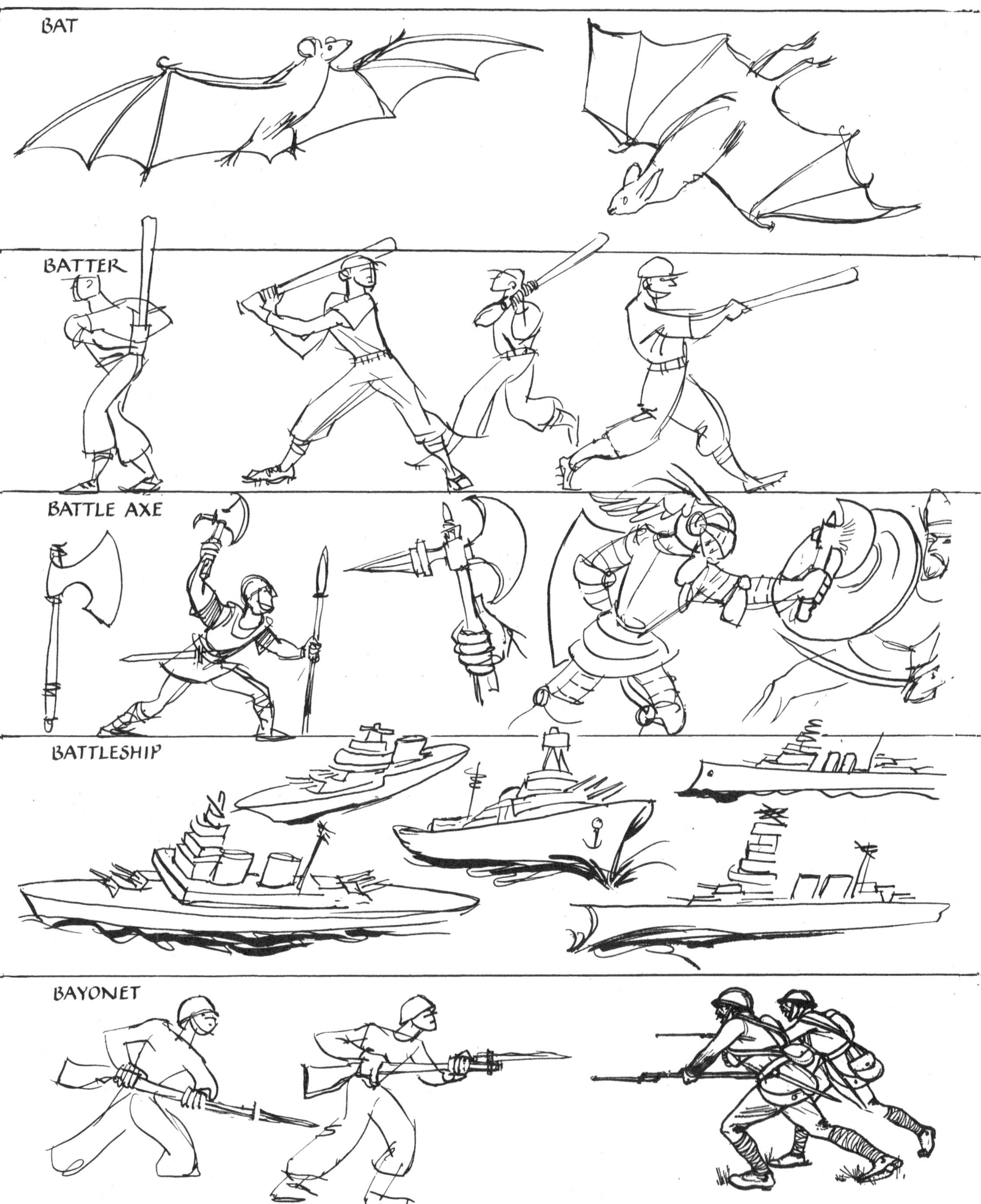
BAT
BATTER
BATTLE AXE
BATTLESHIP
BAYONET

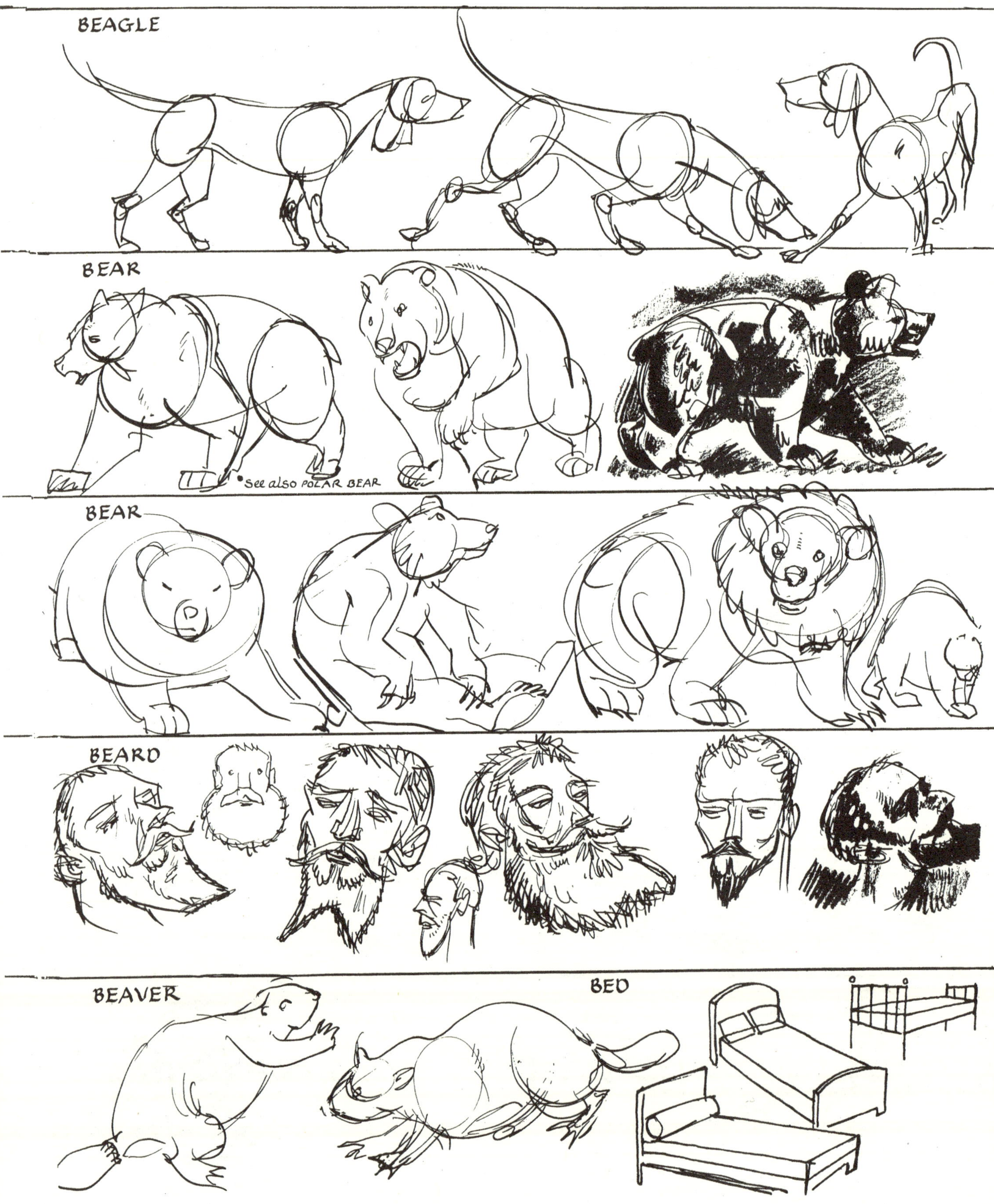
BEAGLE
BEAR
See also POLAR BEAR
BEAR
BEARD
BEAVER
BED

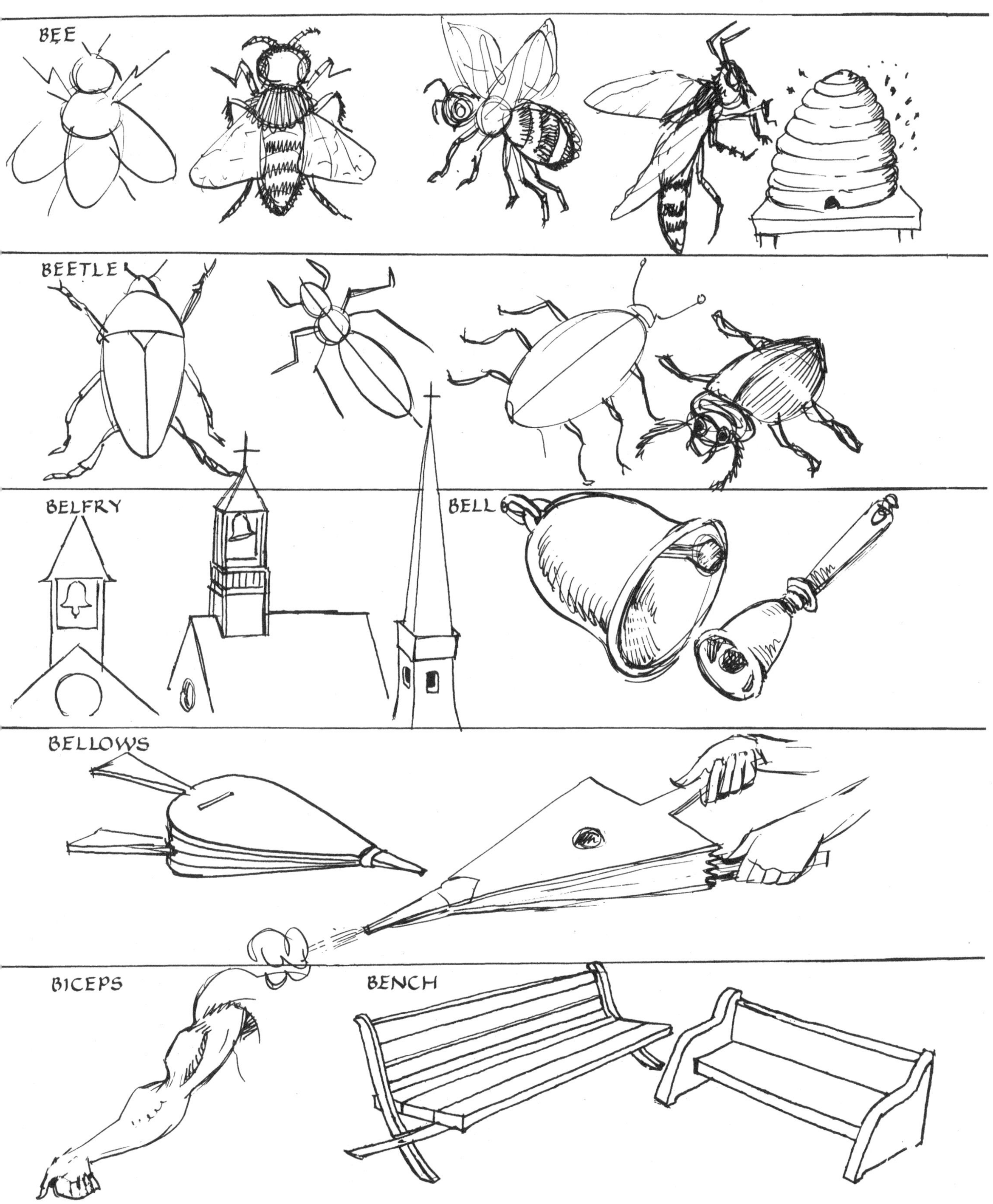
BEE
BEETLE
BELFRY
BELL
BELLOWS
BICEPS
BENCH

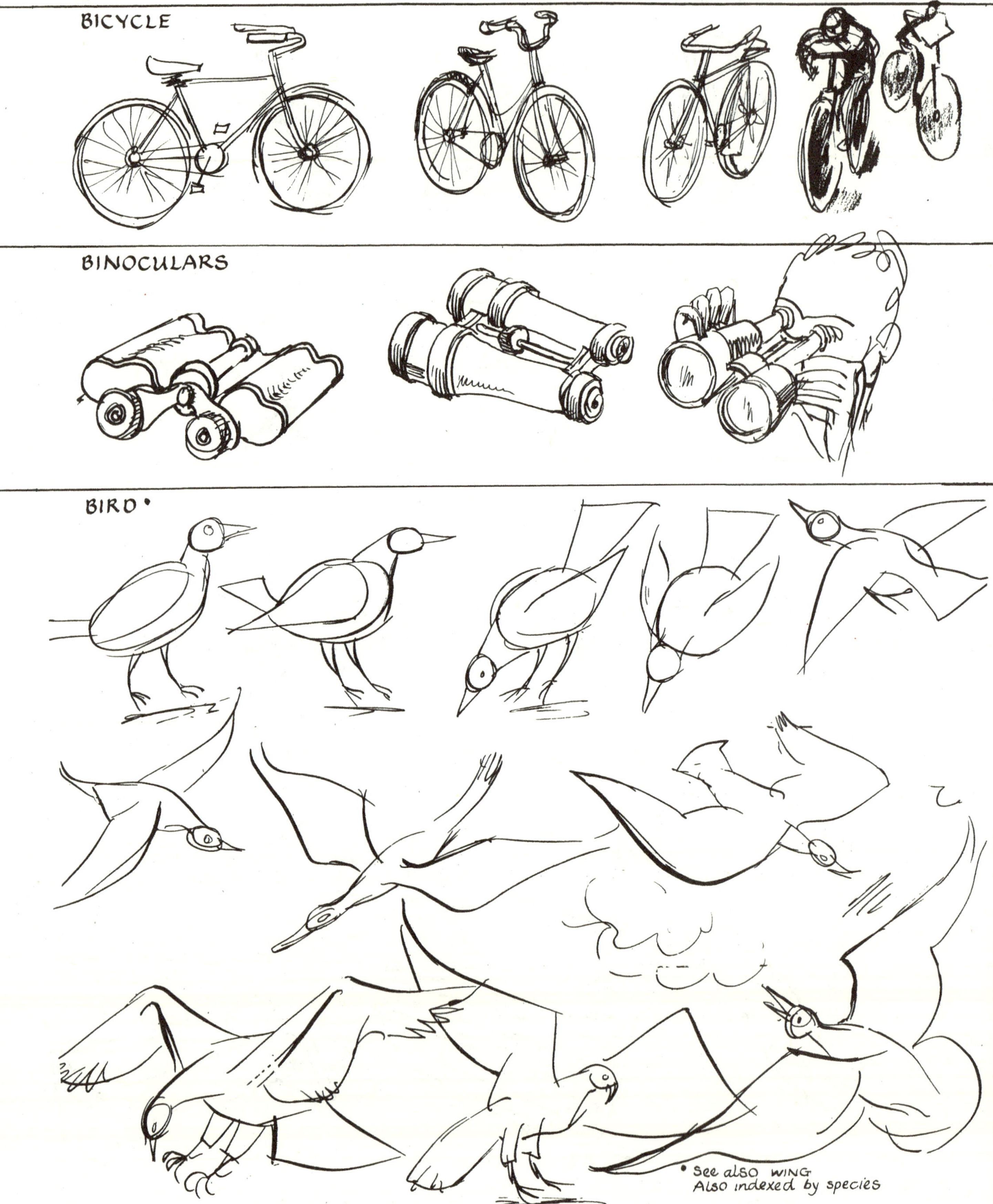
BICYCLE
BINOCULARS
BIRD •
• See also WING
Also indexed by species

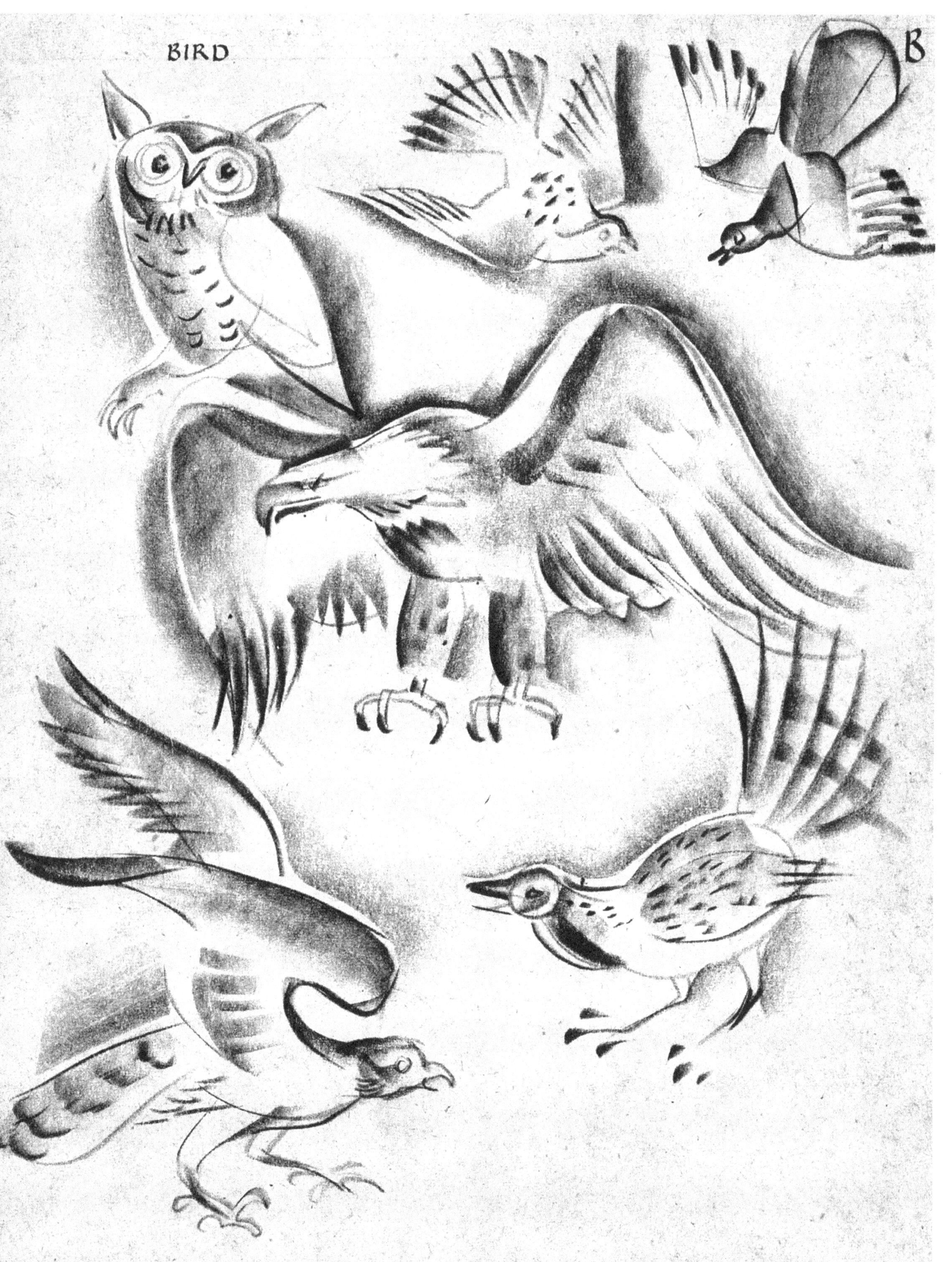
BIRD
B

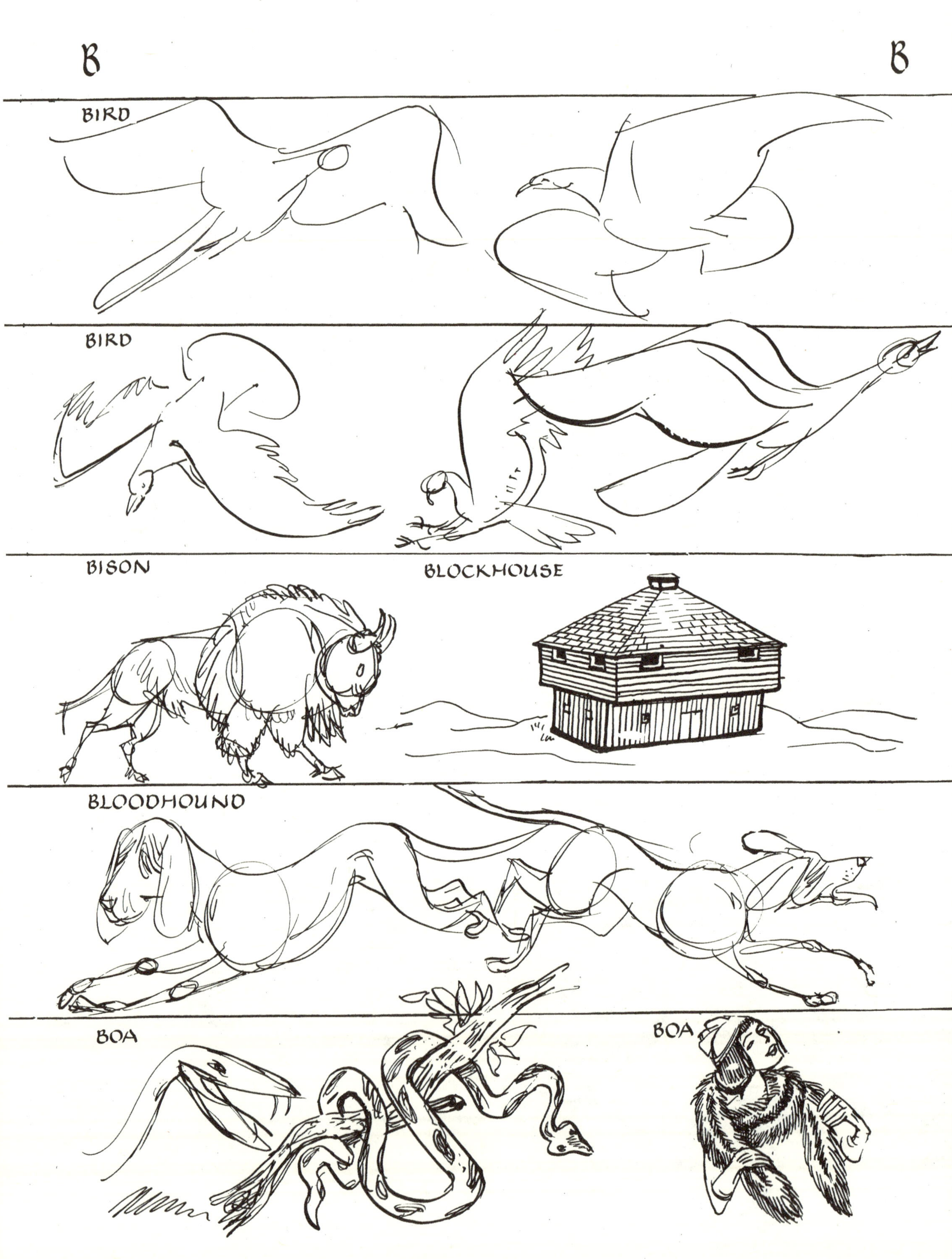
BIRD
BIRD
BISON
BLOCKHOUSE
BLOODHOUND
BOA
BOA

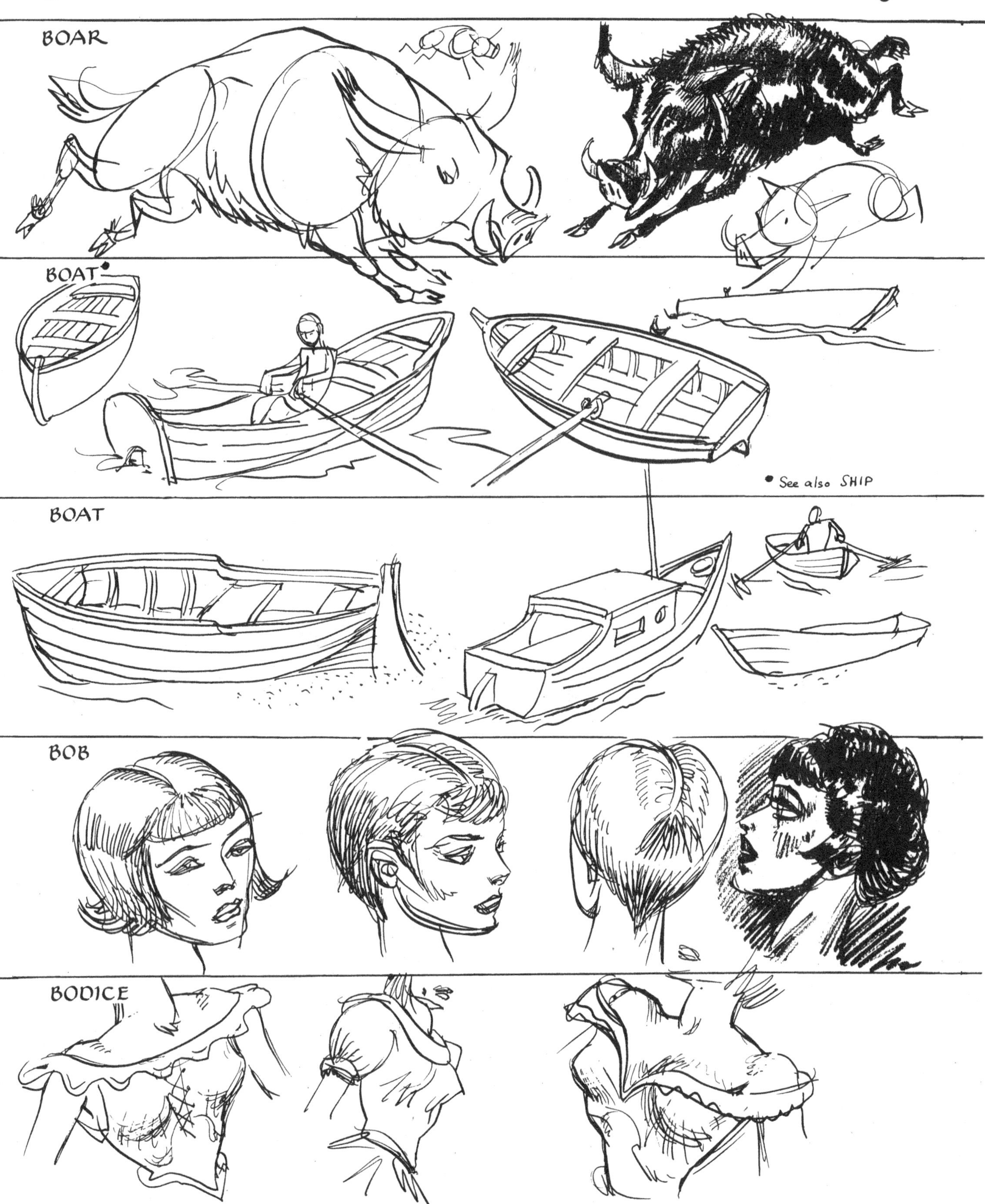
BOAR
BOAT•
• See also SHIP
BOAT
BOB
BODICE

BOOK

BOOT

BOTTLE

BOW

BOWL

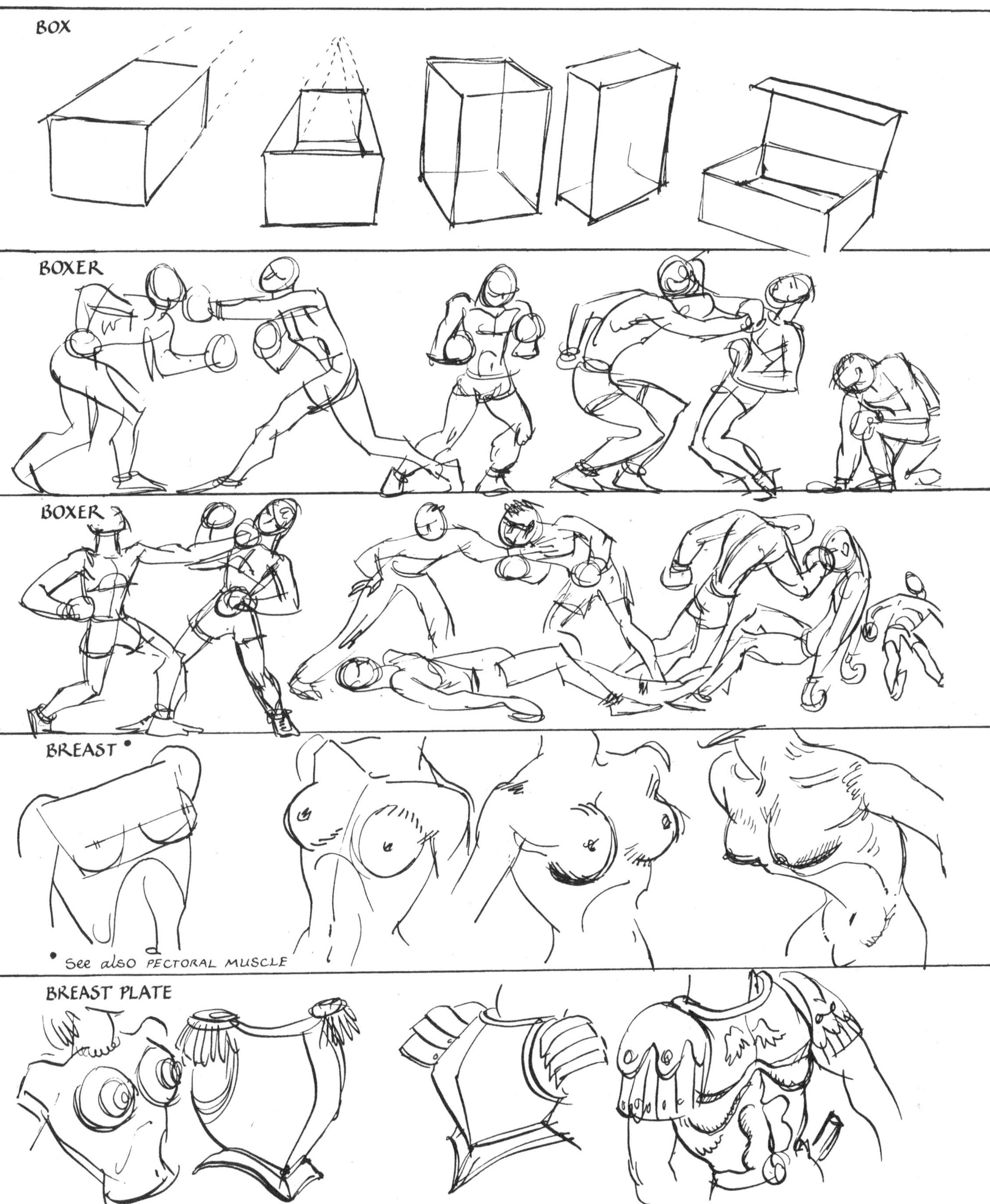
BOX
BOXER
BOXER
BREAST •
• See also PECTORAL MUSCLE
BREAST PLATE

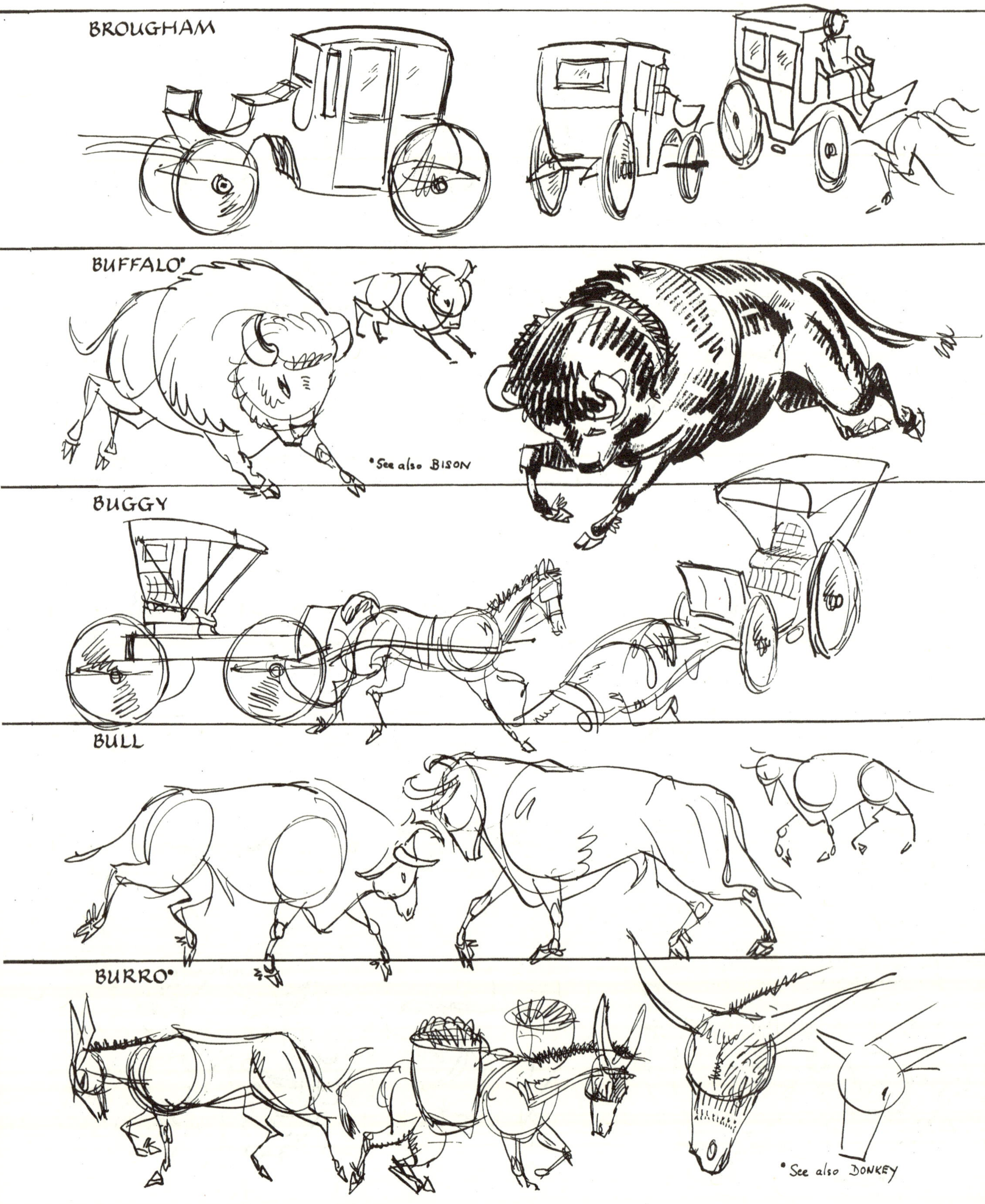
BROUGHAM
BUFFALO*
*See also BISON
BUGGY
BULL
BURRO*
*See also DONKEY

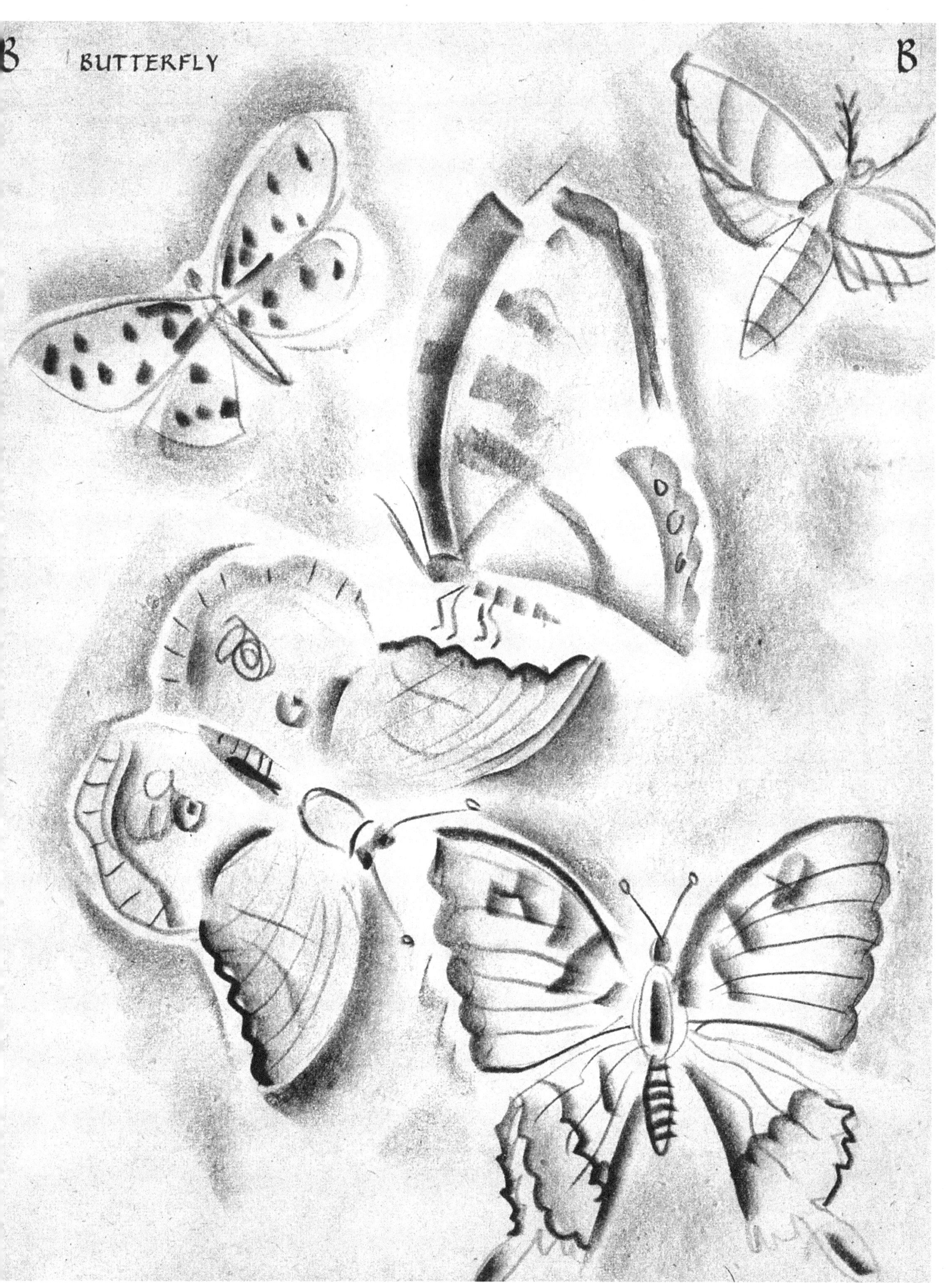
B
BUTTERFLY
B

 B-C

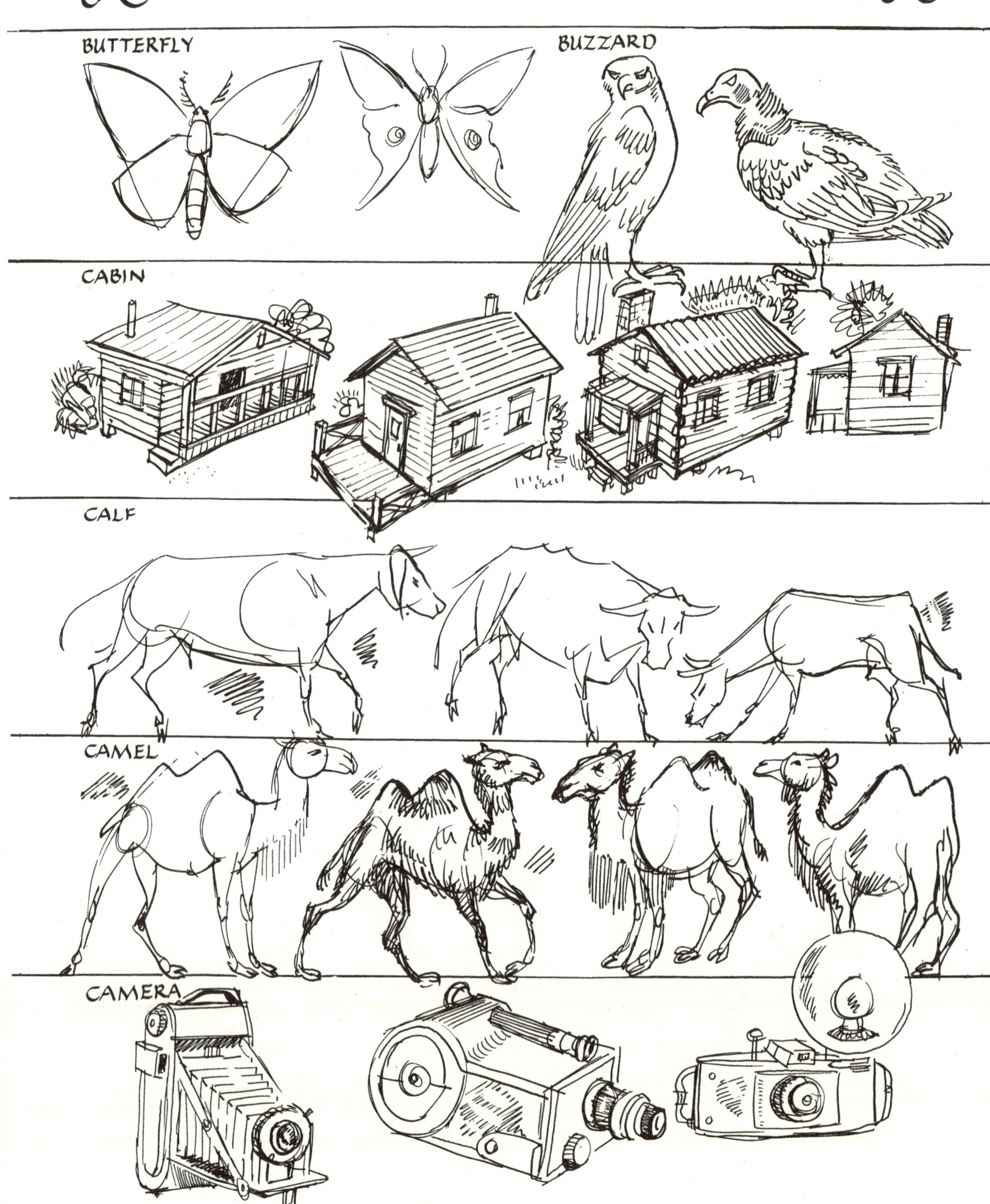

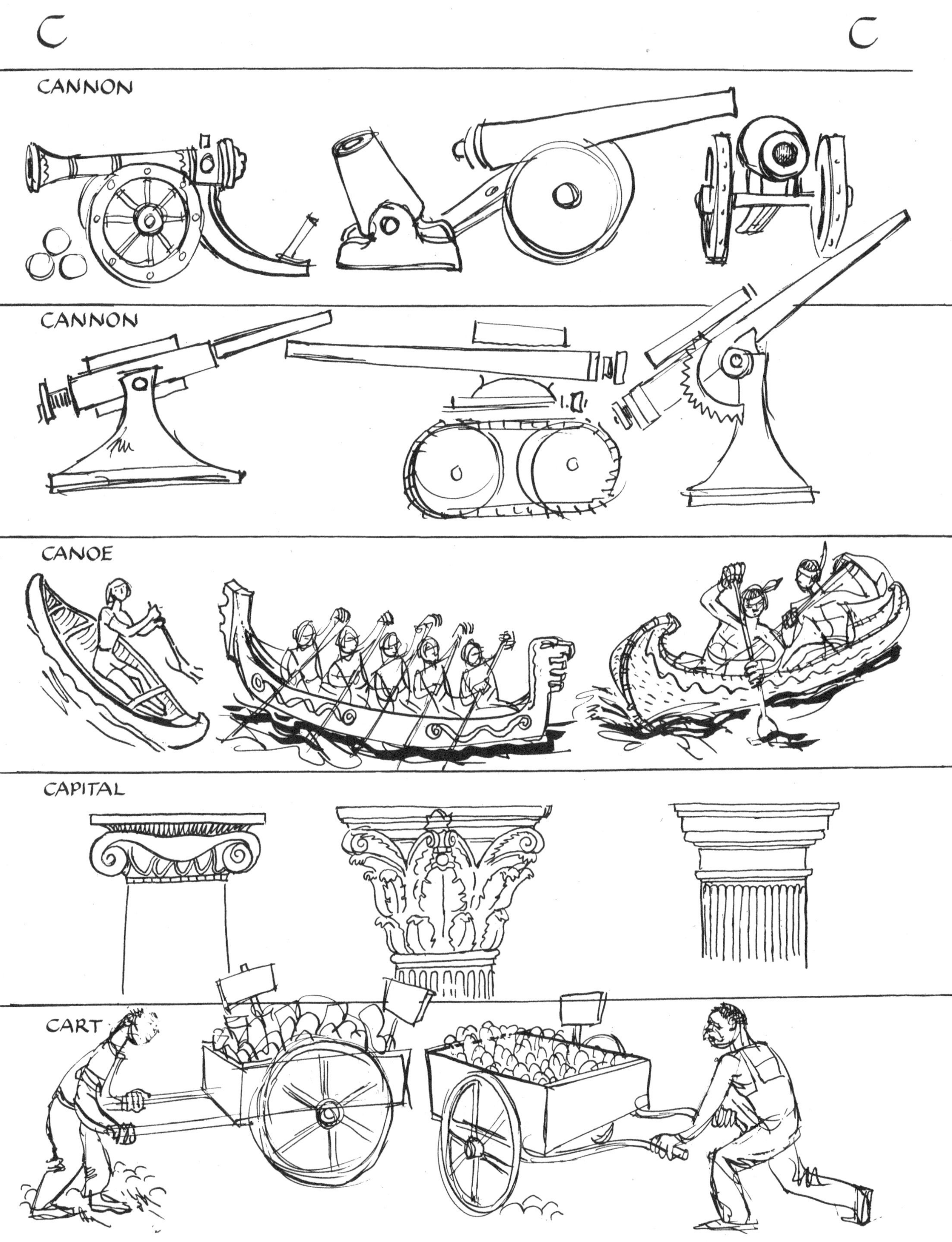
CANNON
CANNON
CANOE
CAPITAL
CART

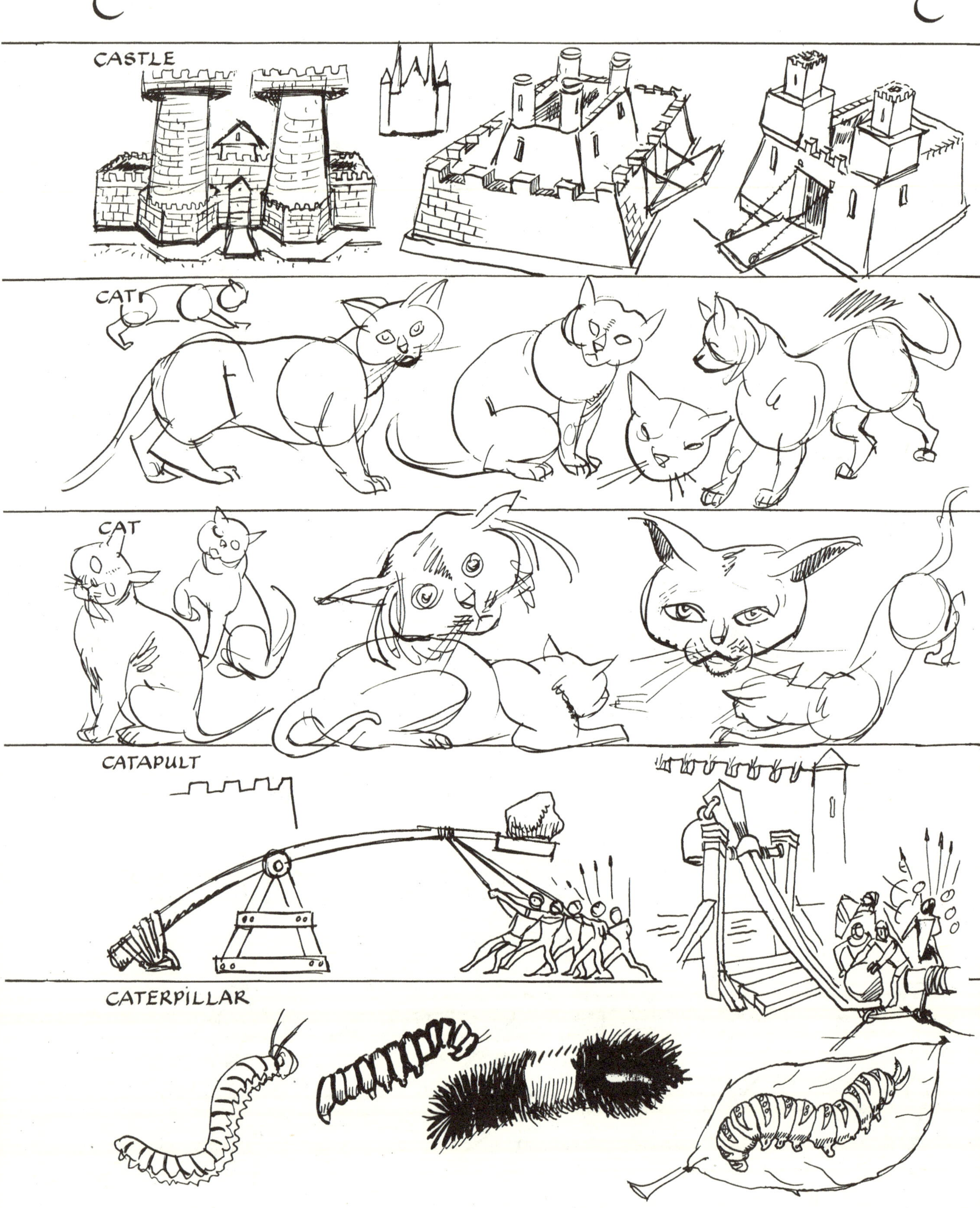
CASTLE
CAT
CAT
CATAPULT
CATERPILLAR

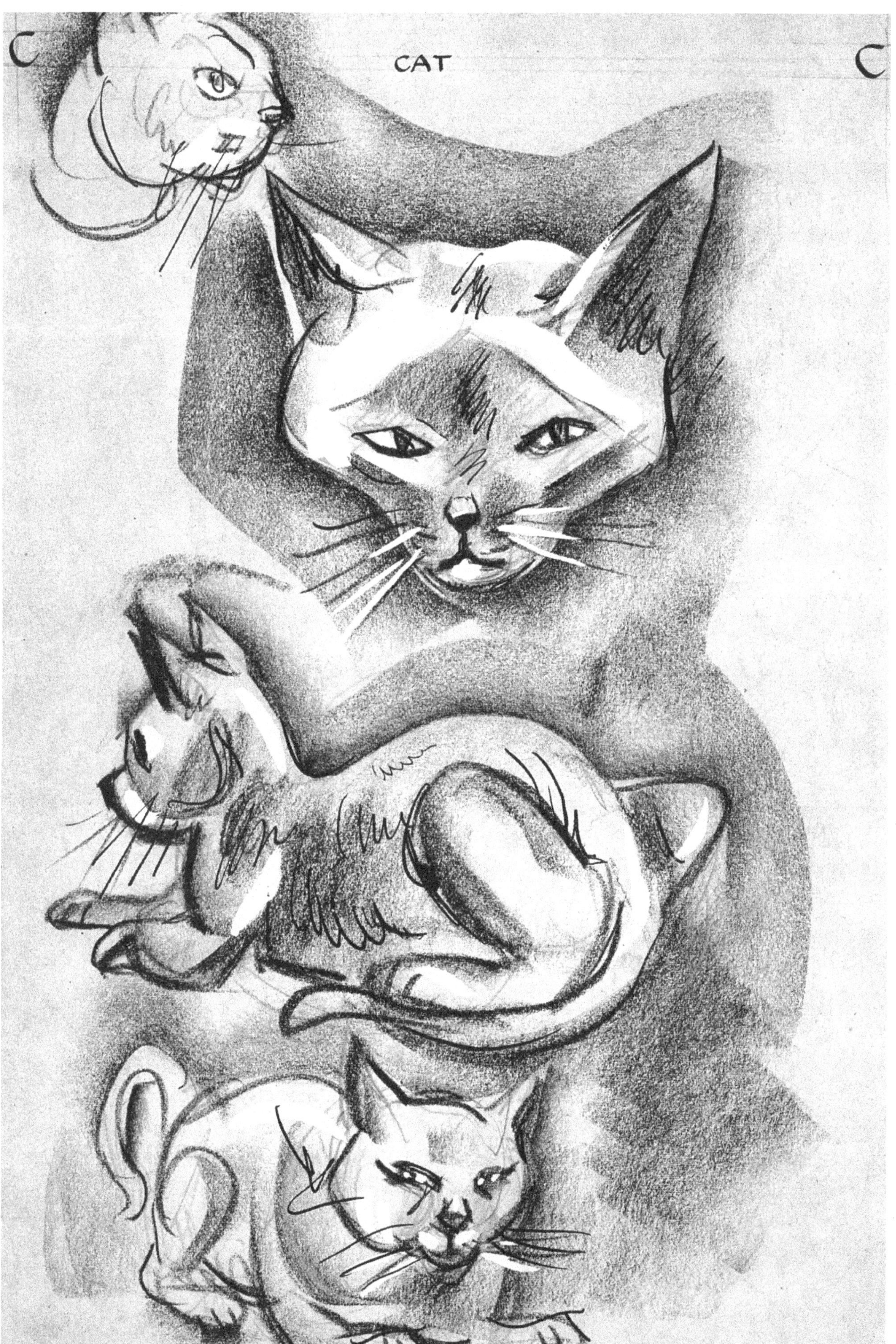
C
CAT
C

C C

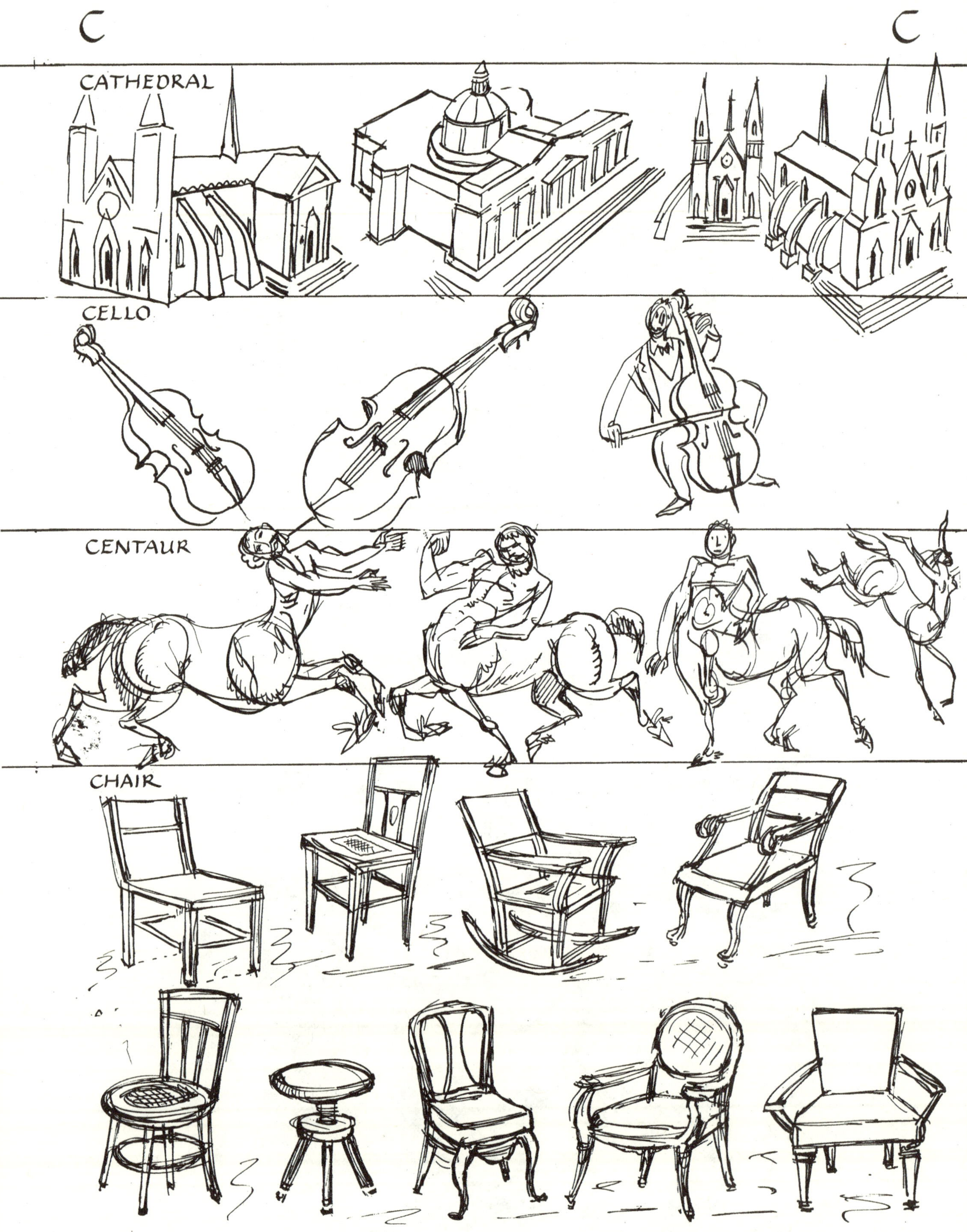

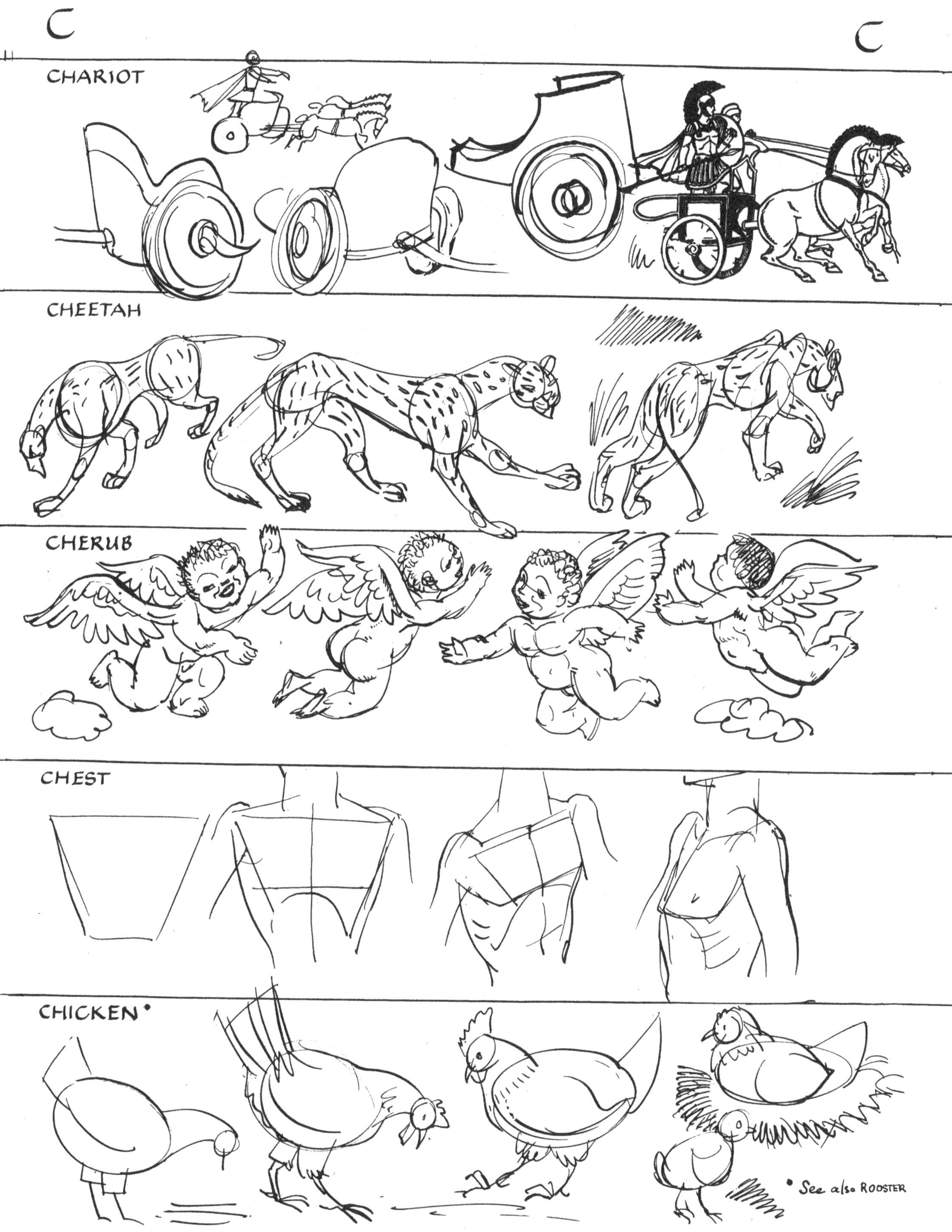
CHARIOT
CHEETAH
CHERUB
CHEST
CHICKEN *
* See also ROOSTER

CHILDREN

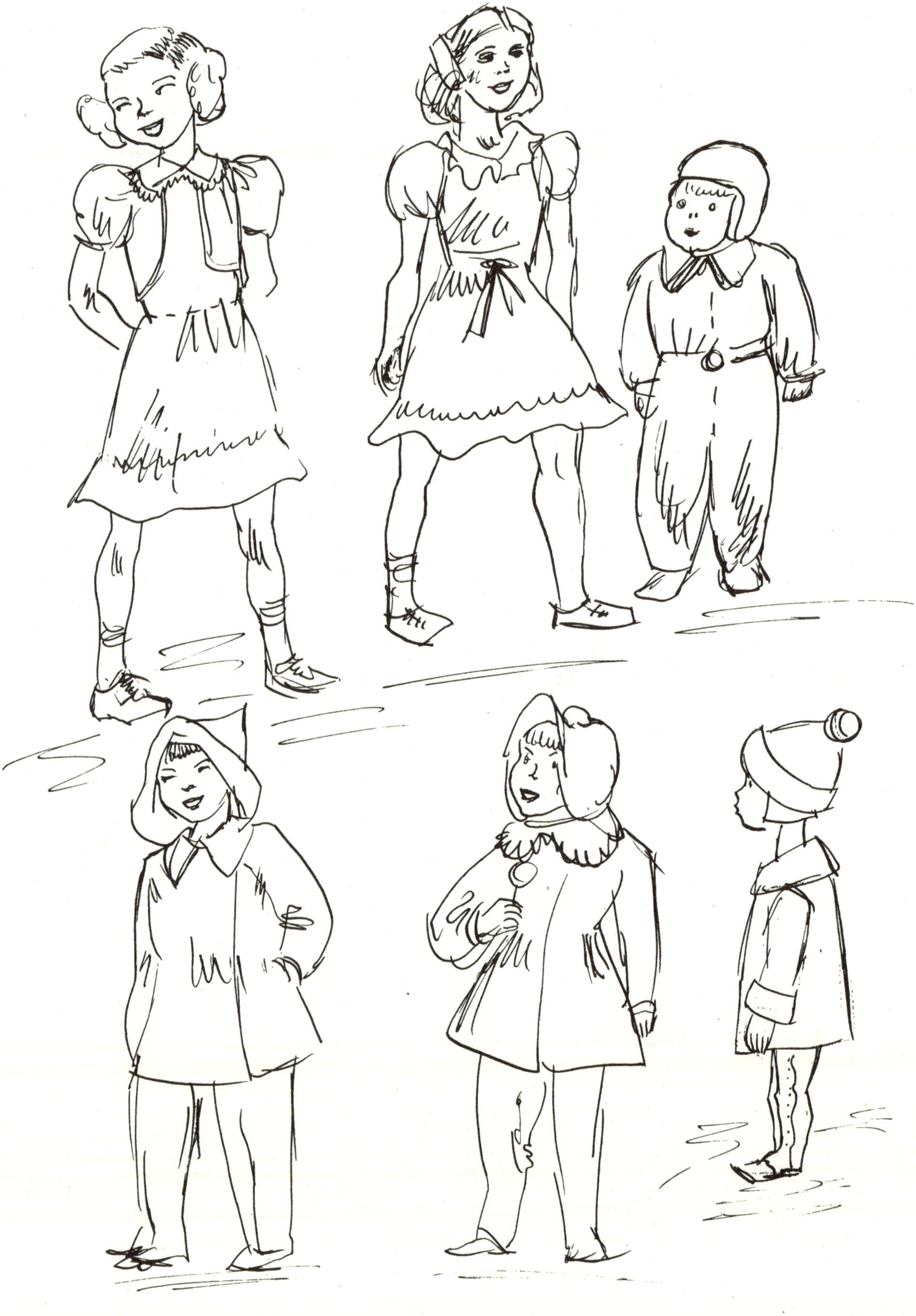

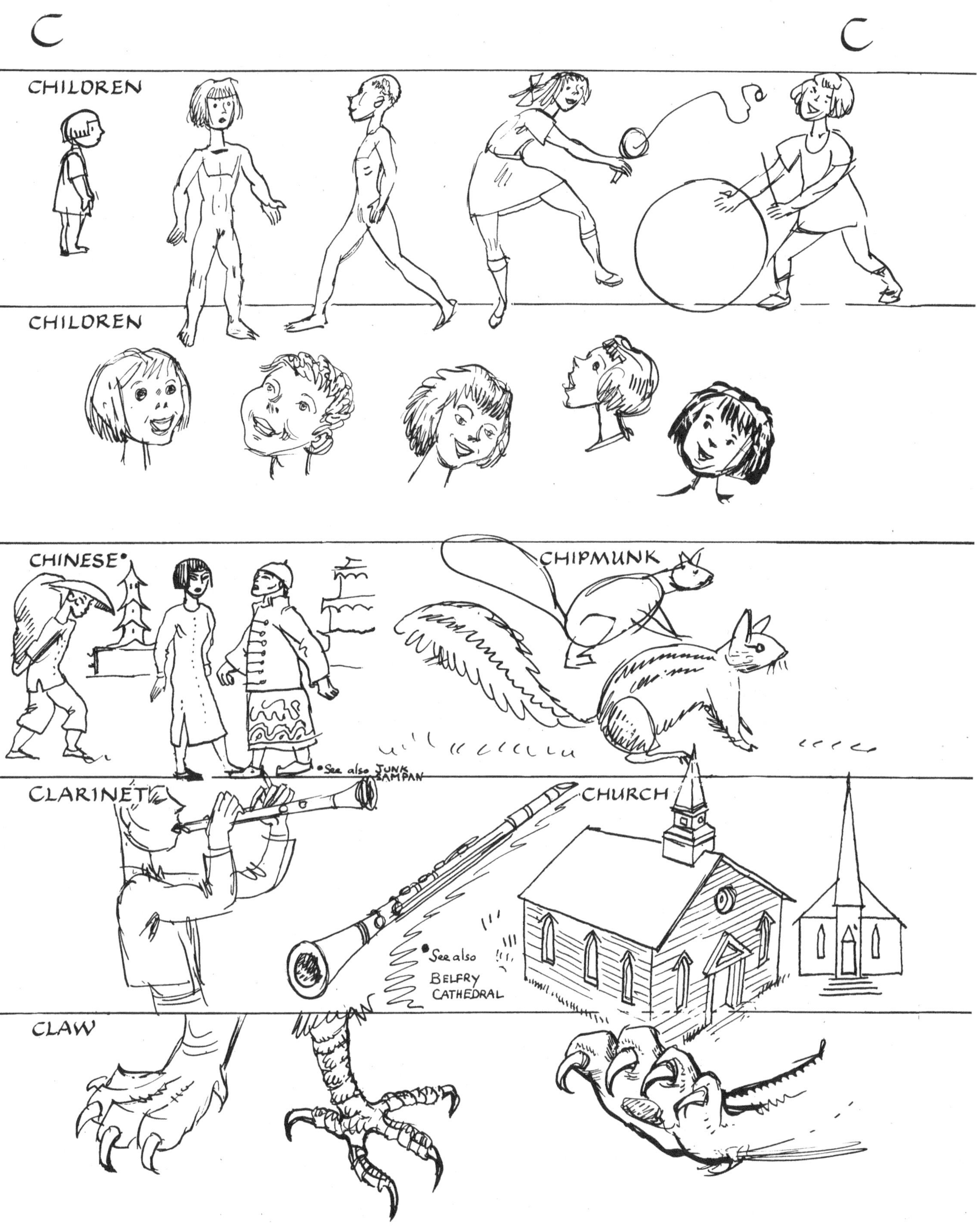
CHILDREN
CHILDREN
CHINESE•
CHIPMUNK
•See also JUNK
SAMPAN
CLARINET
CHURCH
•See also
BELFRY
CATHEDRAL
CLAW

CLOTHES

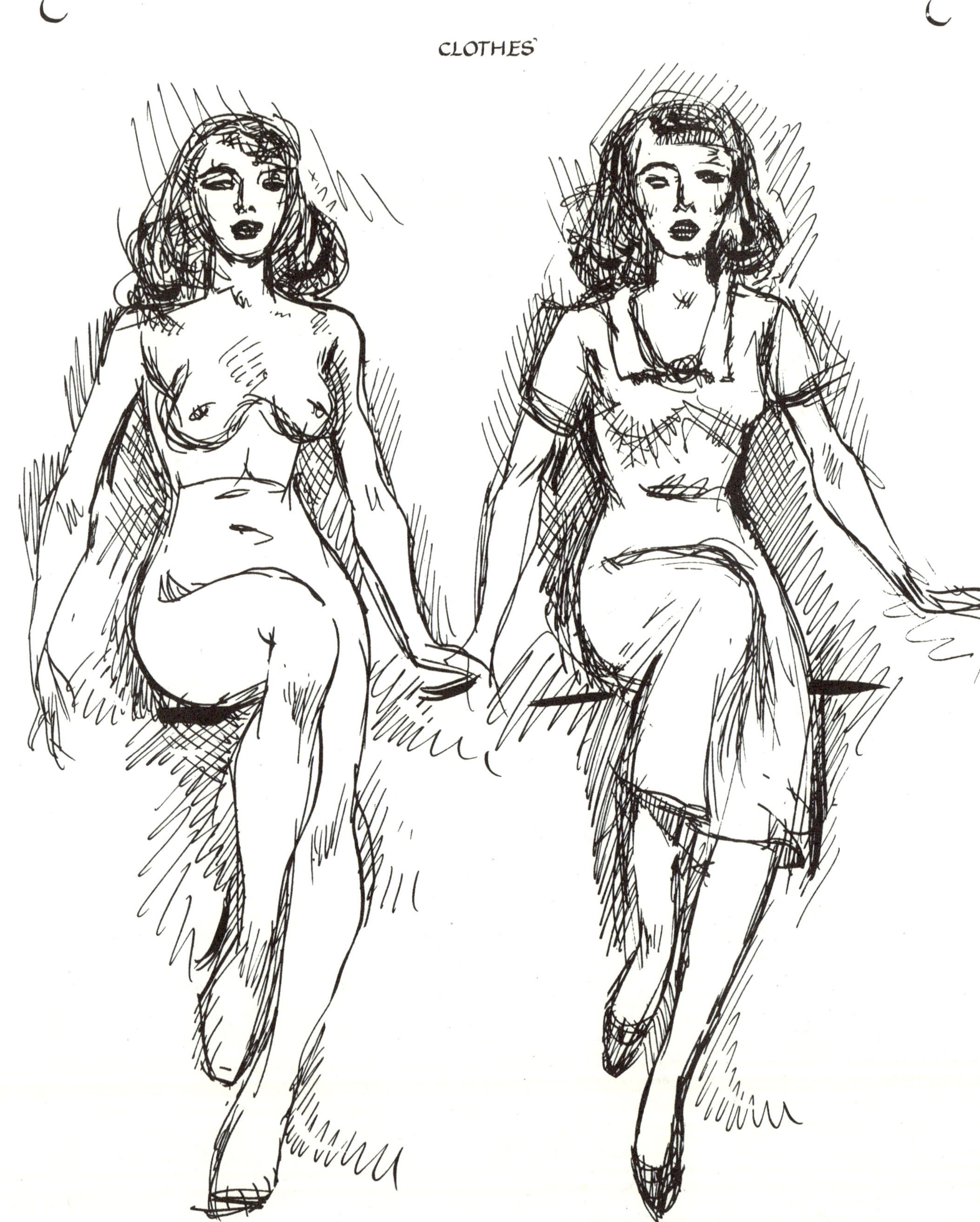

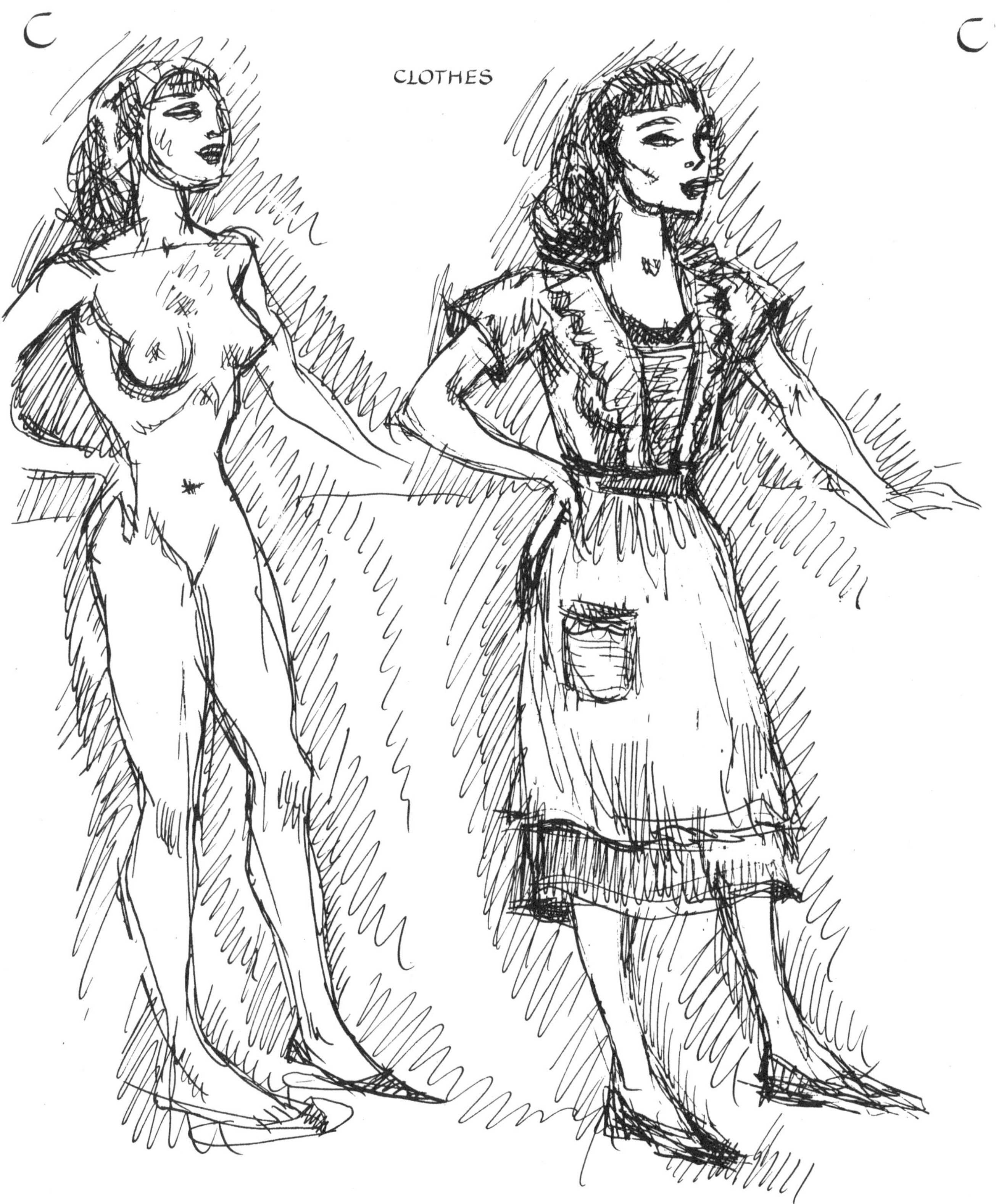
CLOTHES

C

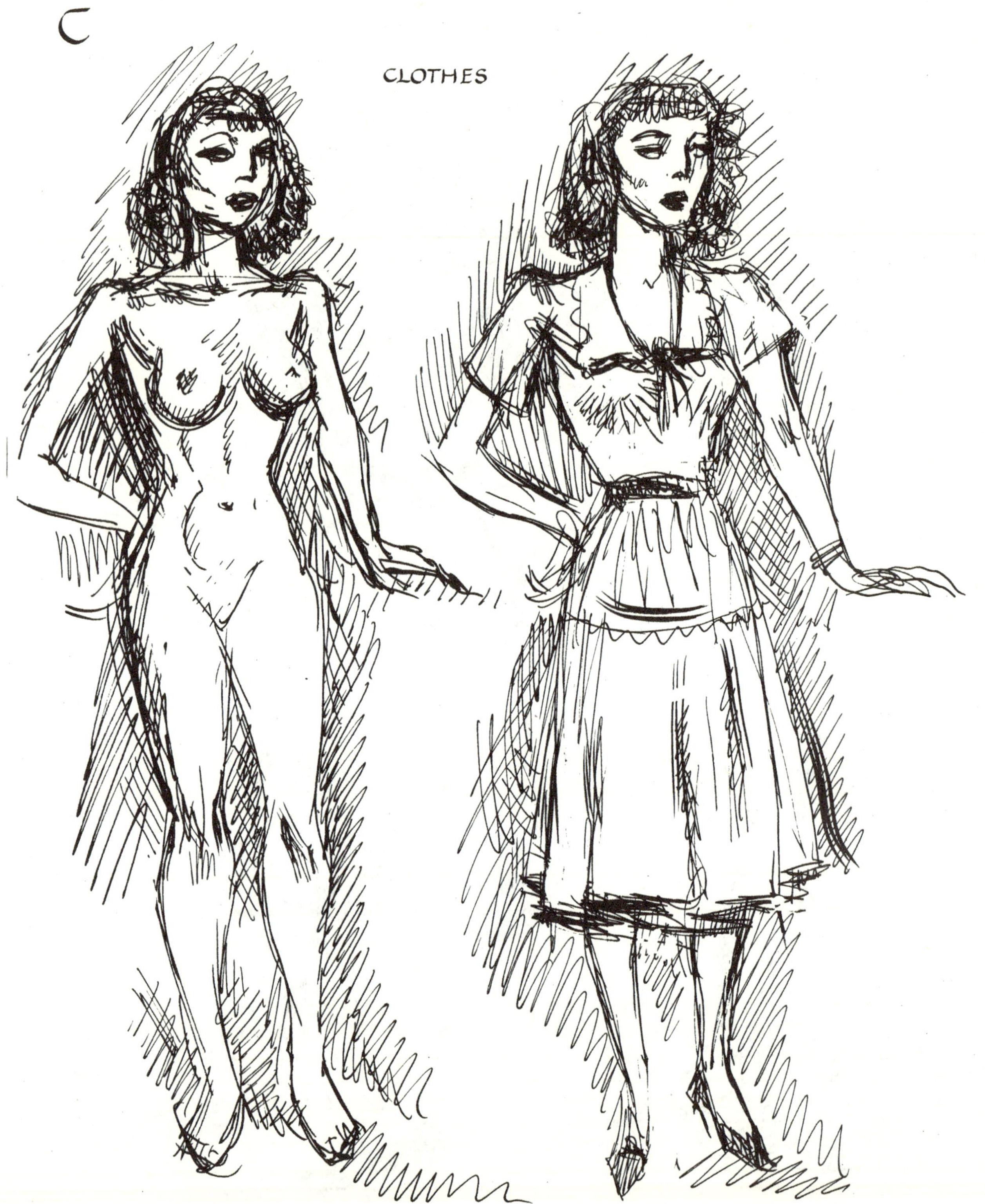

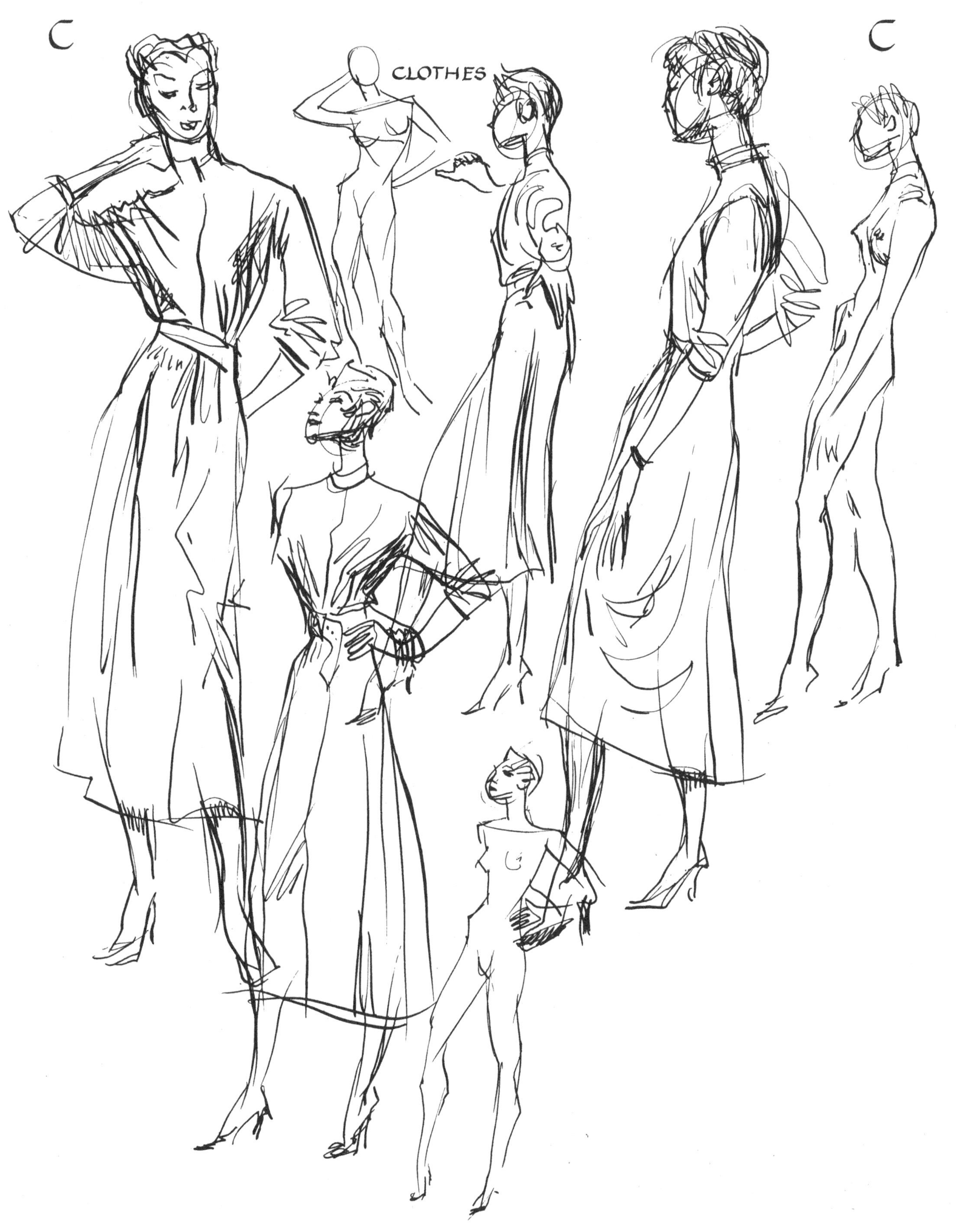
CLOTHES

CLOTHES

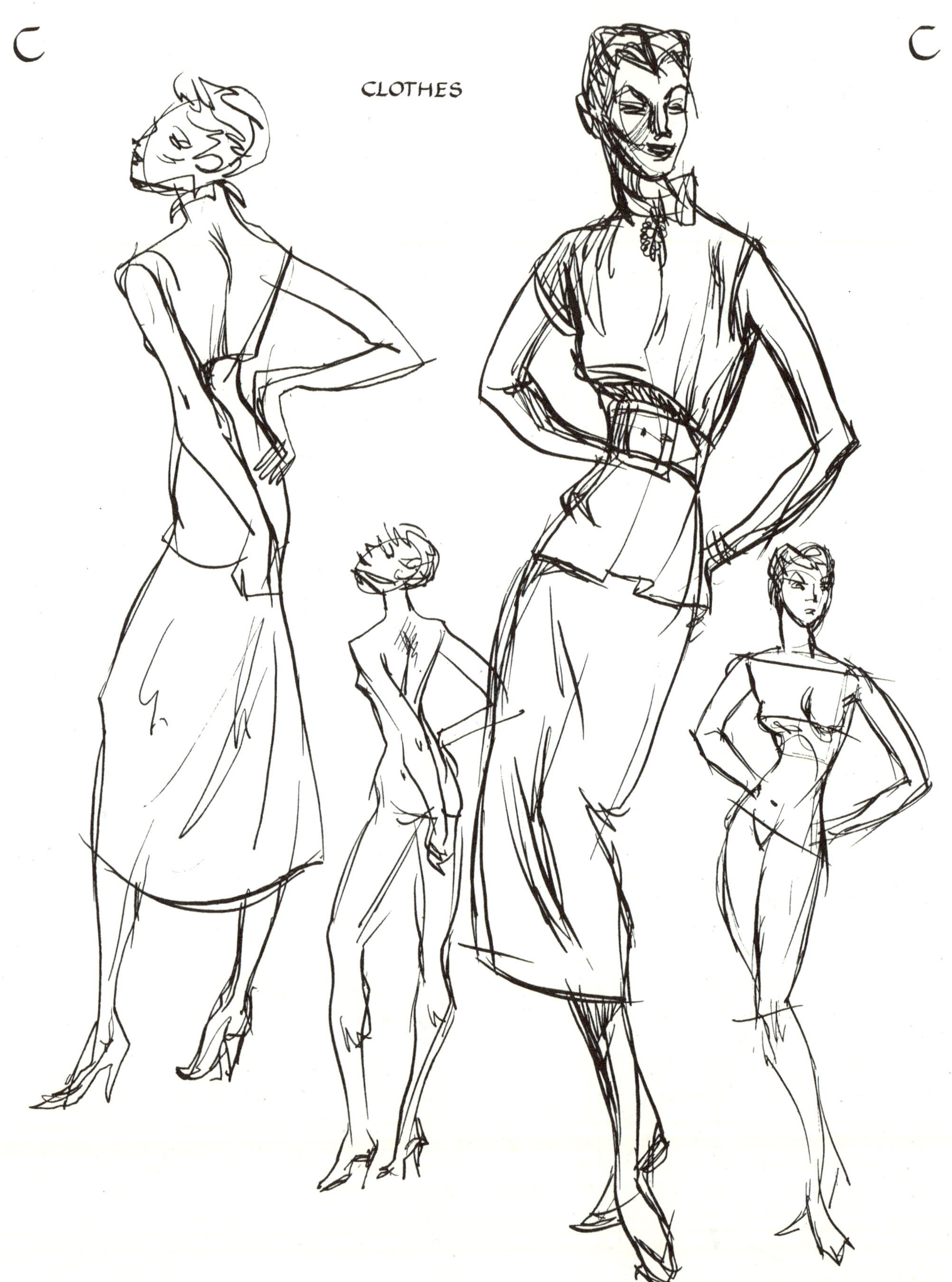

CLOTHES

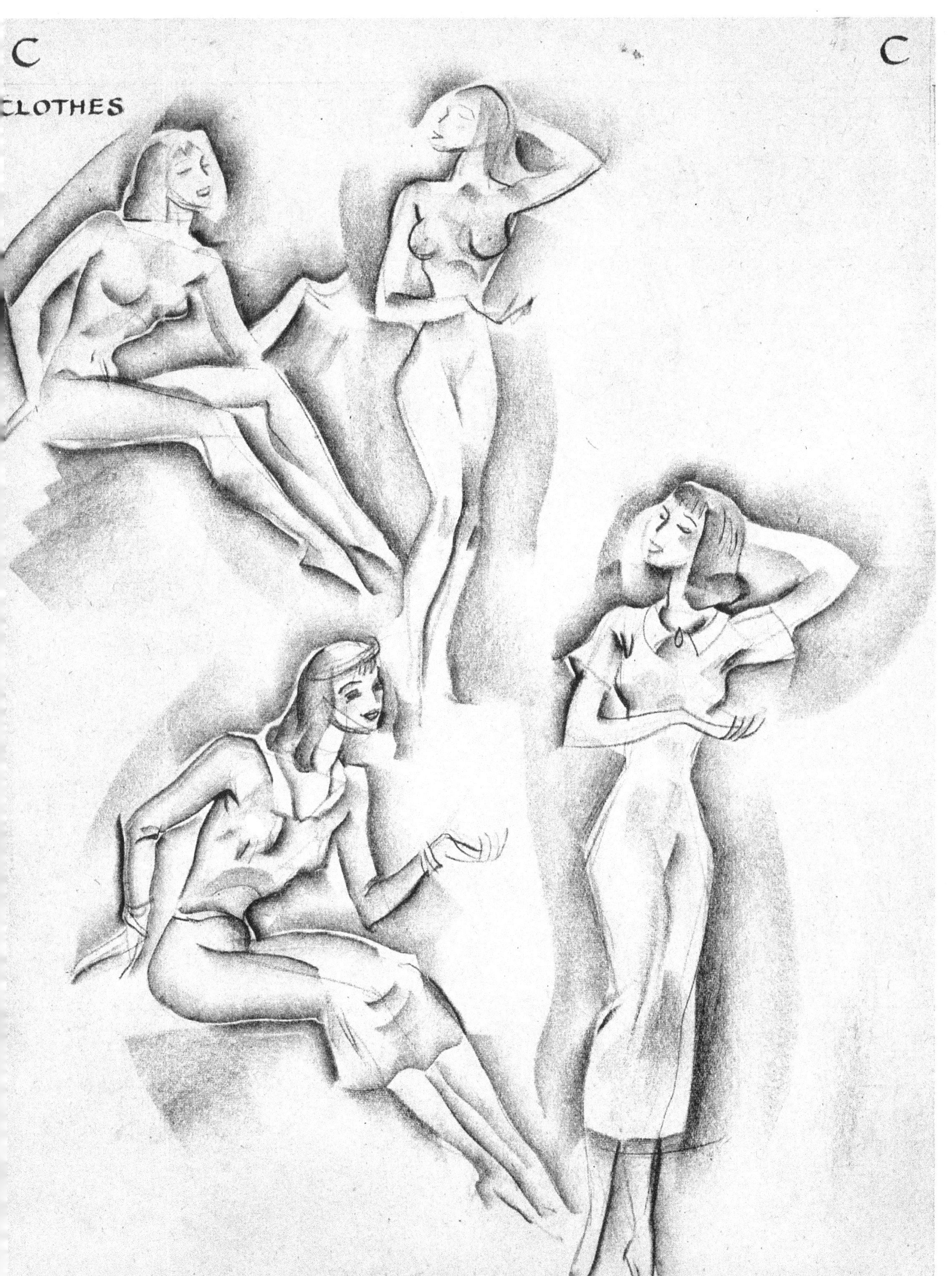

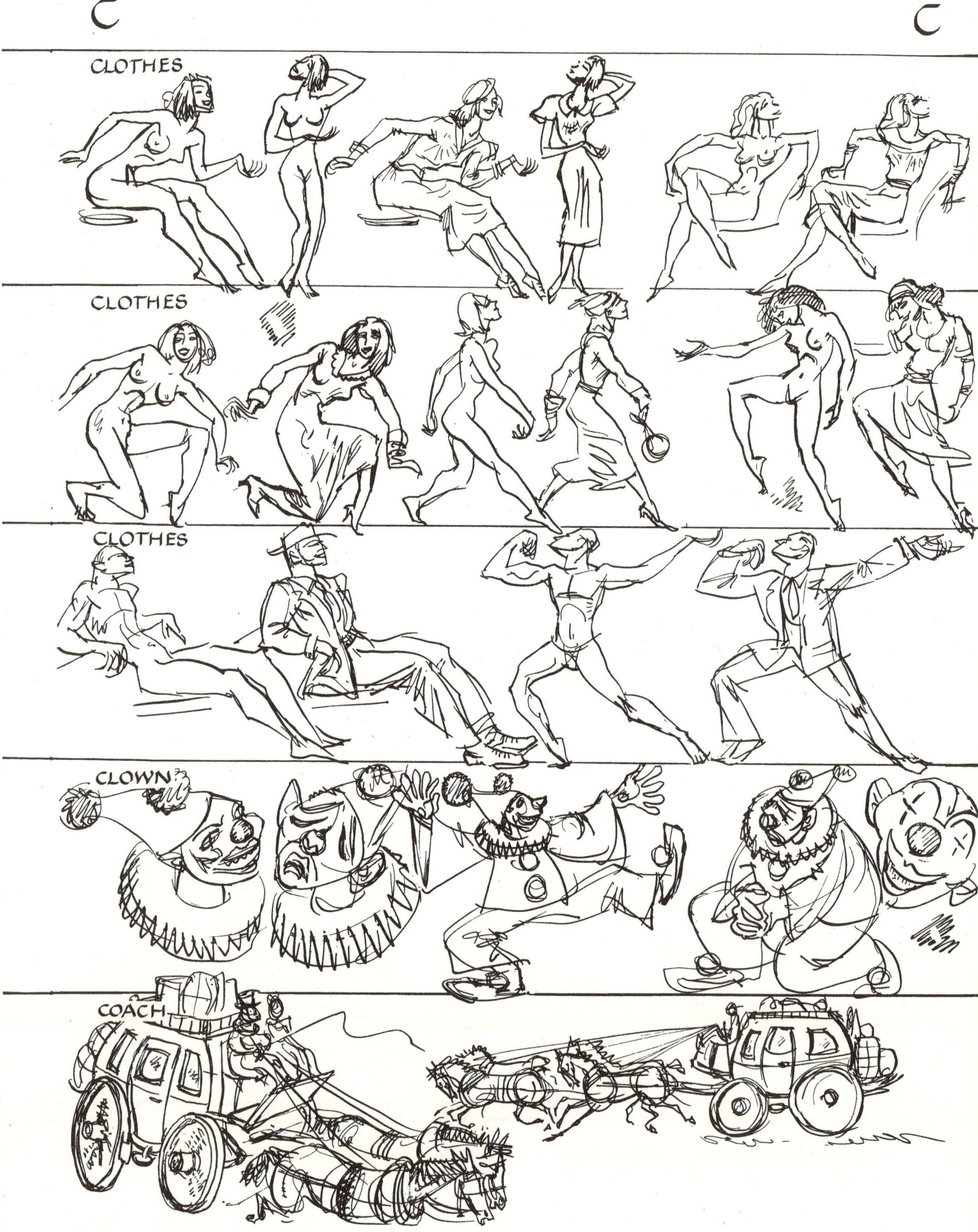
CLOTHES
CLOTHES
CLOTHES
CLOWN
COACH

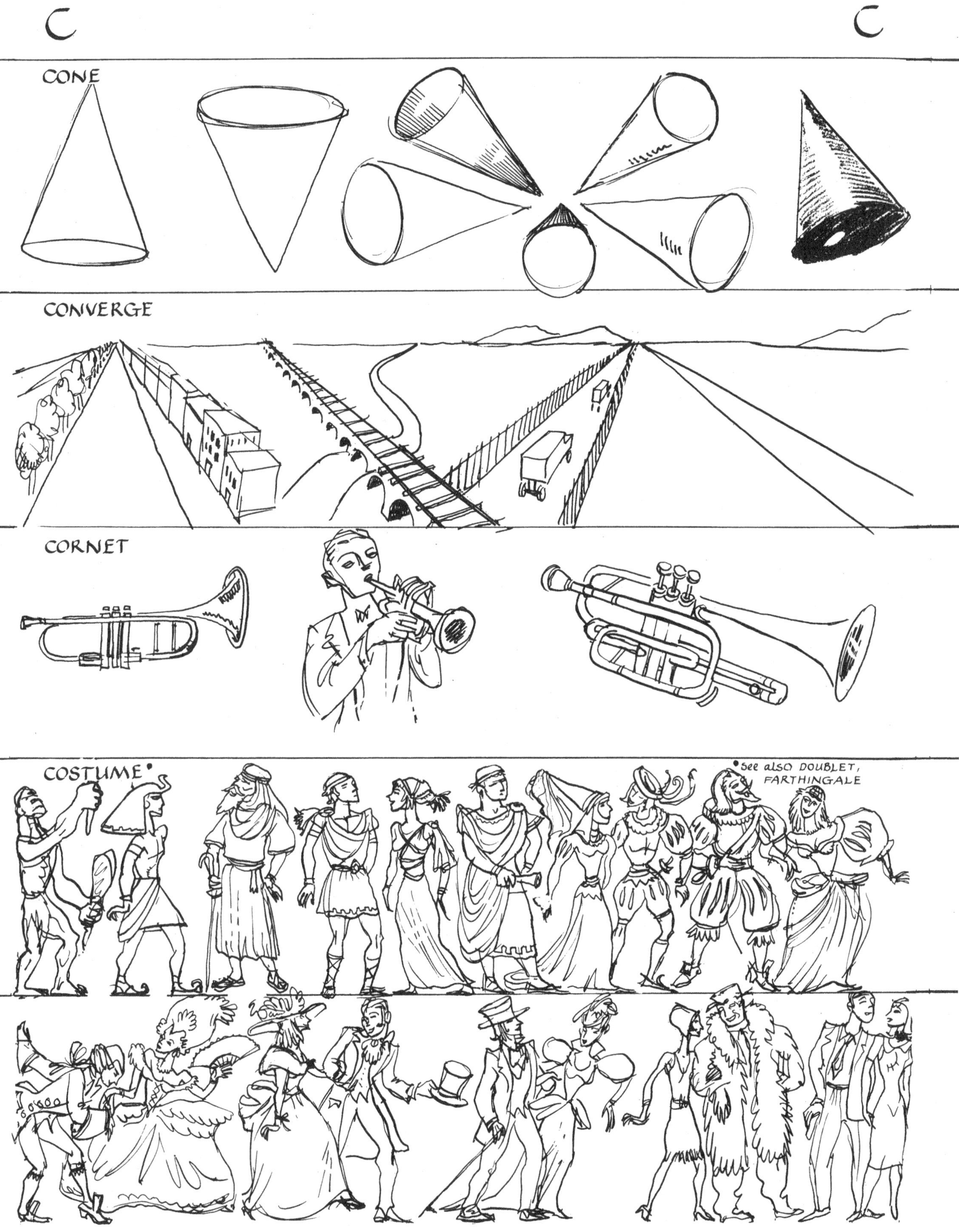
CONE
CONVERGE
CORNET
COSTUME*
*see also DOUBLET, FARTHINGALE

COSTUME

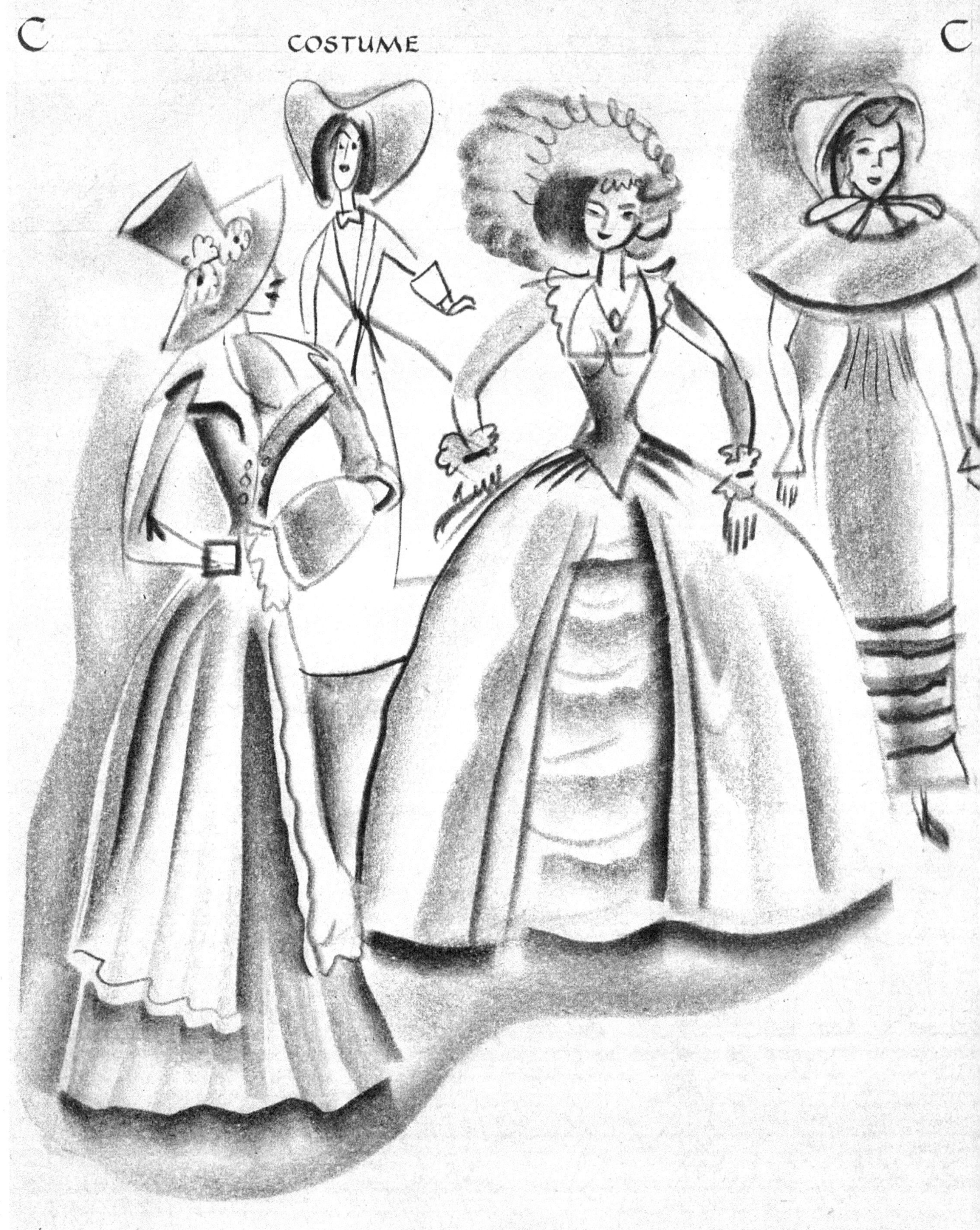

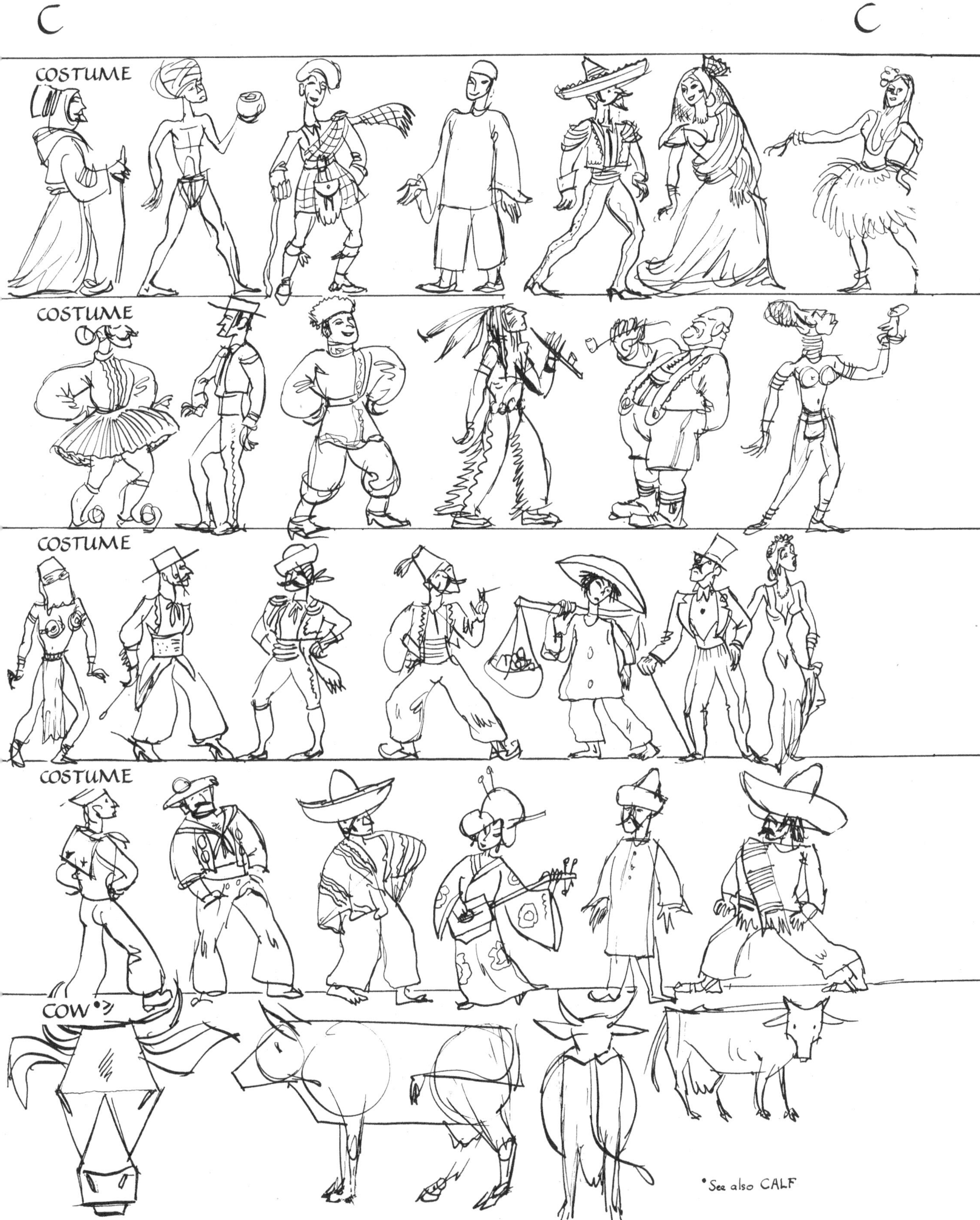

*See also CALF

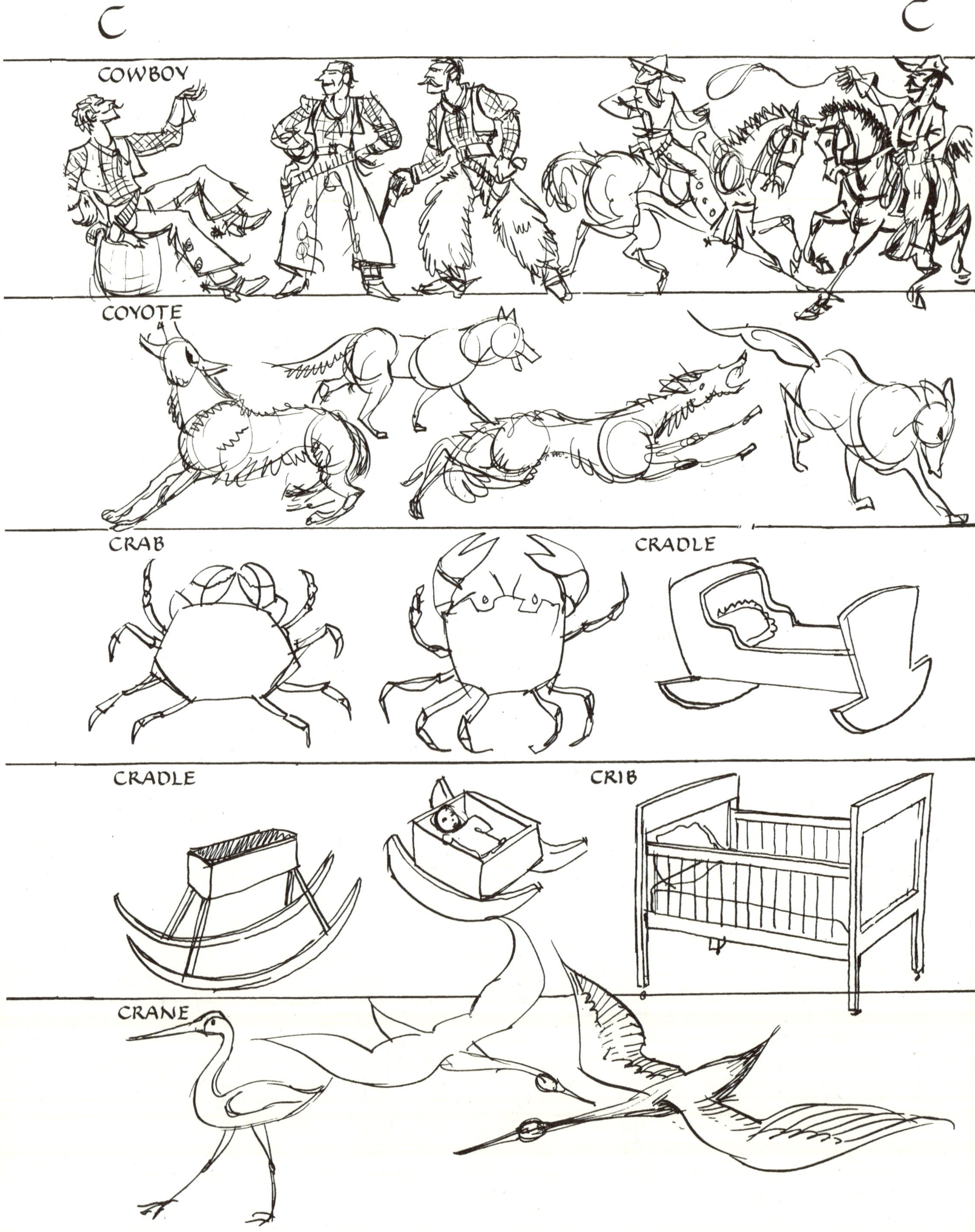
COWBOY
COYOTE
CRAB
CRADLE
CRADLE
CRIB
CRANE

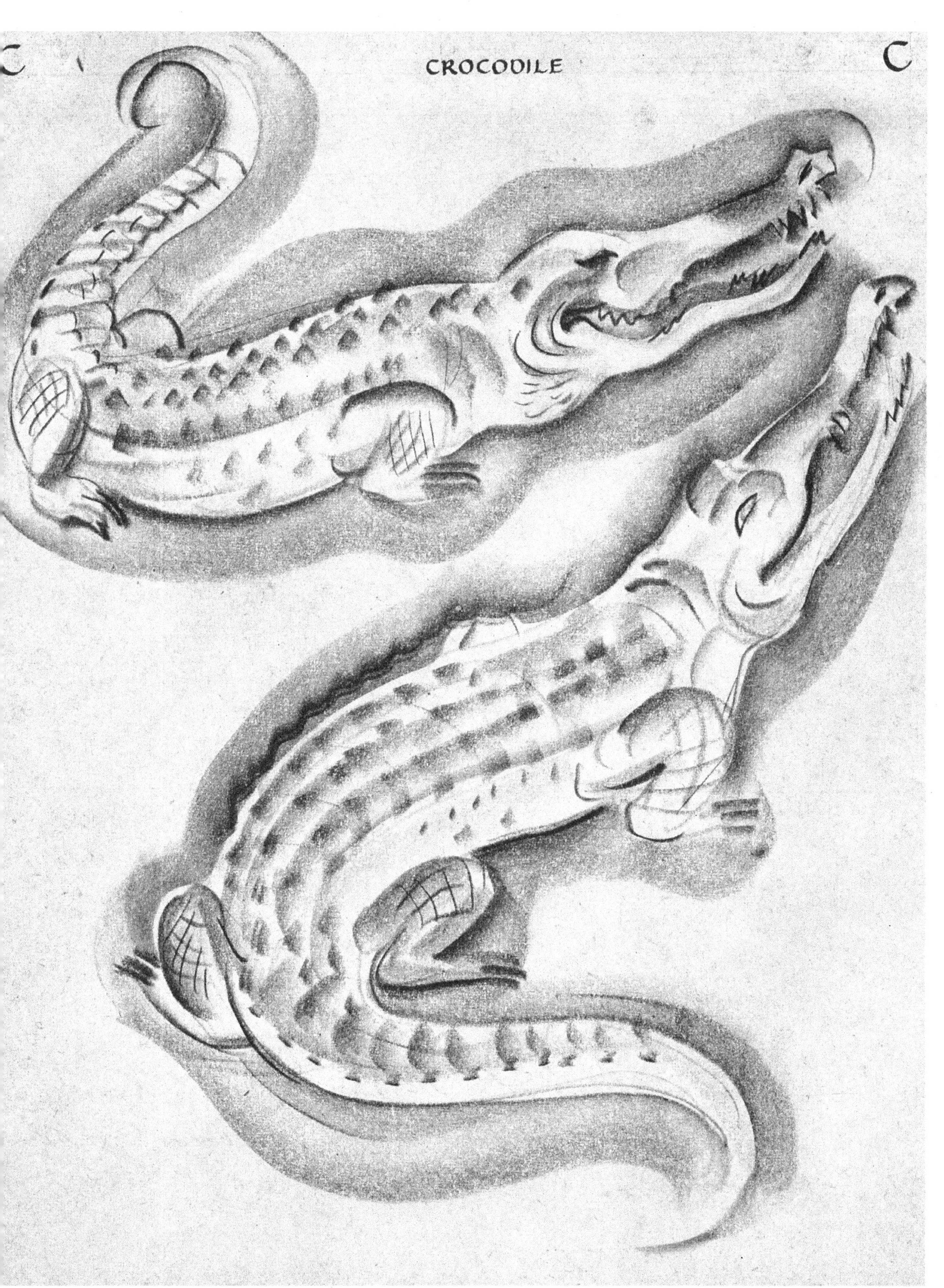
C
CROCODILE
C

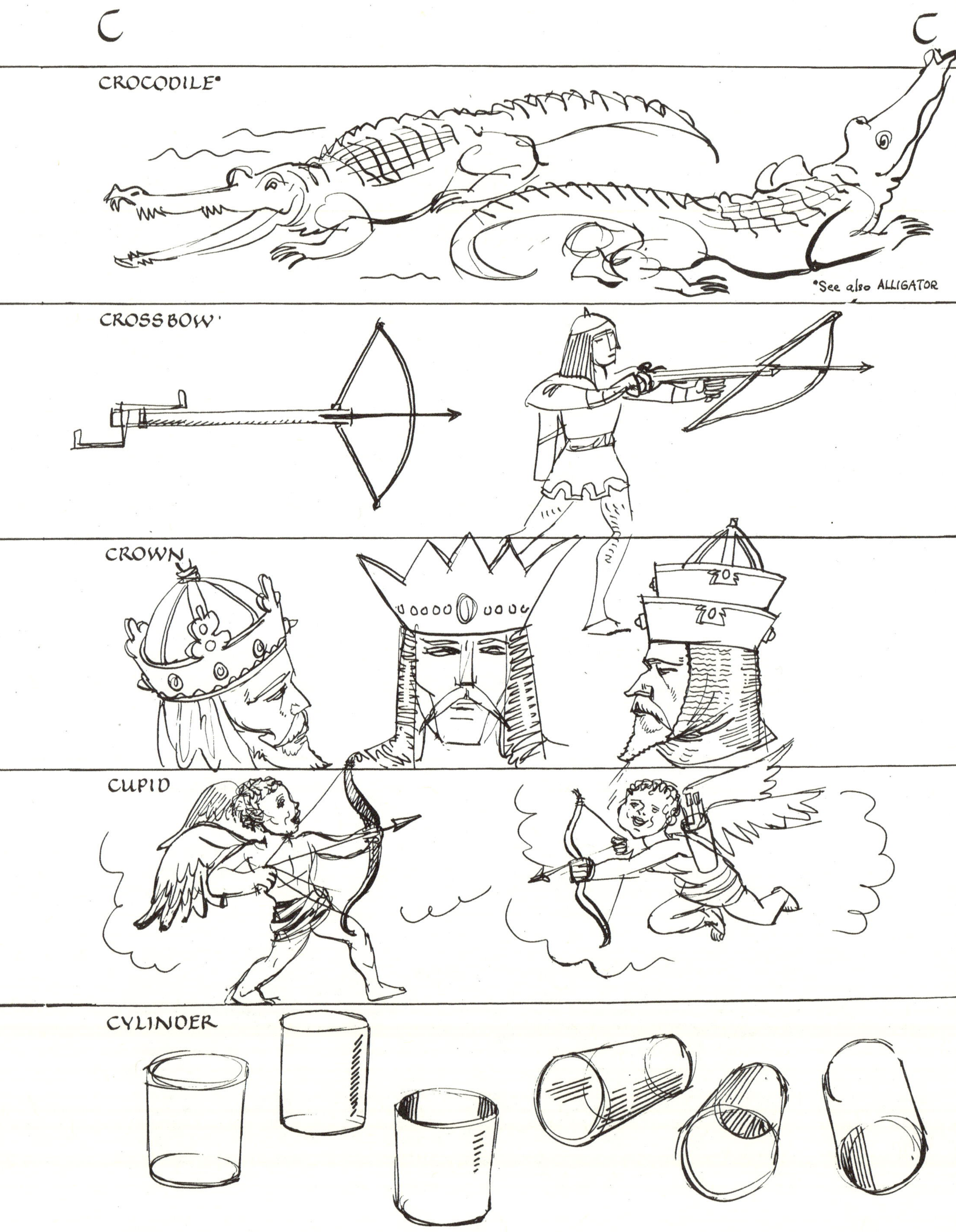
CROCODILE*
*See also ALLIGATOR
CROSSBOW
CROWN
CUPID
CYLINDER

DANCE

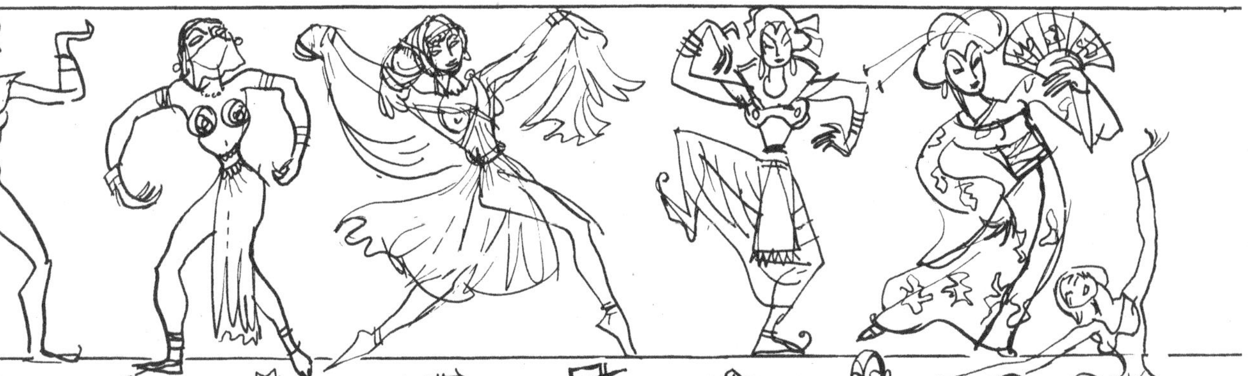

DANCE

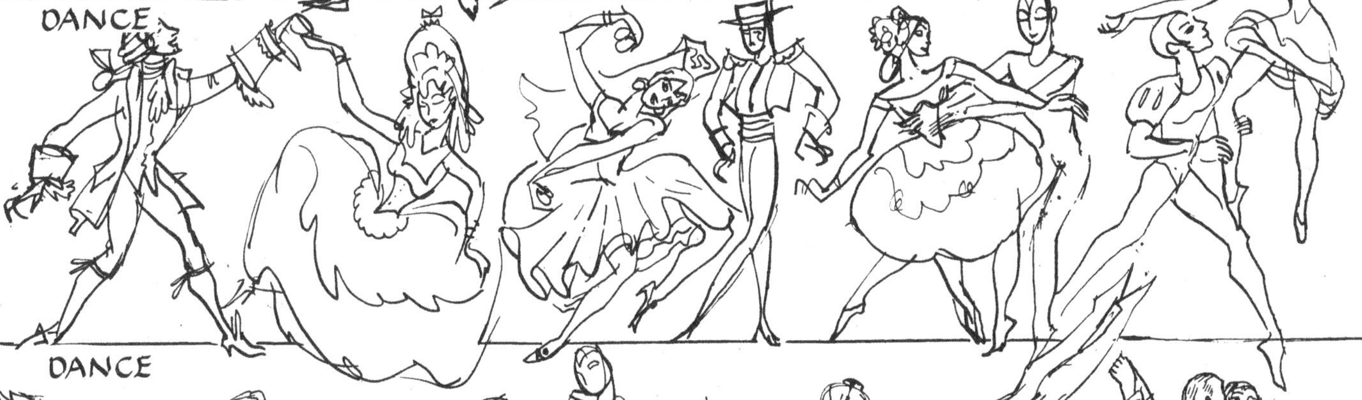

DANCE

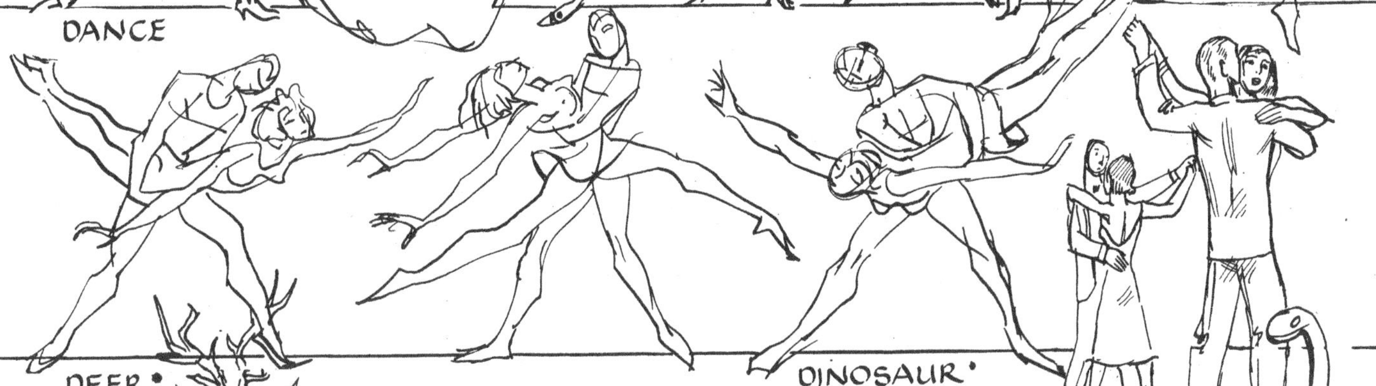

DEER •

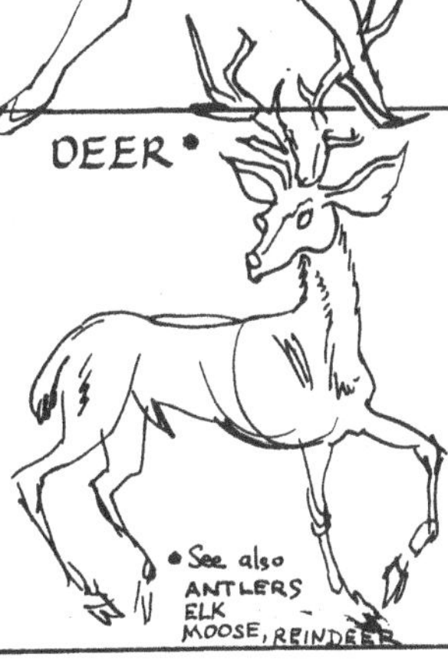

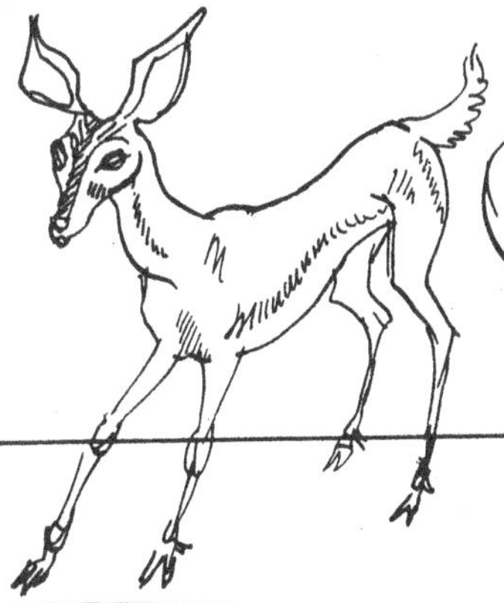

• See also
ANTLERS
ELK
MOOSE, REINDEER

DINOSAUR •

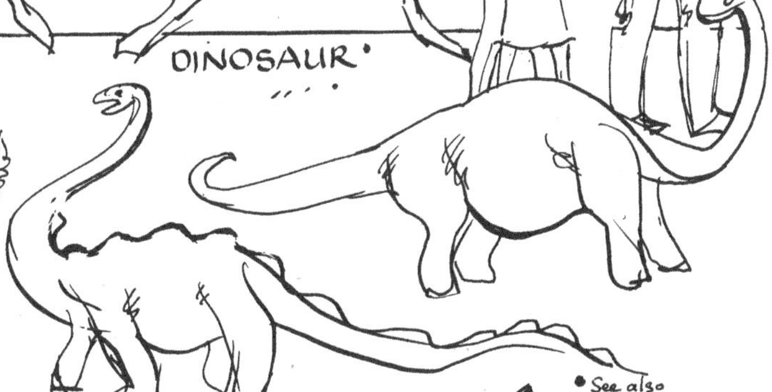

• See also
PREHISTORIC ANIMALS

DIRIGIBLE

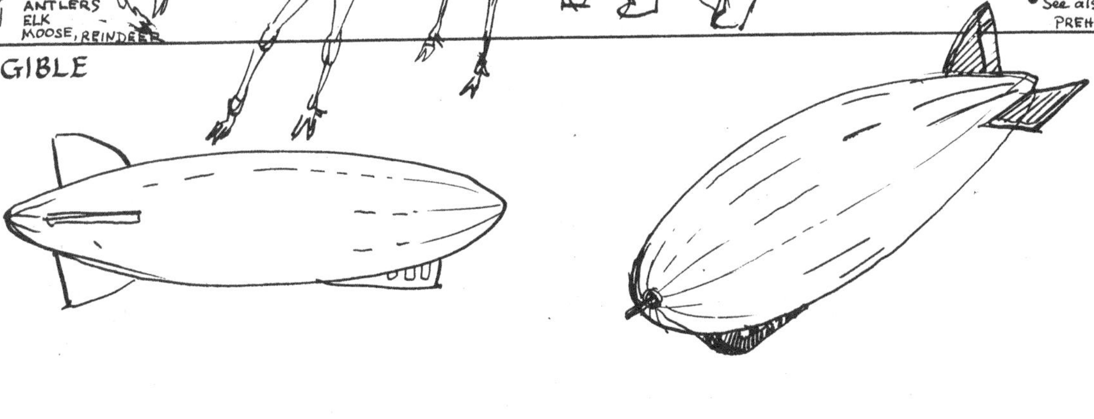

DISH

DIVE

DOG*

*Also indexed by BREEDS, ALSO, PUPPY

D

D

DOG

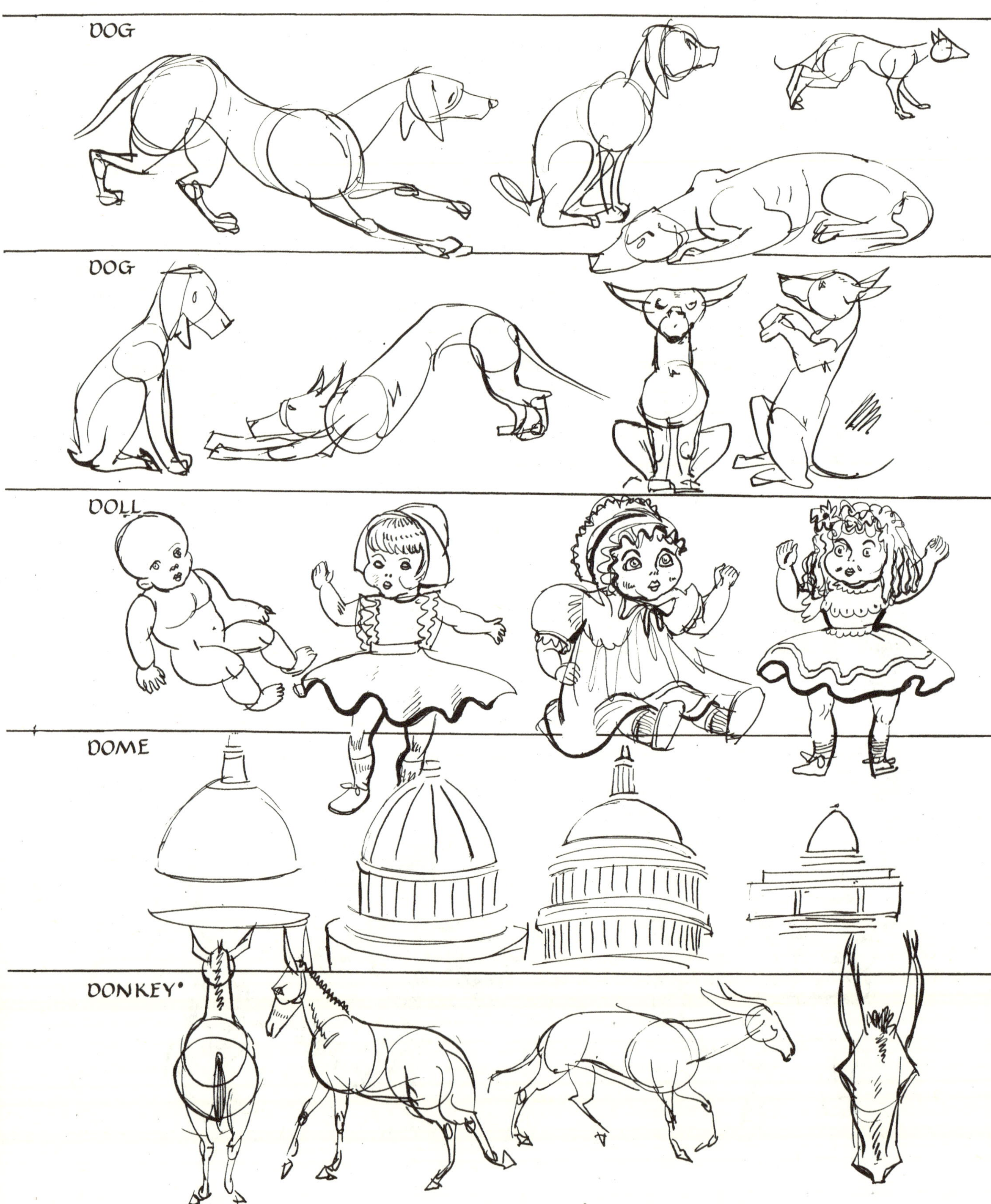

*See also ASS, BURRO

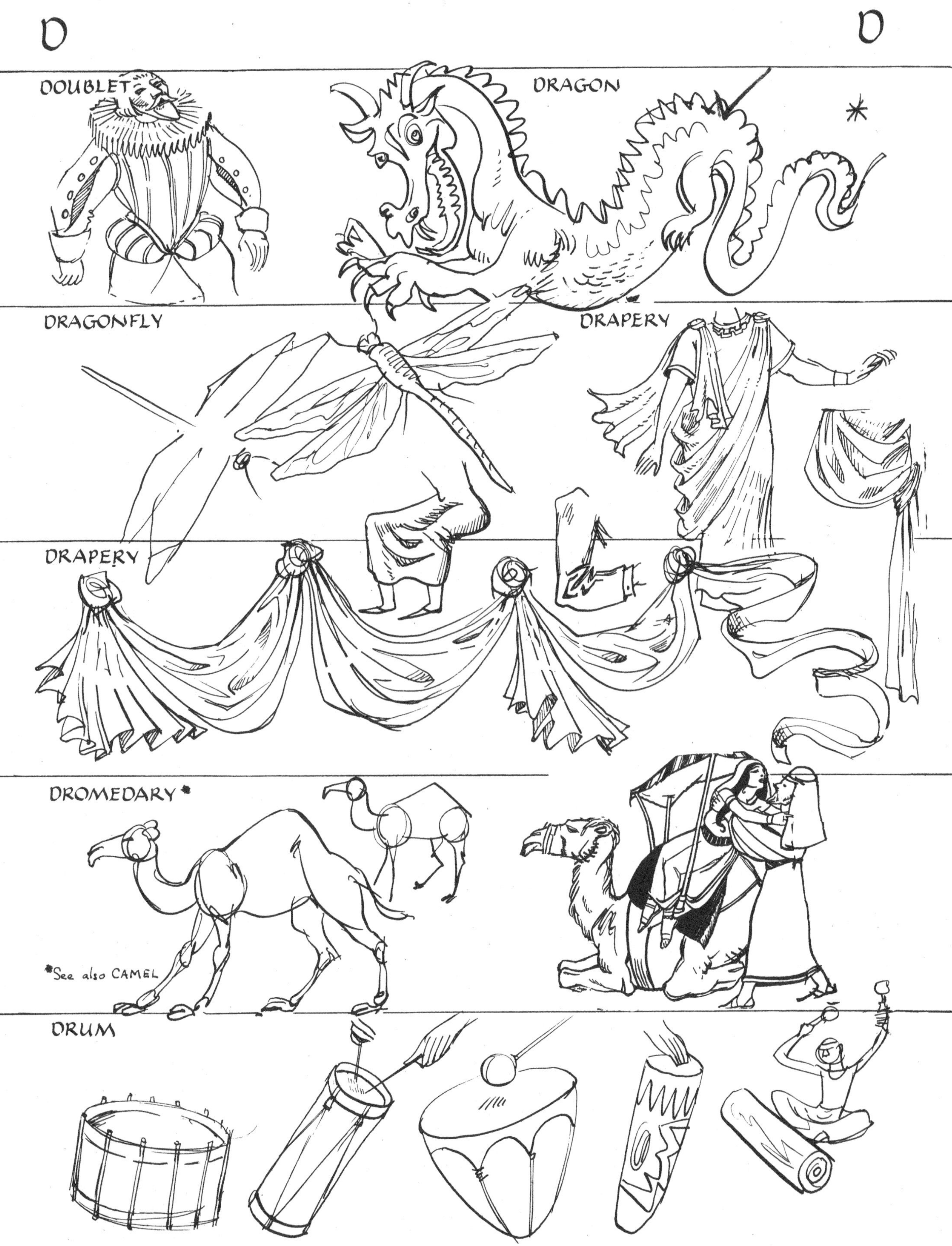
DOUBLET
DRAGON
DRAGONFLY
DRAPERY
DRAPERY
DROMEDARY*
*See also CAMEL
DRUM

 D-E

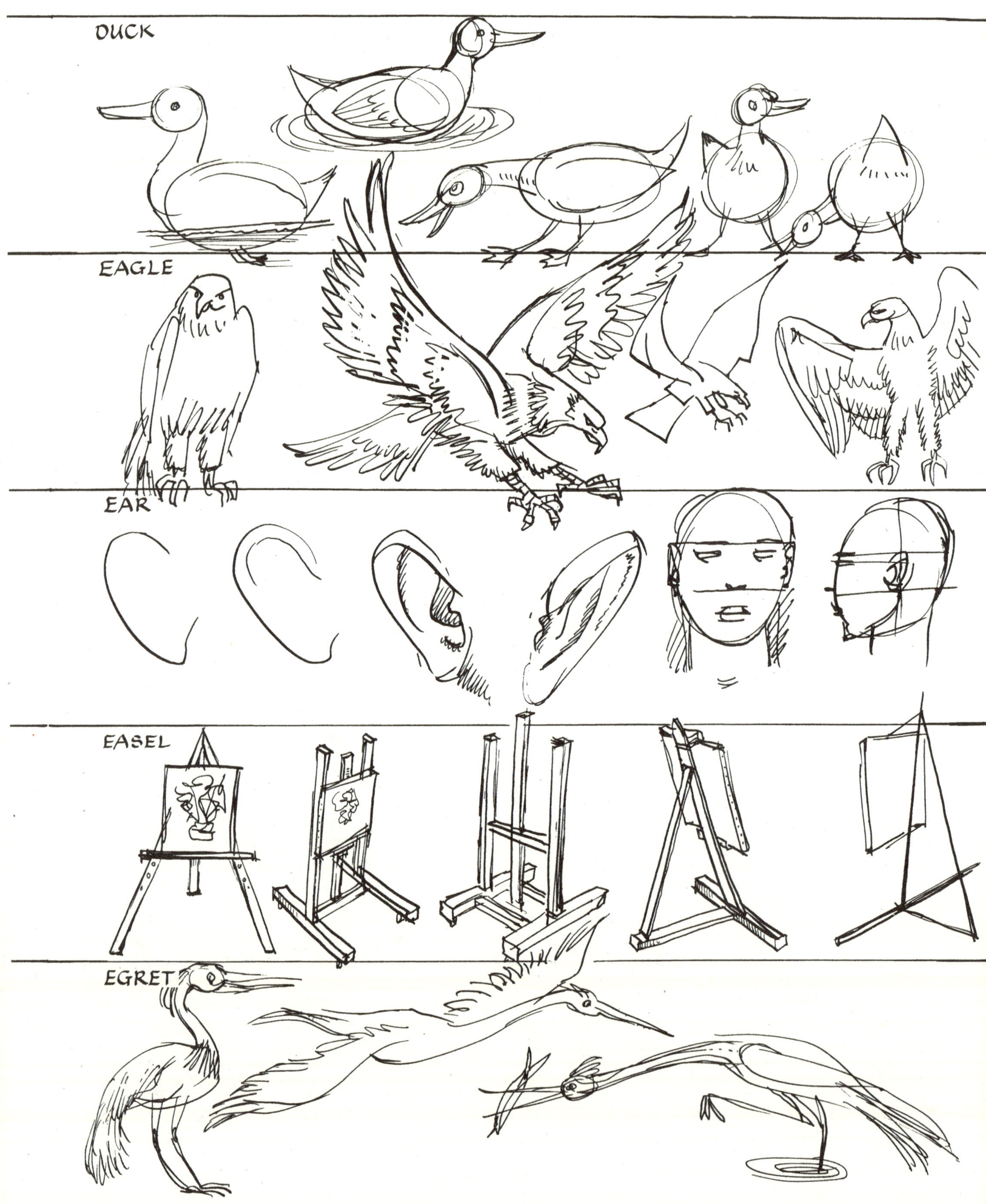

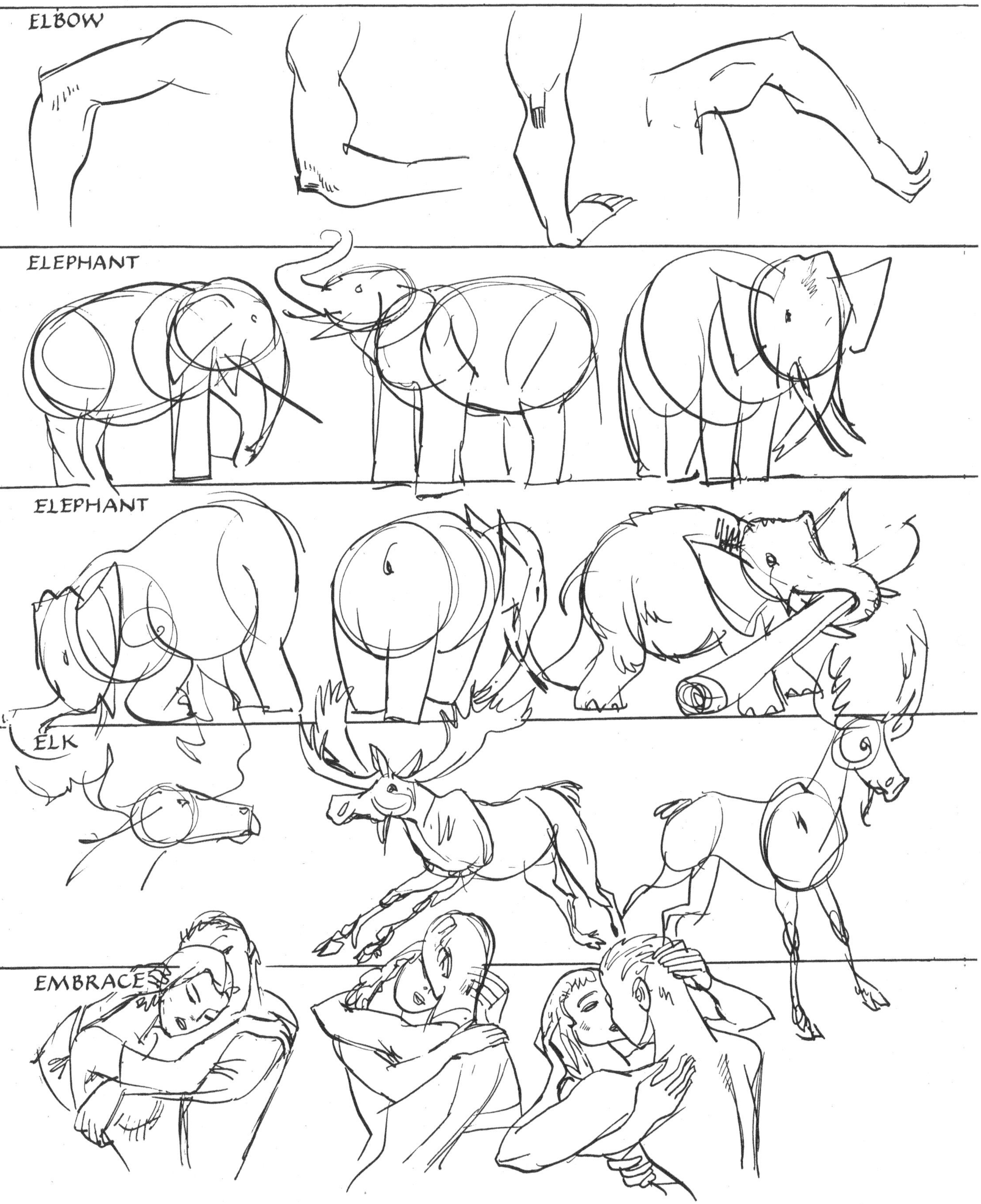

ELBOW

ELEPHANT

ELEPHANT

ELK

EMBRACE

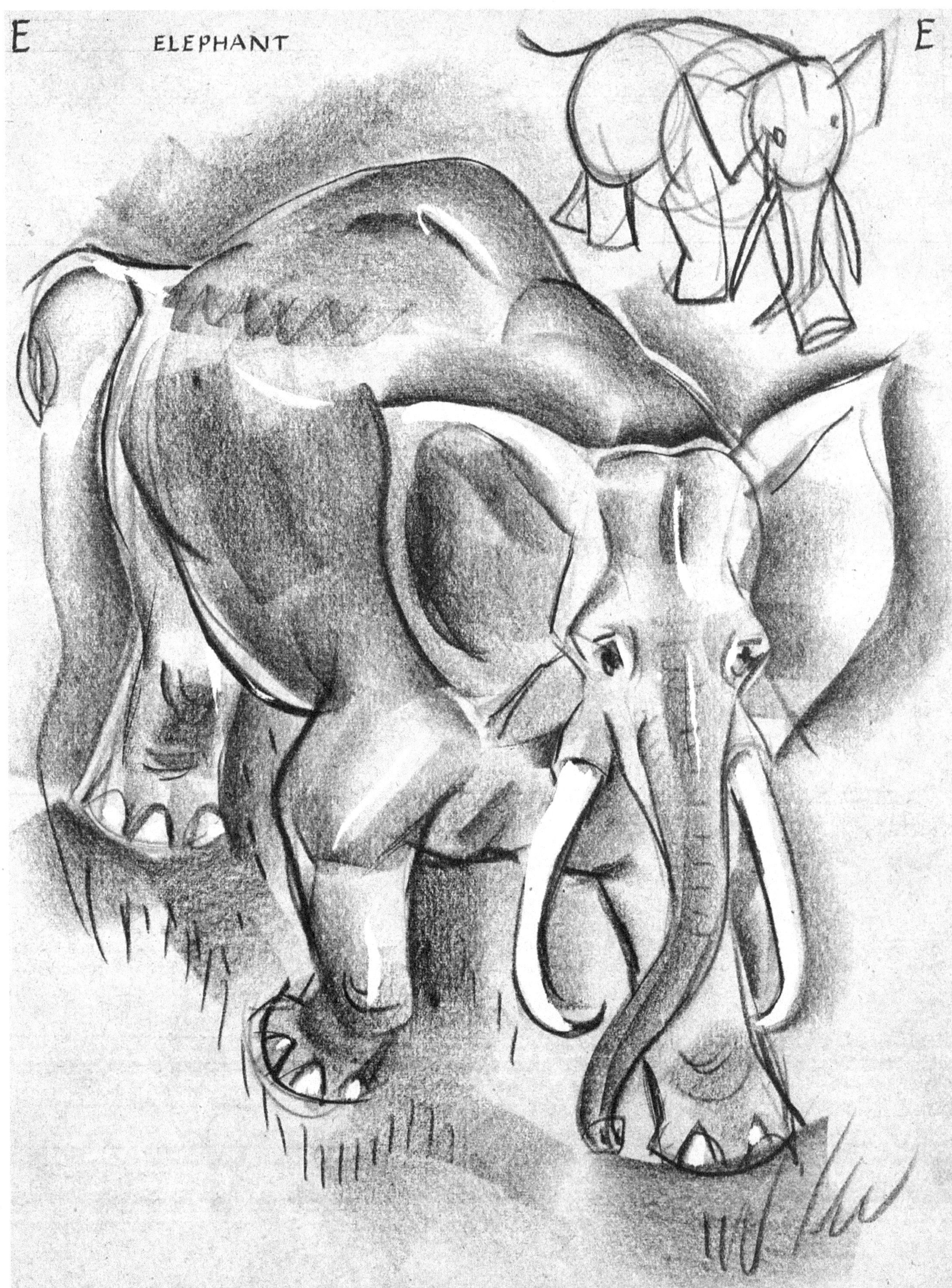
E
ELEPHANT
E

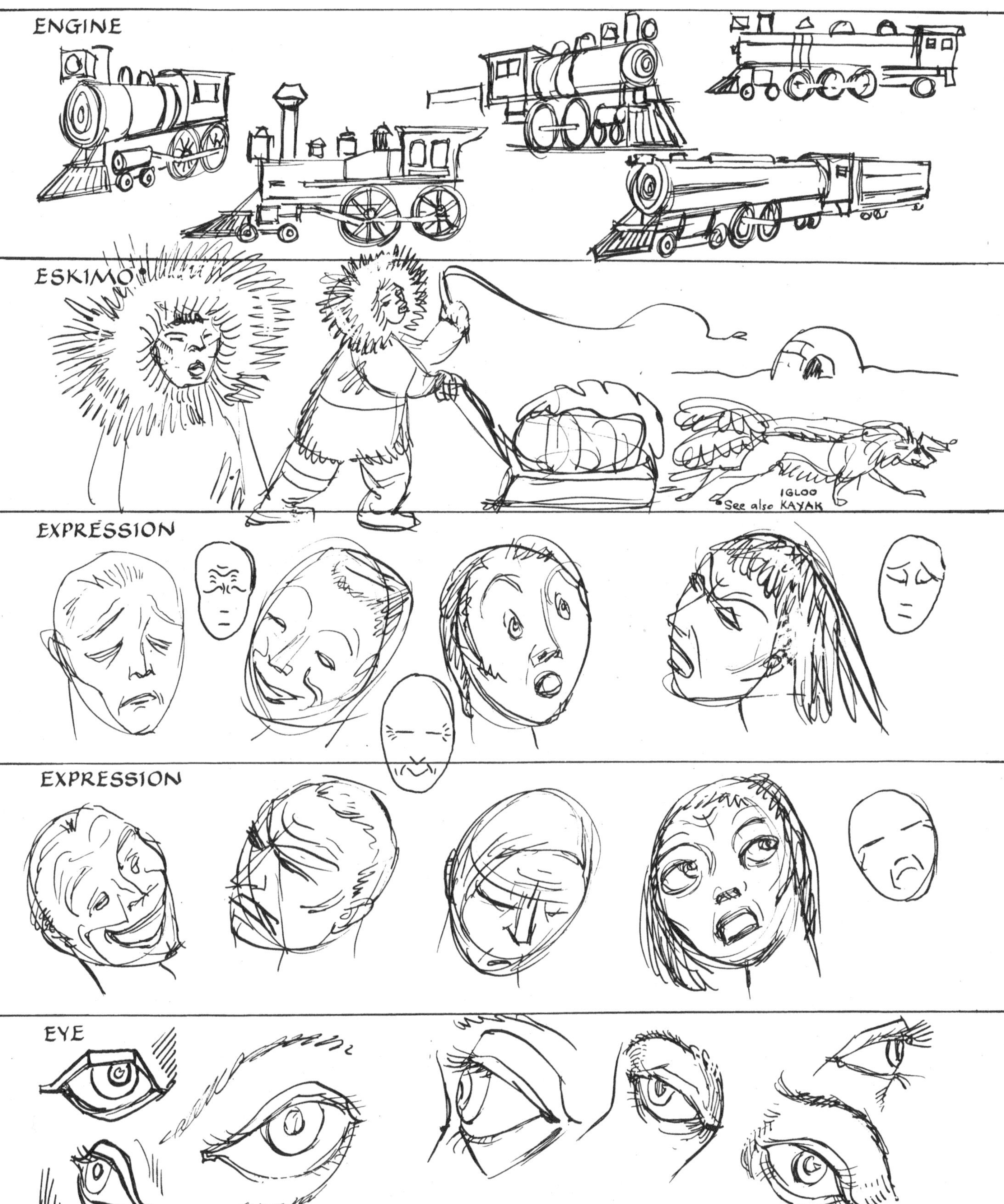
ENGINE
ESKIMO•
IGLOO
•See also KAYAK
EXPRESSION
EXPRESSION
EYE

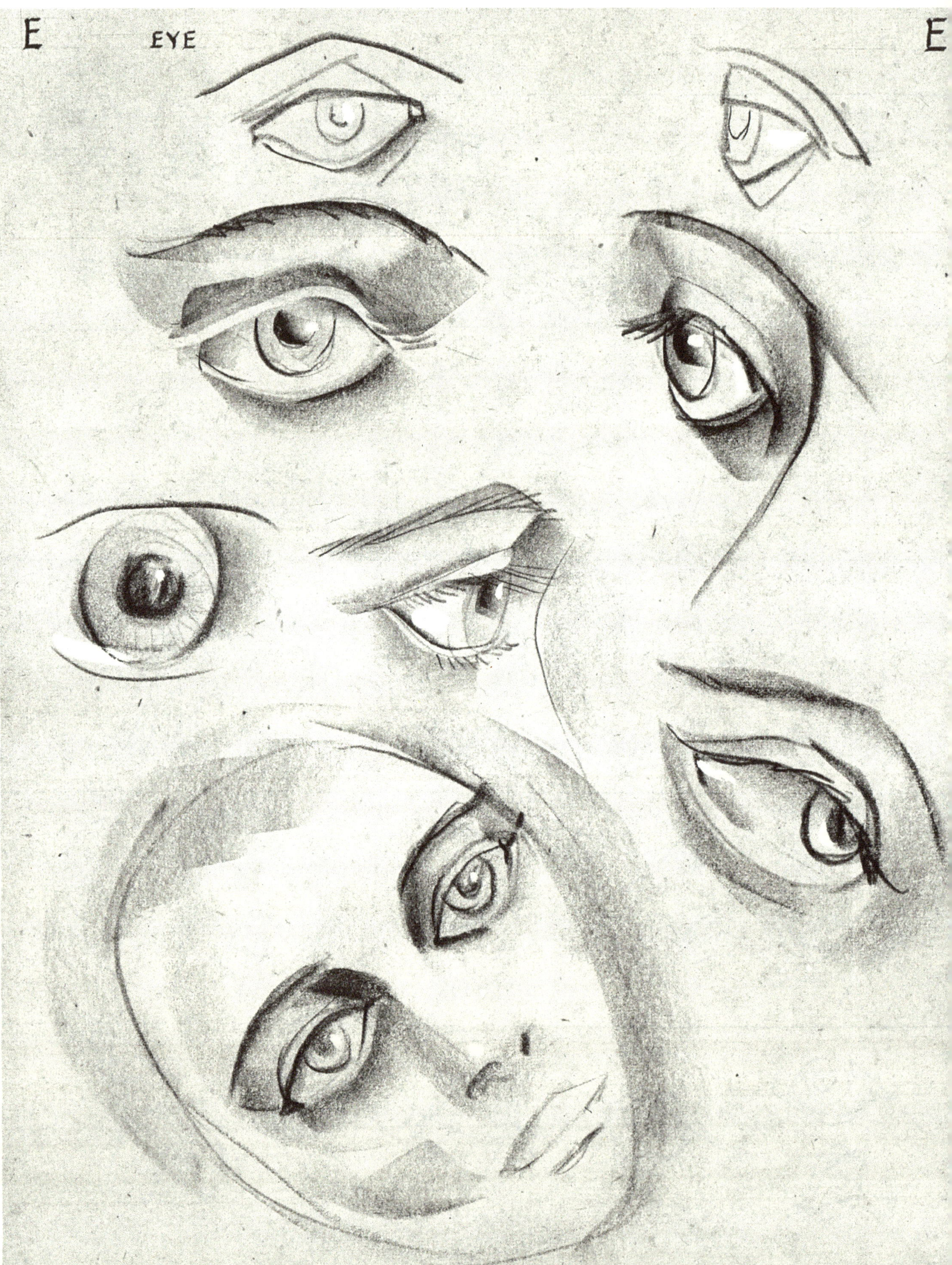
E
EYE
E

FALCON

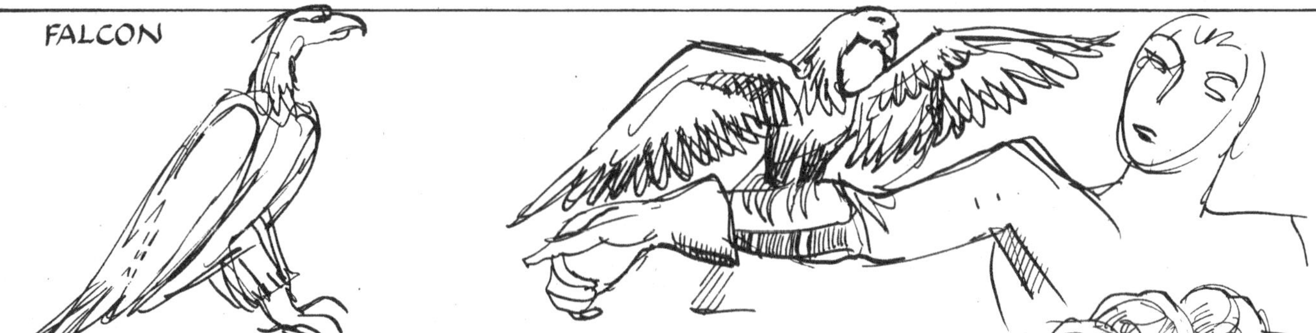

FAN

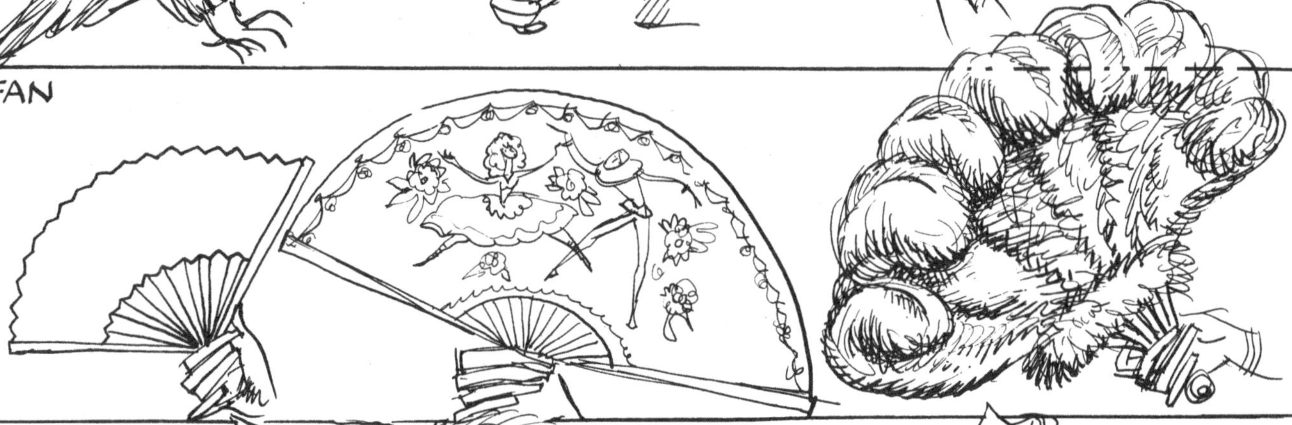

FARMER

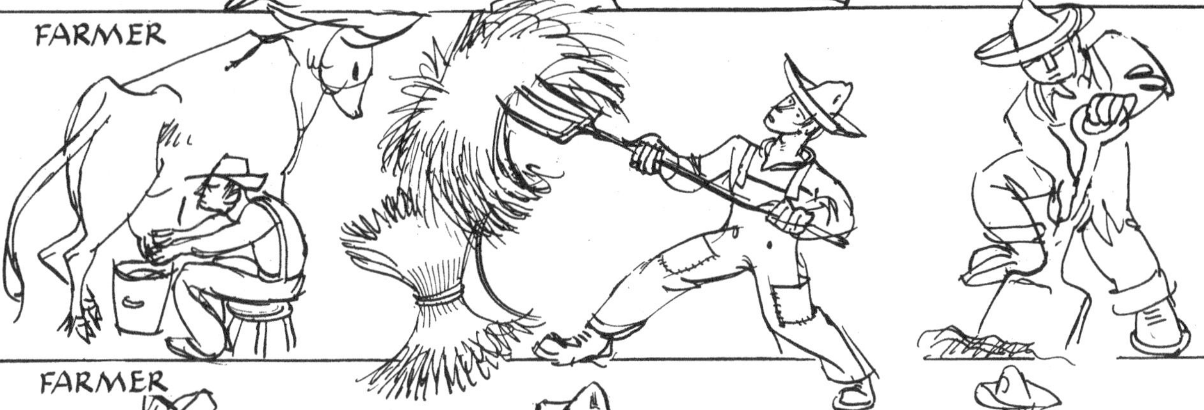

FARMER

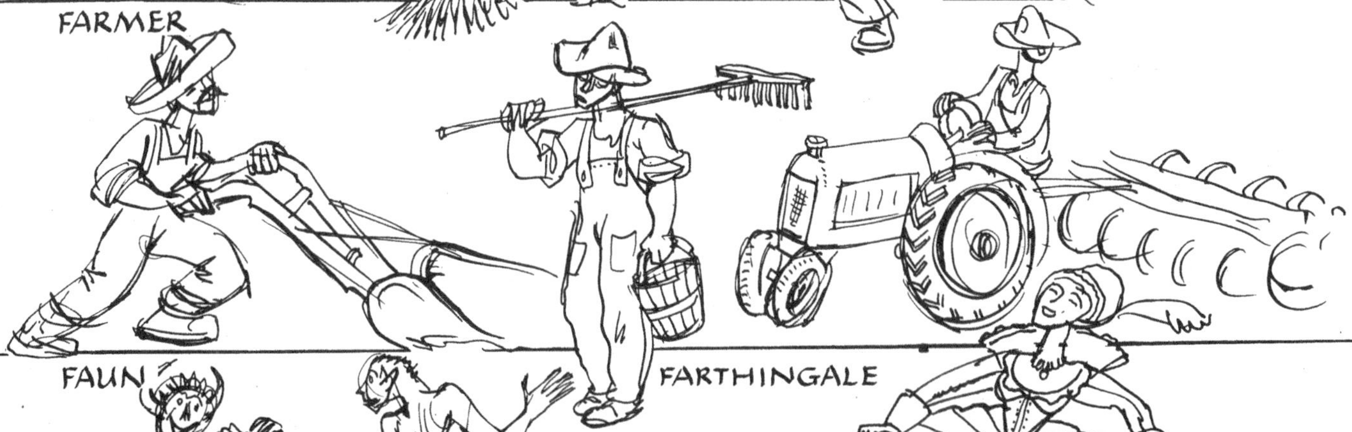

FAUN

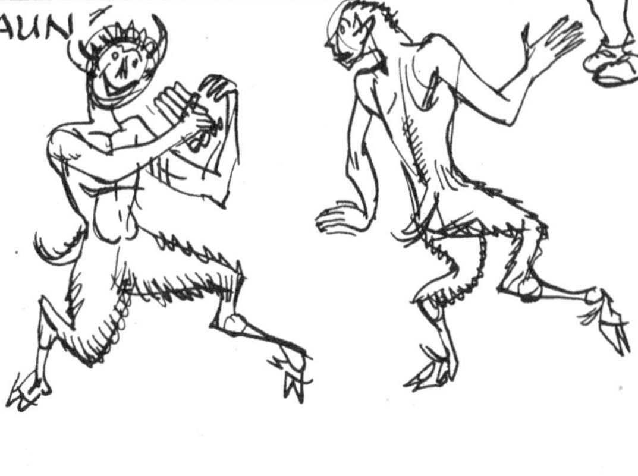

FARTHINGALE

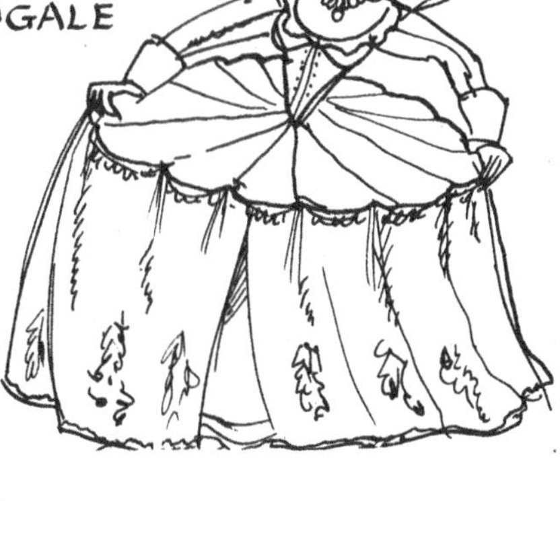

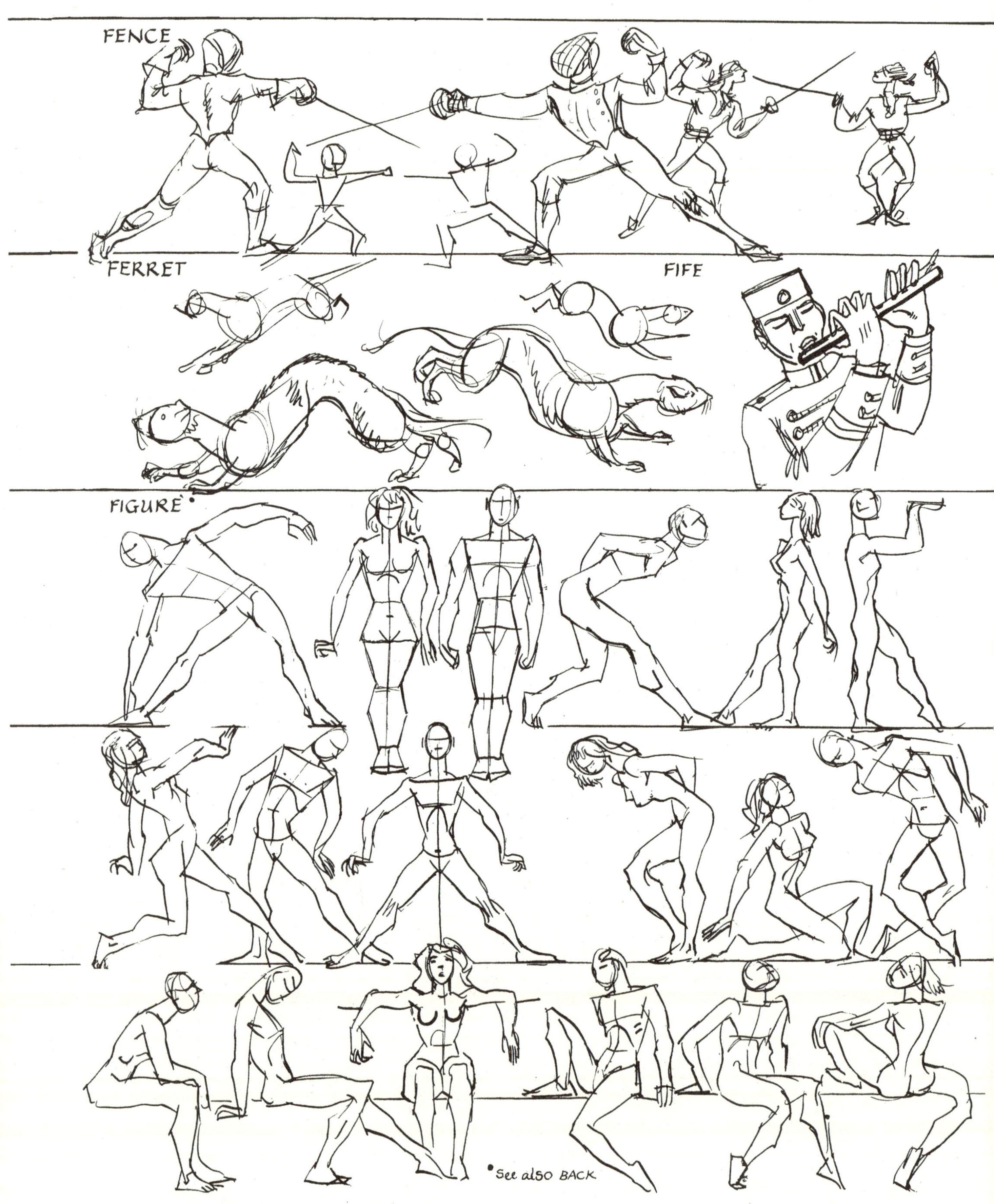
FENCE
FERRET
FIFE
FIGURE•
•See also BACK

FIGURE

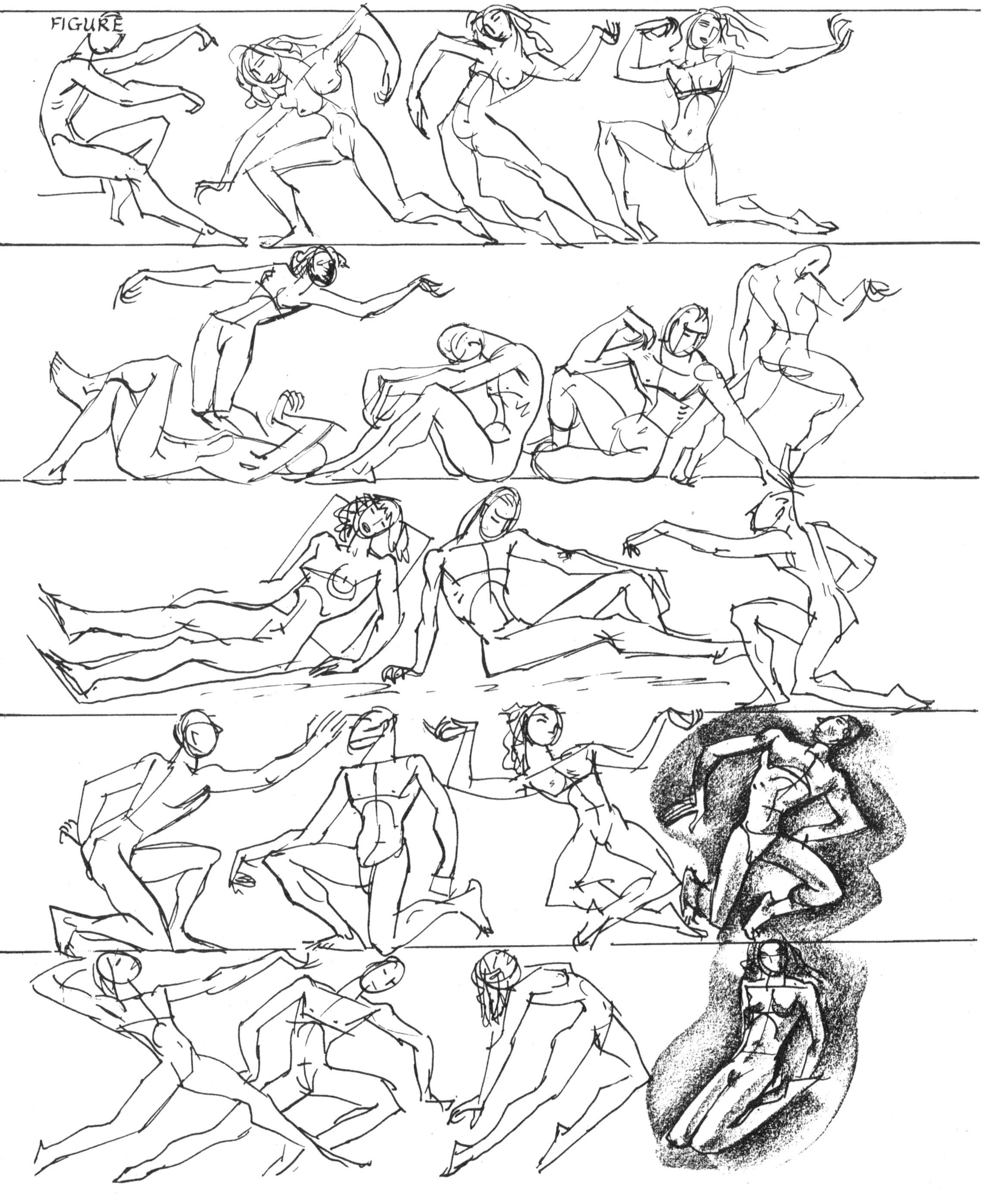

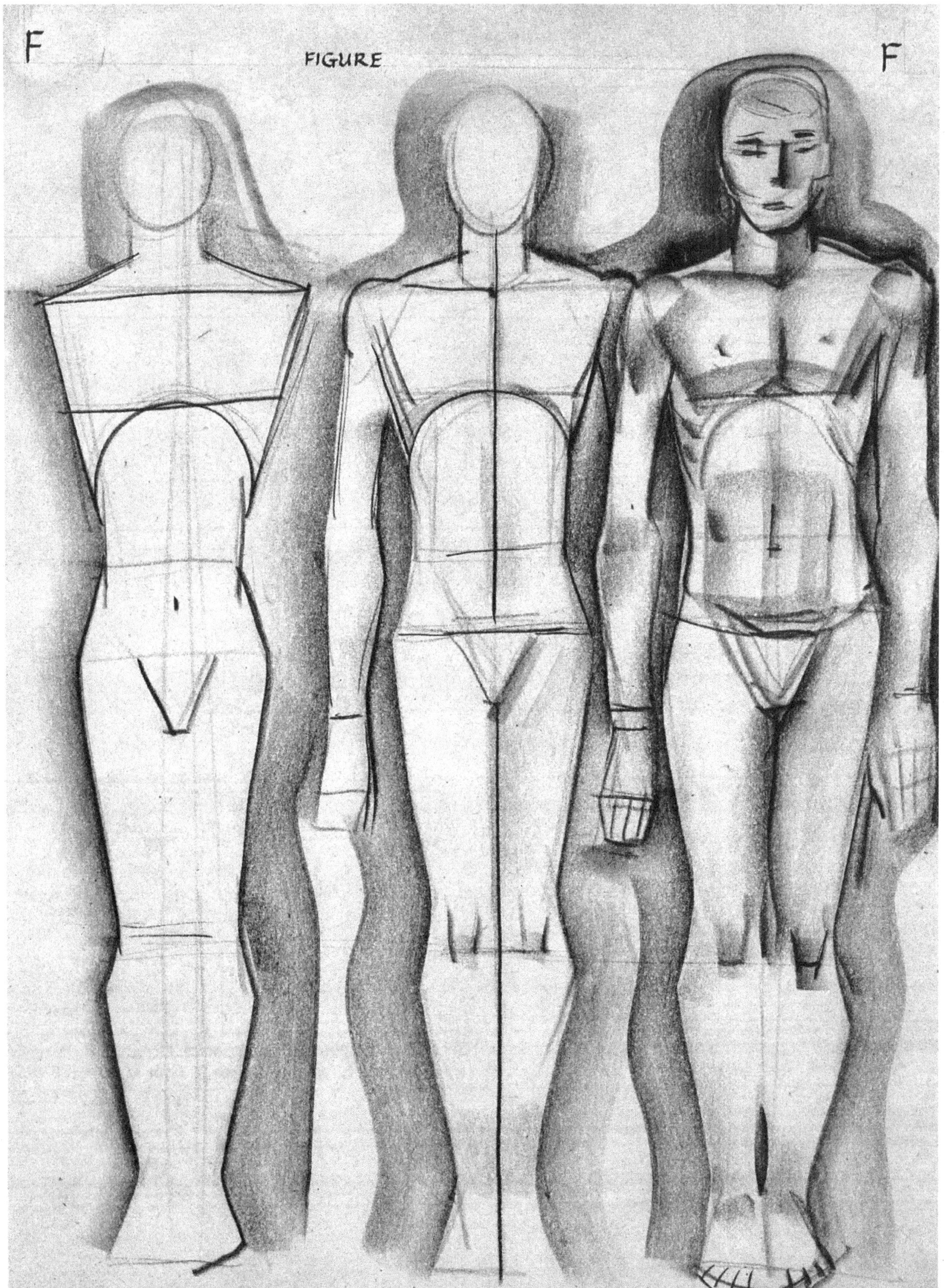
F
FIGURE
F

FIGURE

F

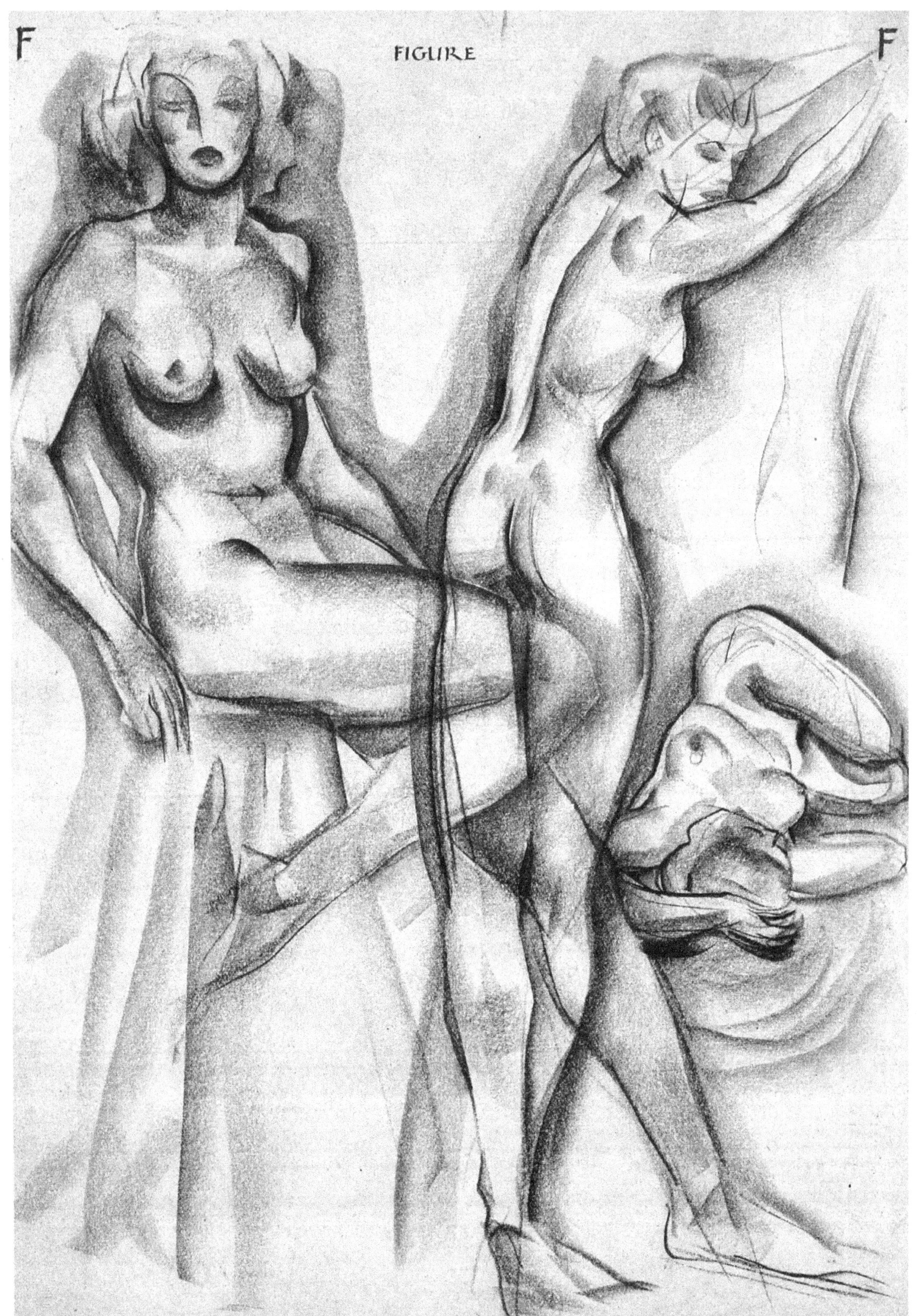

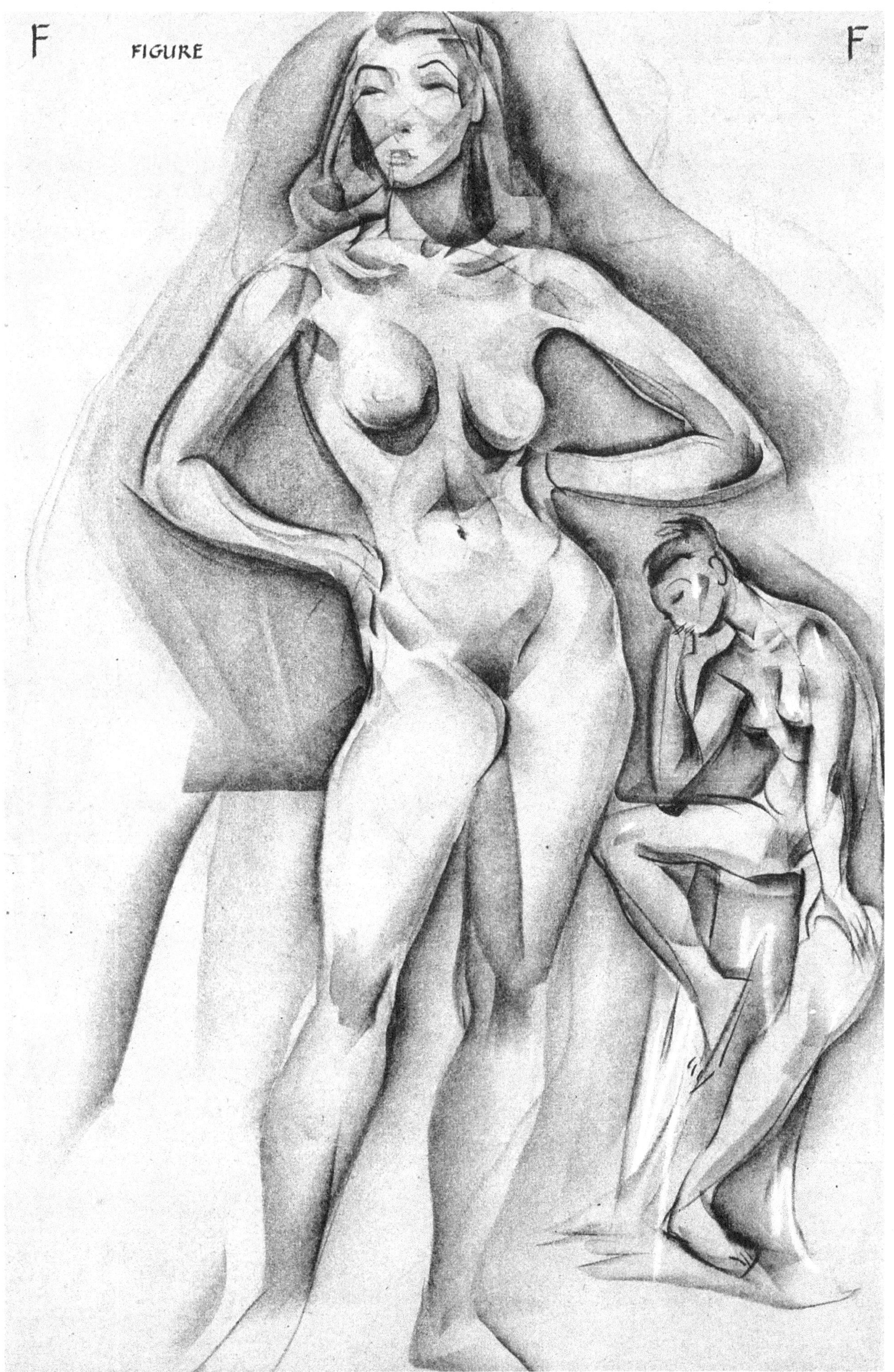
F
FIGURE
F

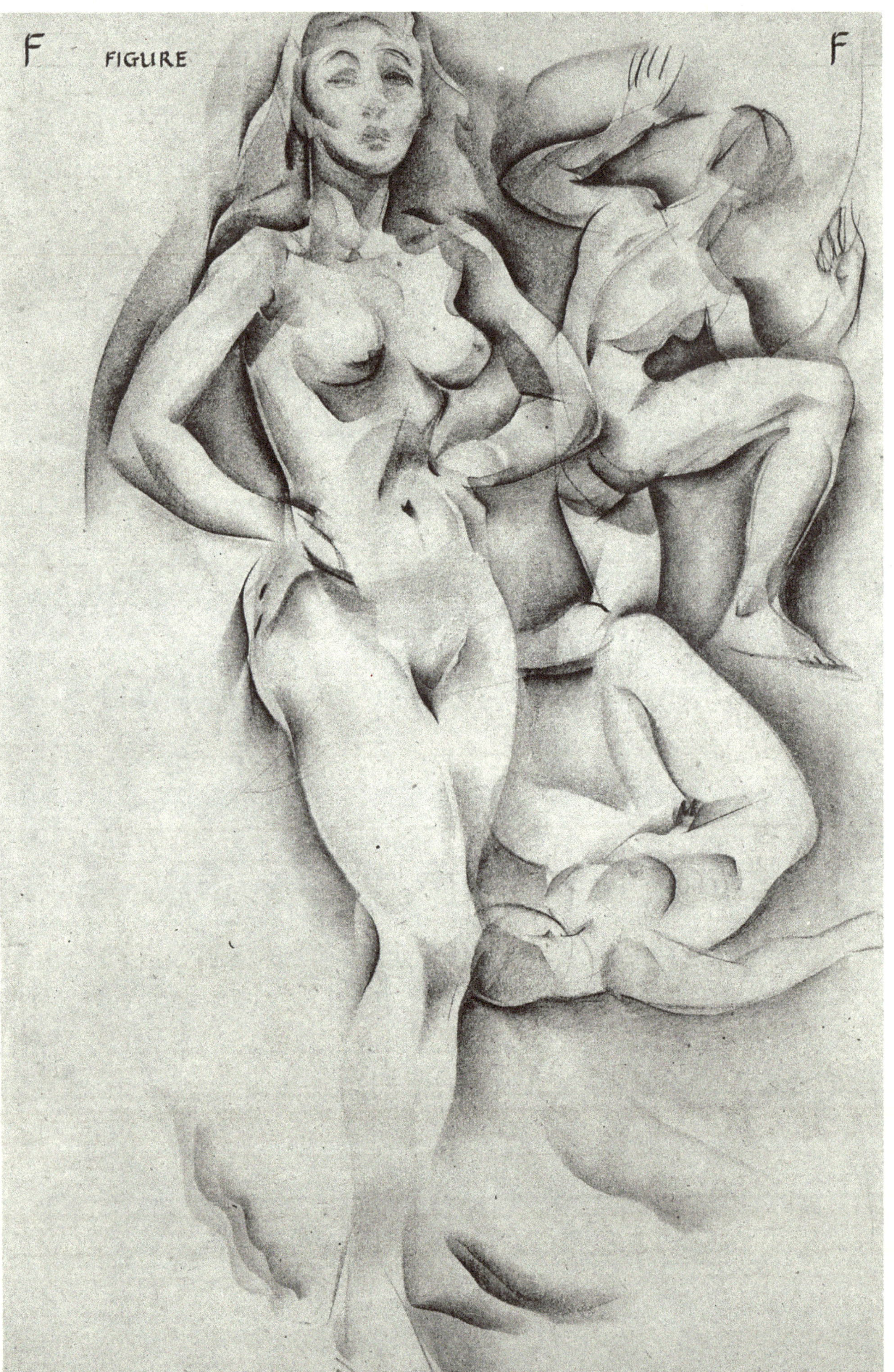
F
FIGURE
F

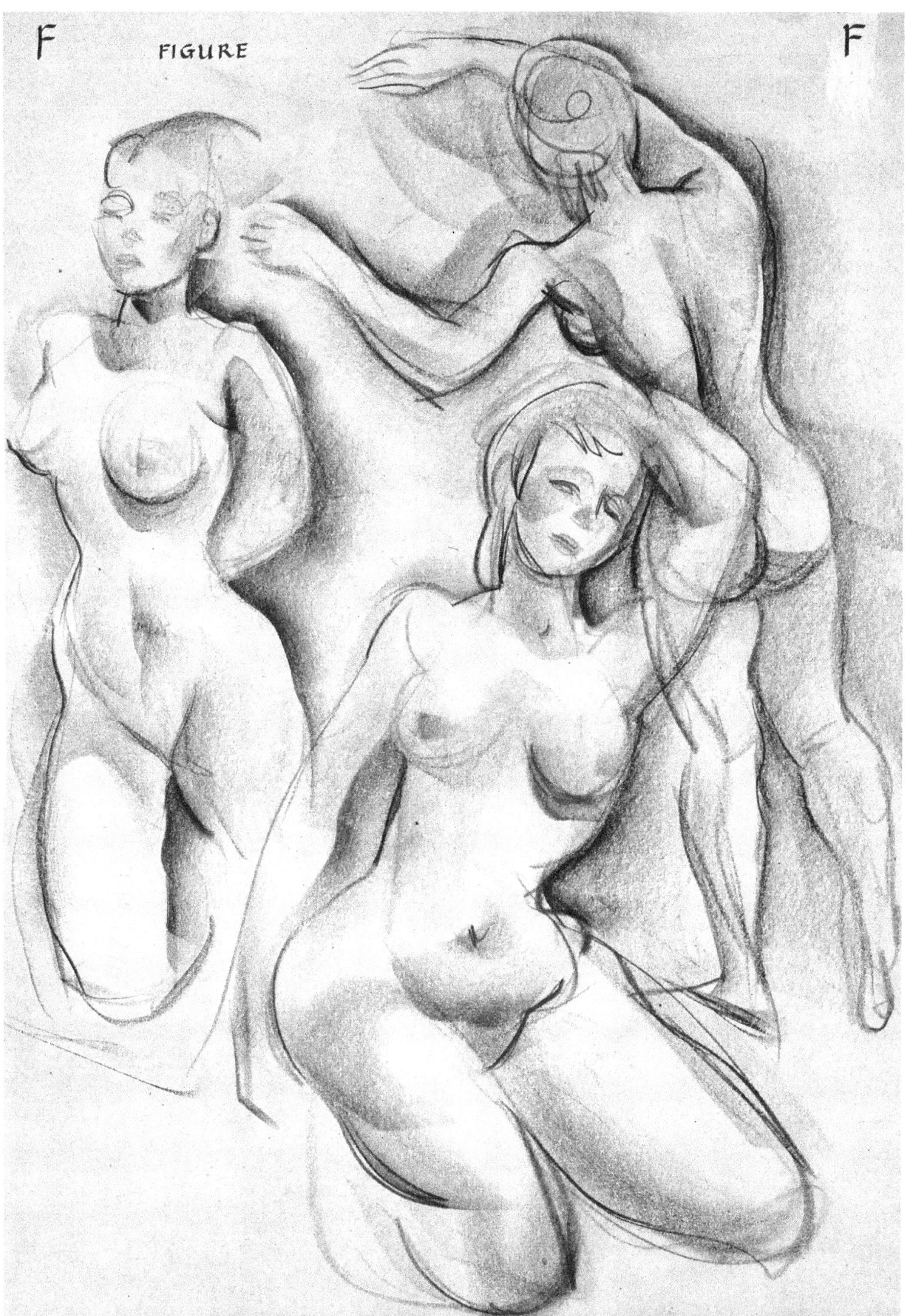
F
FIGURE
F

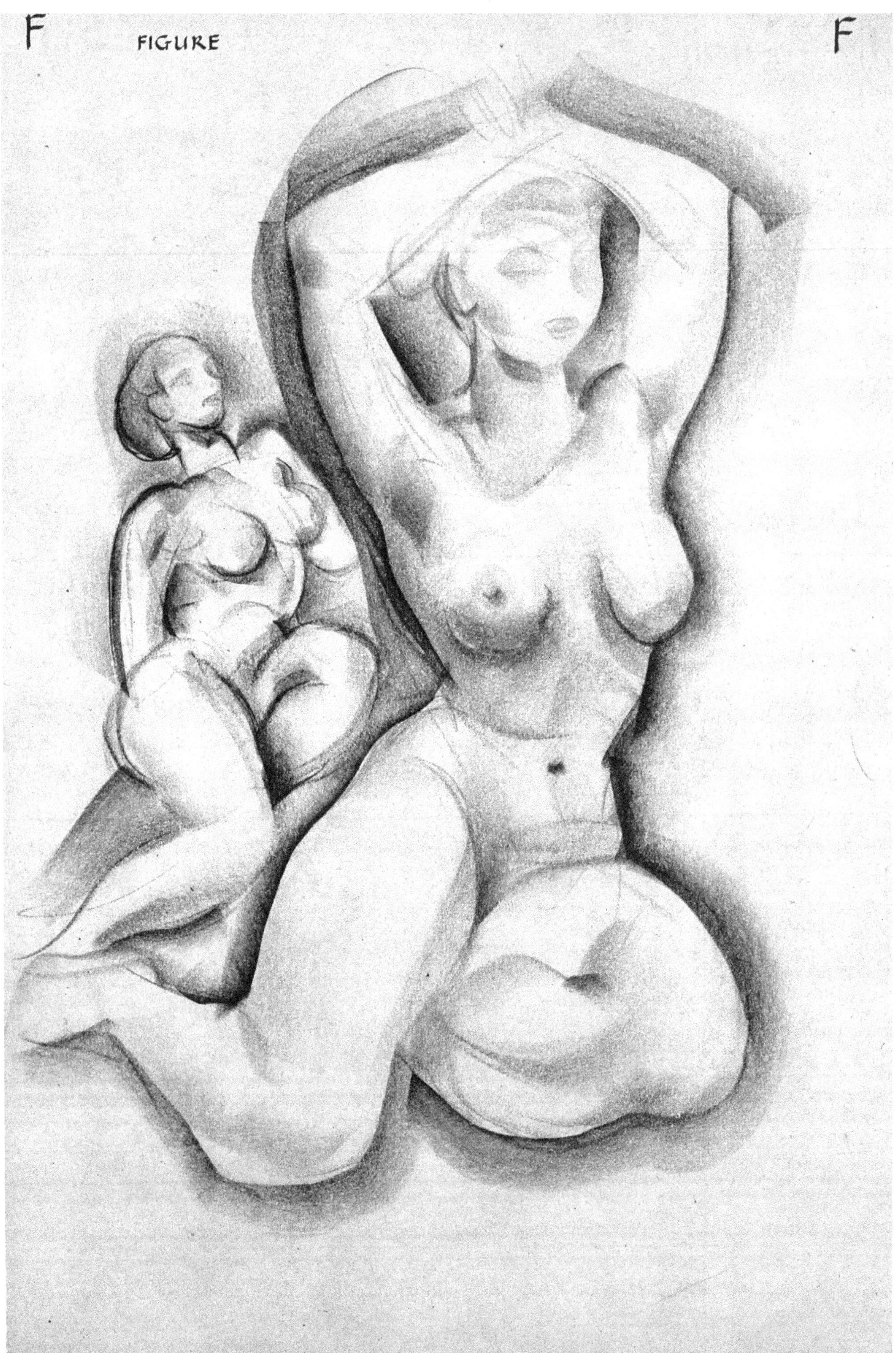
F
FIGURE
F

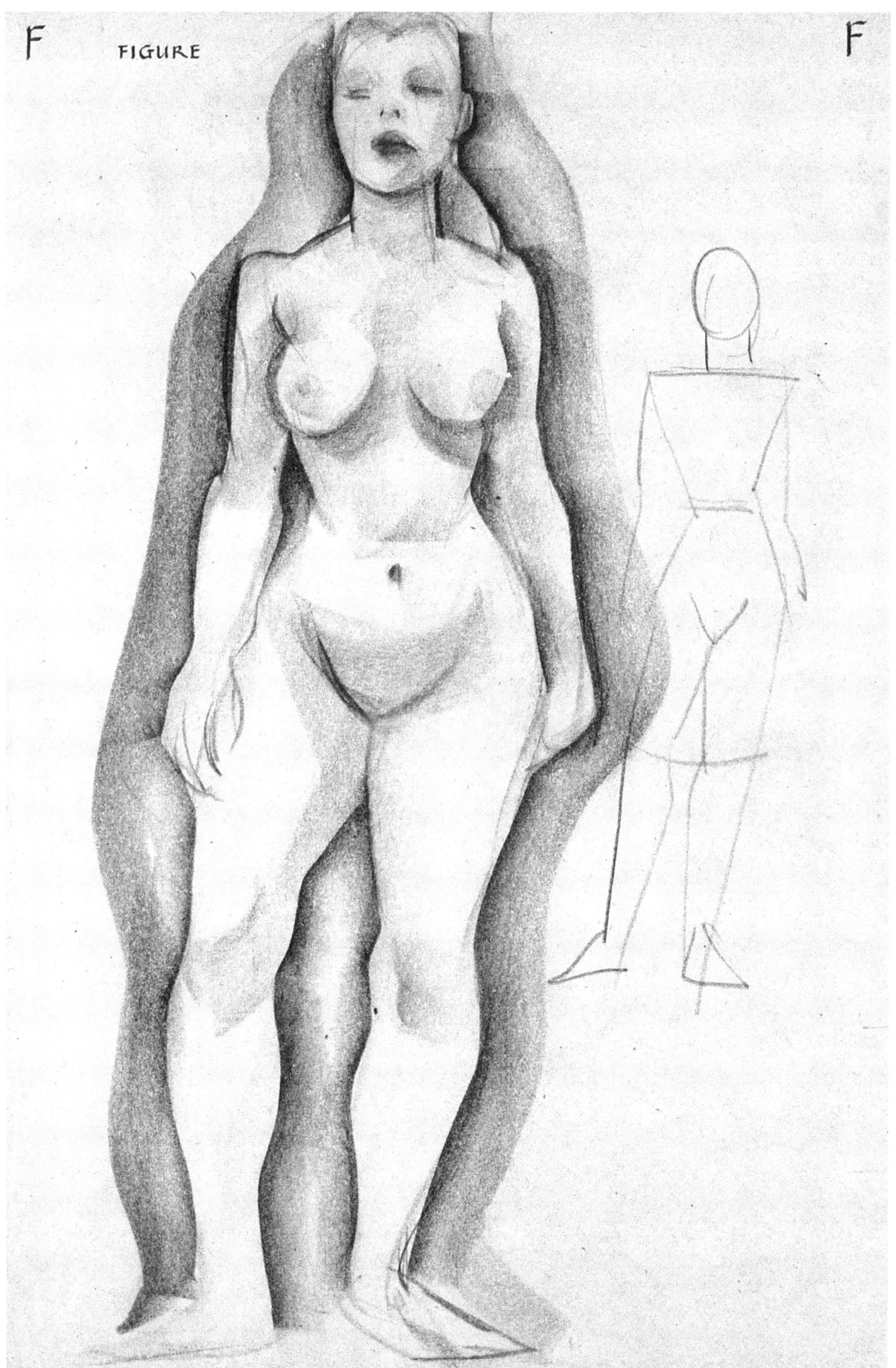
F
FIGURE
F

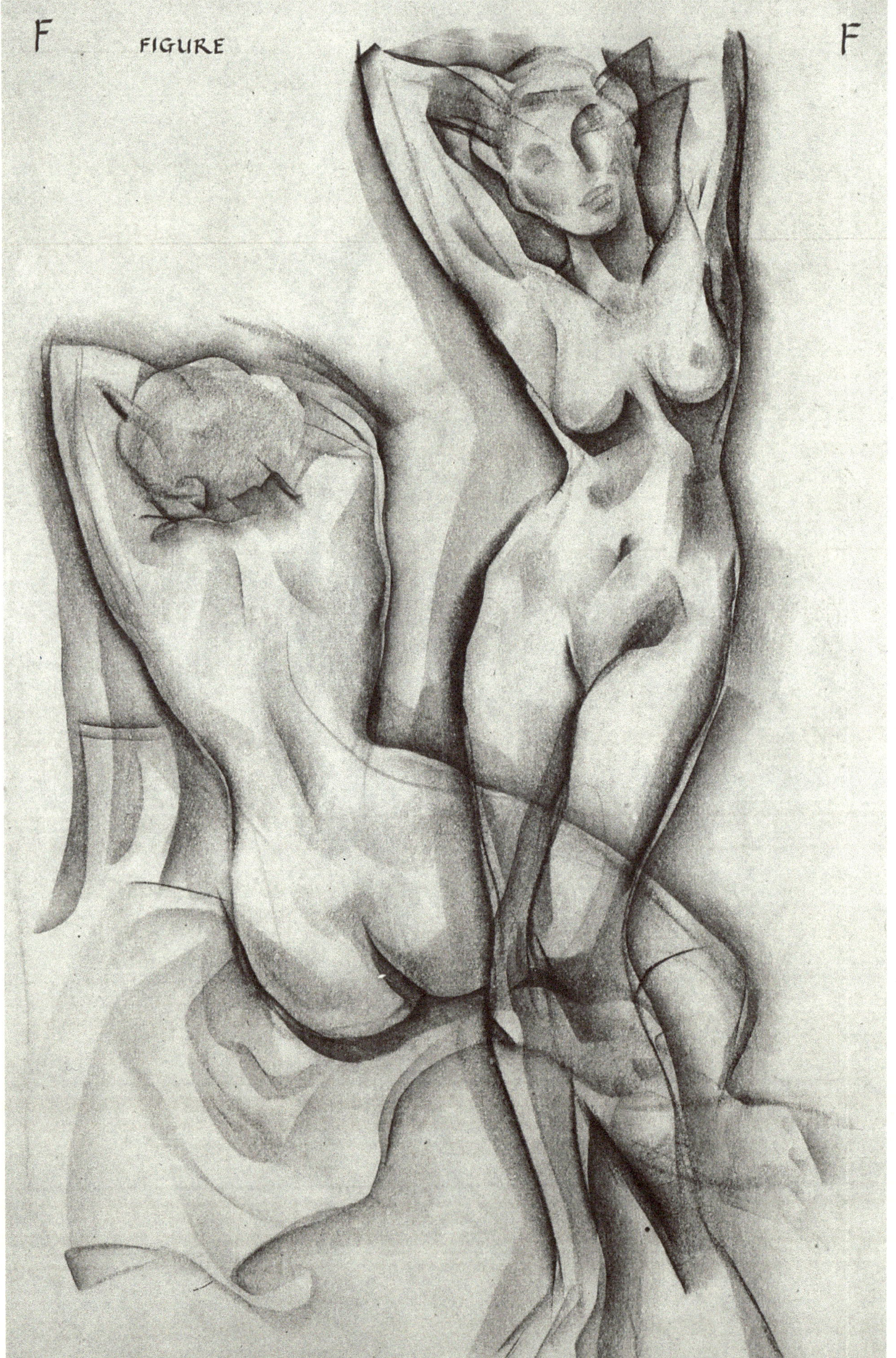
F
FIGURE
F

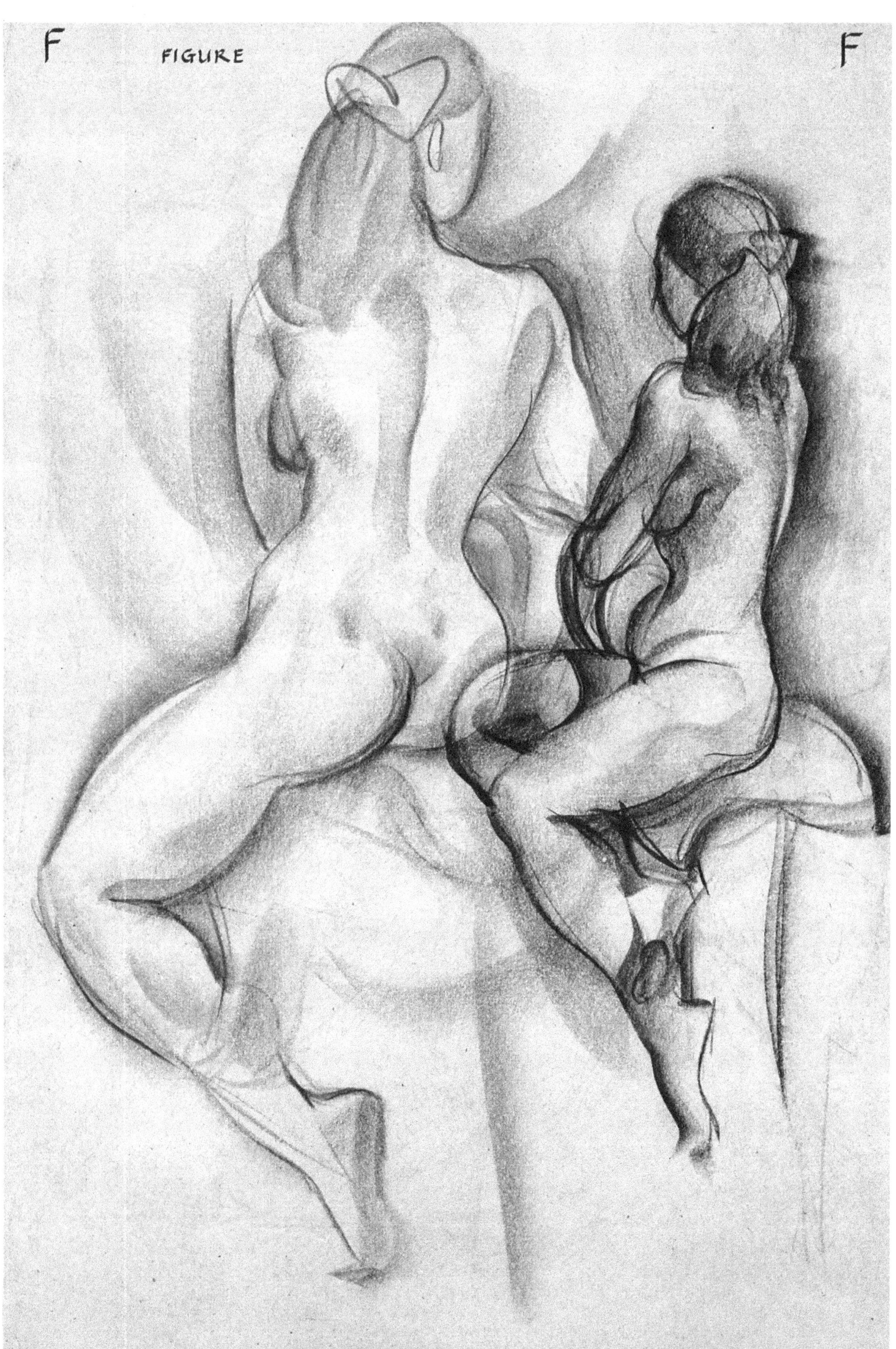
F
FIGURE
F

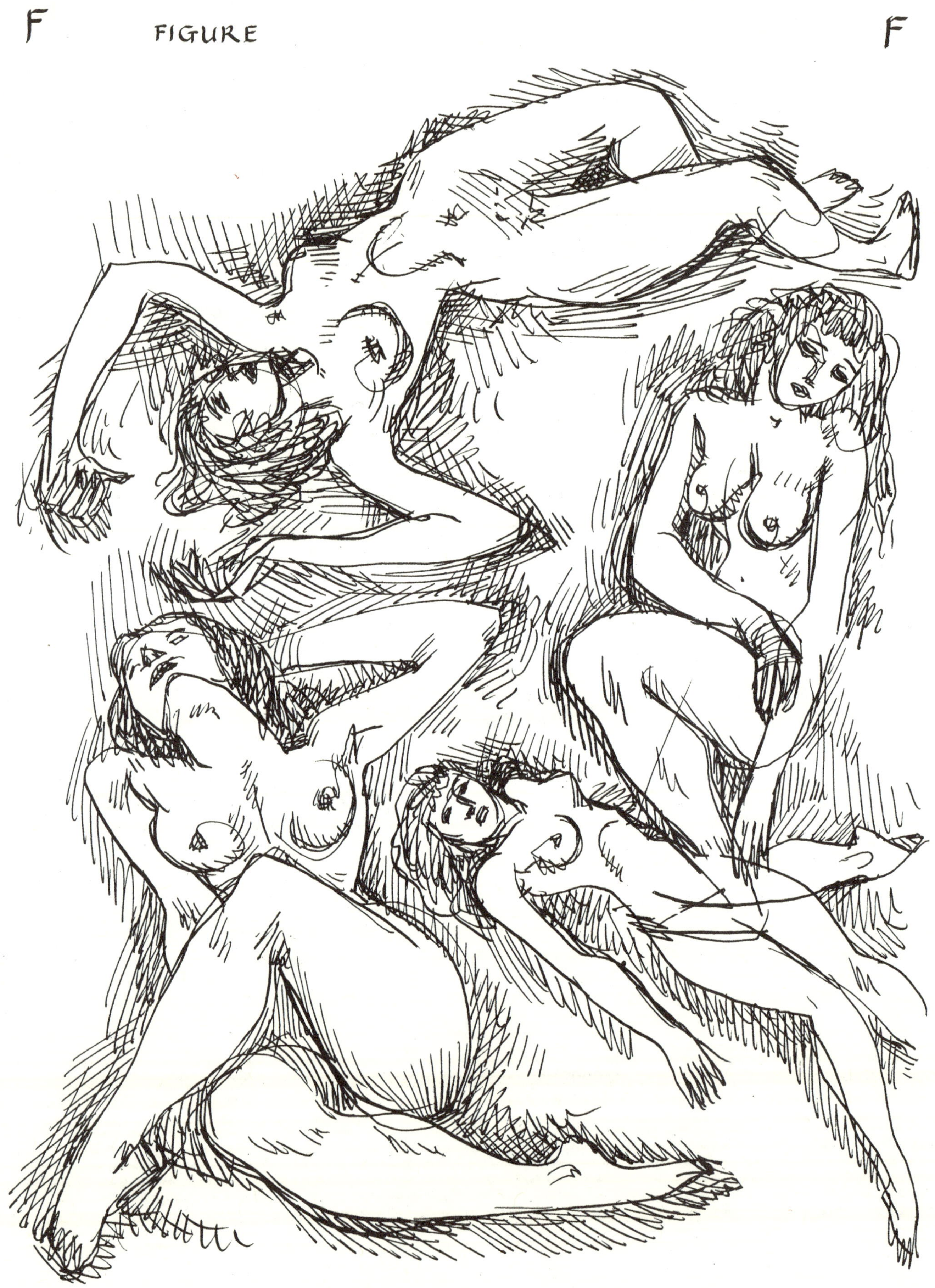
F
FIGURE
F

FIGURE

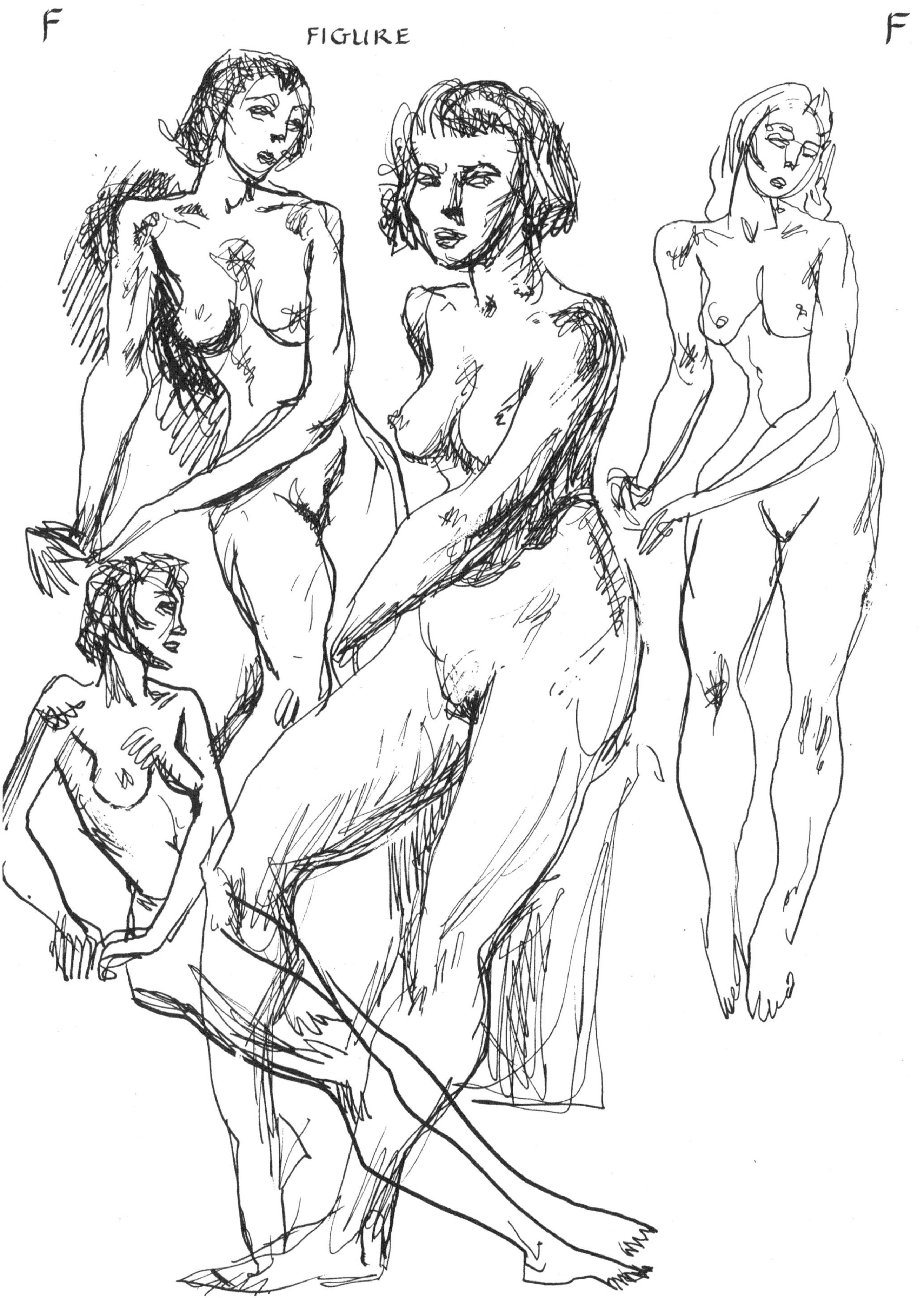

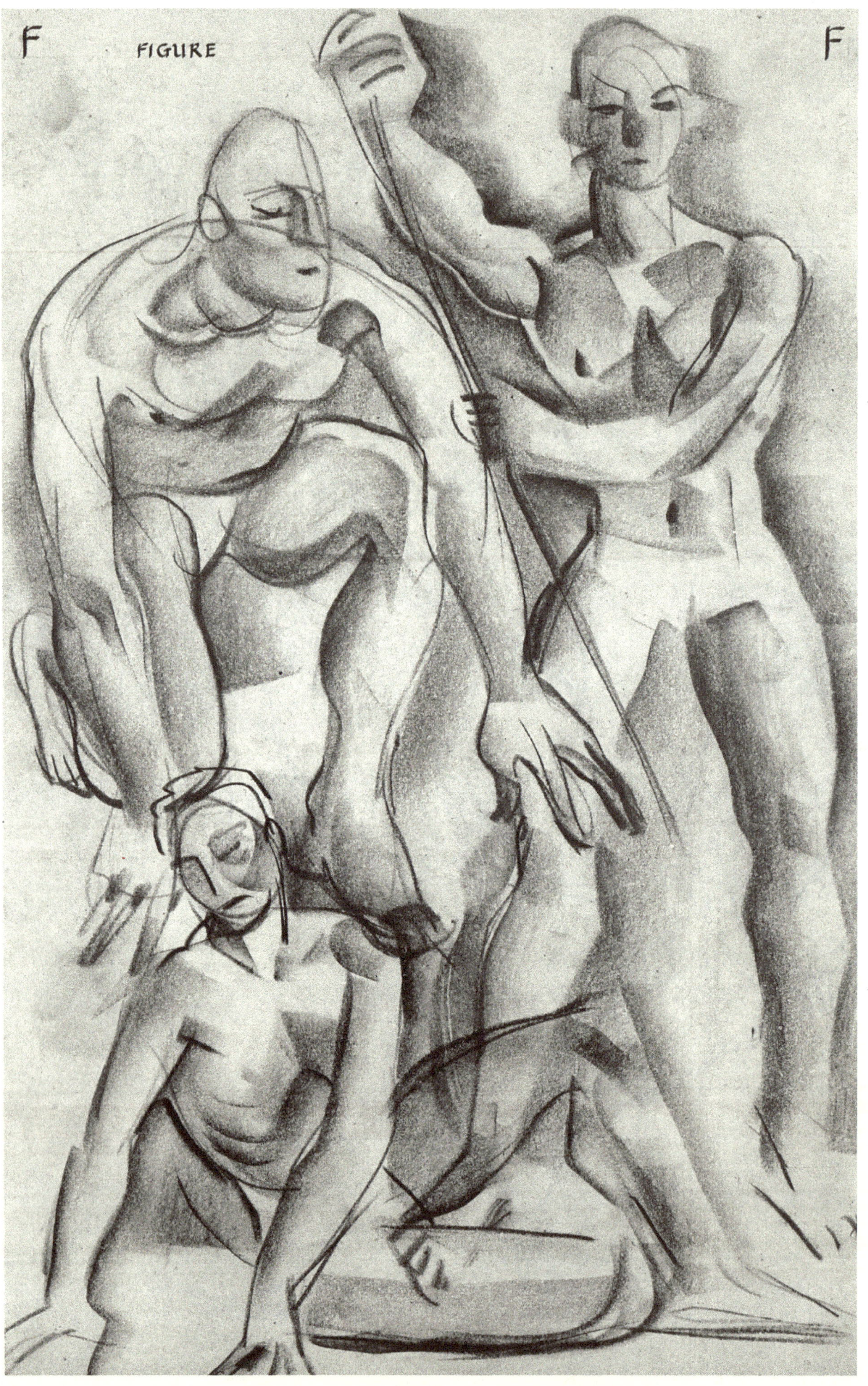
F
FIGURE
F

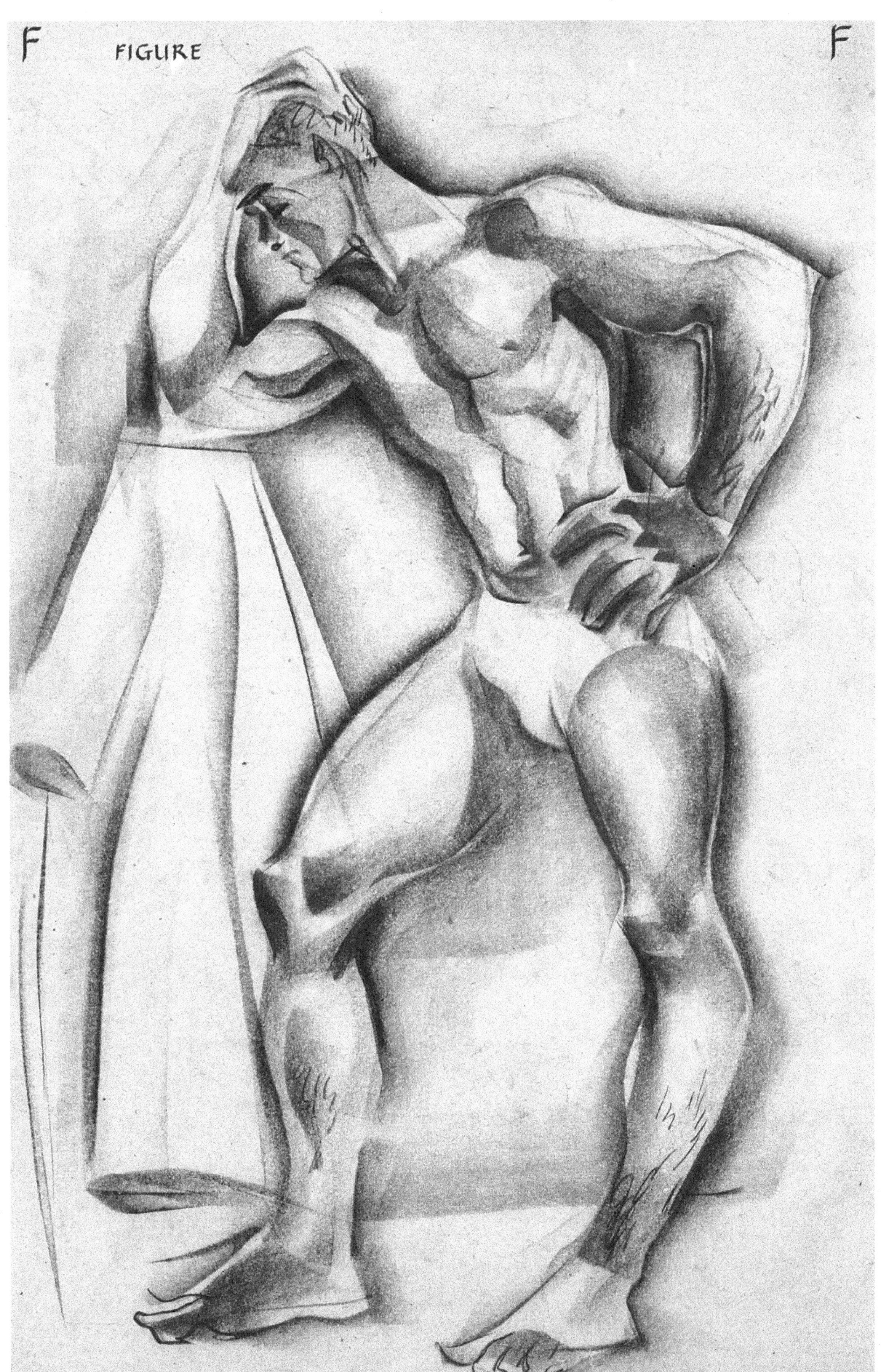
F
FIGURE
F

FIGURE

F

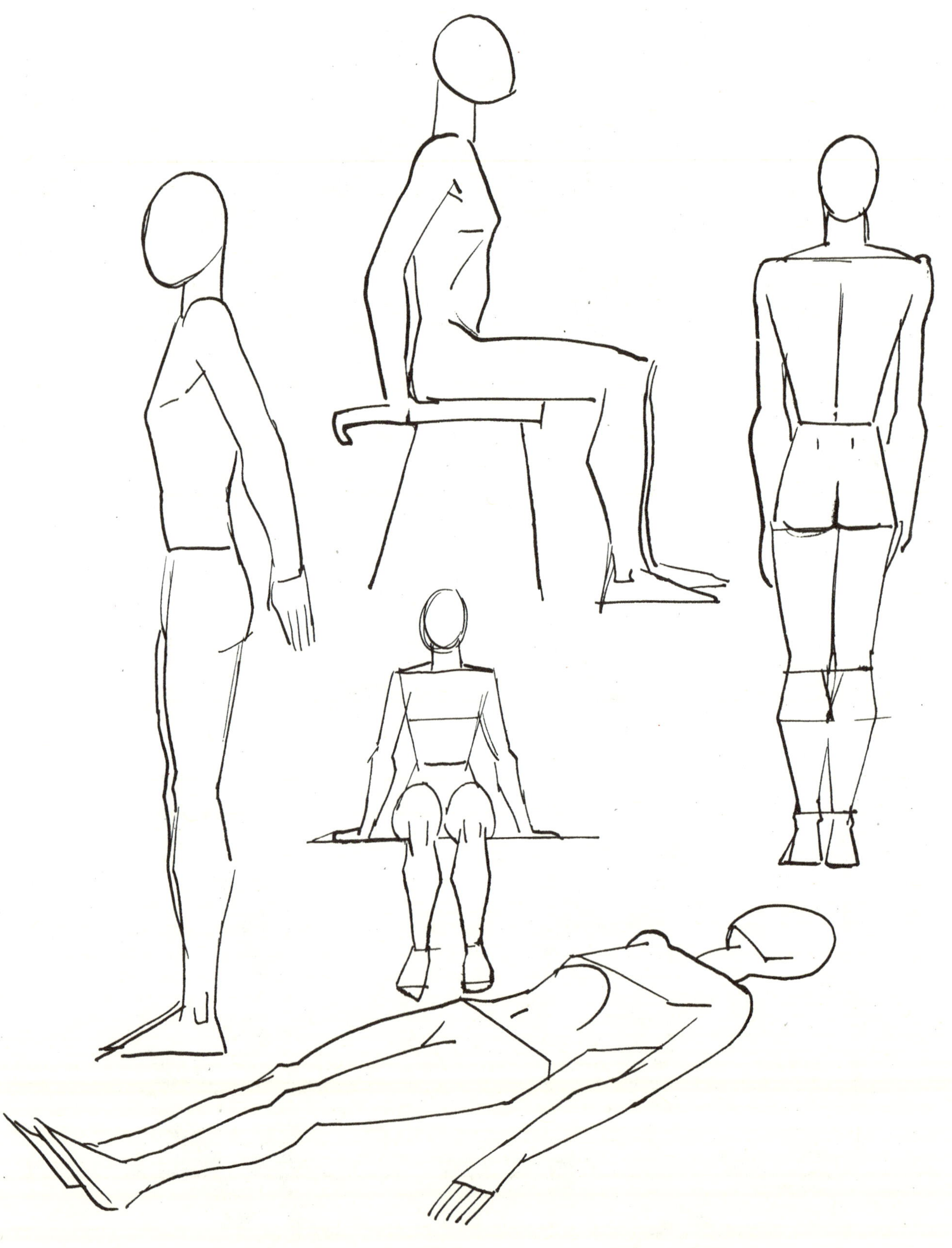

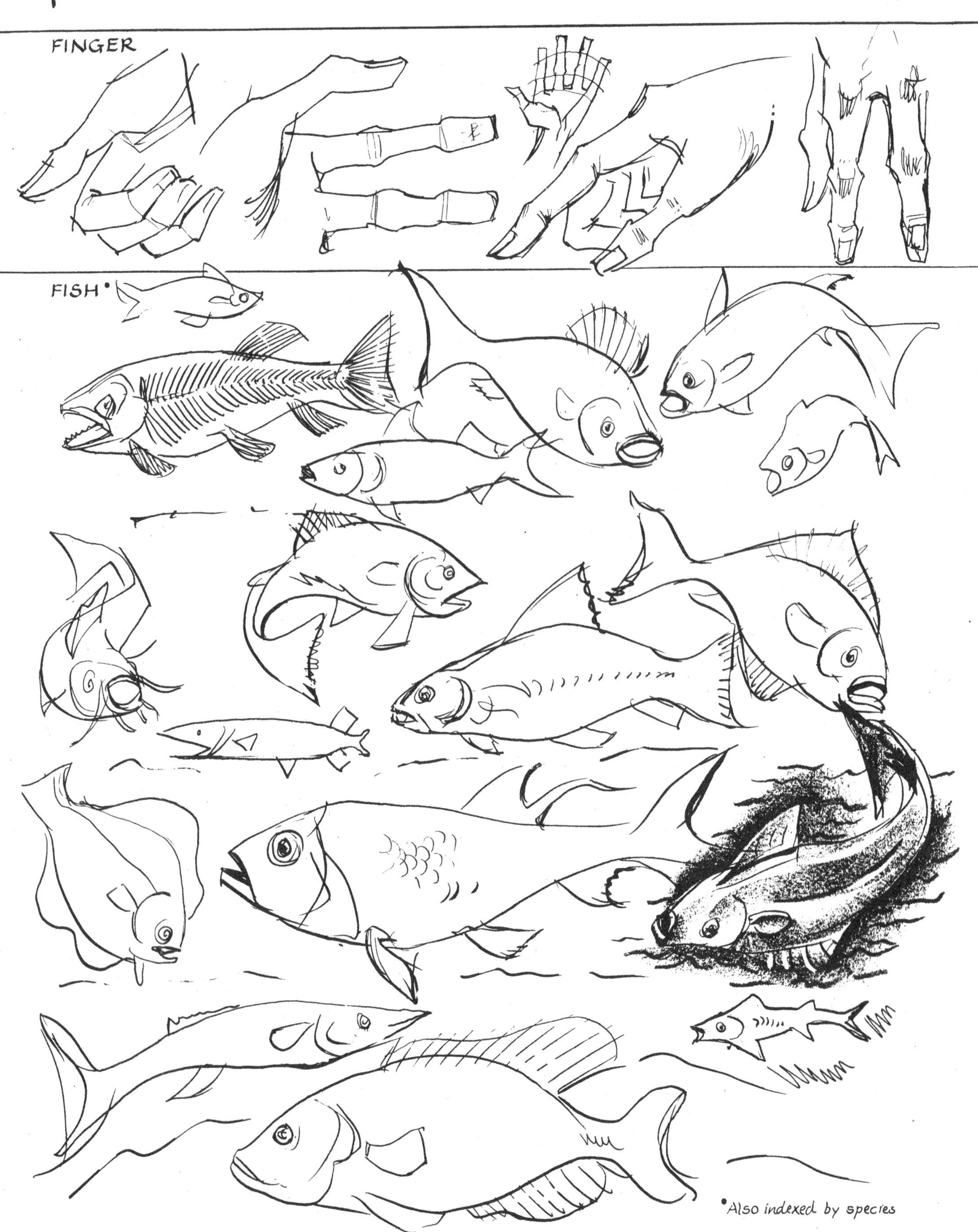
FINGER
FISH*
*Also indexed by species

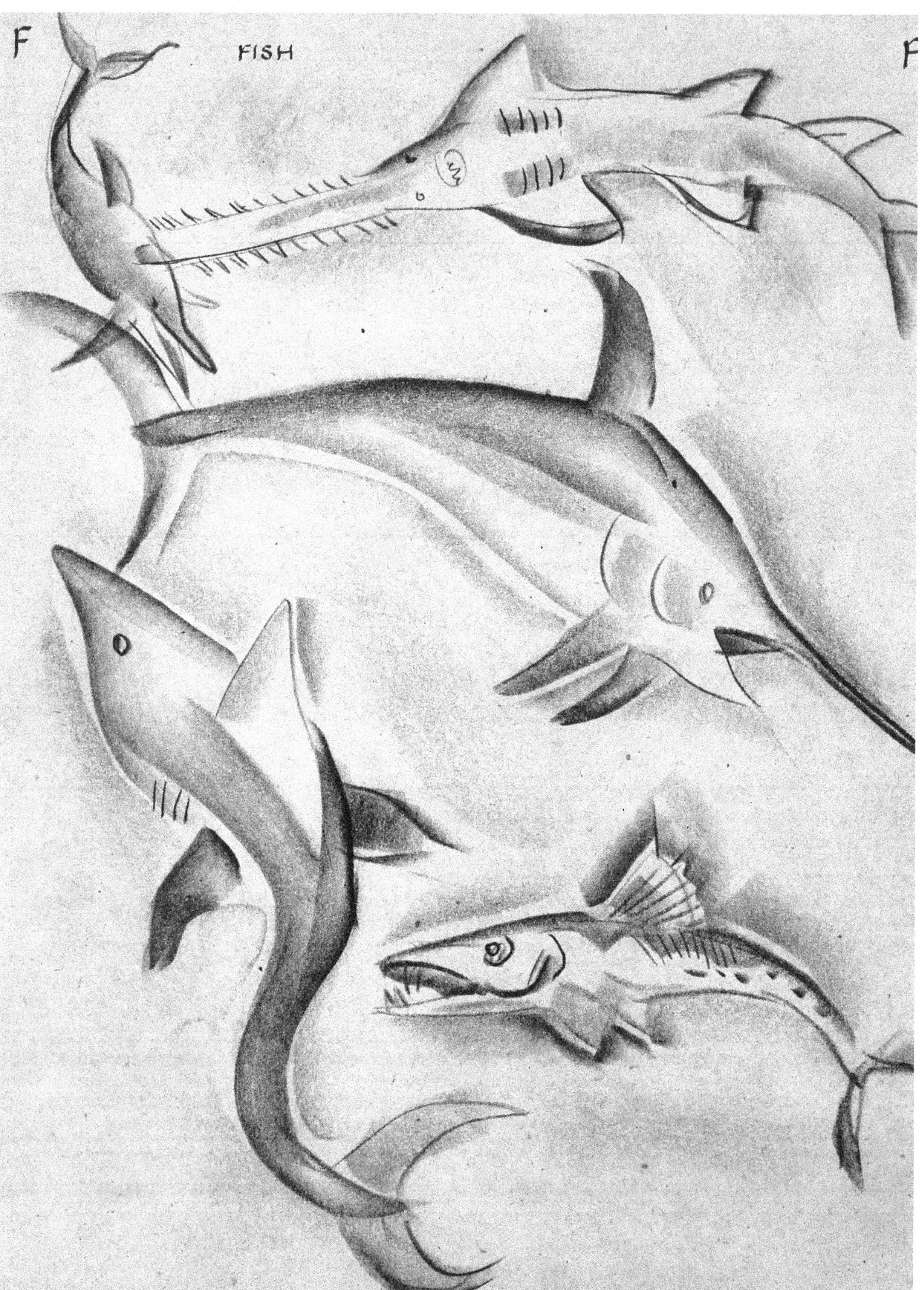
F
FISH
F

FISHING

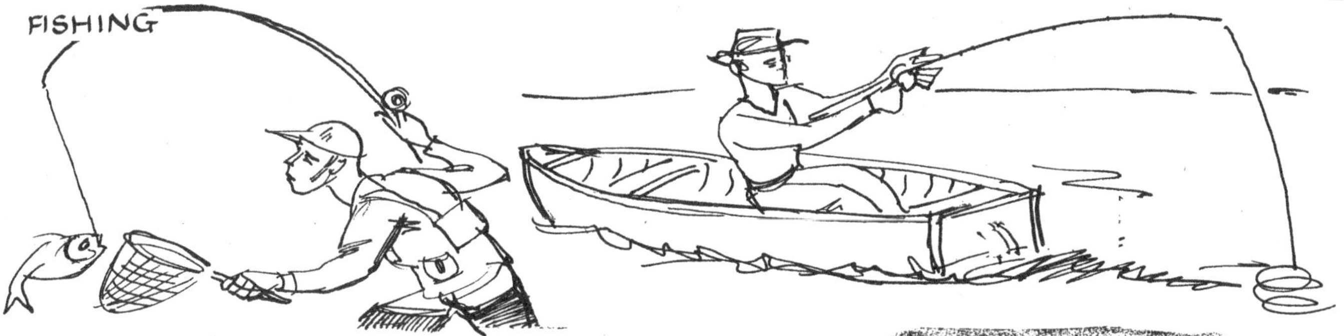

FLAG

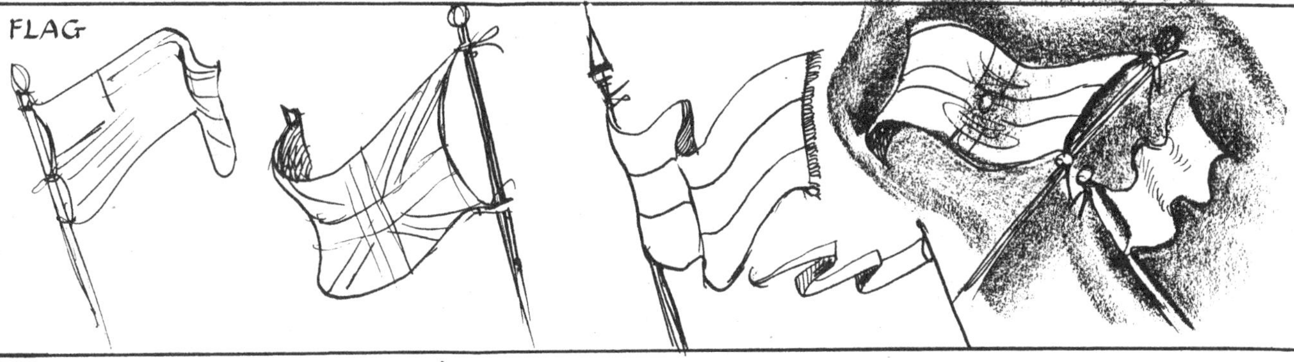

FLAMINGO

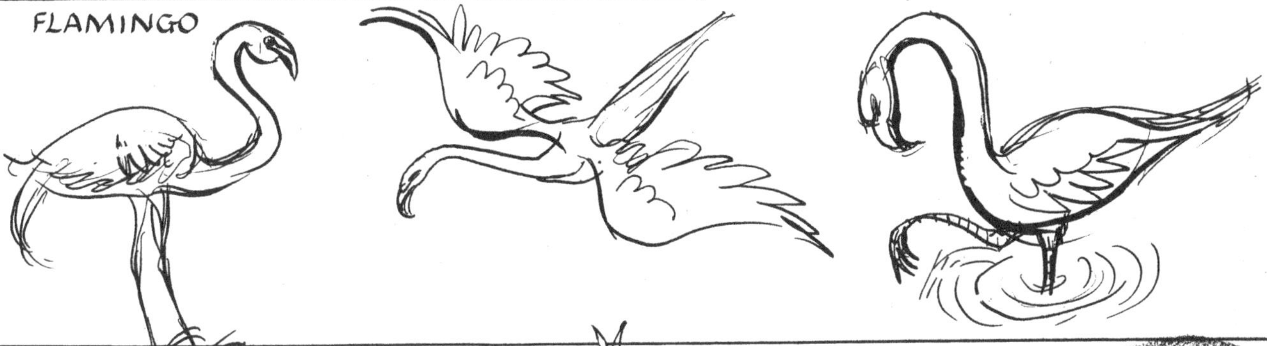

FLOWER

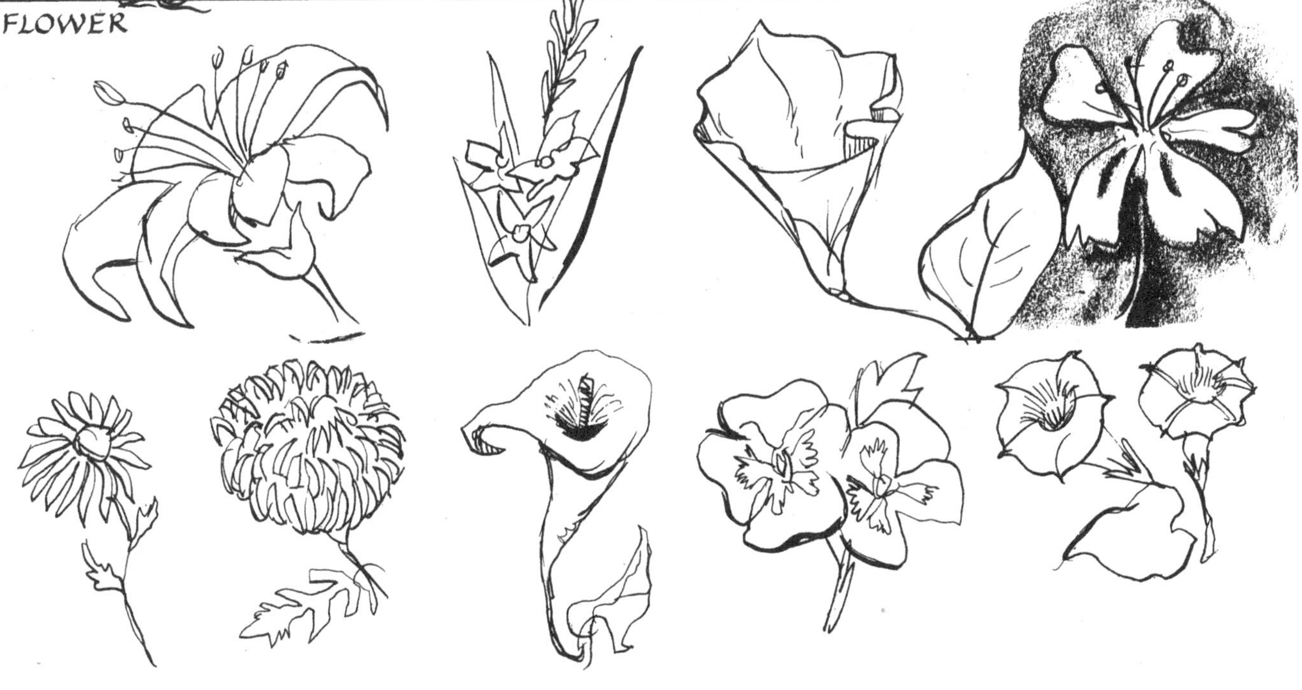

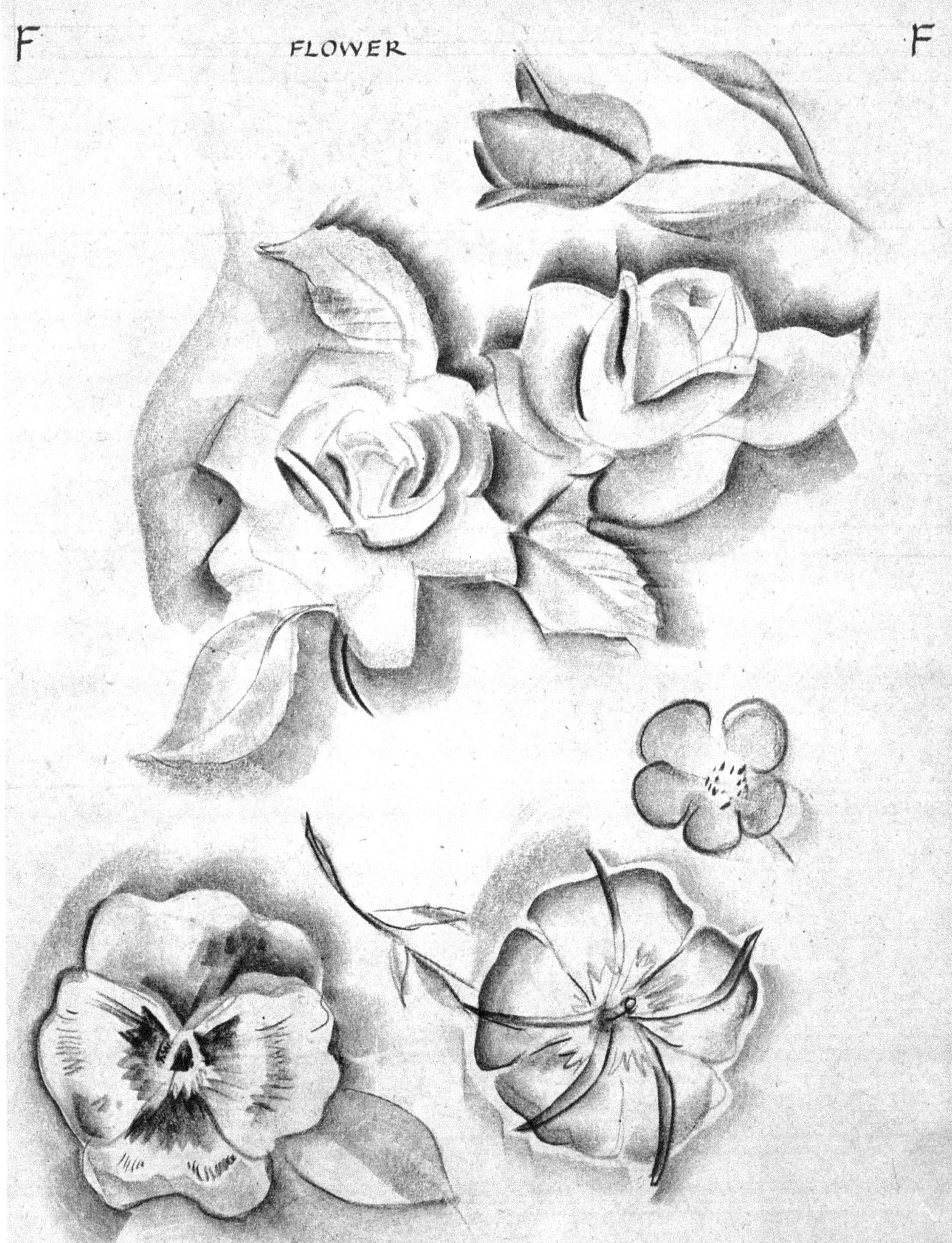
F
FLOWER
F

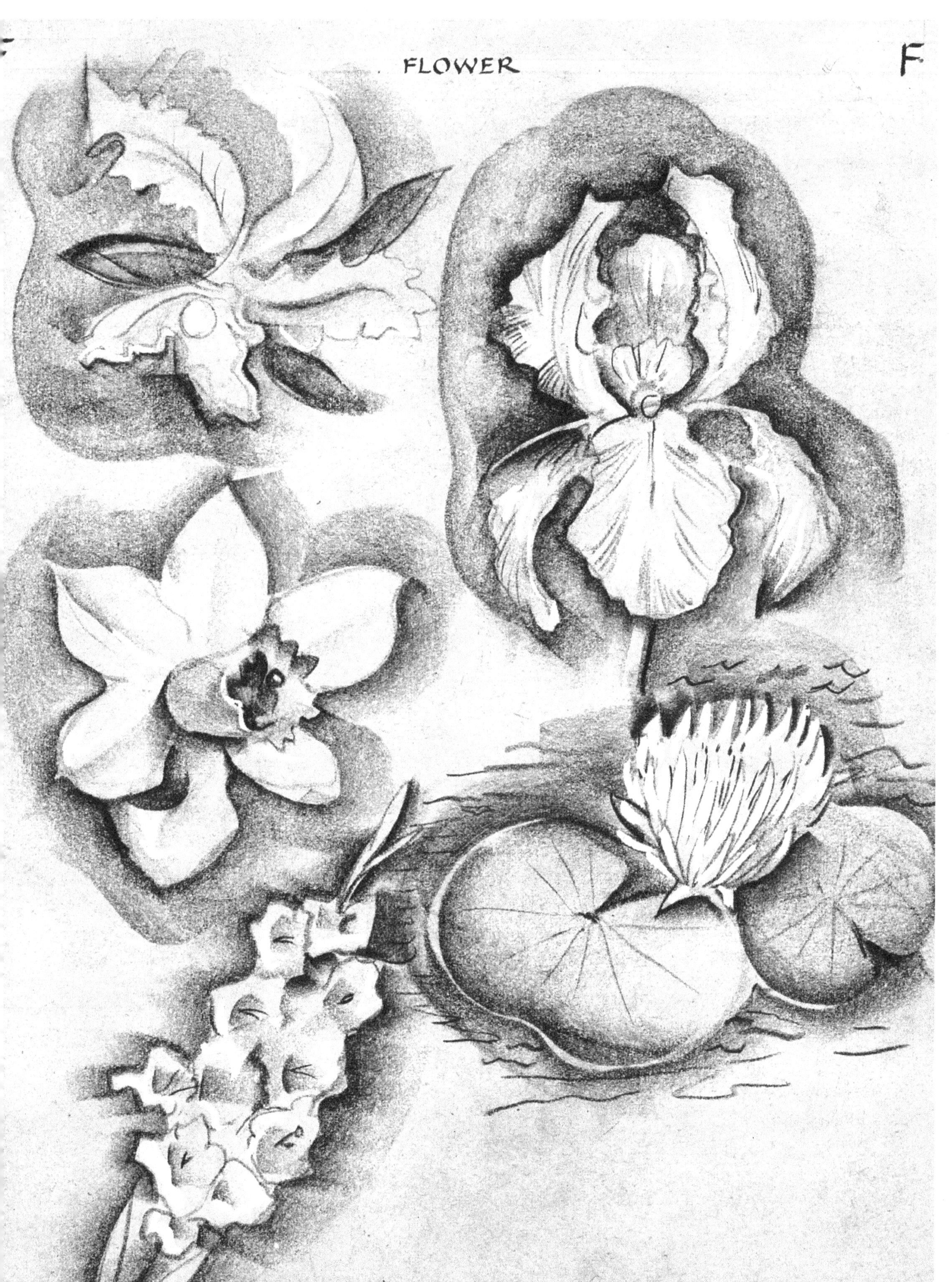
FLOWER
F

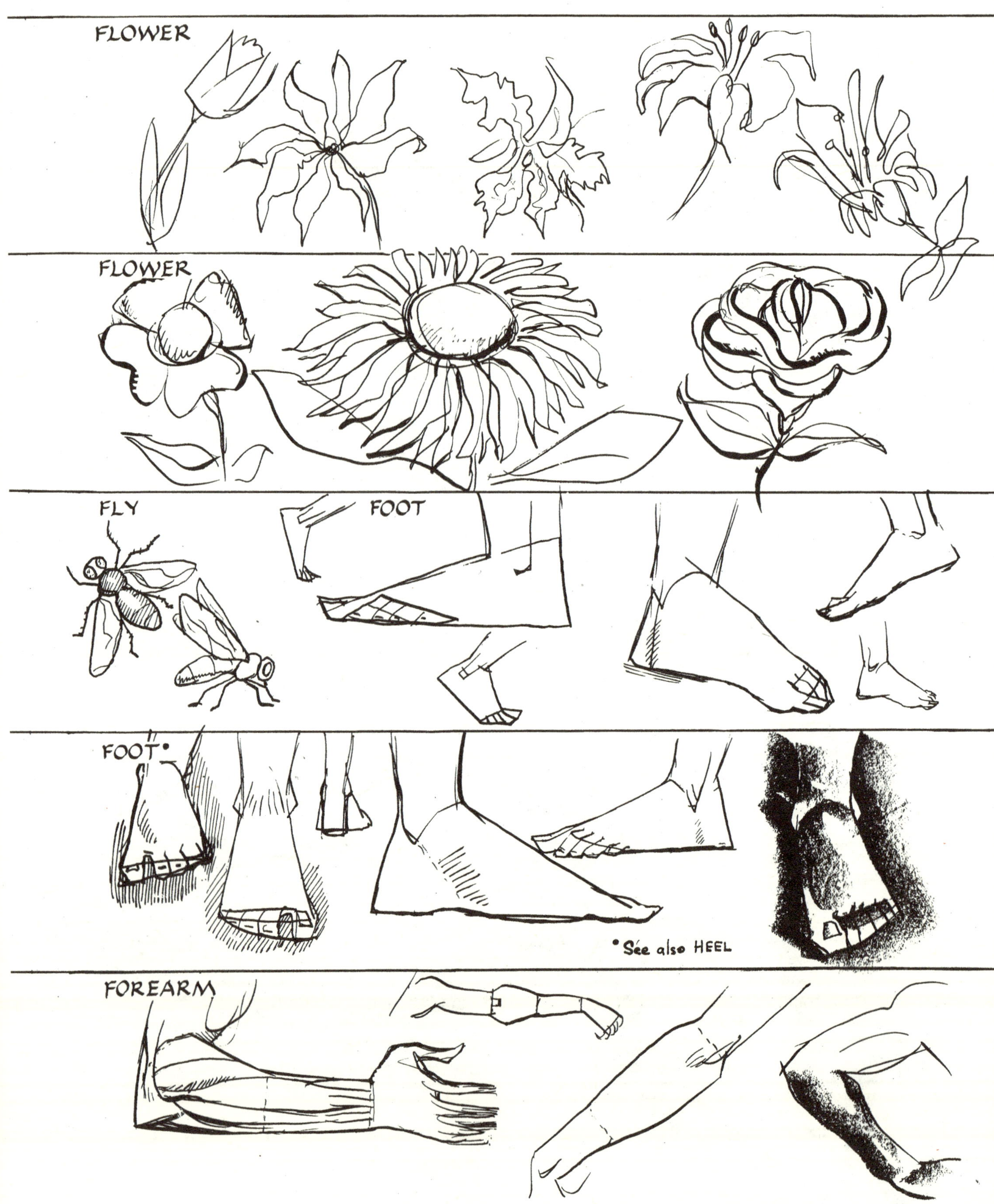
FLOWER
FLOWER
FLY
FOOT
FOOT*
*See also HEEL
FOREARM

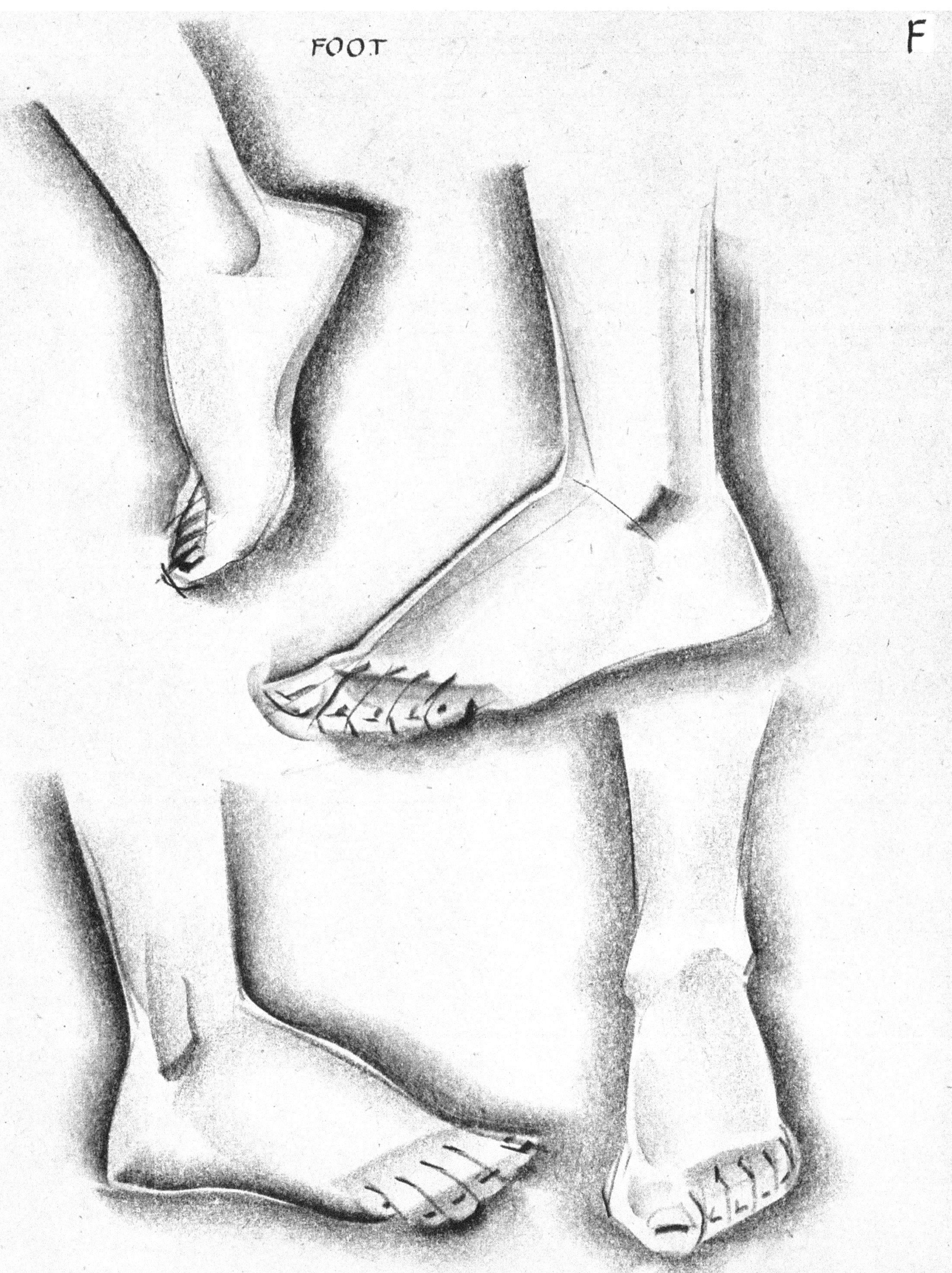
FOOT
F

FOX

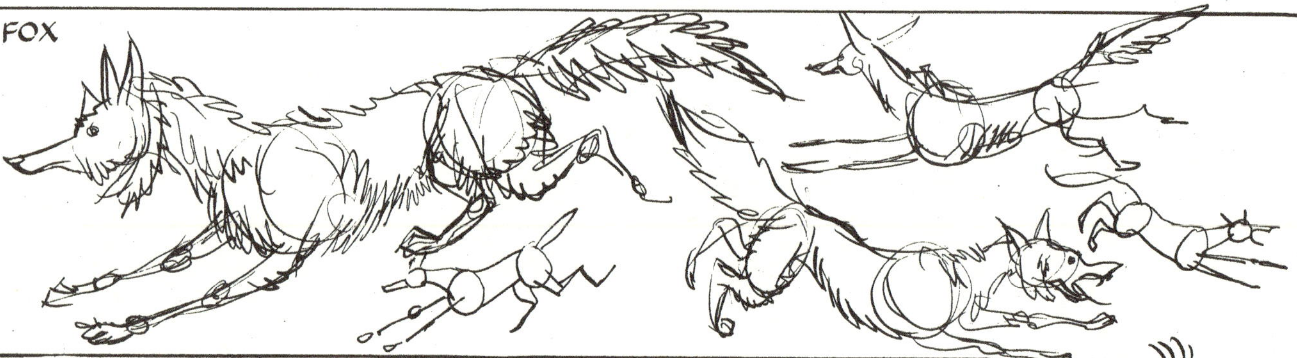

FROG

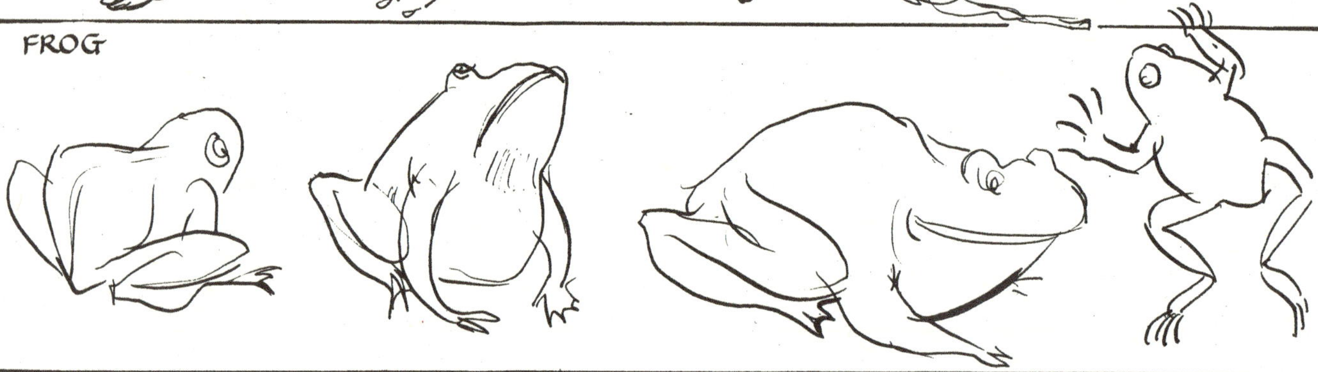

FRUIT

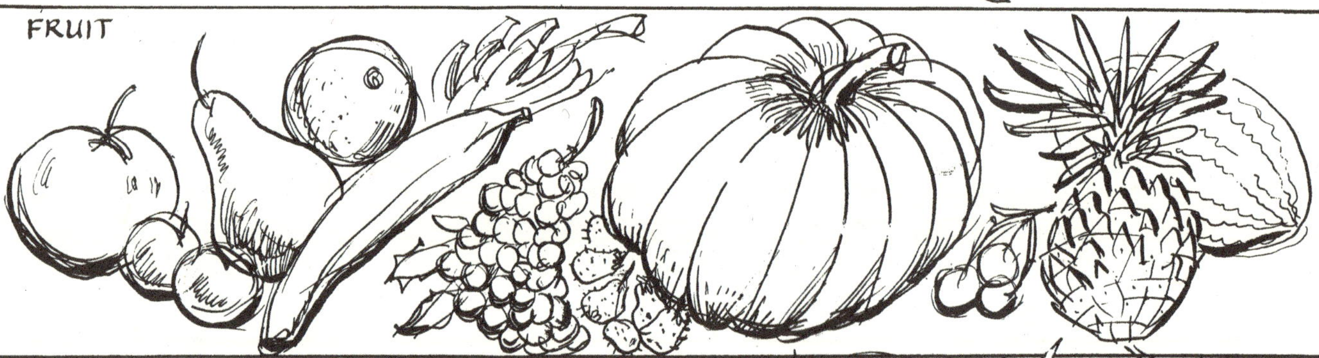

GARGOYLE

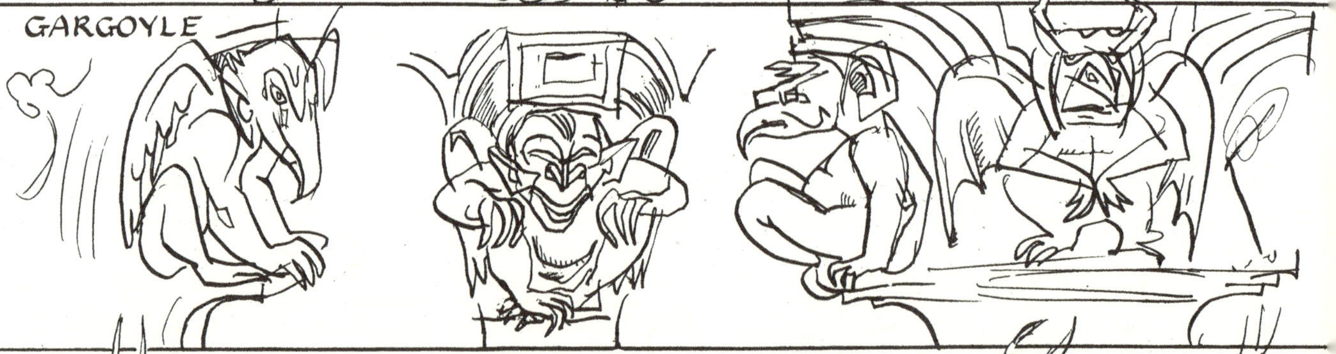

GAZELLE

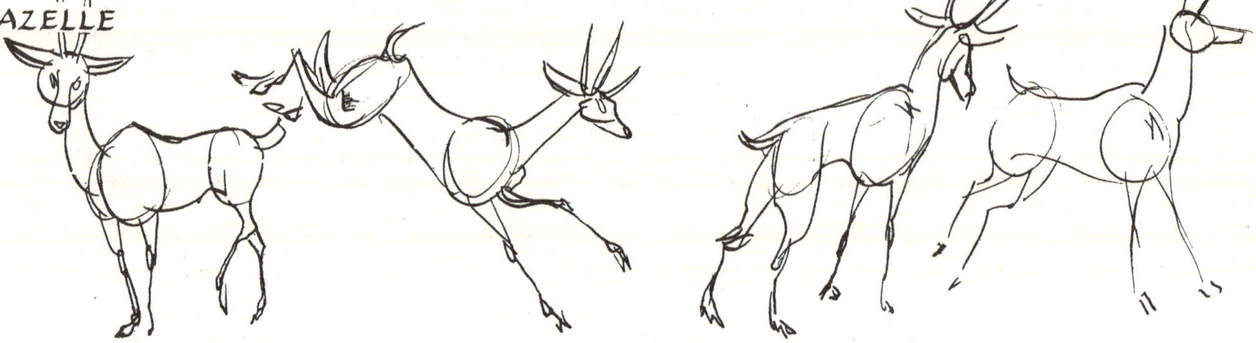

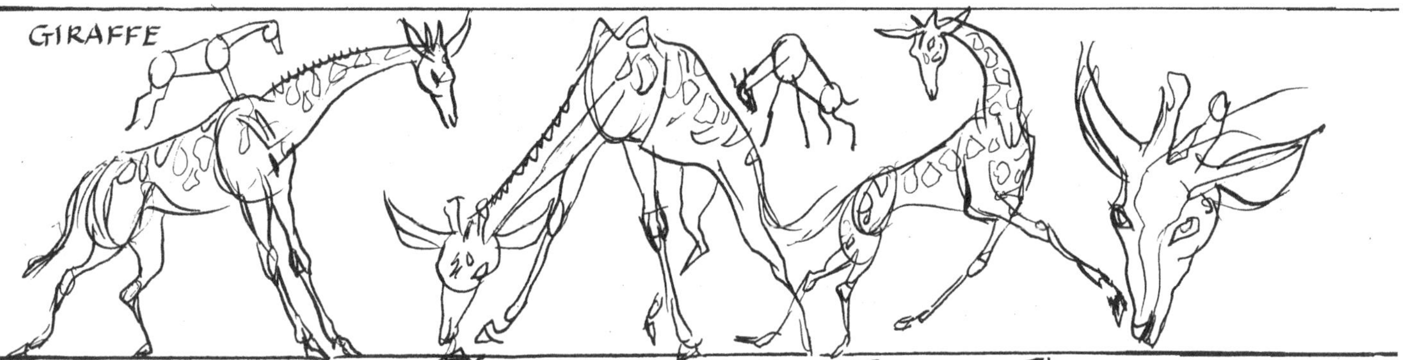

GIRAFFE

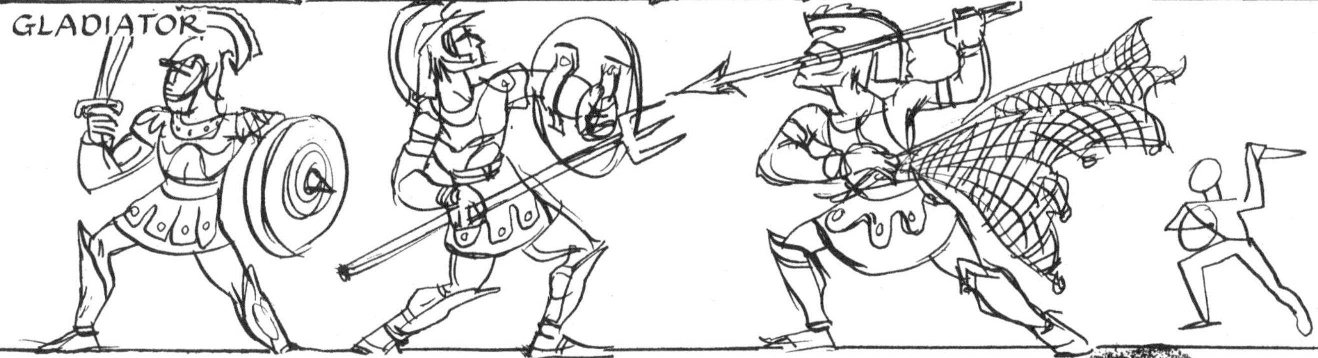

GLADIATOR

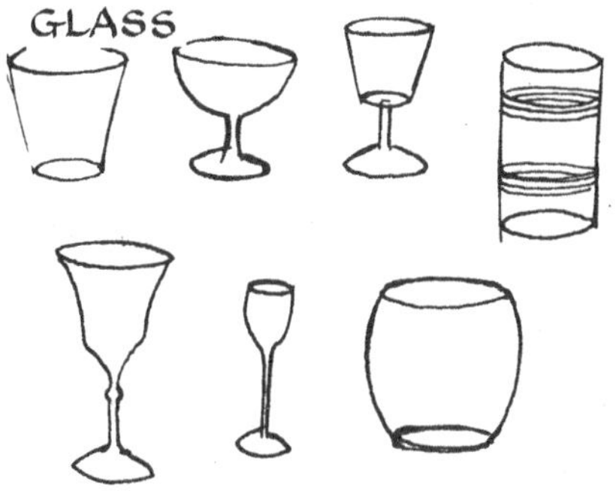

GLASS

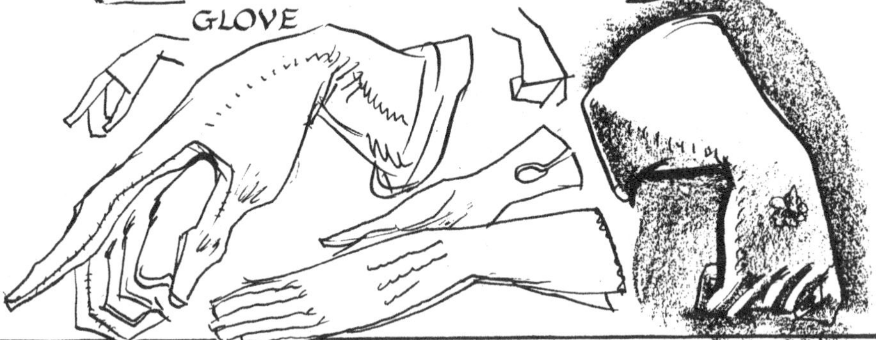

GLOVE

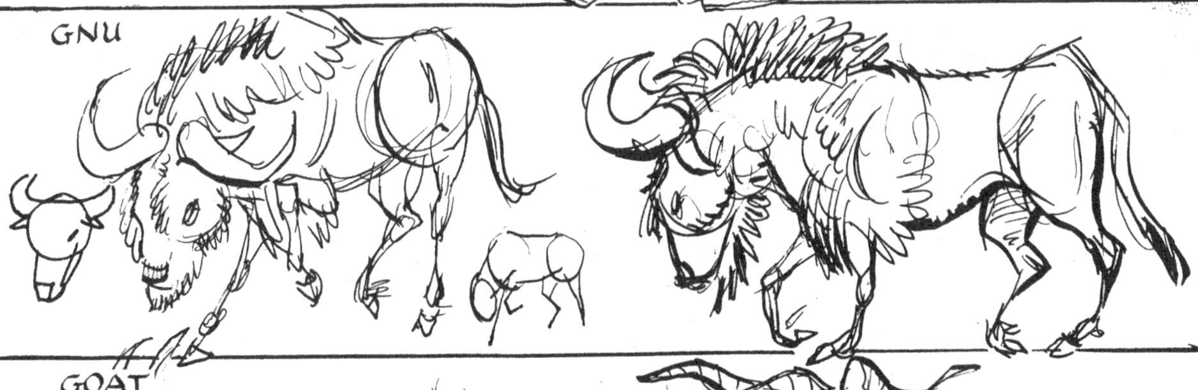

GNU

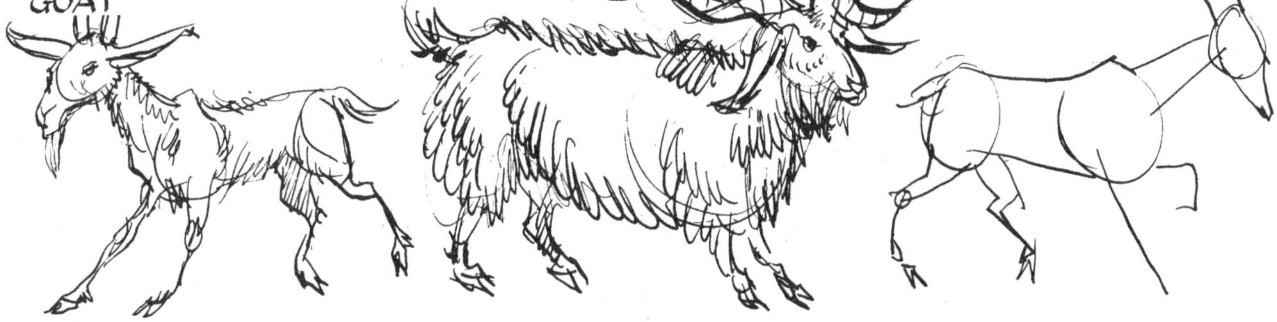

GOAT

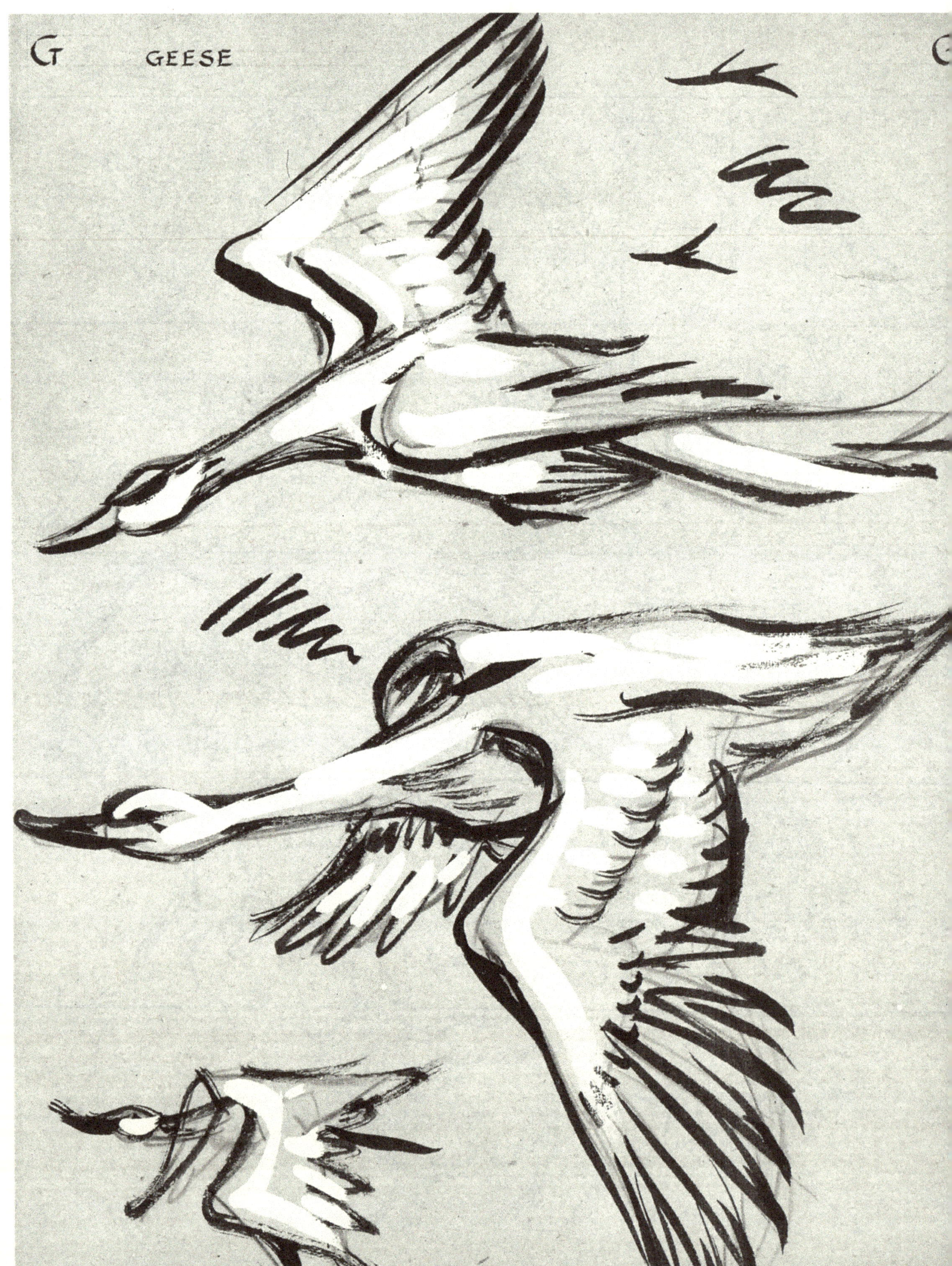
G
GEESE

GOLF

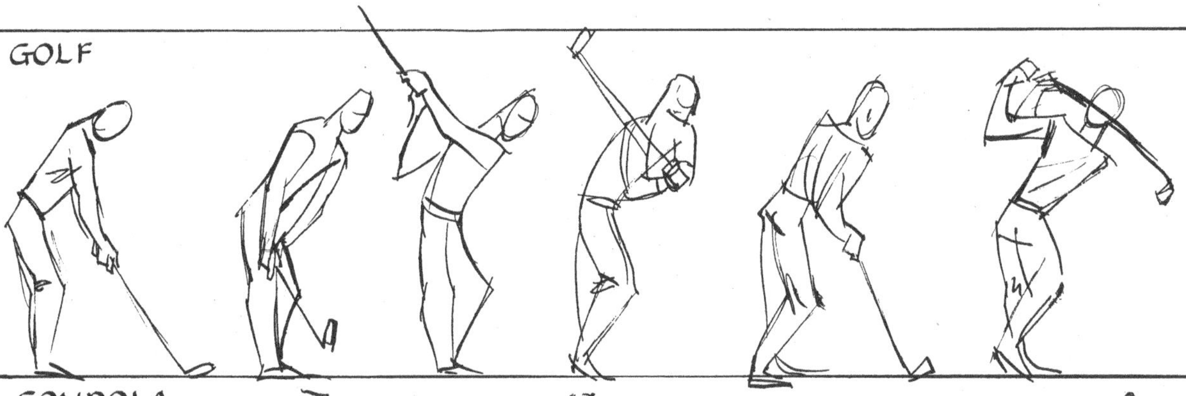

GONDOLA

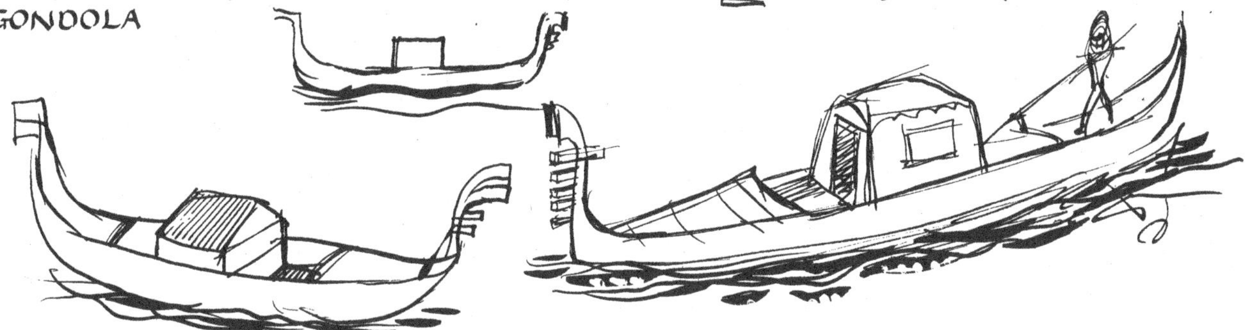

GOOSE

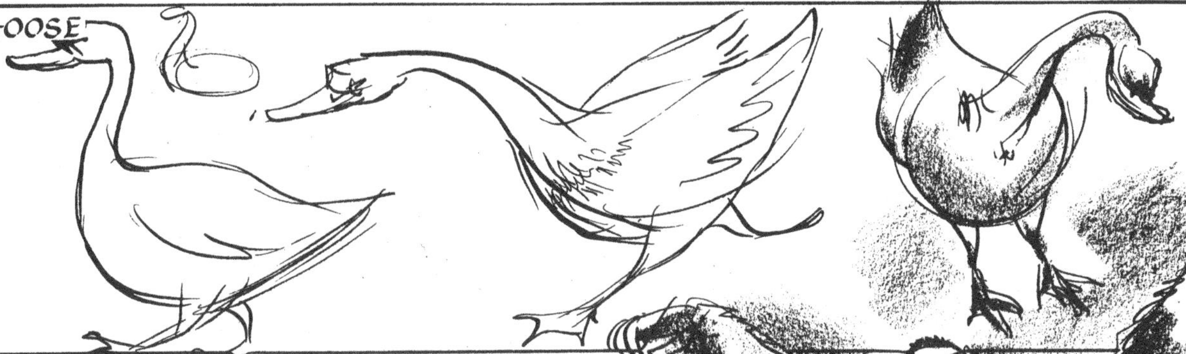

GORILLA

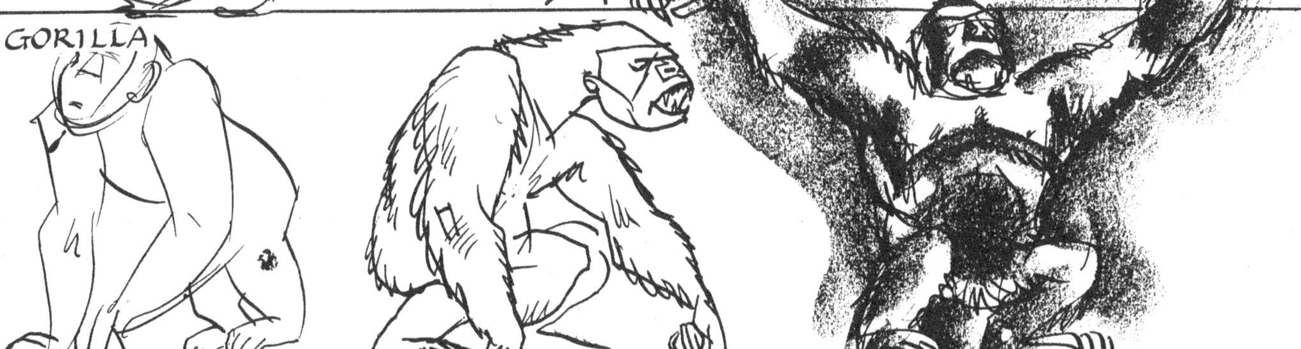

GREAT DANE

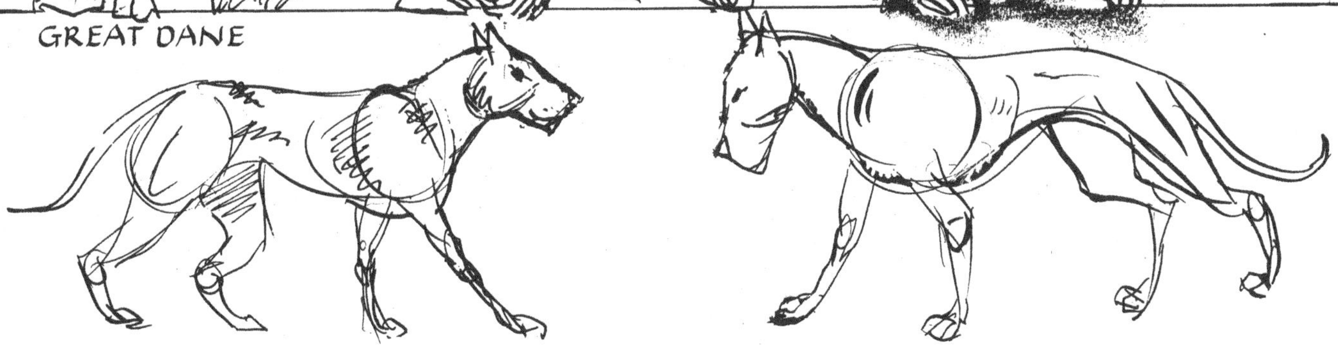

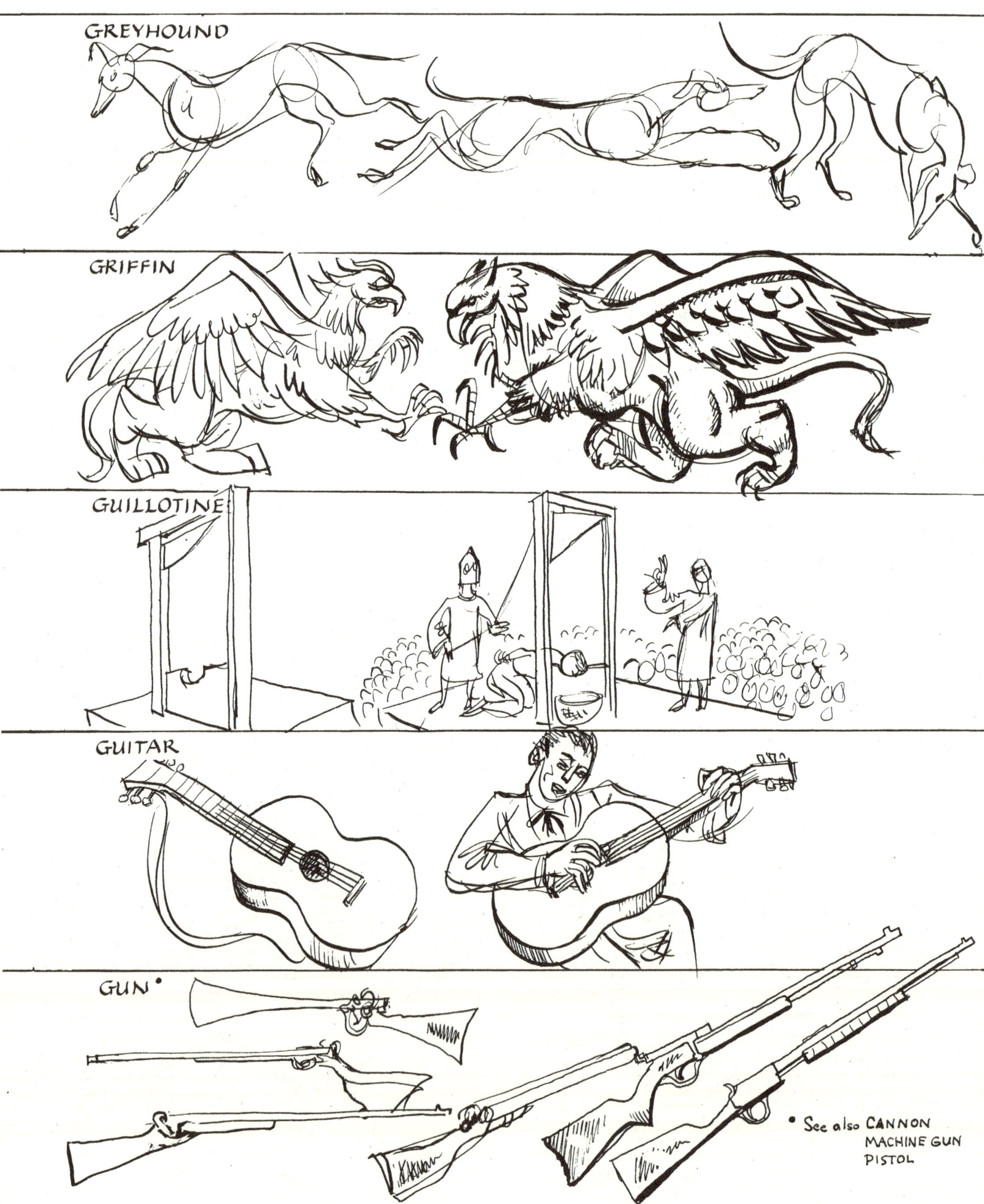
GREYHOUND
GRIFFIN
GUILLOTINE
GUITAR
GUN•
• See also CANNON
MACHINE GUN
PISTOL

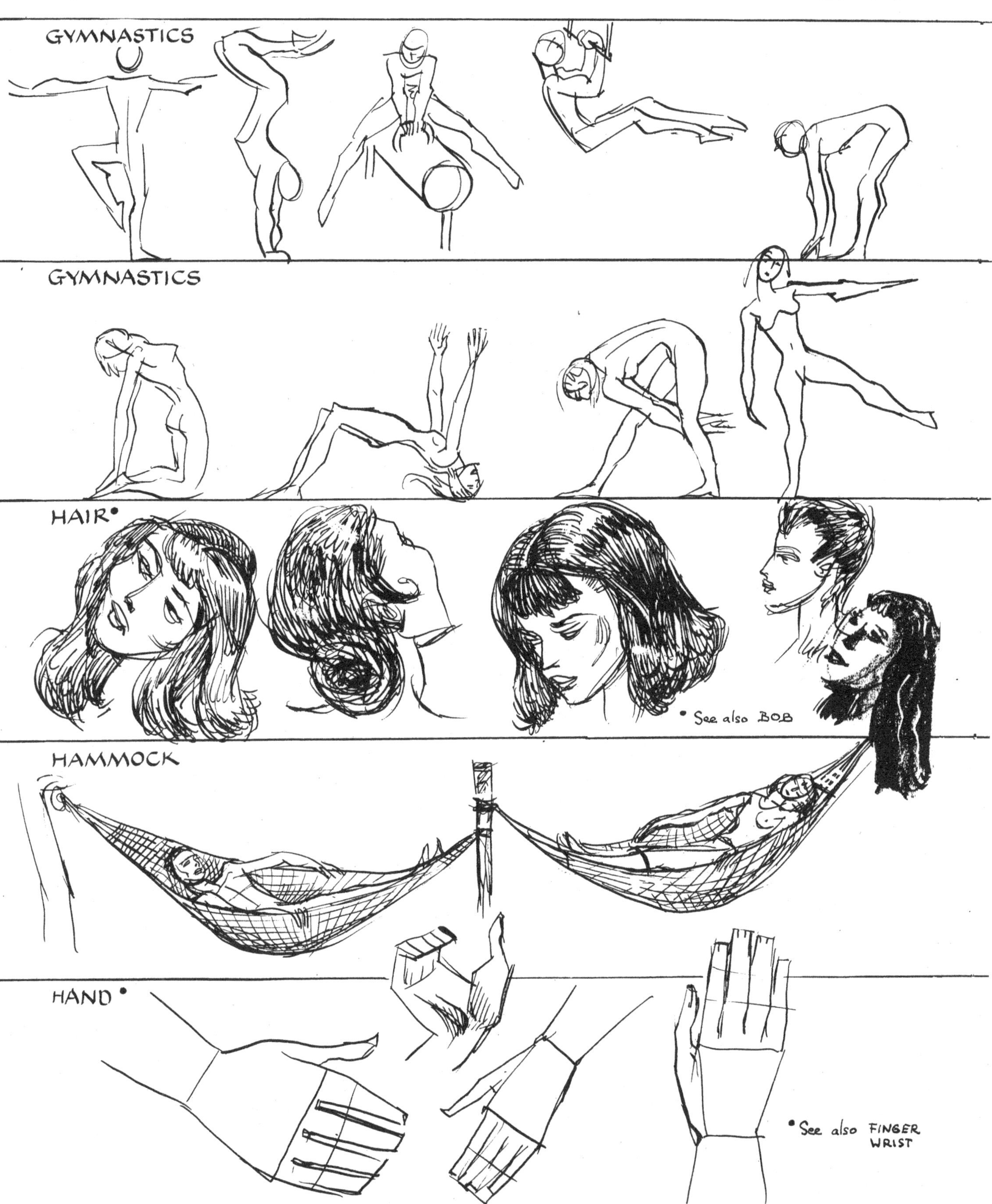
GYMNASTICS
GYMNASTICS
HAIR•
• See also BOB
HAMMOCK
HAND •
• See also FINGER
WRIST

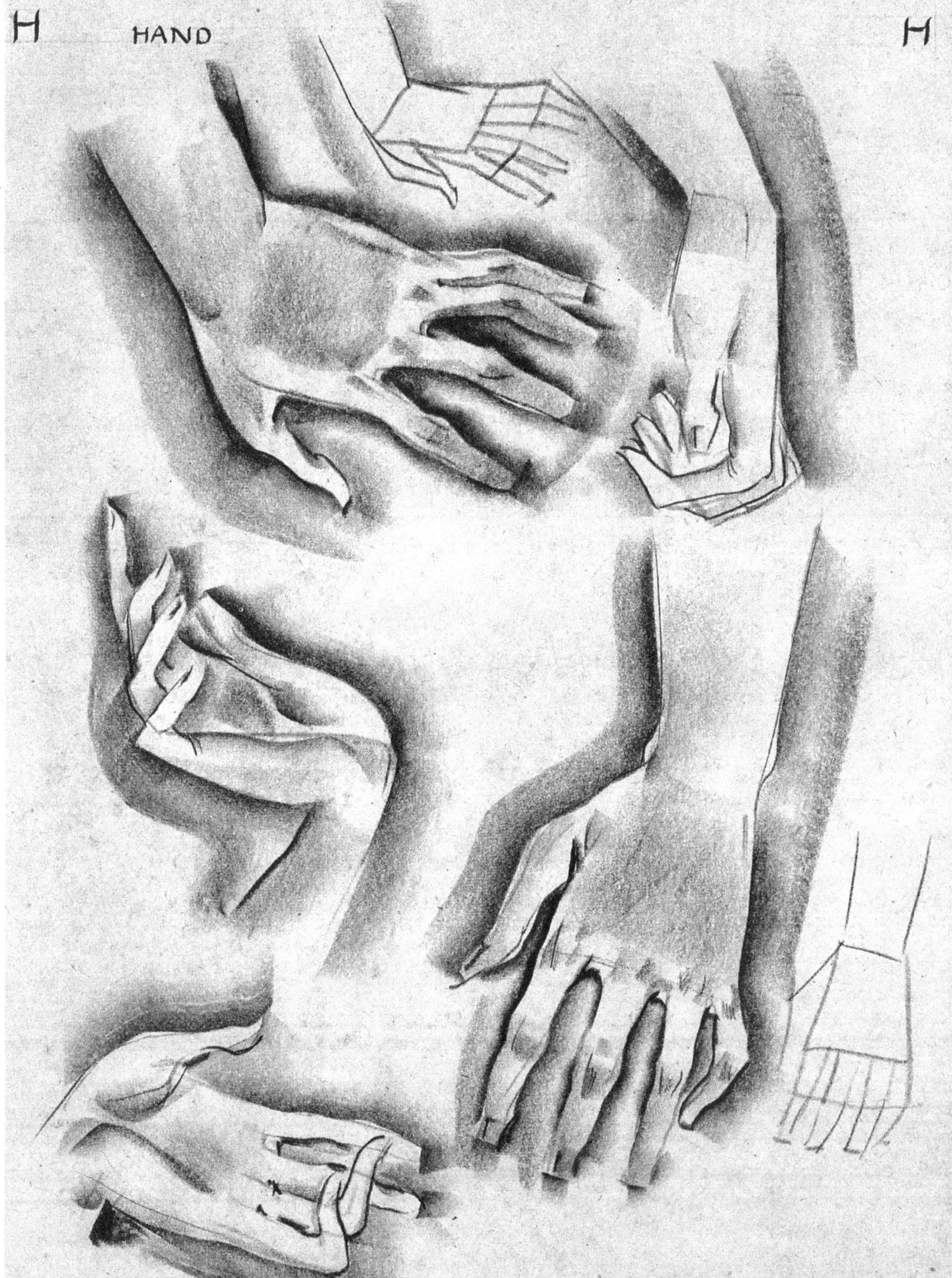
H
HAND
H

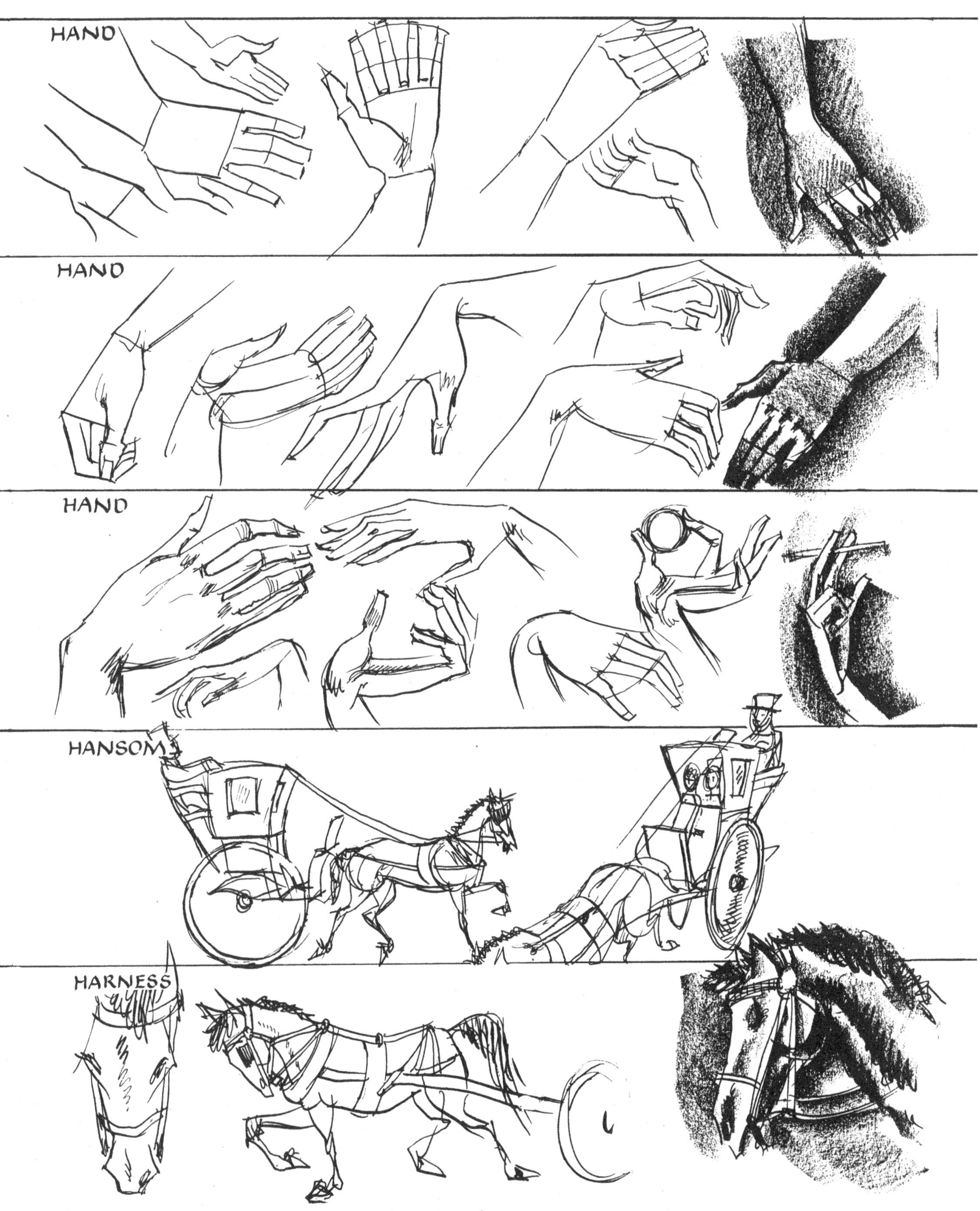
HAND
HAND
HAND
HANSOM
HARNESS

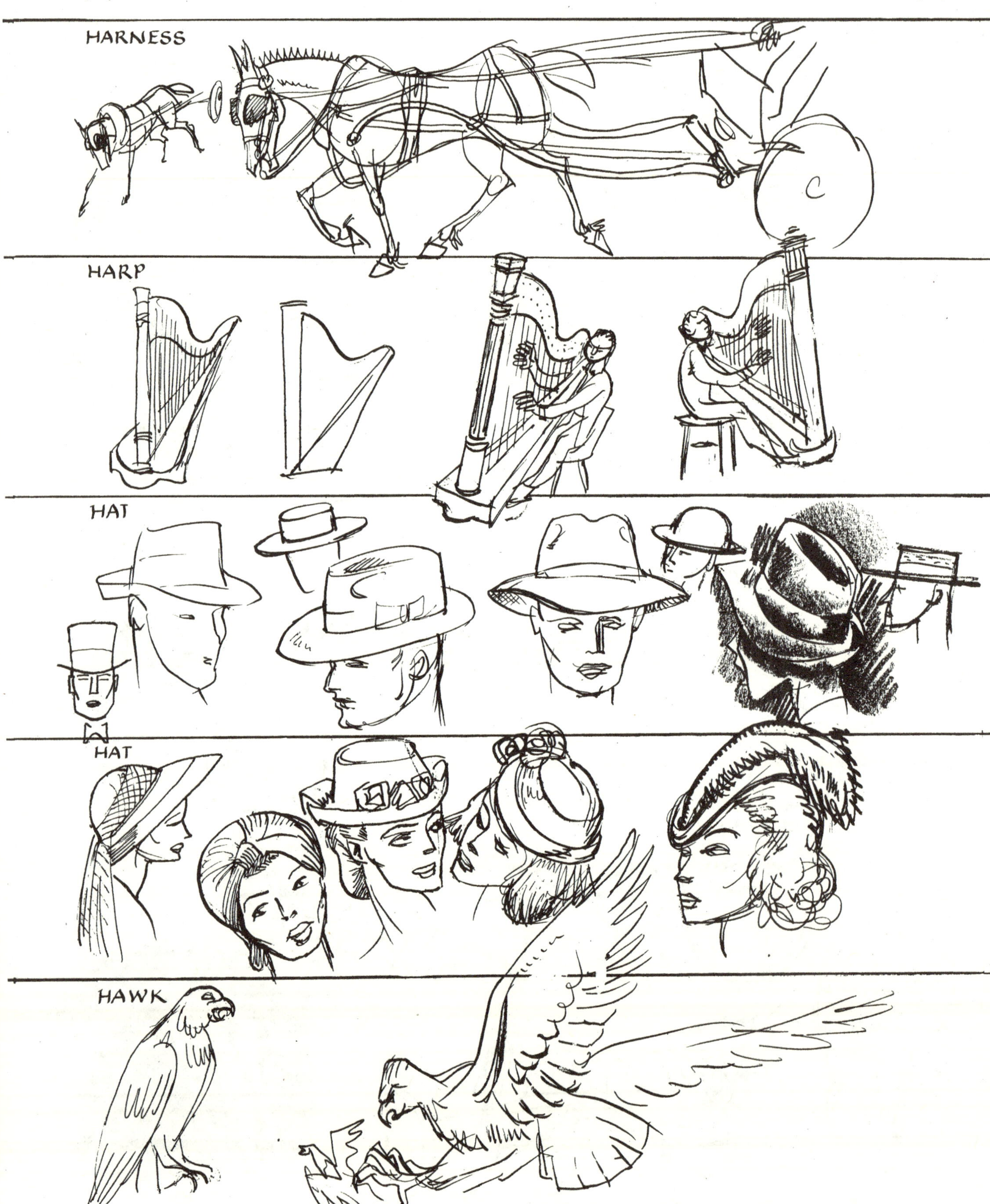
HARNESS
HARP
HAT
HAT
HAWK

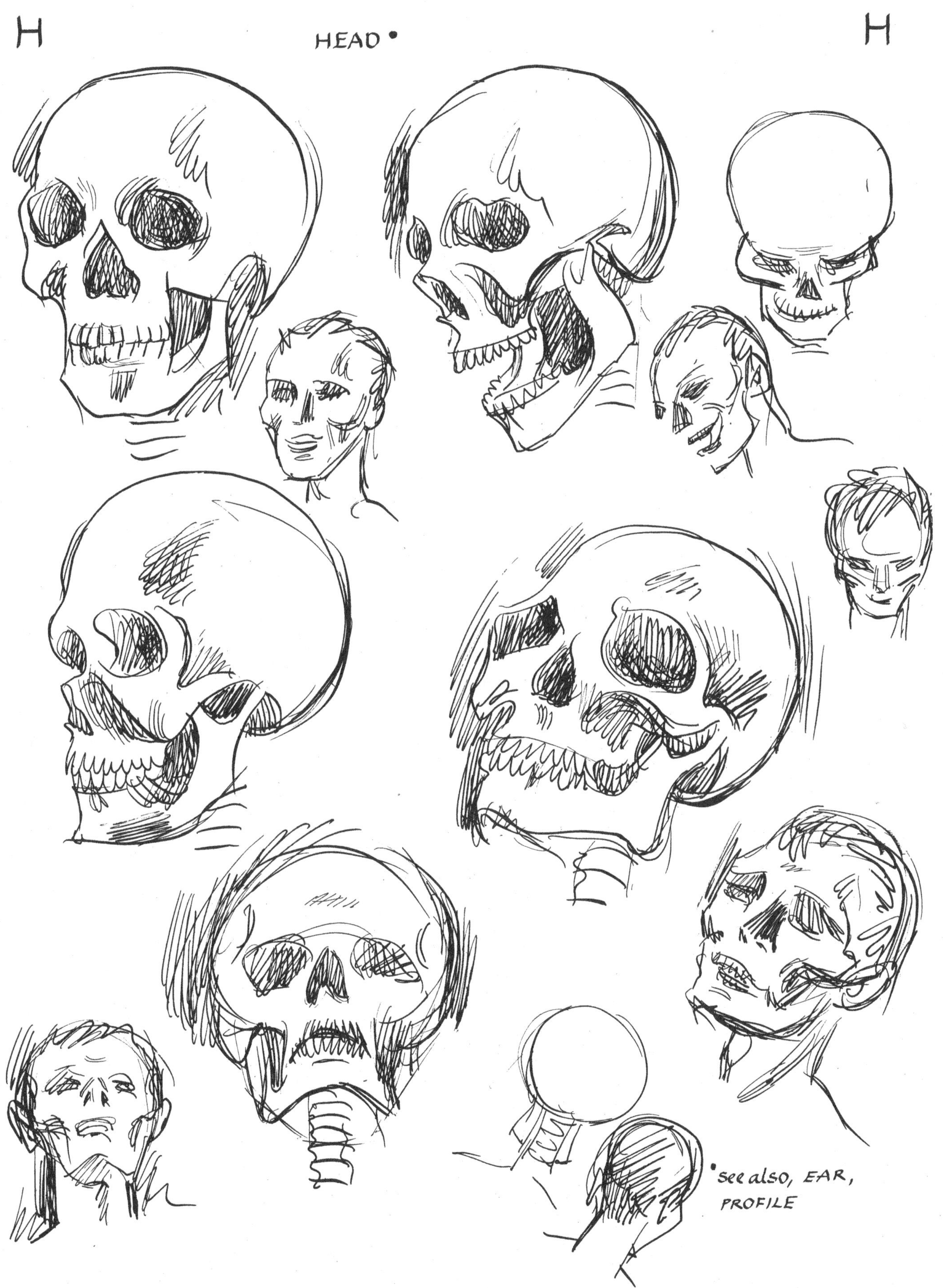
• see also, EAR, PROFILE

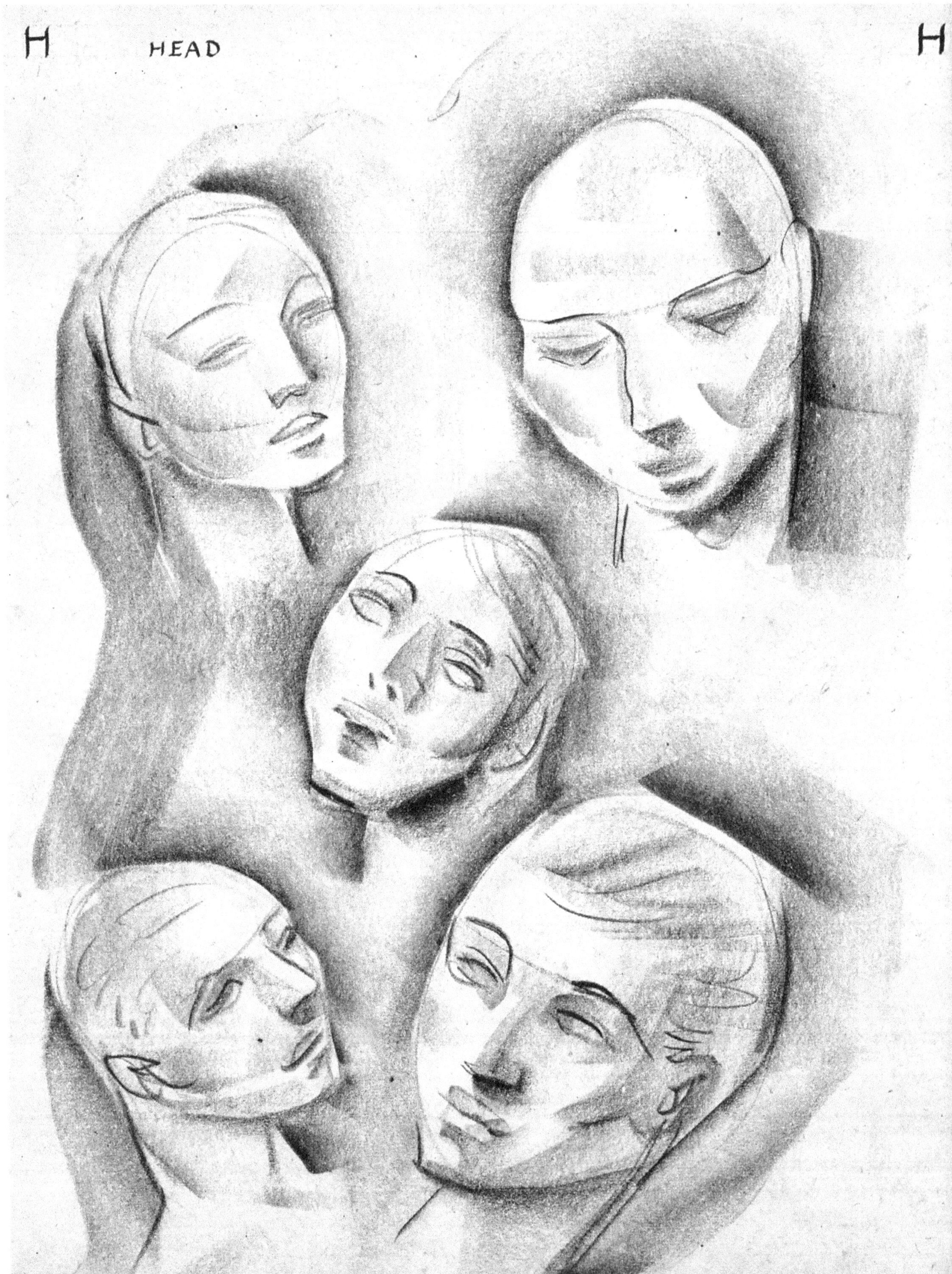

HEAD

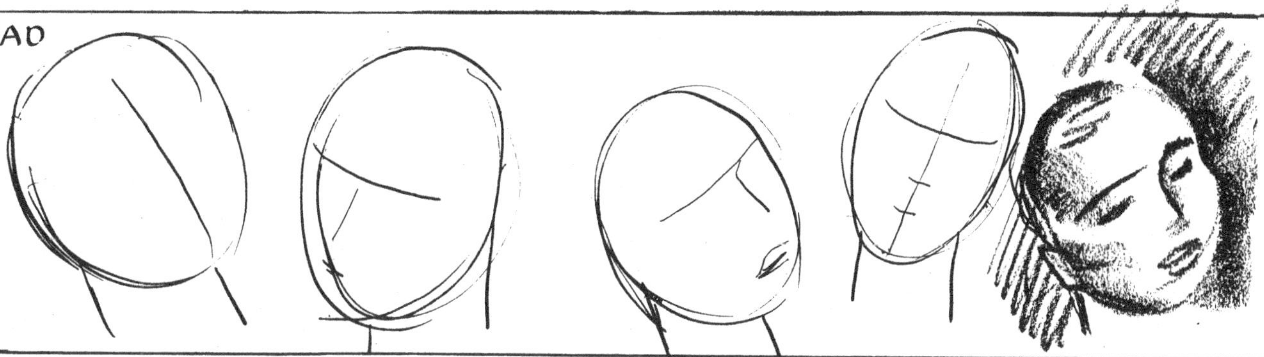

HEAD

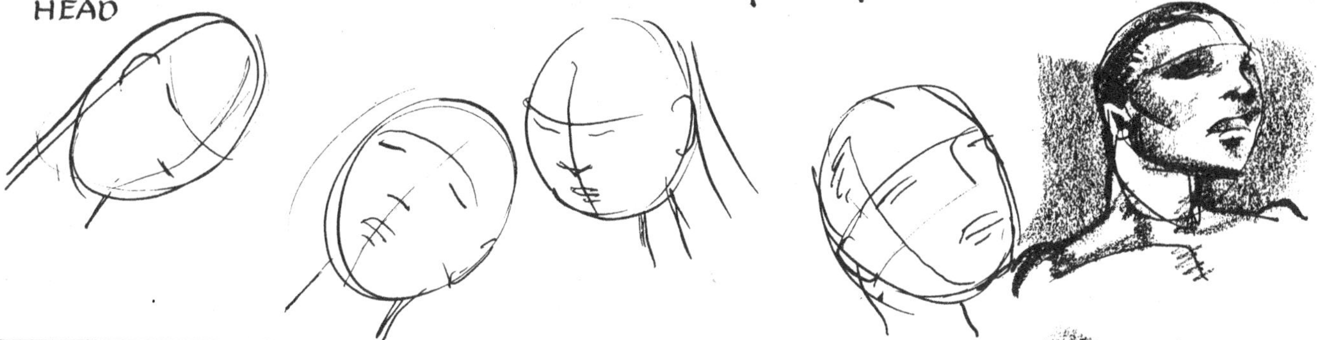

HEAD

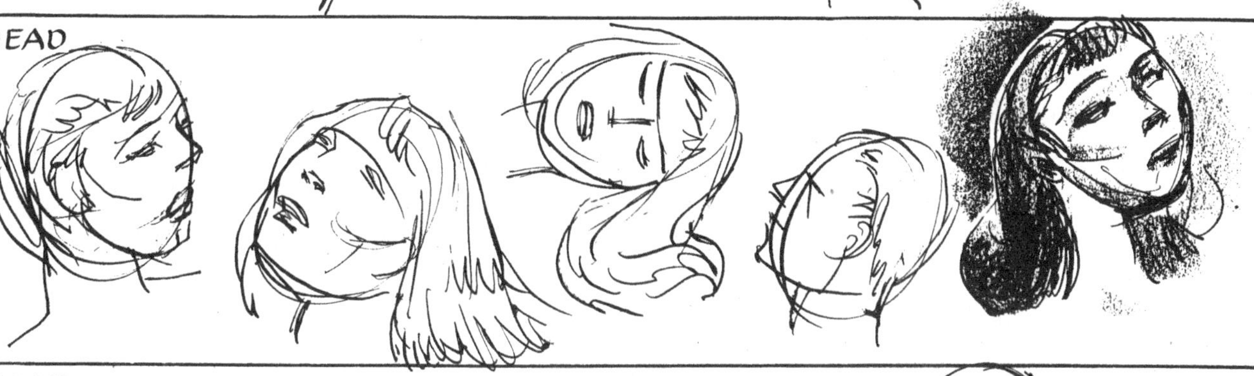

HEAD

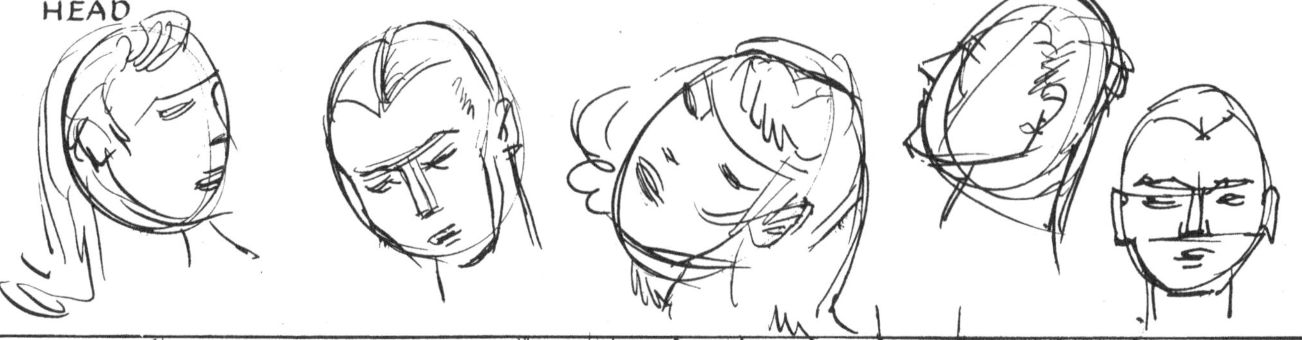

HEEL

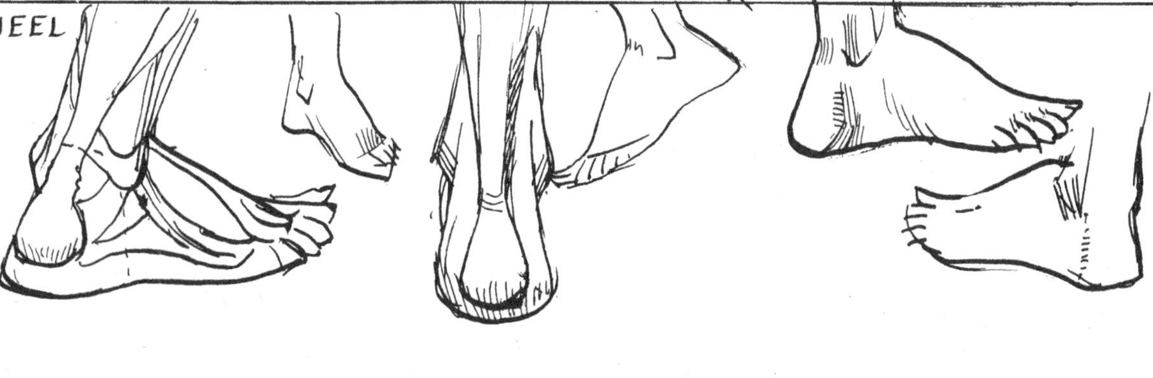

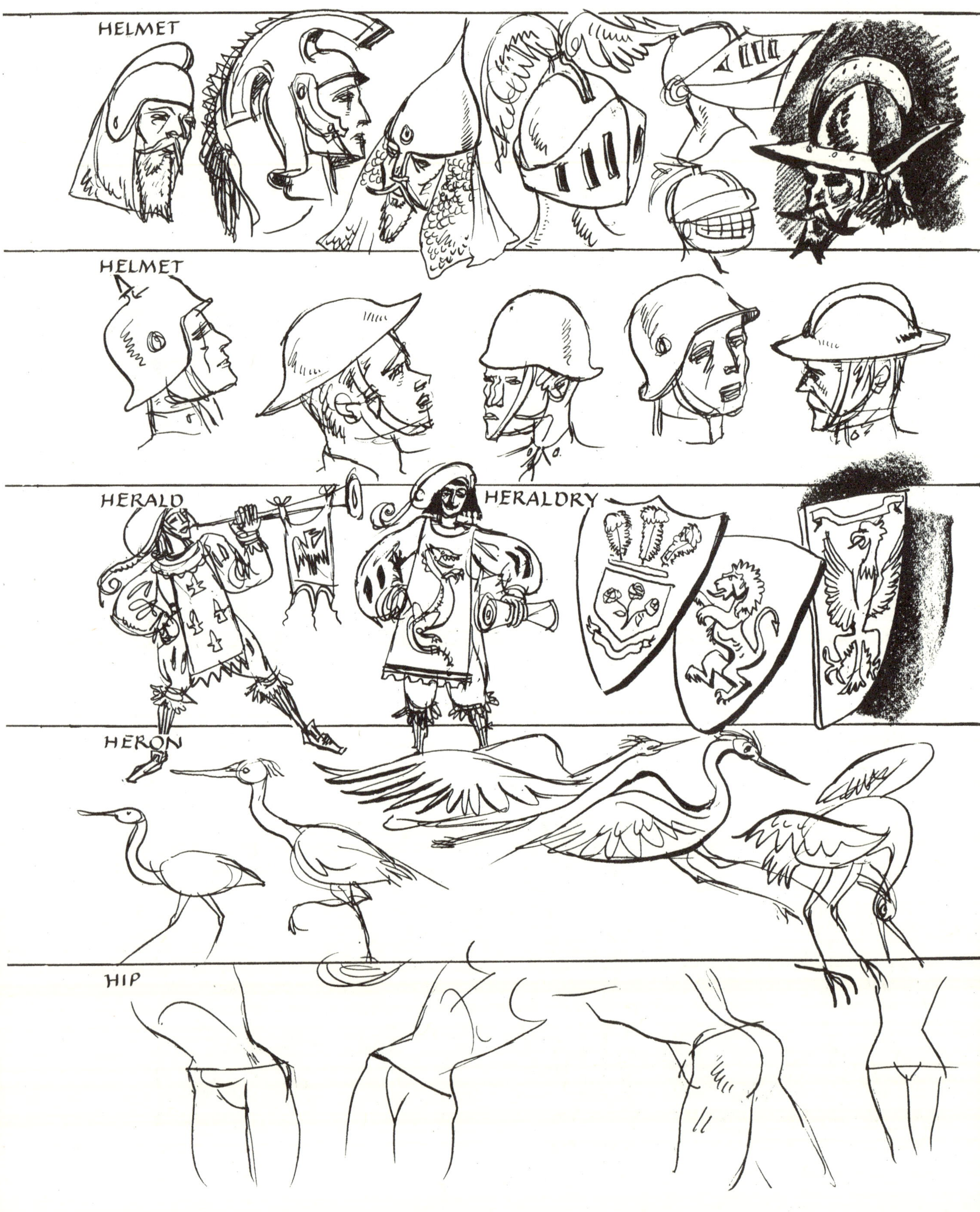
HELMET
HELMET
HERALD
HERALDRY
HERON
HIP

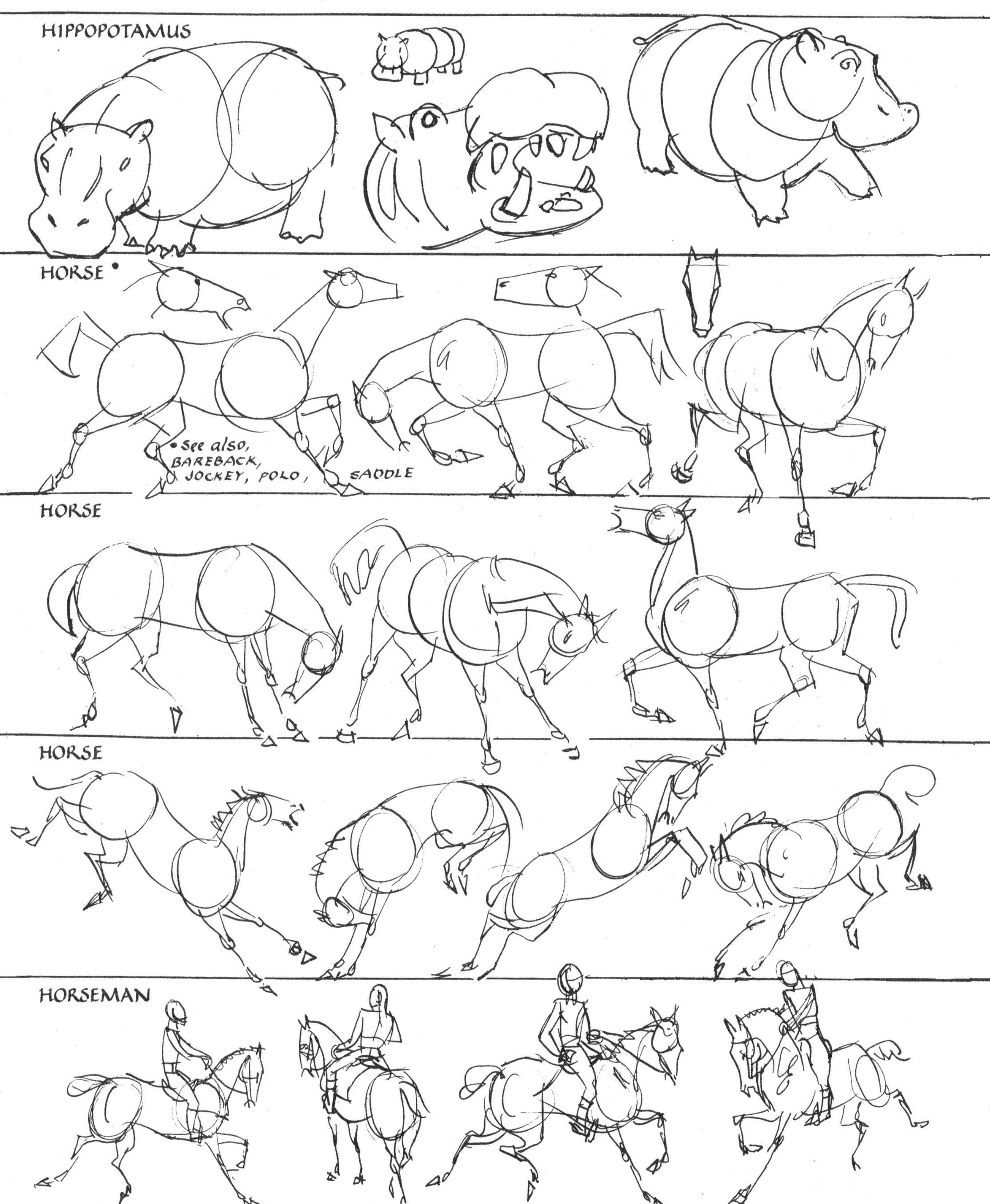
HIPPOPOTAMUS
HORSE •
• See also, BAREBACK, JOCKEY, POLO, SADDLE
HORSE
HORSE
HORSEMAN

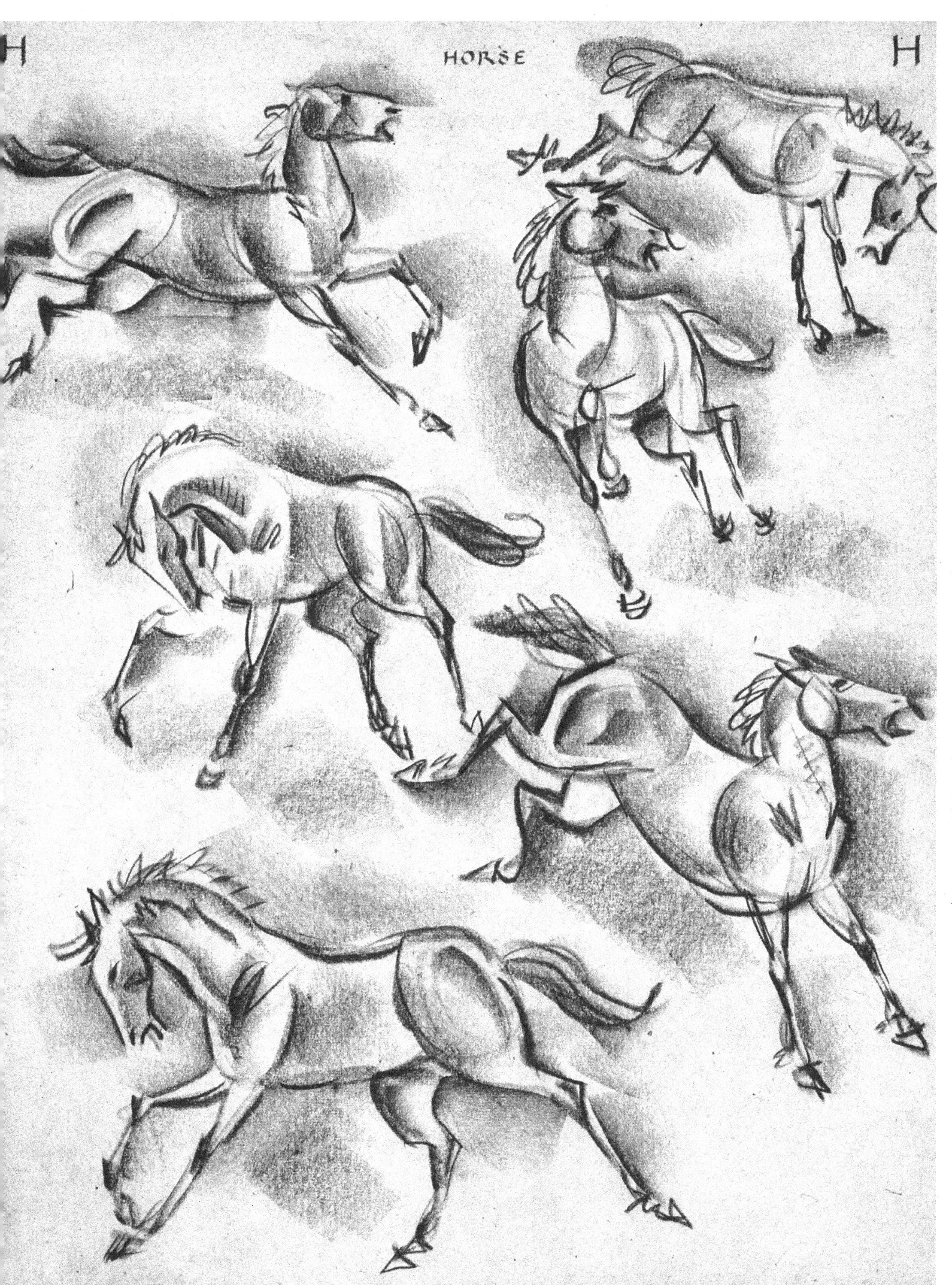
H
HORSE
H

HOUSE

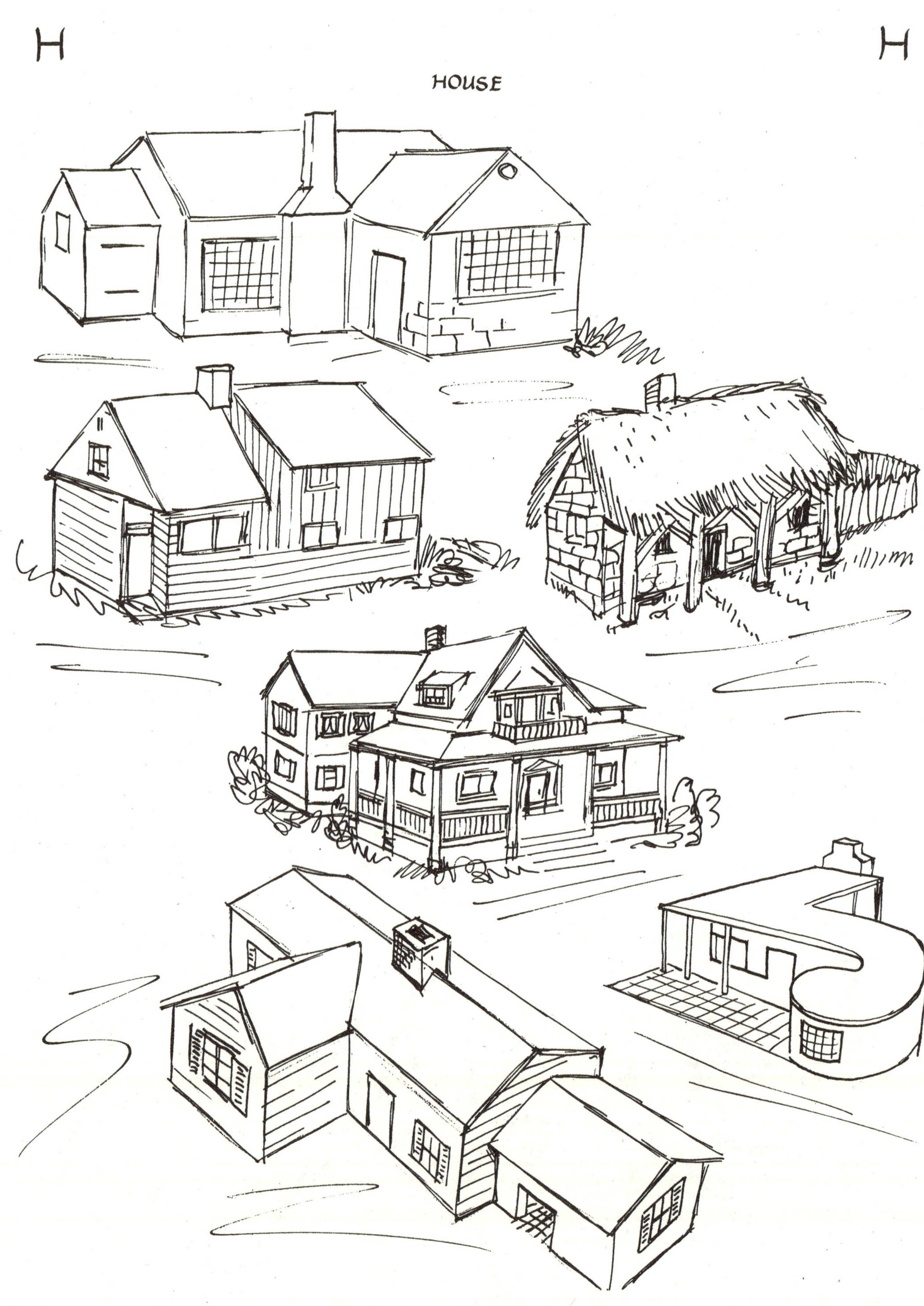

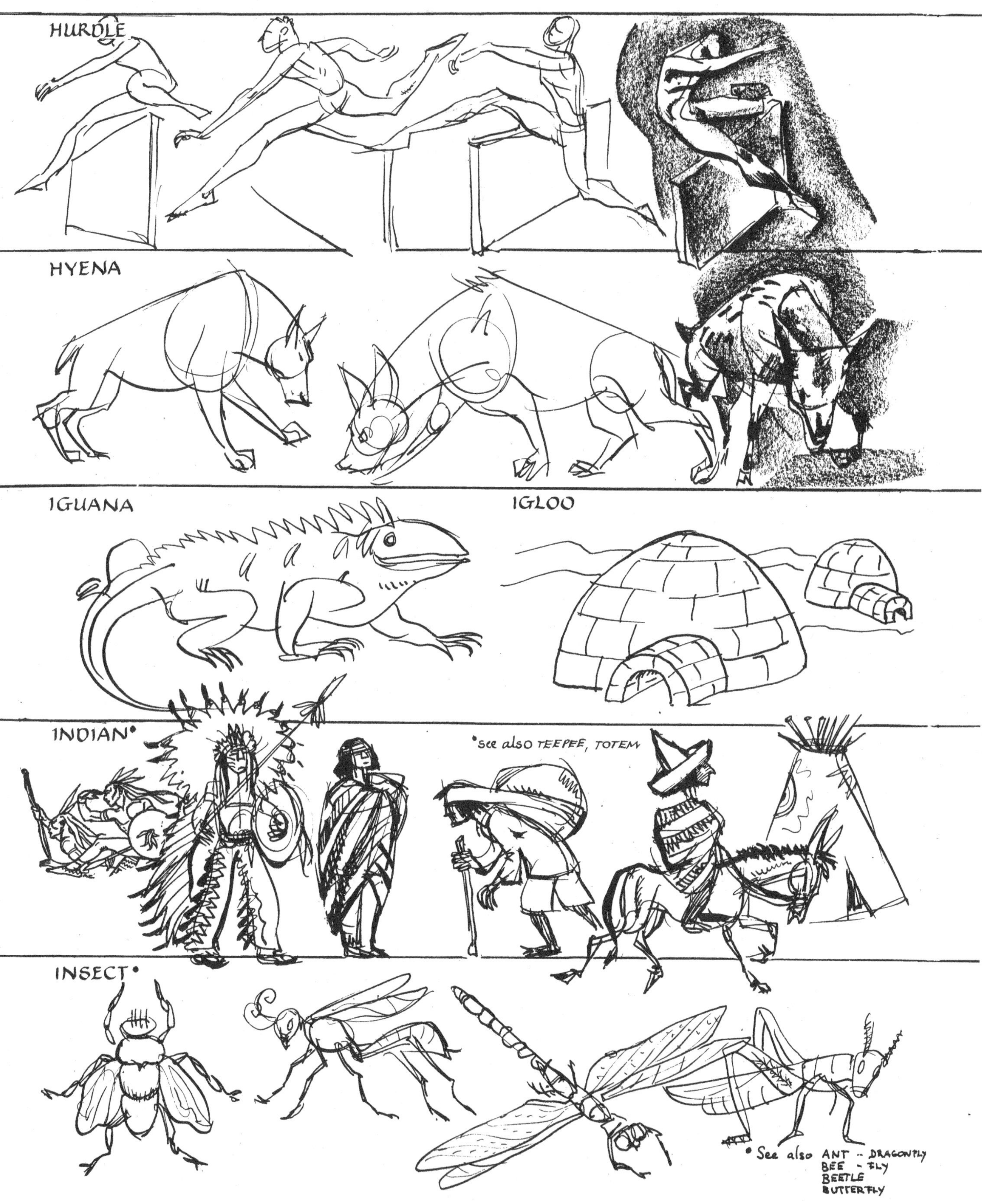

HURDLE
HYENA
IGUANA
IGLOO
INDIAN*
*see also TEEPEE, TOTEM
INSECT*
* See also ANT - DRAGONFLY
BEE - FLY
BEETLE
BUTTERFLY

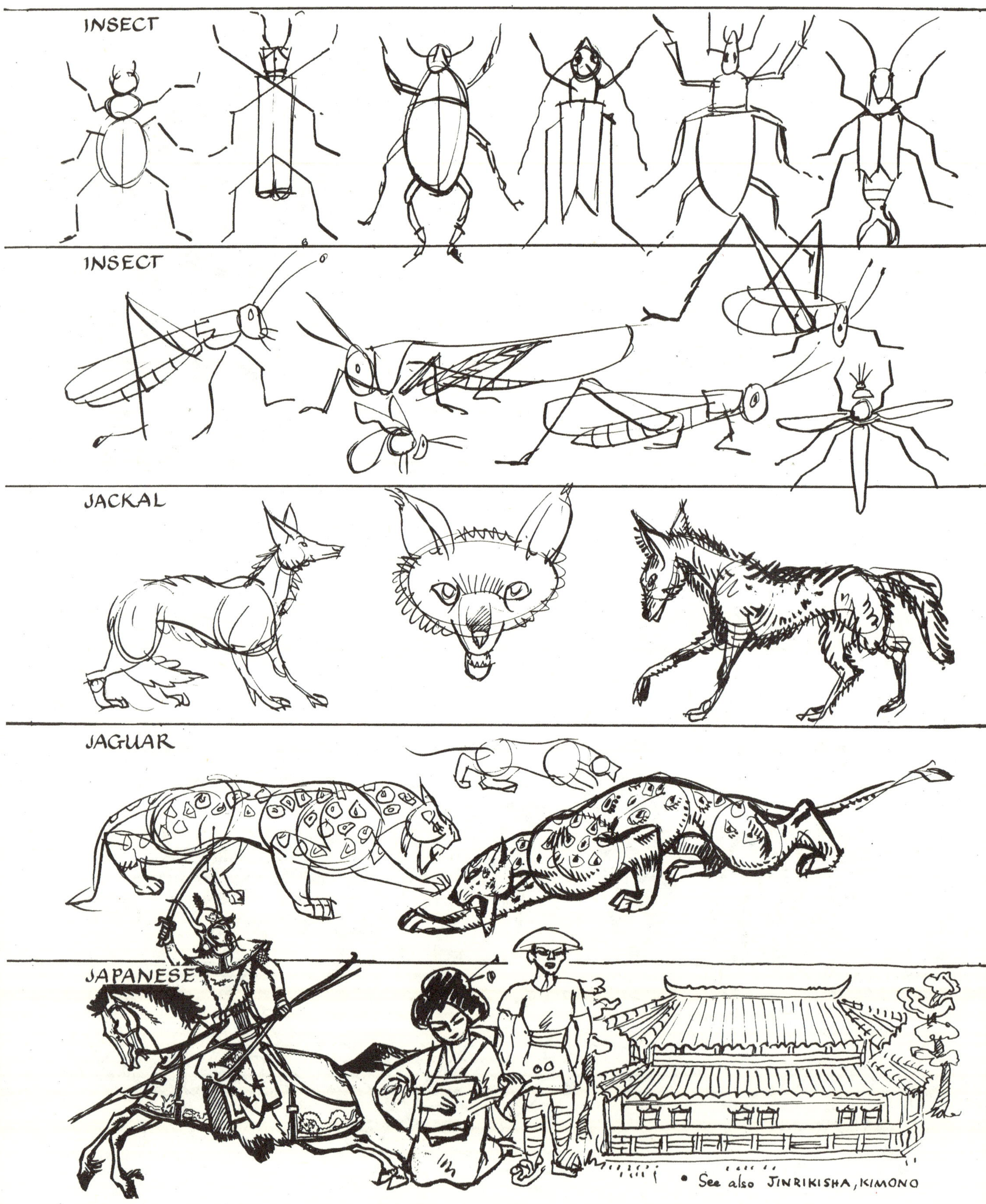

• See also JINRIKISHA, KIMONO

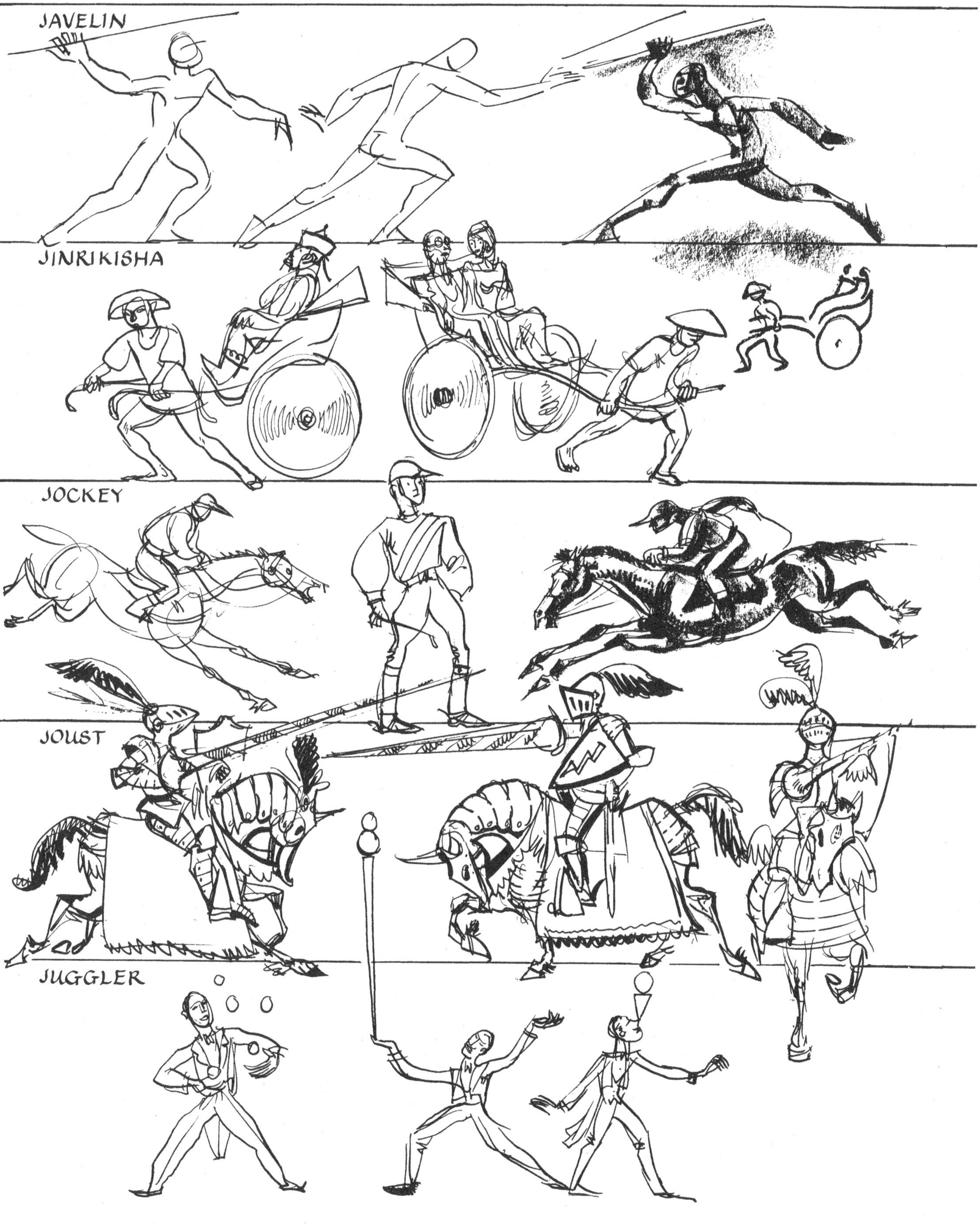

JAVELIN

JINRIKISHA

JOCKEY

JOUST

JUGGLER

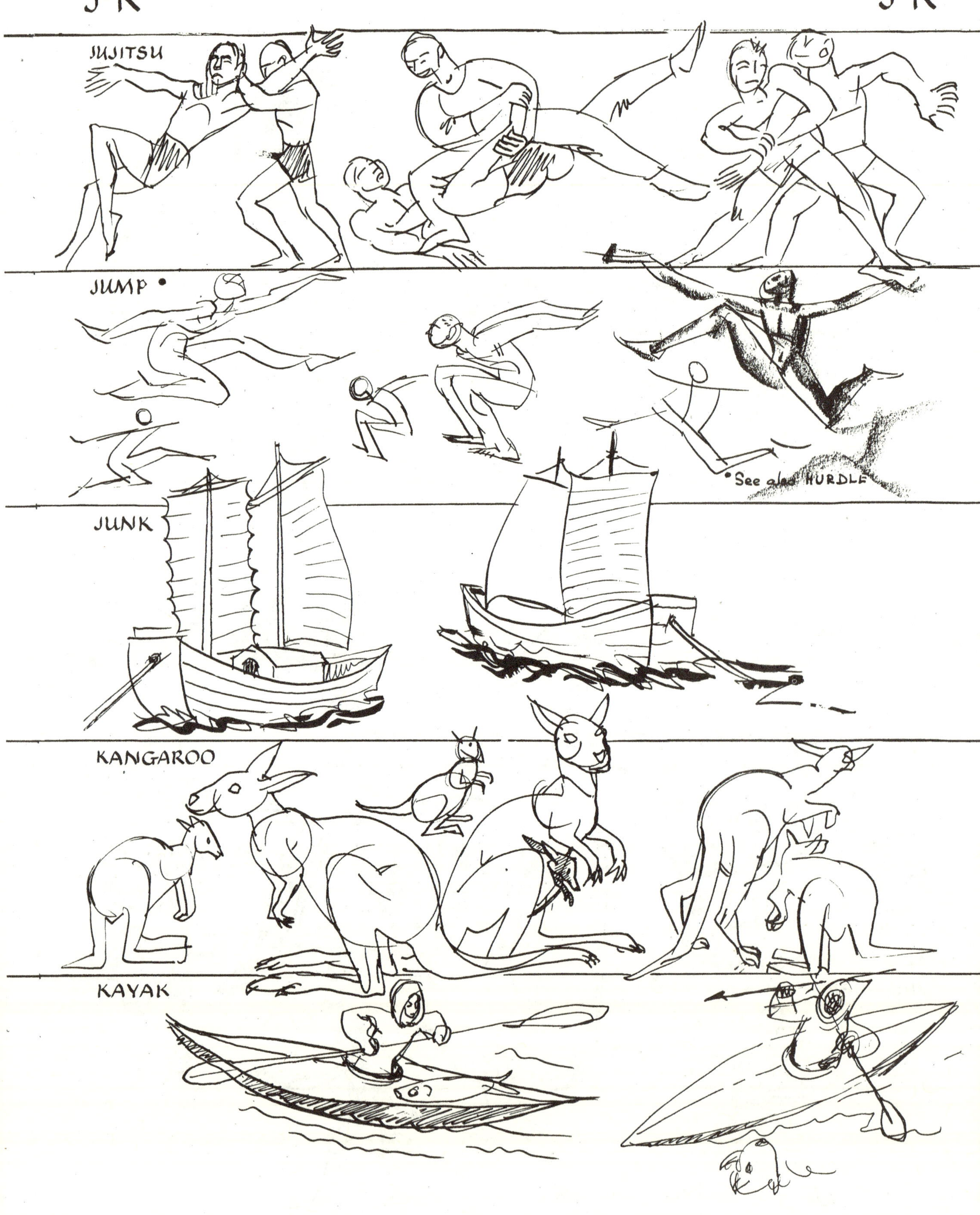

JUJITSU
JUMP •
• See also HURDLE
JUNK
KANGAROO
KAYAK

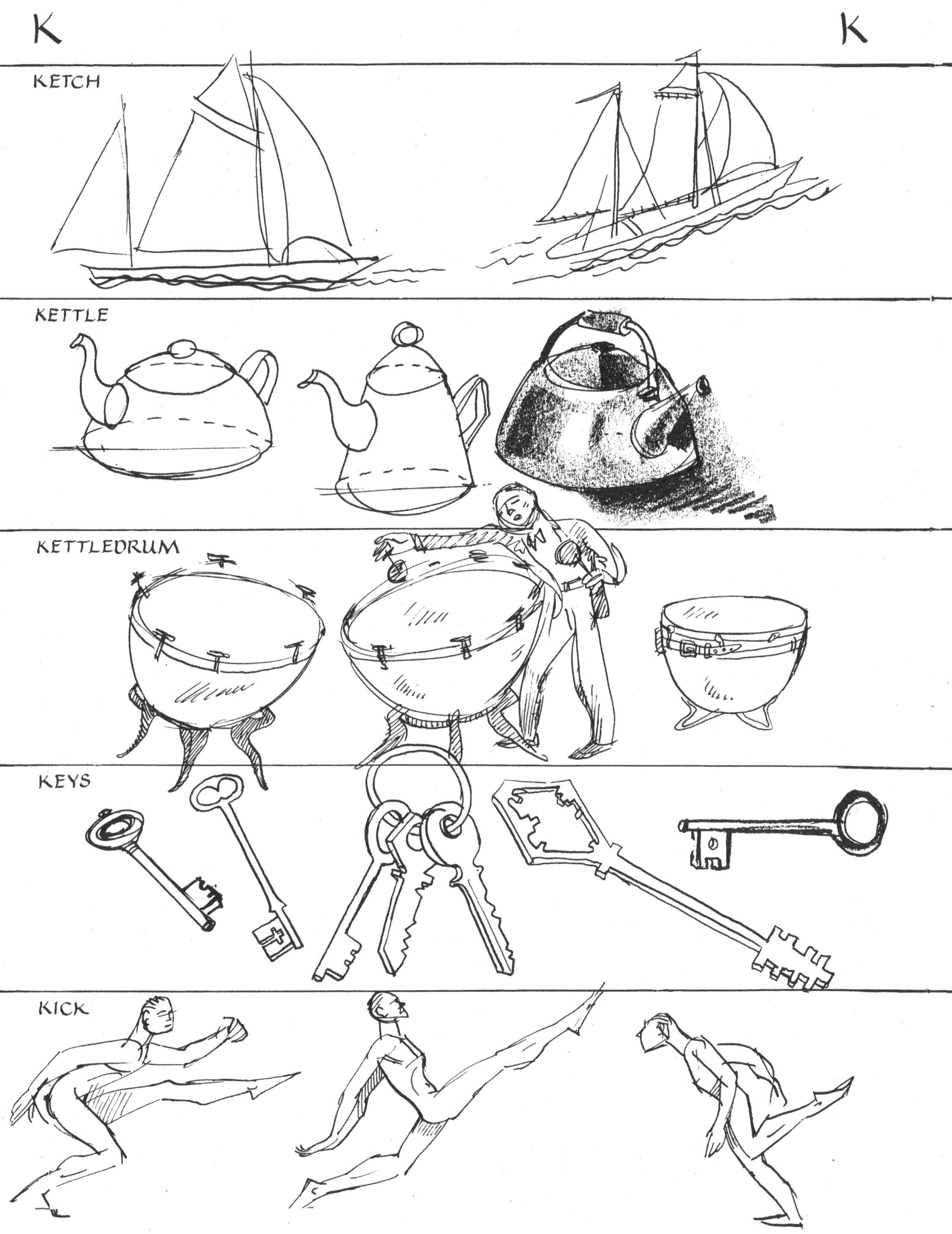
KETCH
KETTLE
KETTLEDRUM
KEYS
KICK

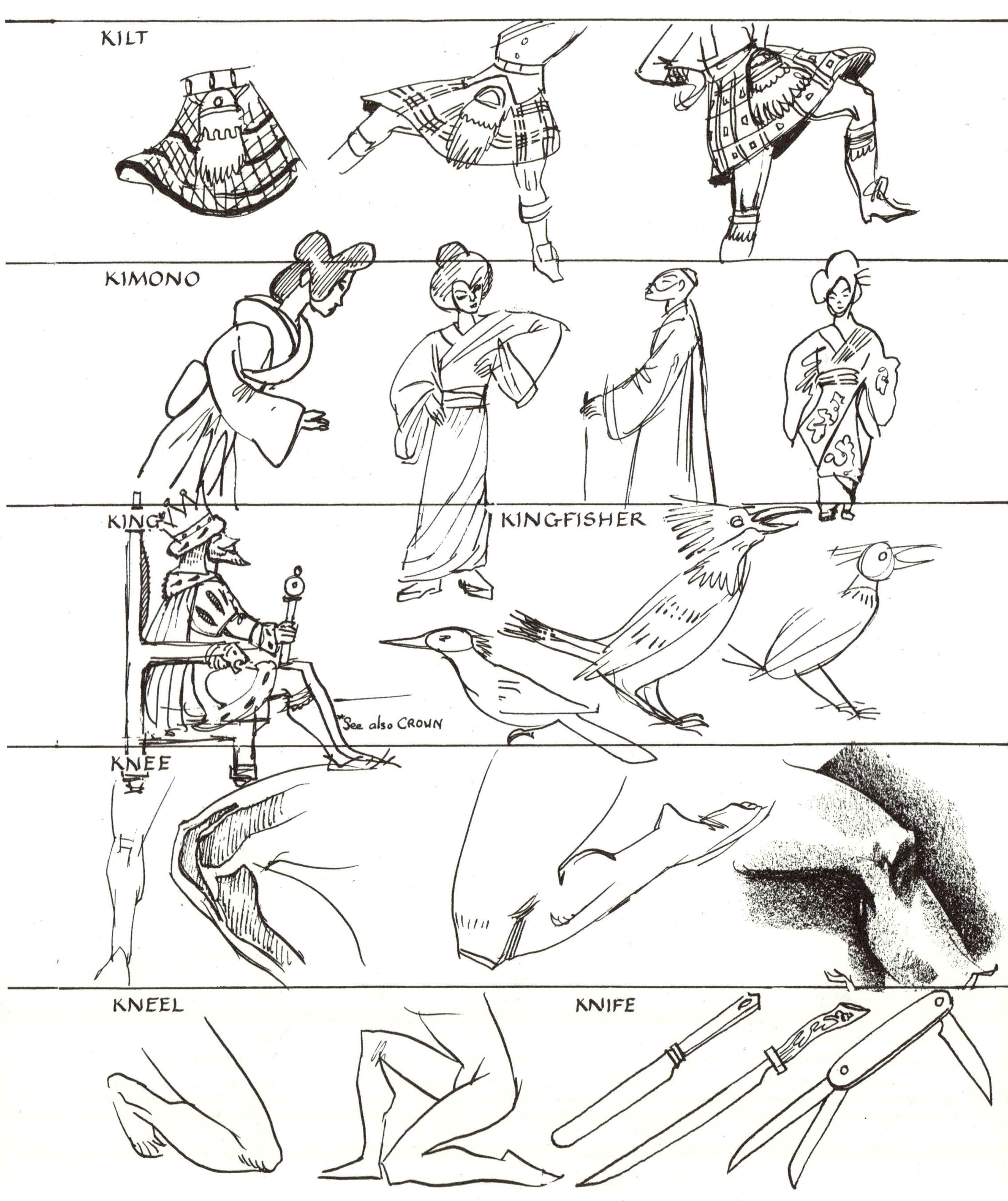
KILT
KIMONO
KING*
KINGFISHER
*See also CROWN
KNEE
KNEEL
KNIFE

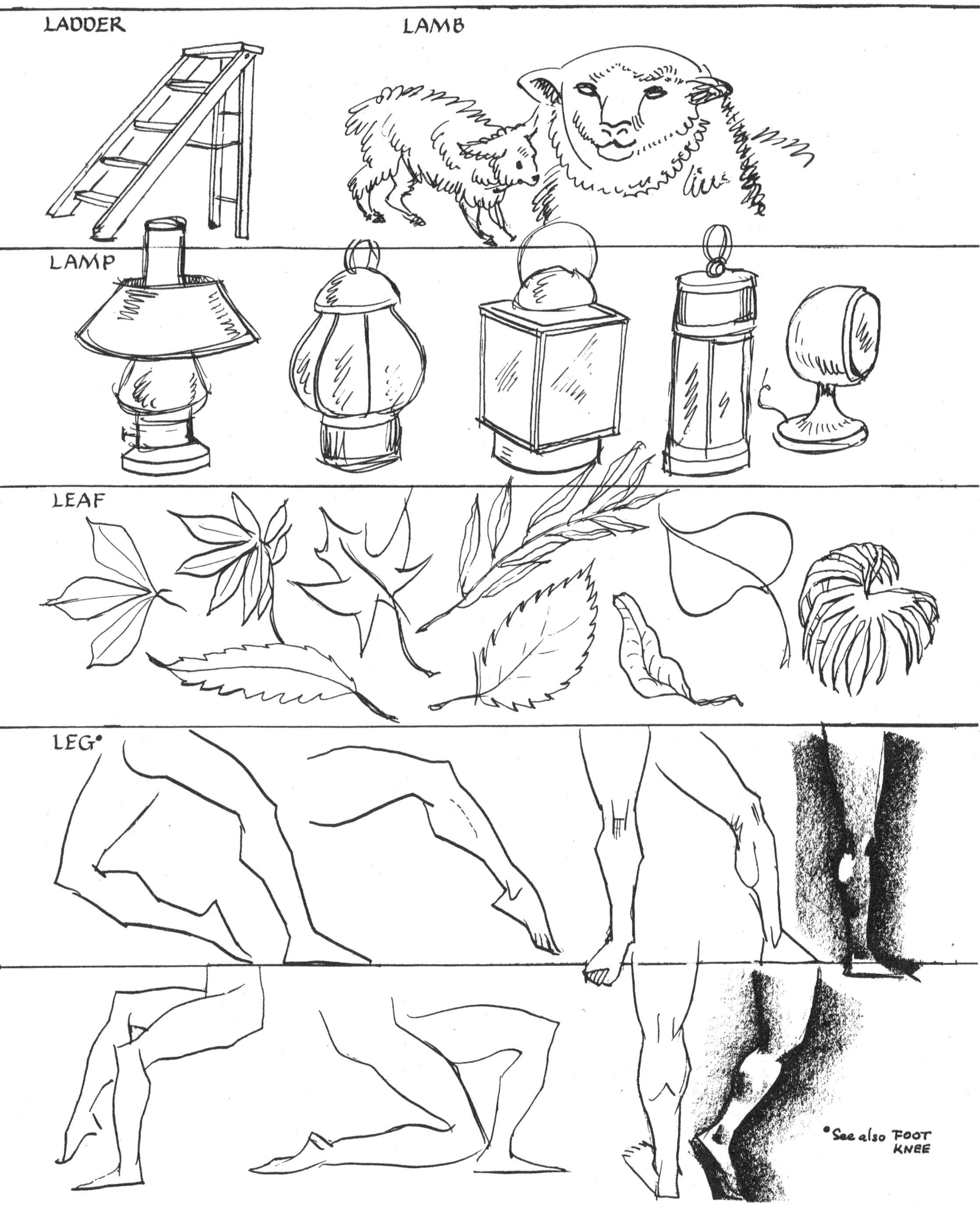

LADDER
LAMB
LAMP
LEAF
LEG*
*See also FOOT
KNEE

L

LEG

L

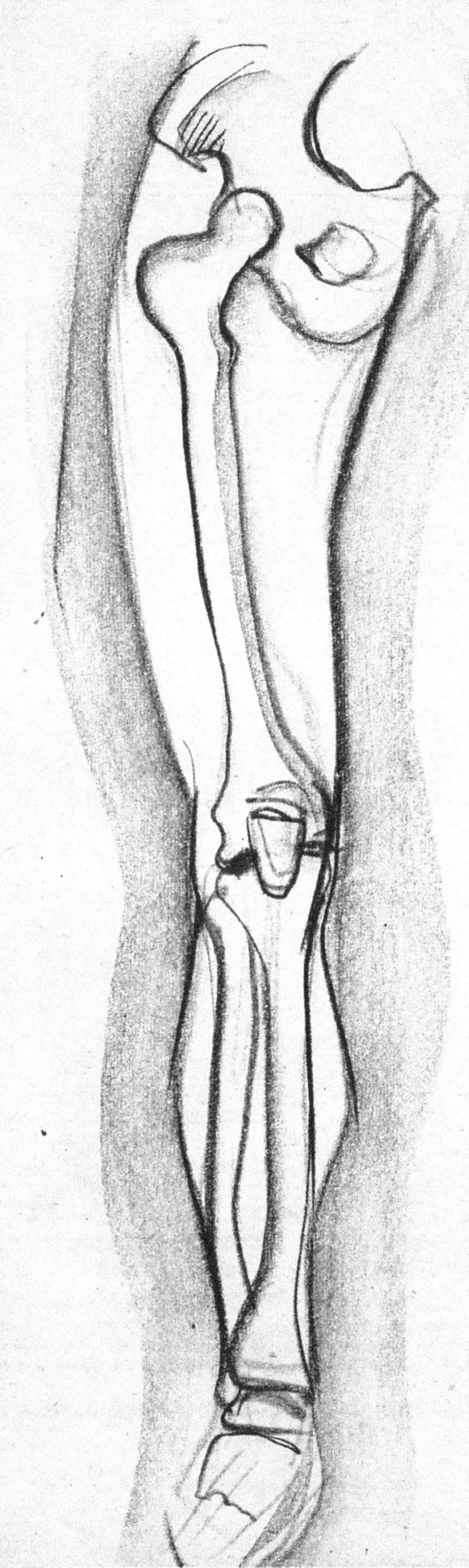

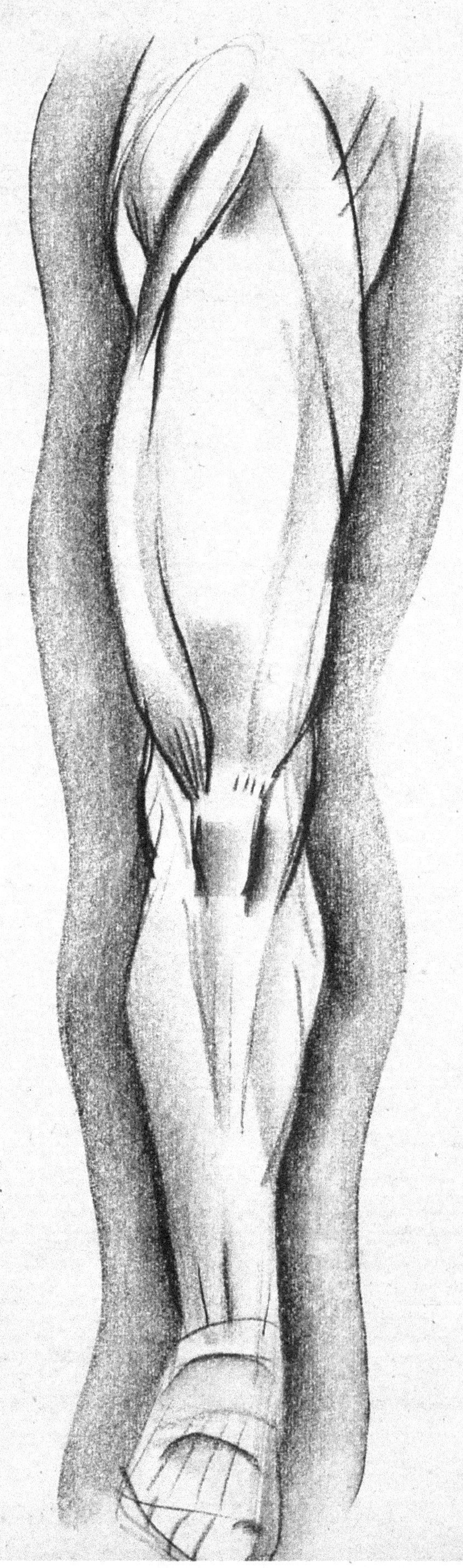

LEG

L

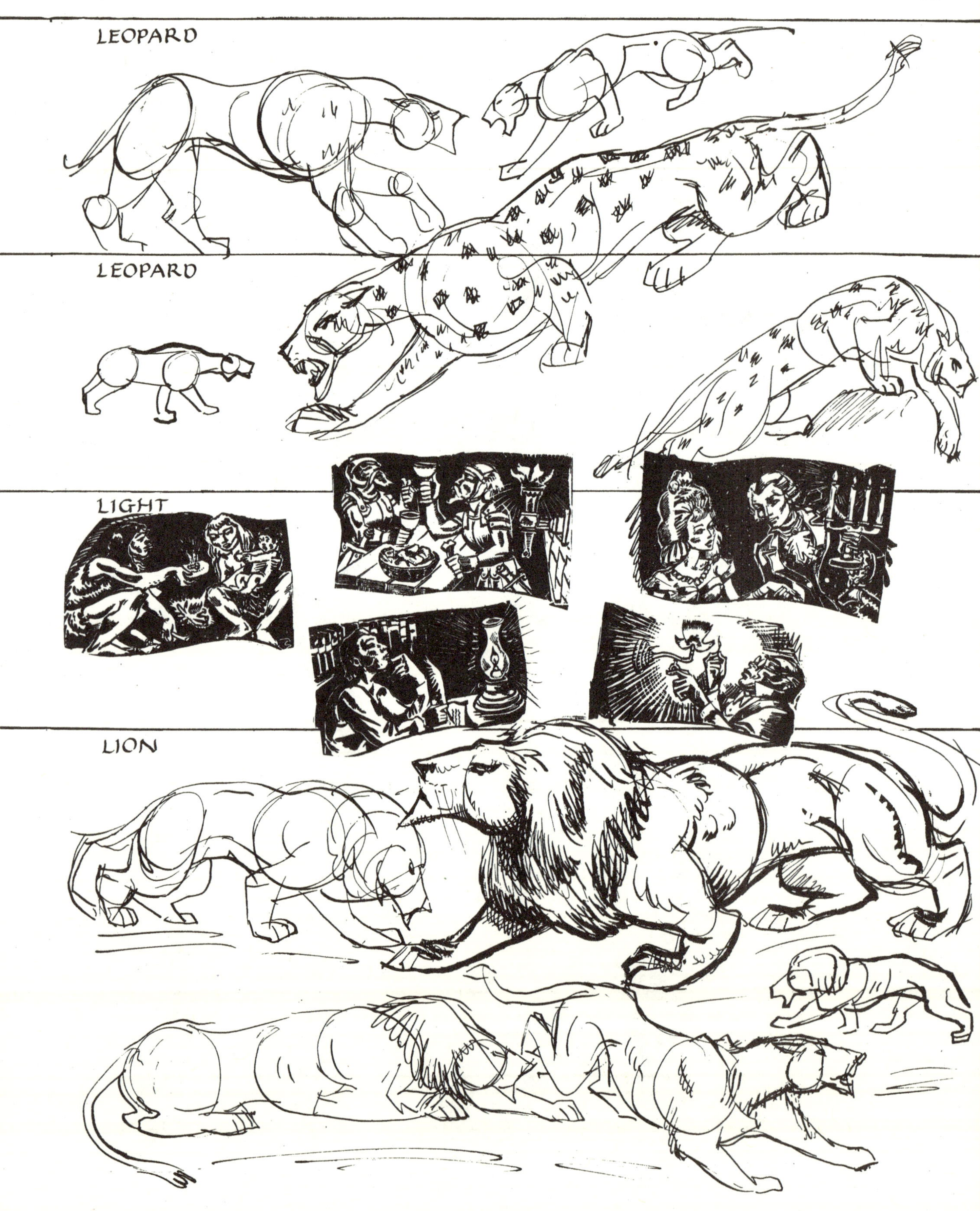
LEOPARD
LEOPARD
LIGHT
LION

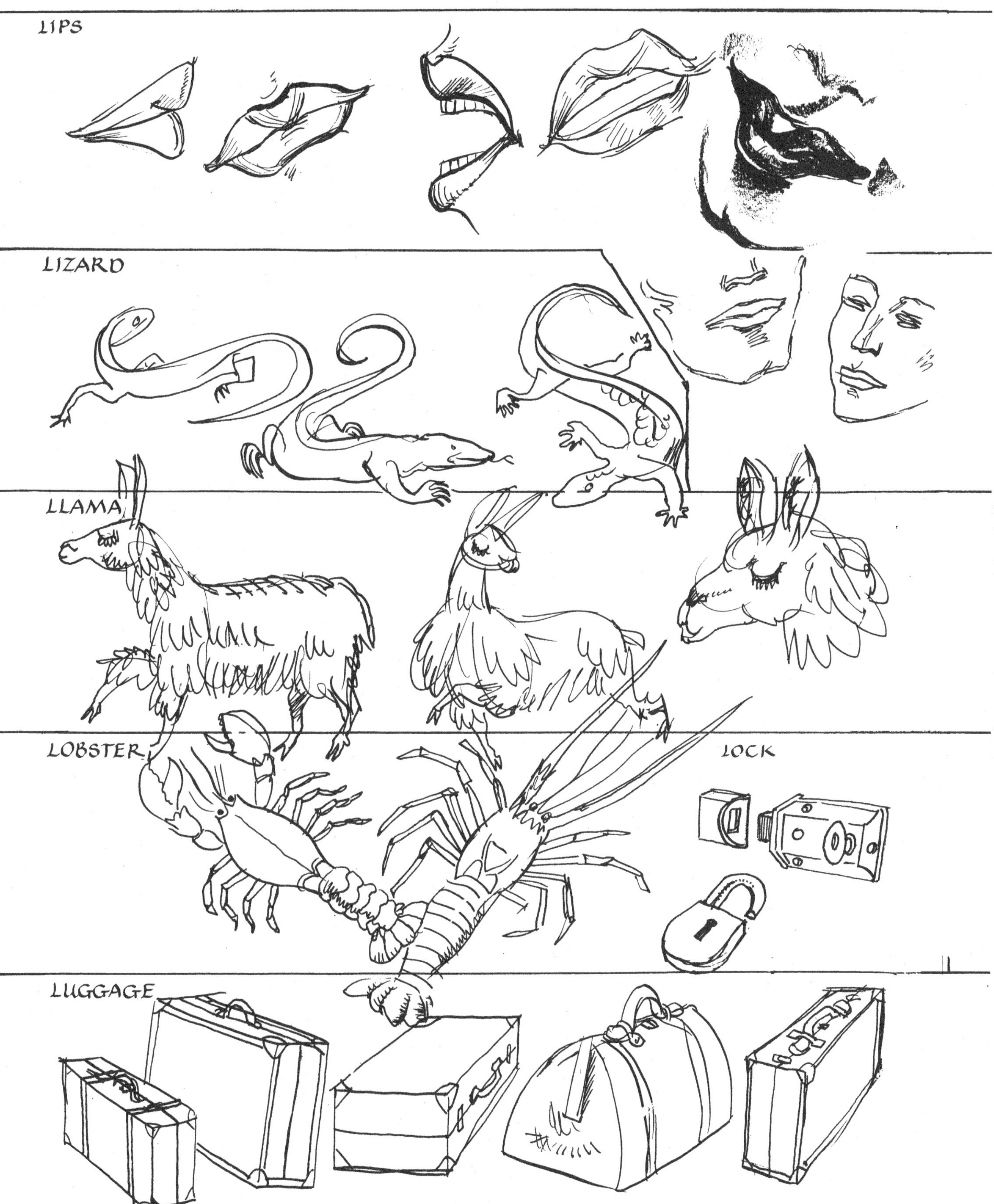
LIPS
LIZARD
LLAMA
LOBSTER
LOCK
LUGGAGE

LYNX

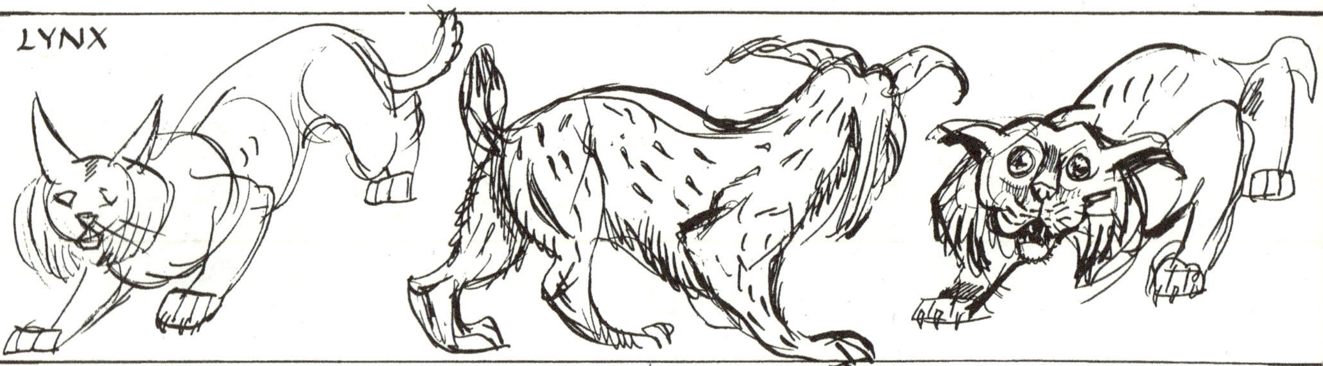

LYRE

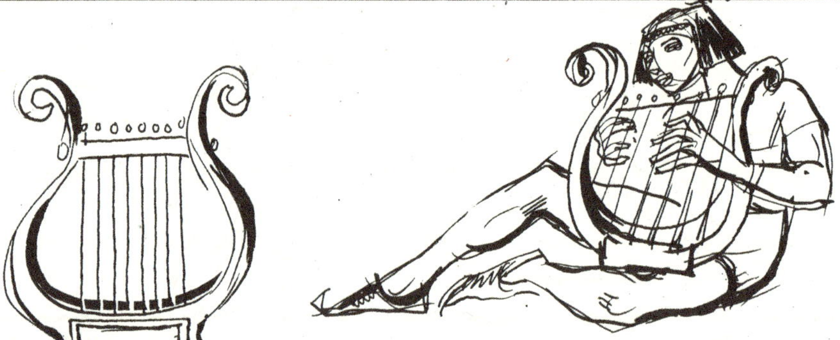

MACHINE GUN

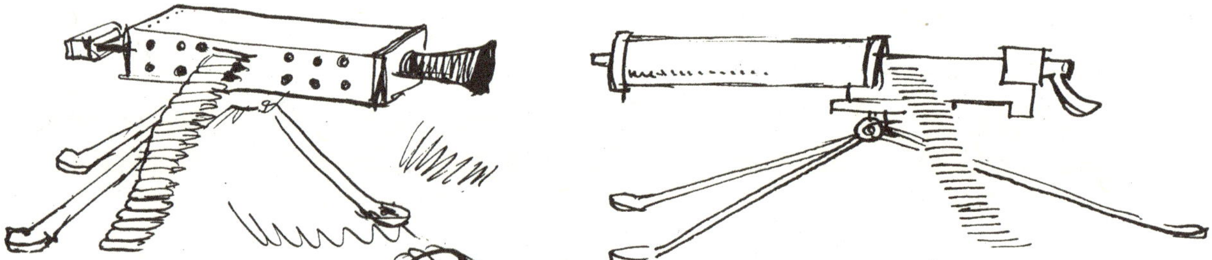

MAMMOTH

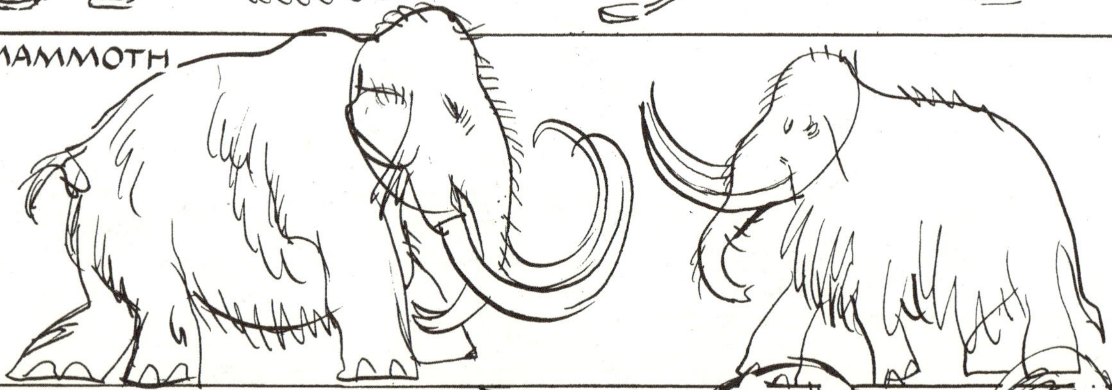

MASK

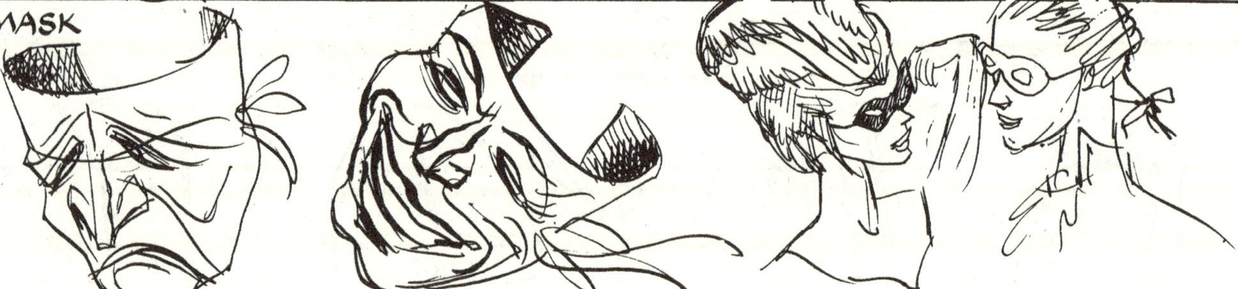

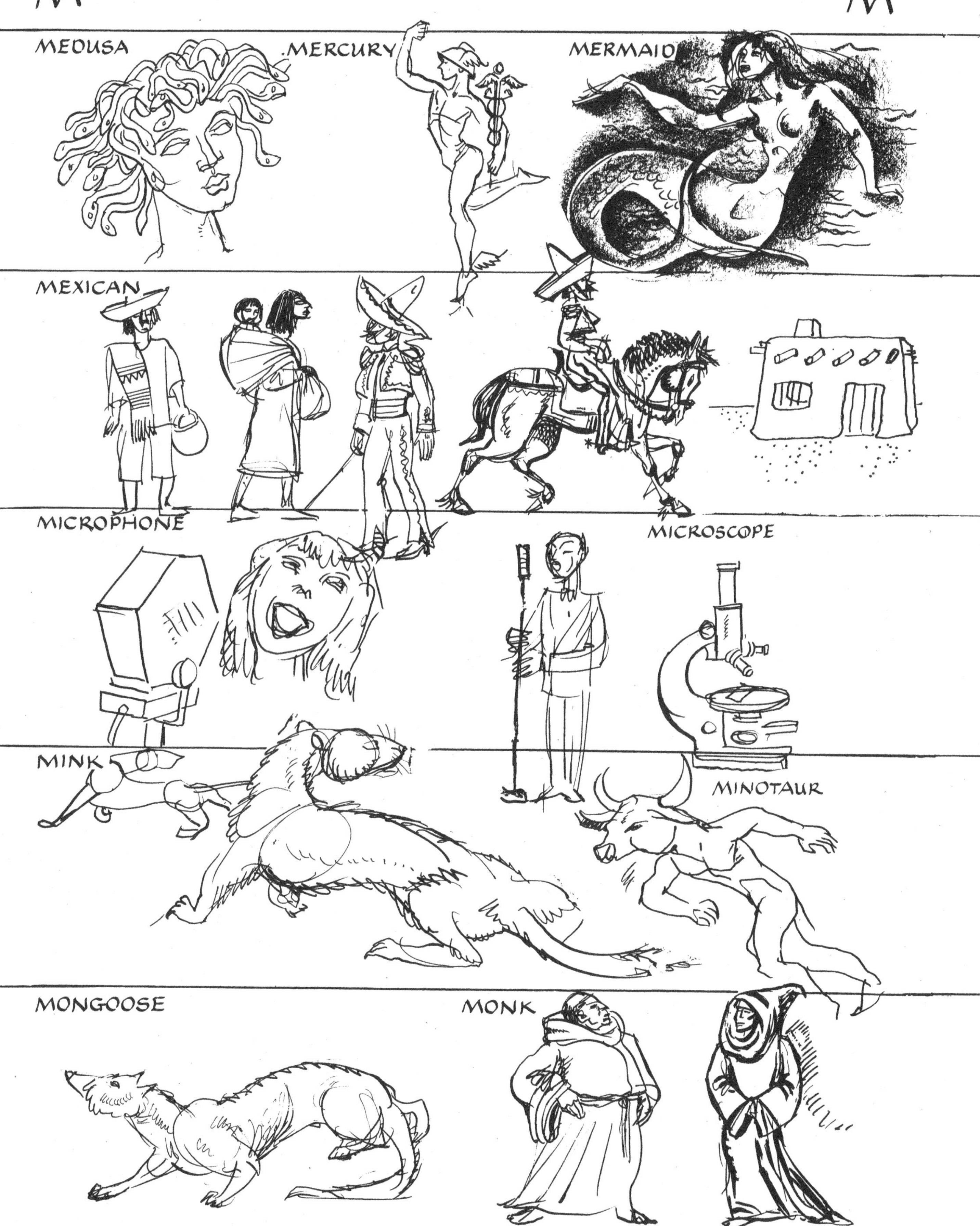
MEDUSA
MERCURY
MERMAID
MEXICAN
MICROPHONE
MICROSCOPE
MINK
MINOTAUR
MONGOOSE
MONK

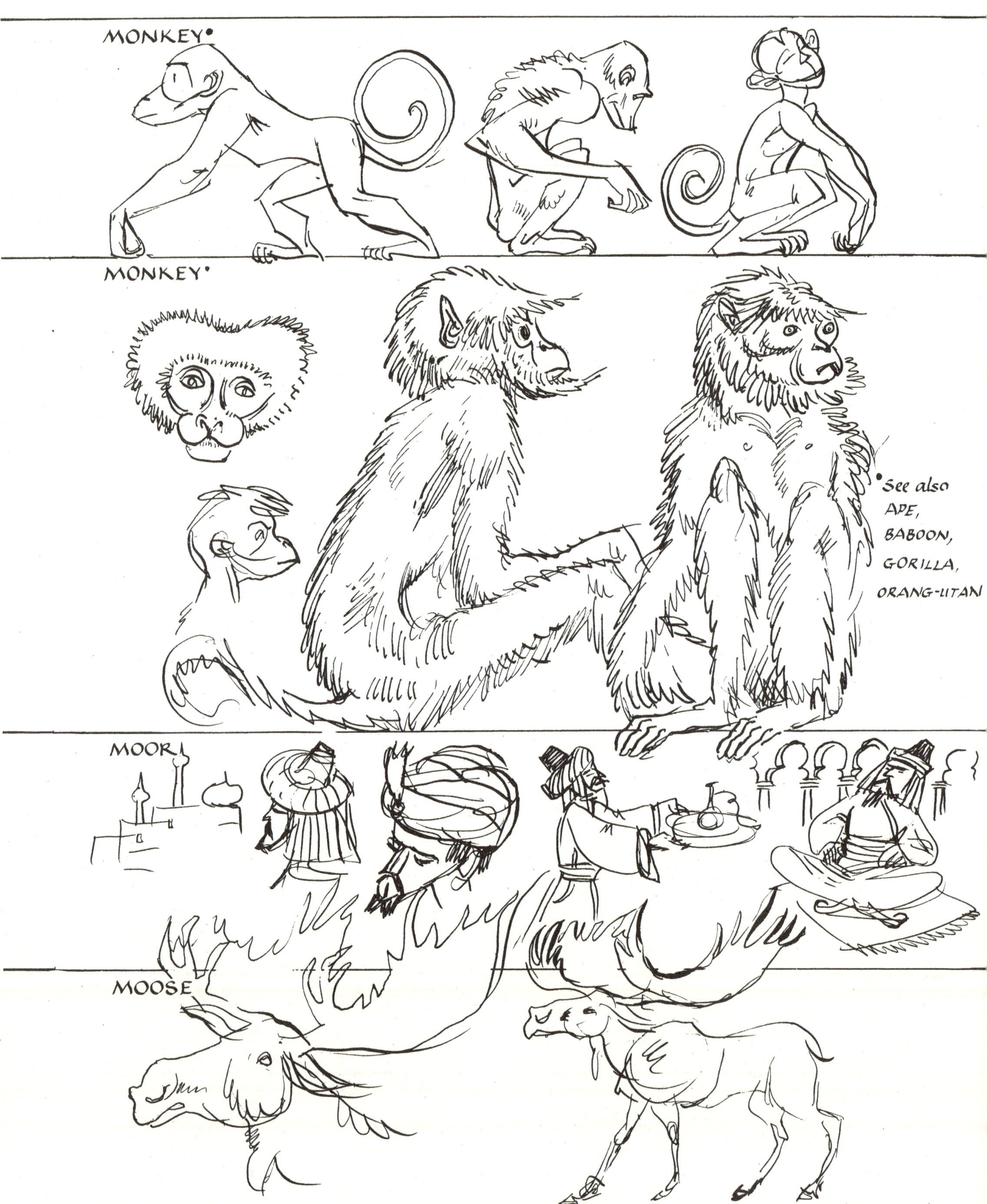
MONKEY•
MONKEY•
•See also
APE,
BABOON,
GORILLA,
ORANG-UTAN
MOOR
MOOSE

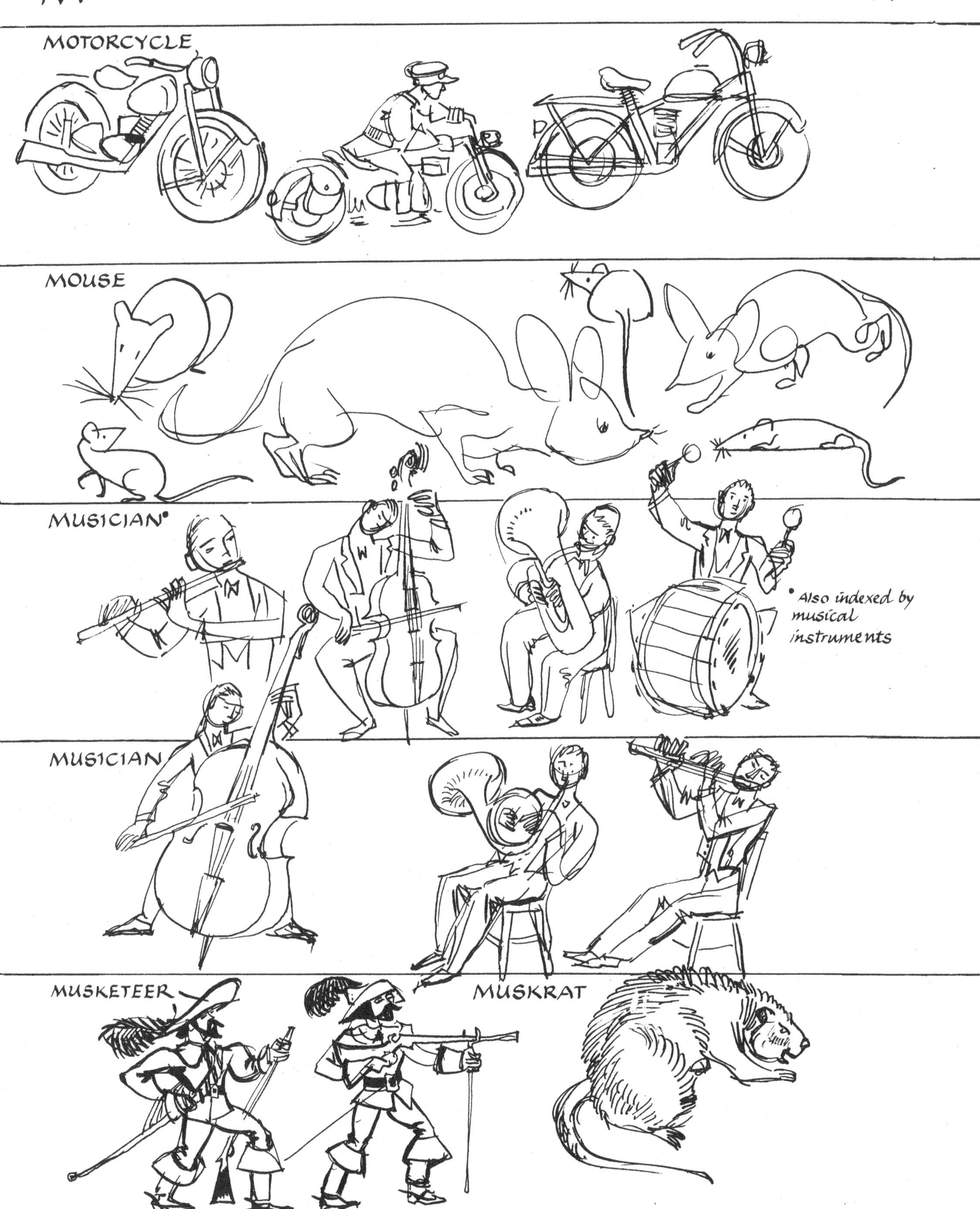
MOTORCYCLE
MOUSE
MUSICIAN•
• Also indexed by musical instruments
MUSICIAN
MUSKETEER
MUSKRAT

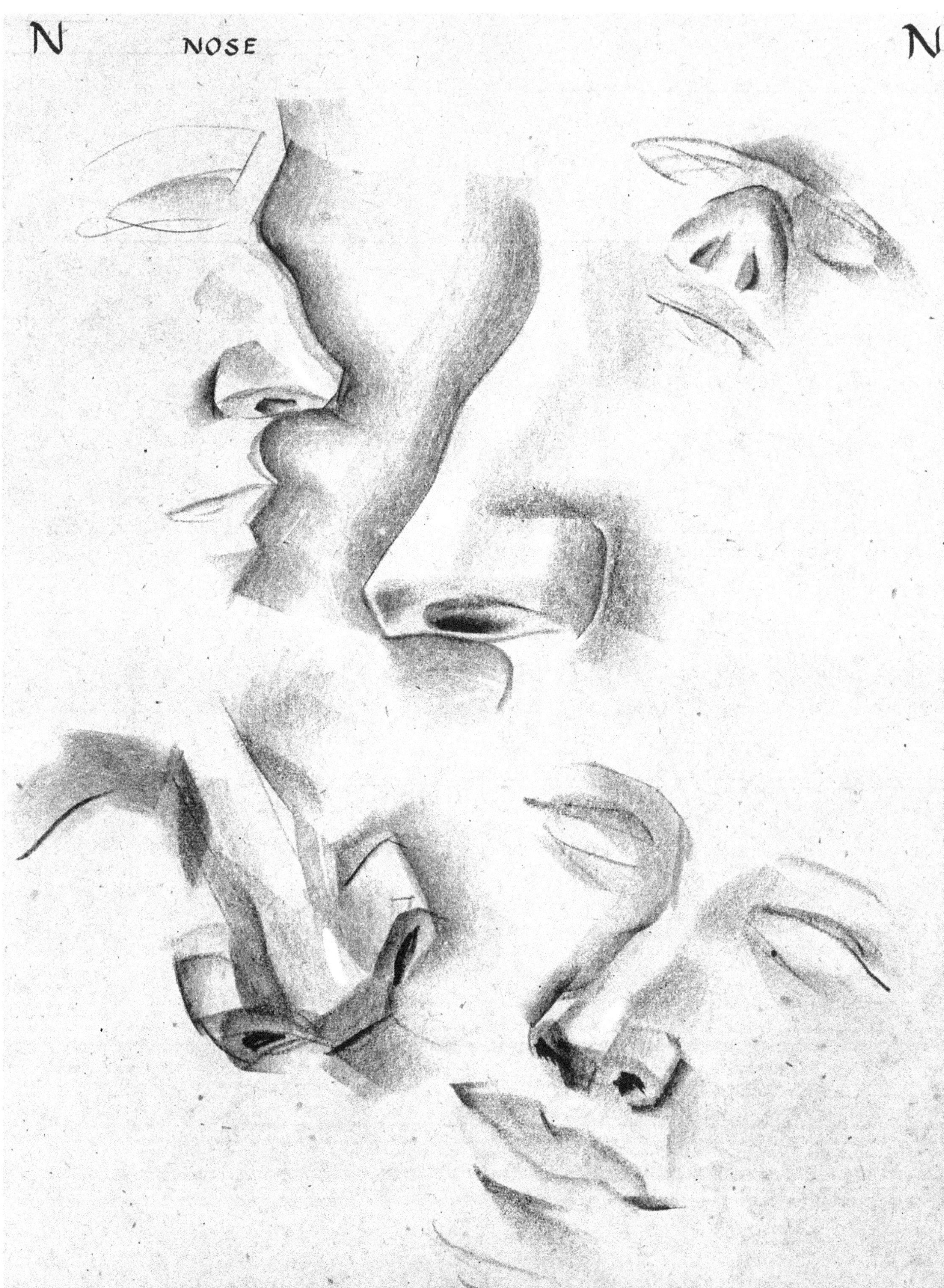
N
NOSE
N

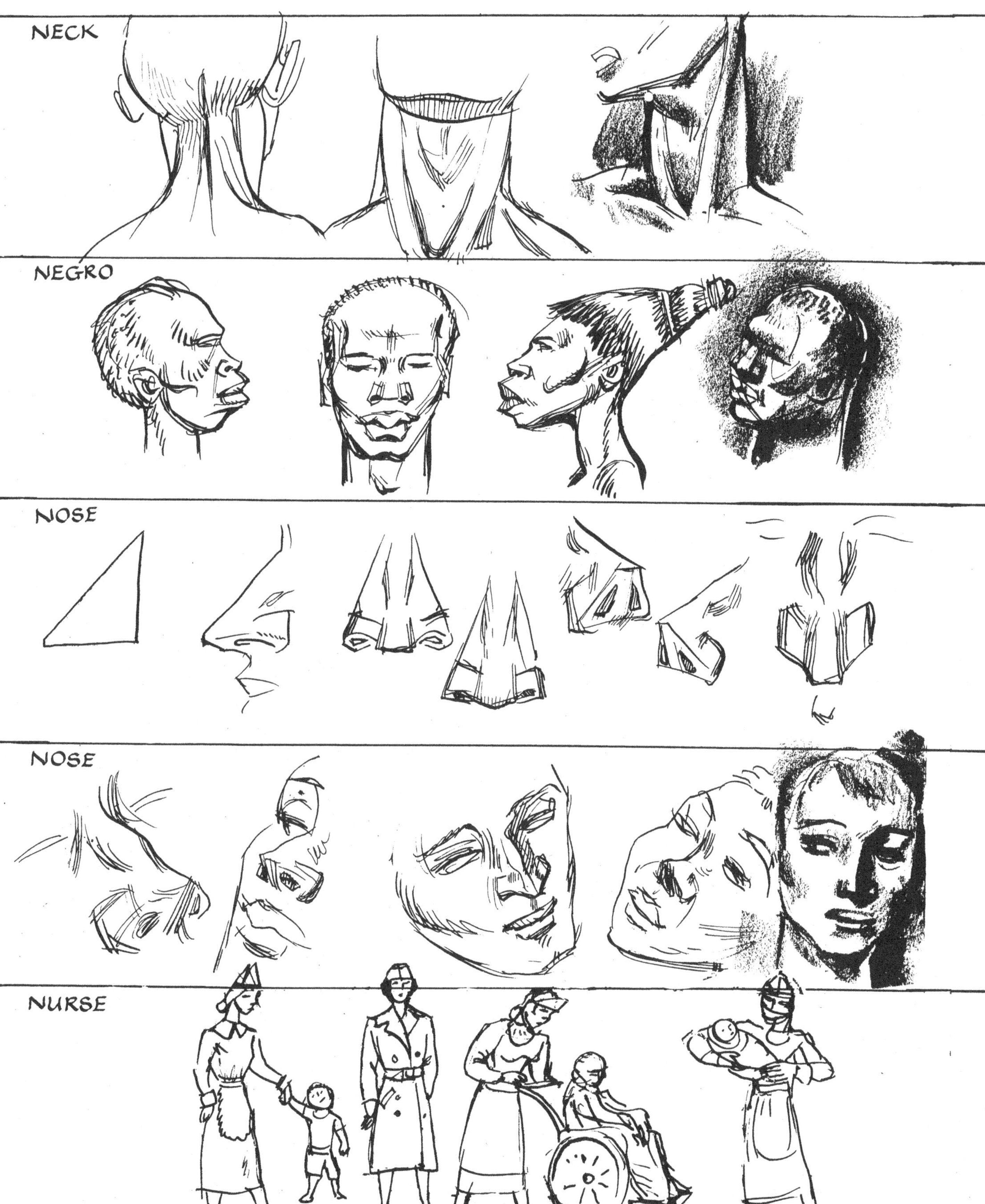
NECK
NEGRO
NOSE
NOSE
NURSE

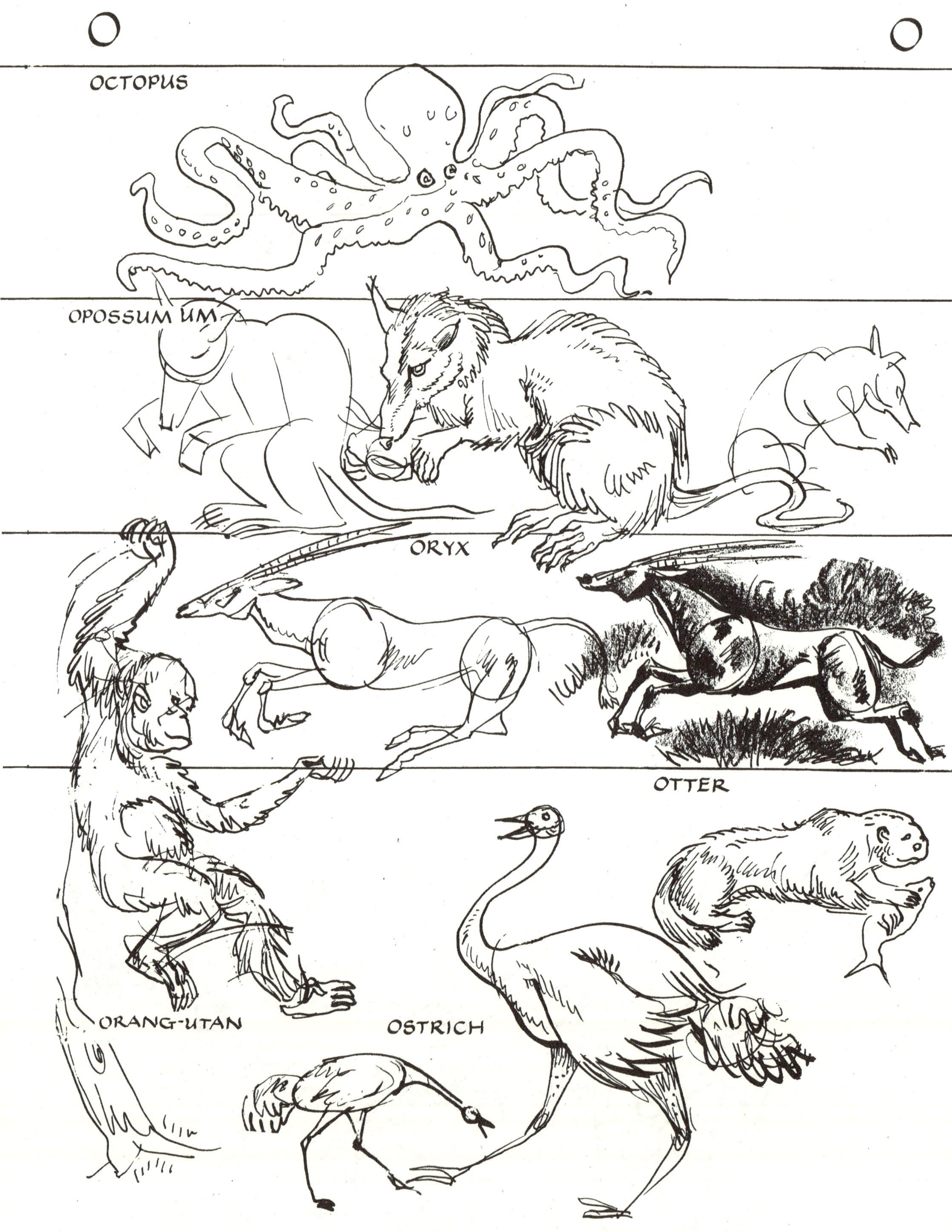
O
O
OCTOPUS
OPOSSUM UM
ORYX
OTTER
ORANG-UTAN
OSTRICH

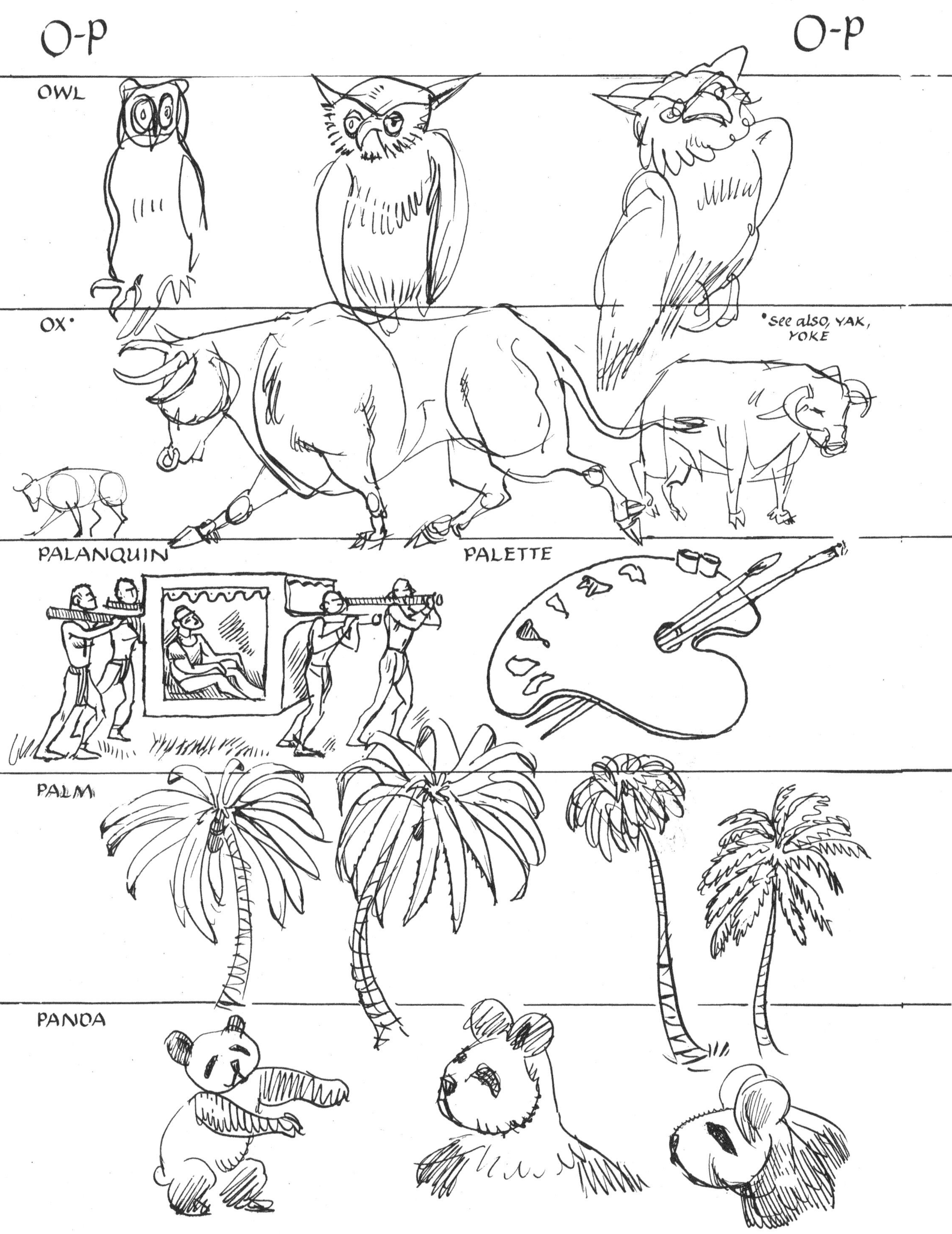

O-p
O-p
OWL
OX*
*See also, YAK, YOKE
PALANQUIN
PALETTE
PALM
PANDA

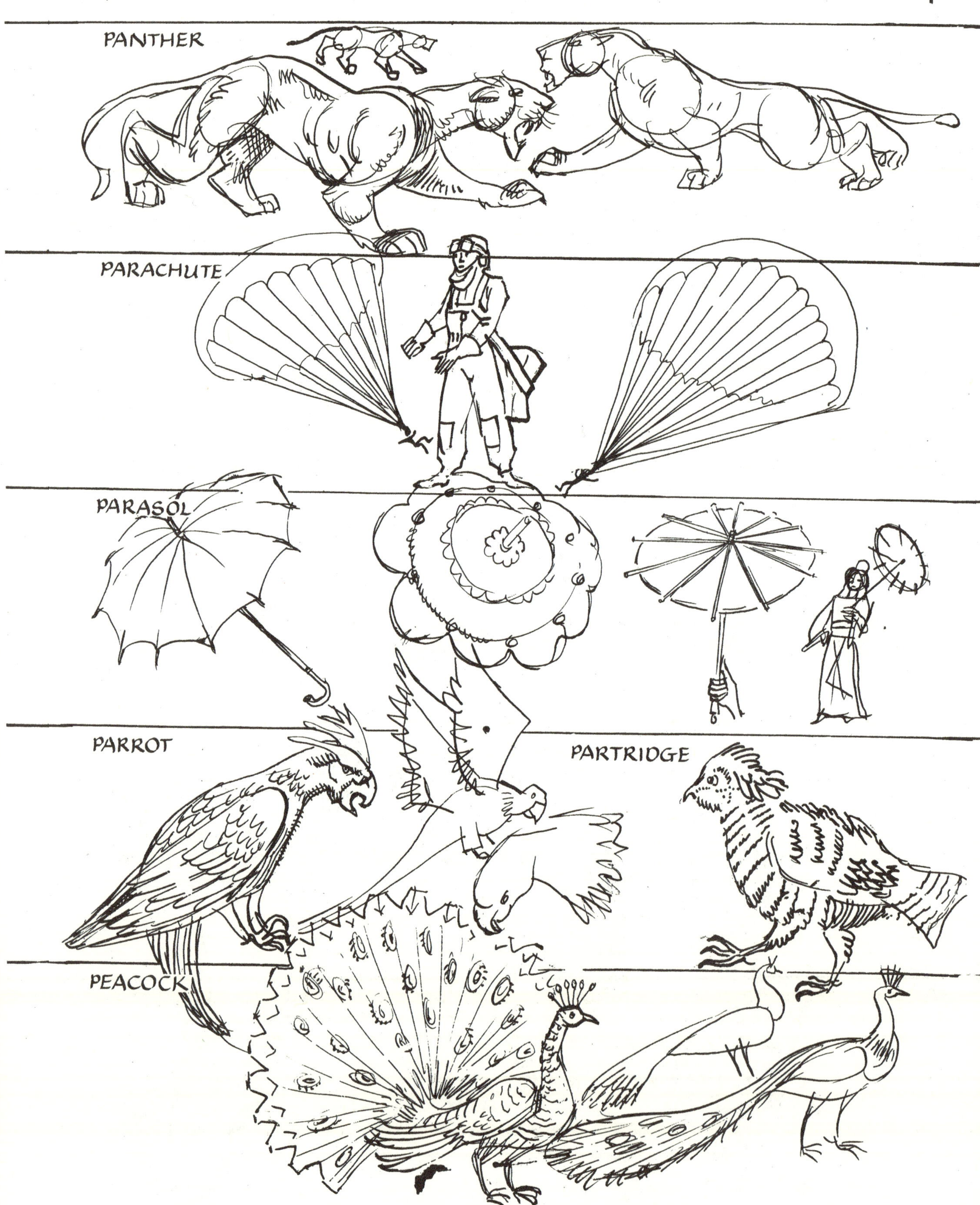
PANTHER
PARACHUTE
PARASOL
PARROT
PARTRIDGE
PEACOCK

PECARY

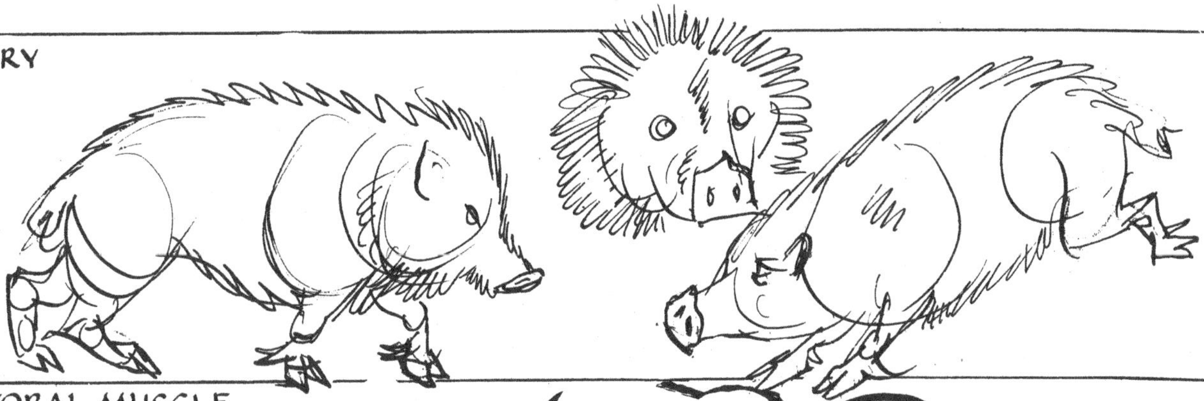

PECTORAL MUSCLE

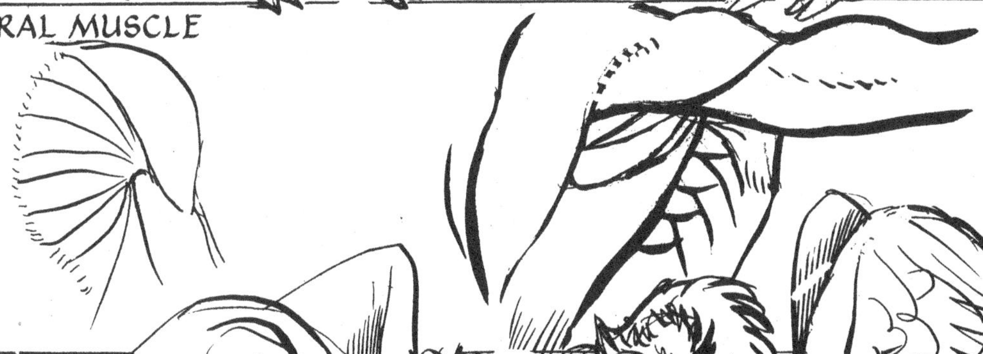

PEGASUS

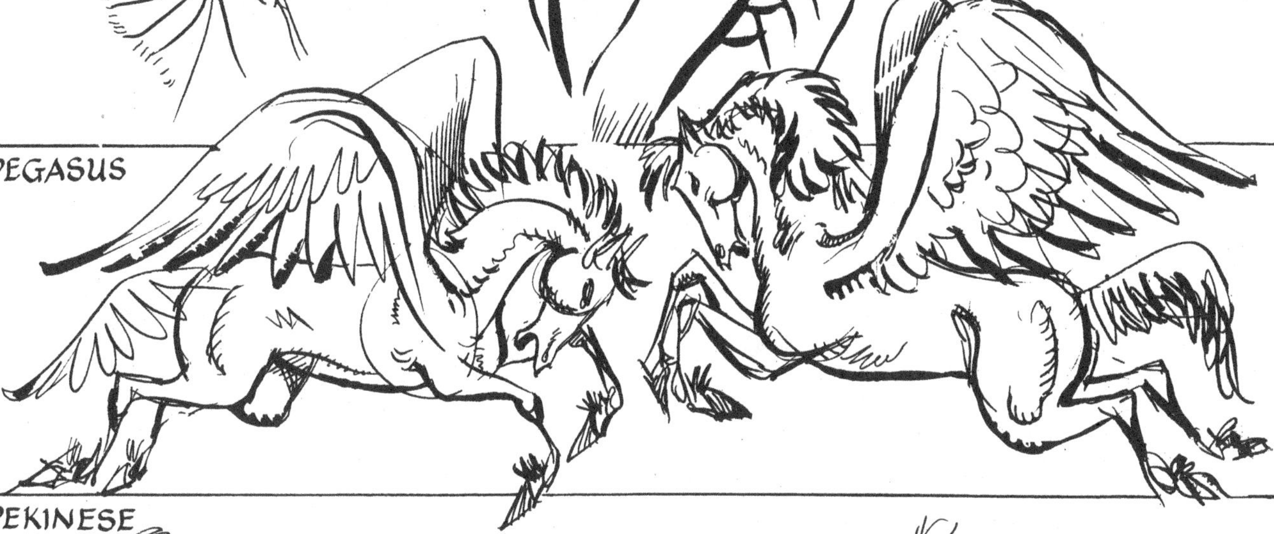

PEKINESE

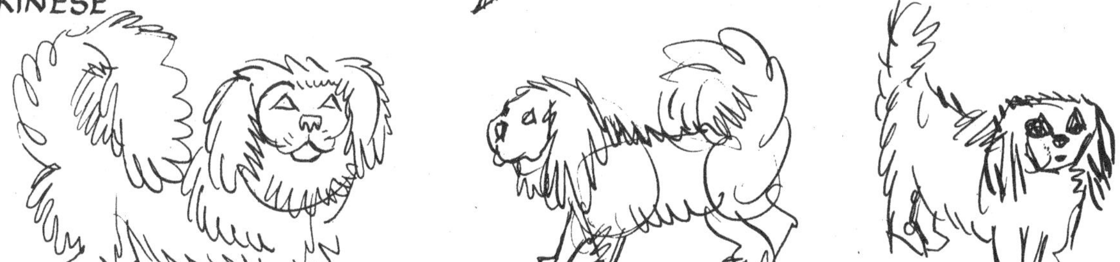

PELICAN

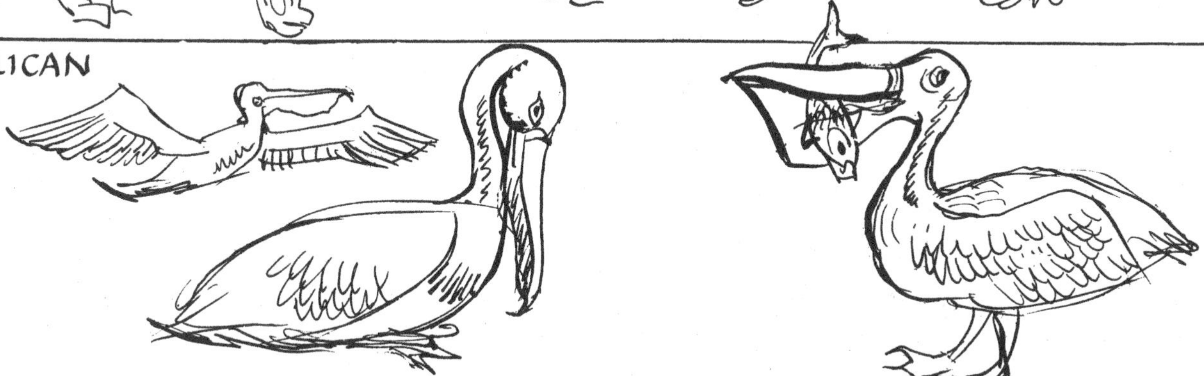

PELVIS

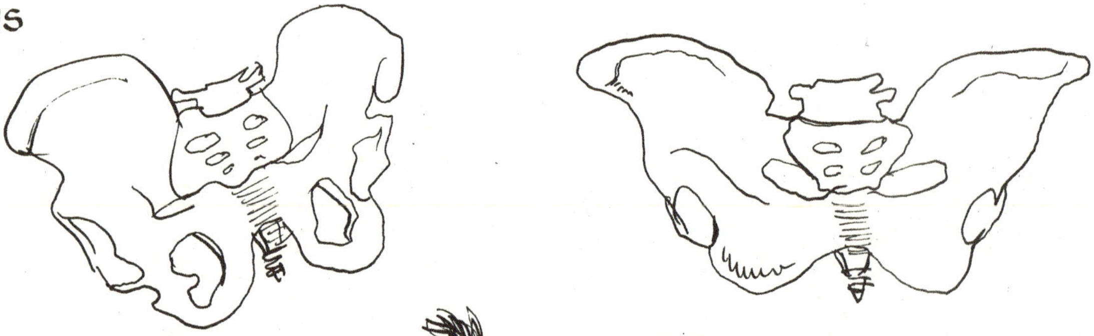

PENGUIN

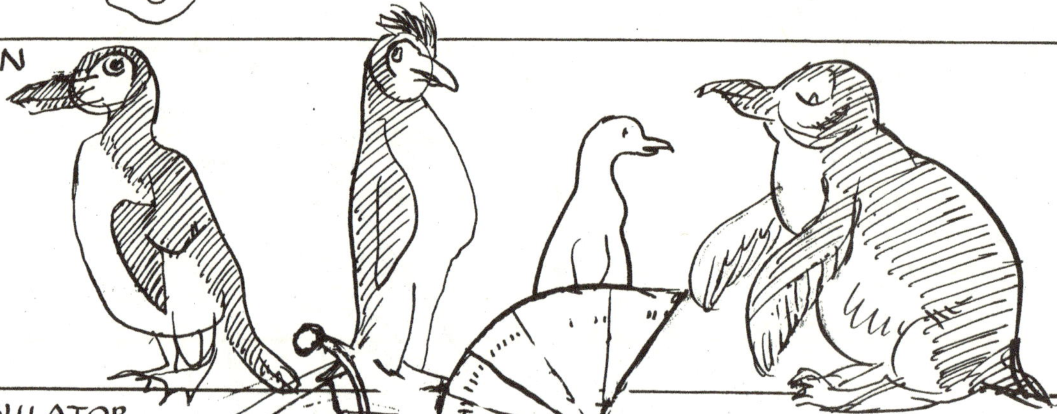

PERAMBULATOR

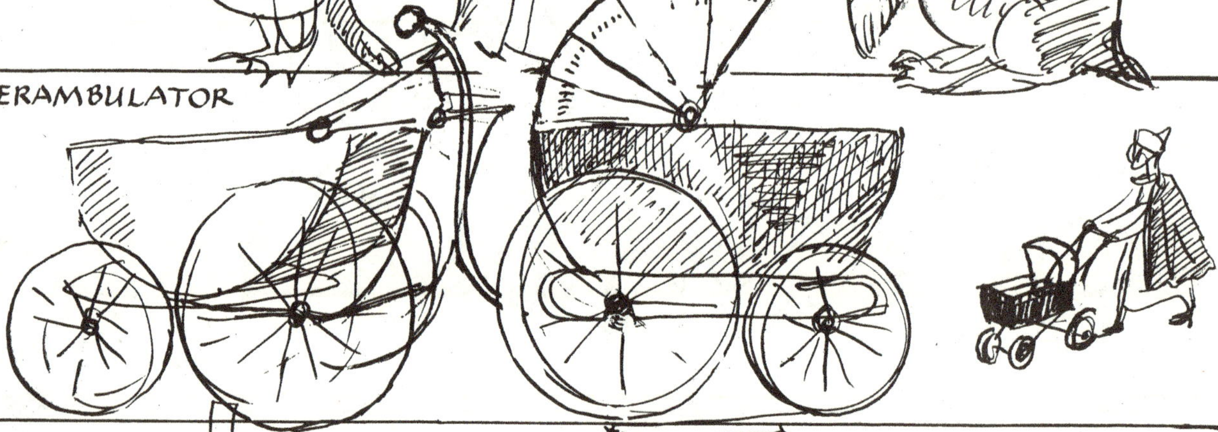

PHAETON

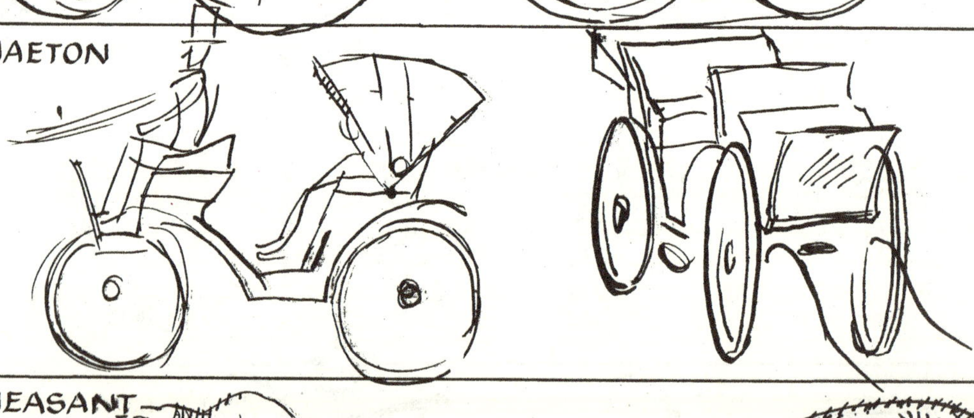

PHEASANT

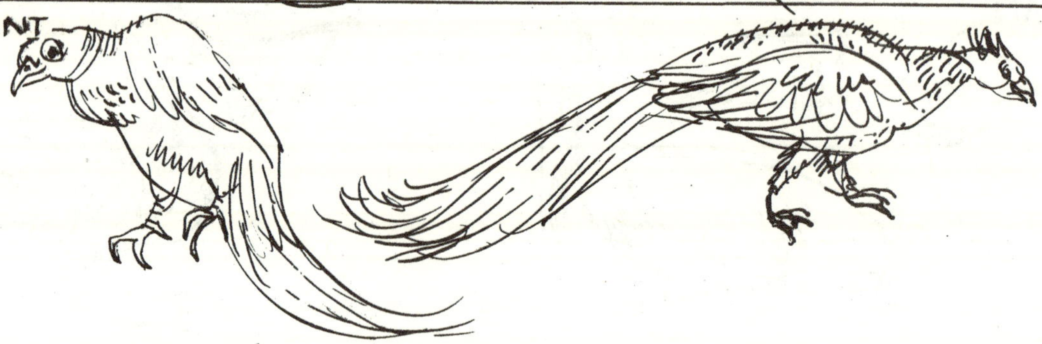

PIANO

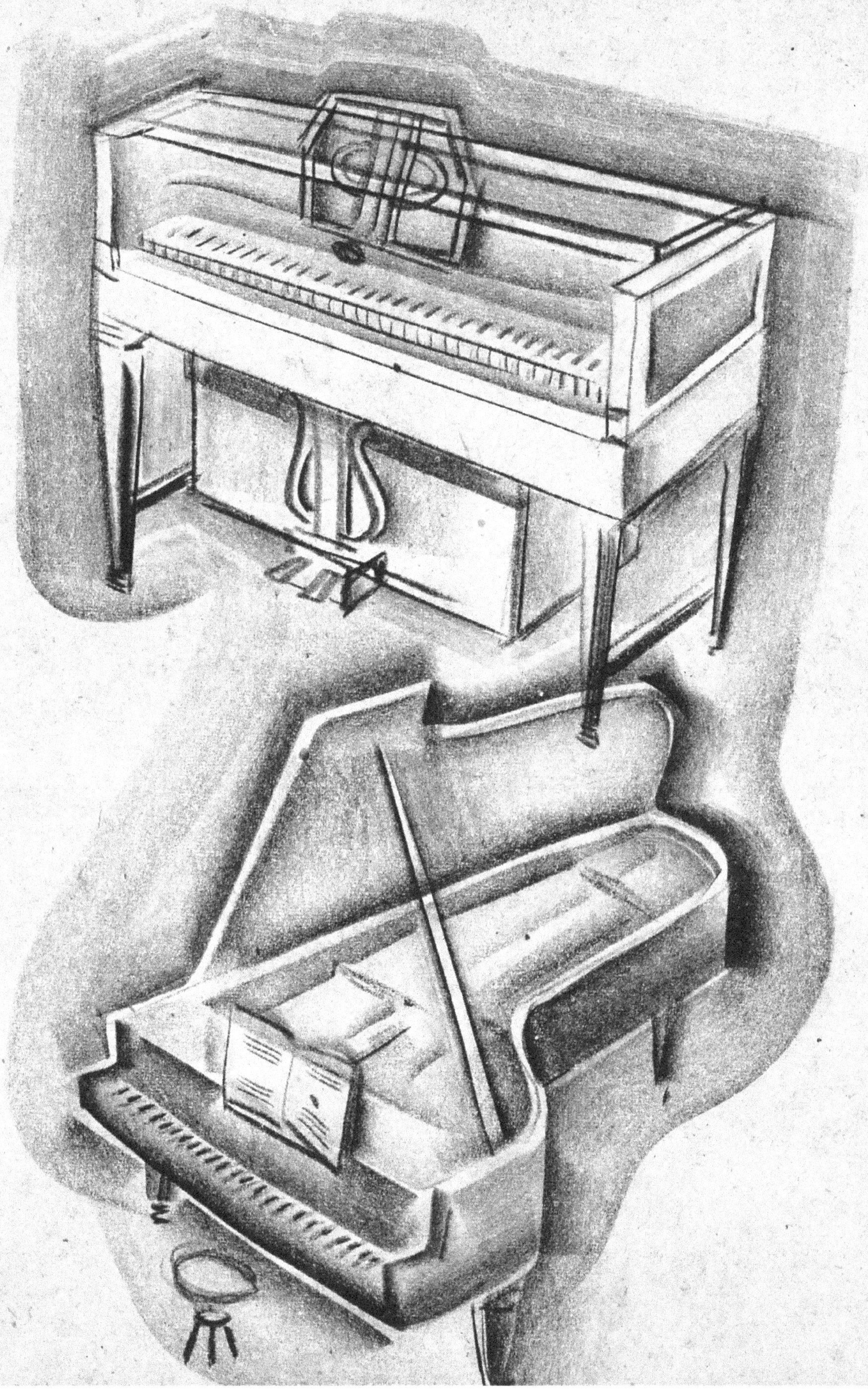

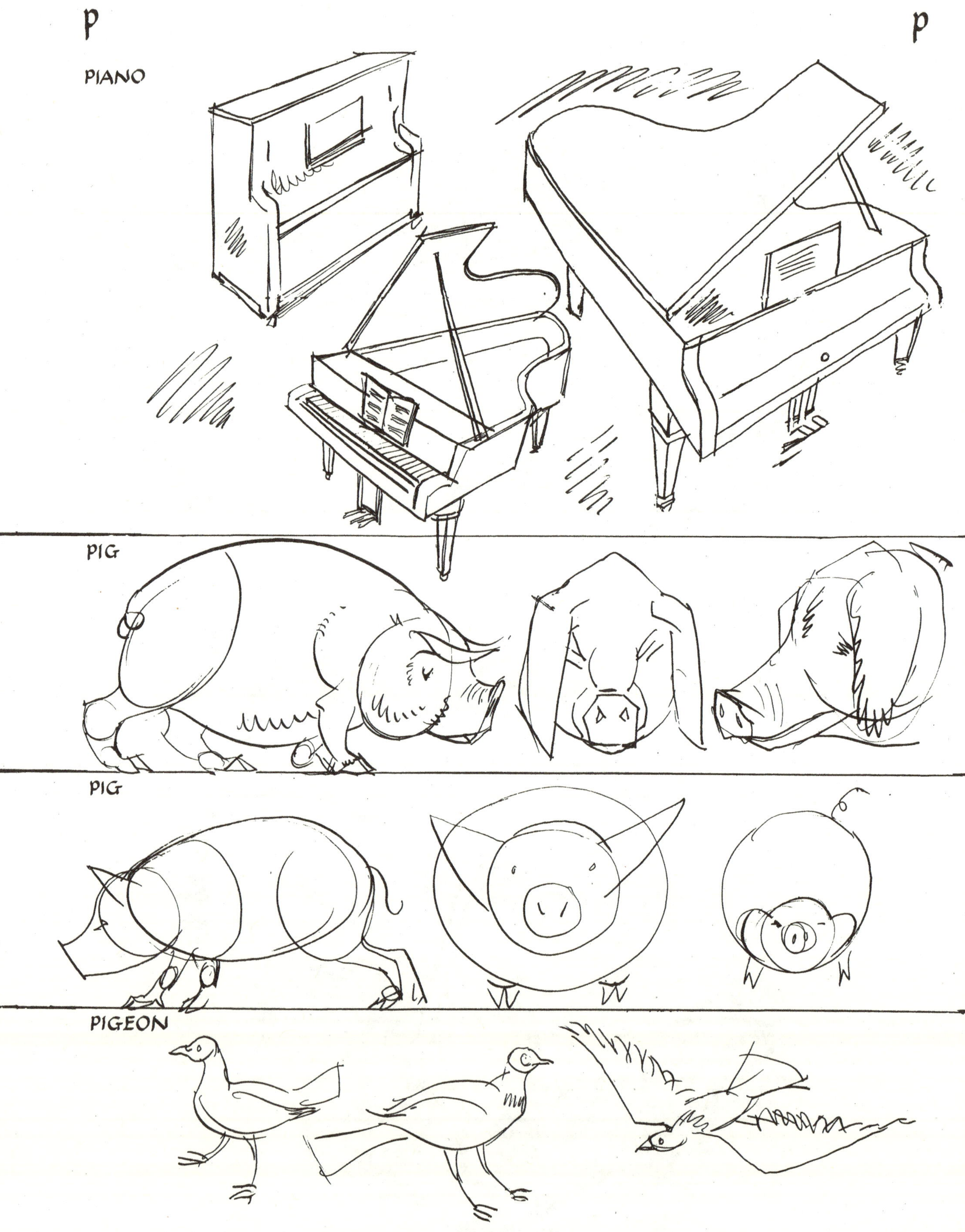
p
p
PIANO
PIG
PIG
PIGEON

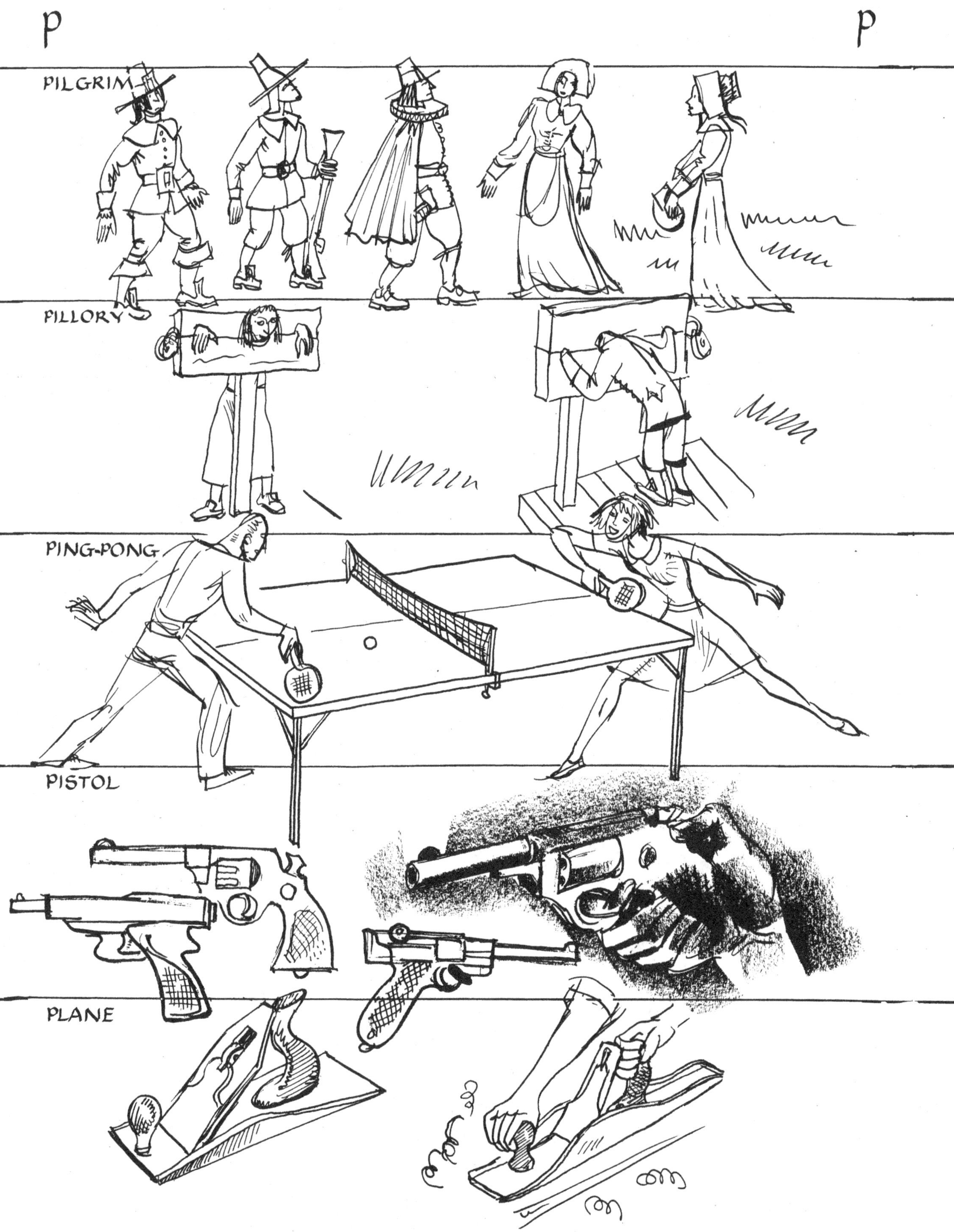
PILGRIM
PILLORY
PING-PONG
PISTOL
PLANE

POINTER

POLAR BEAR

POLE VAULT

POLICEMAN

POLO

POODLE

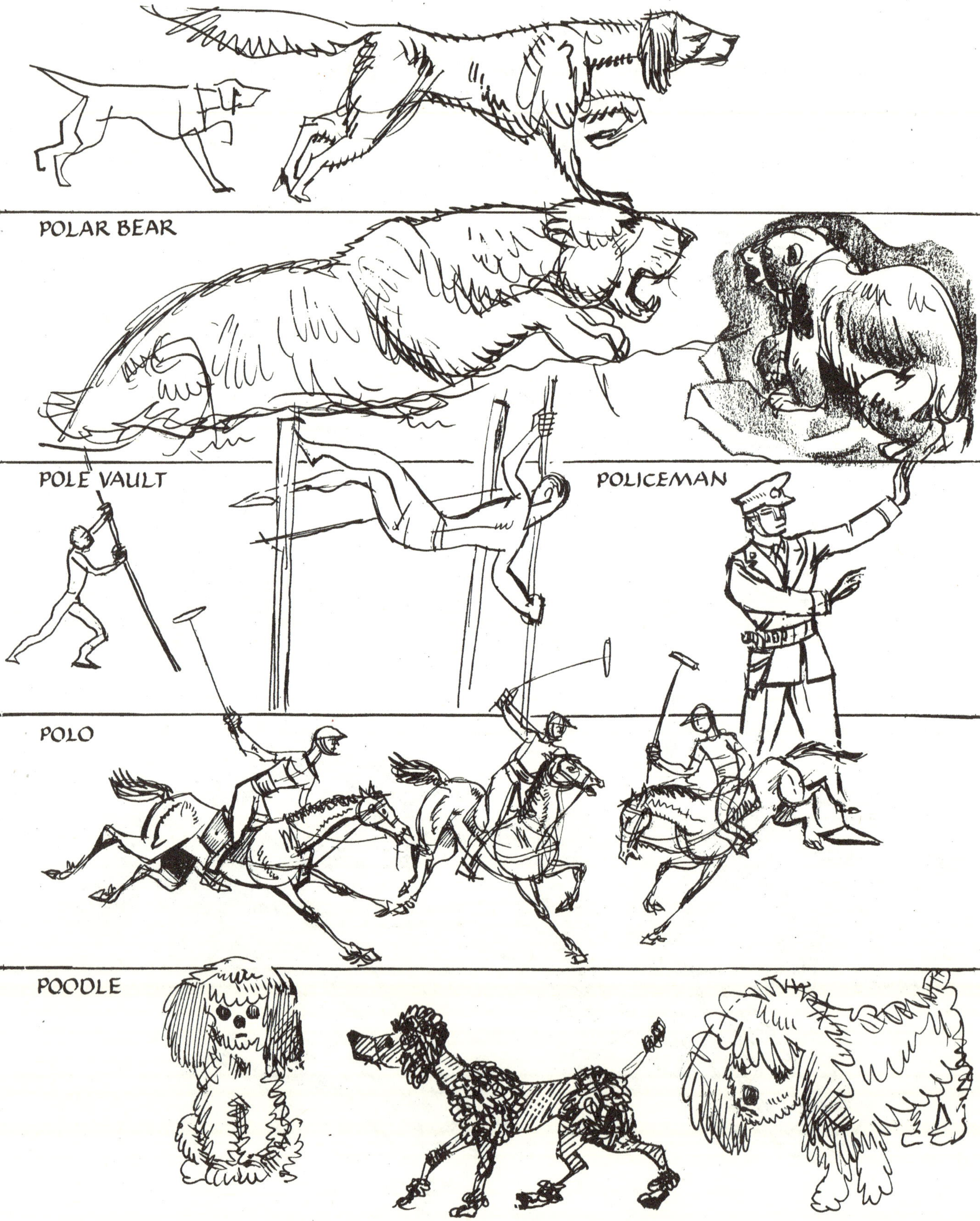

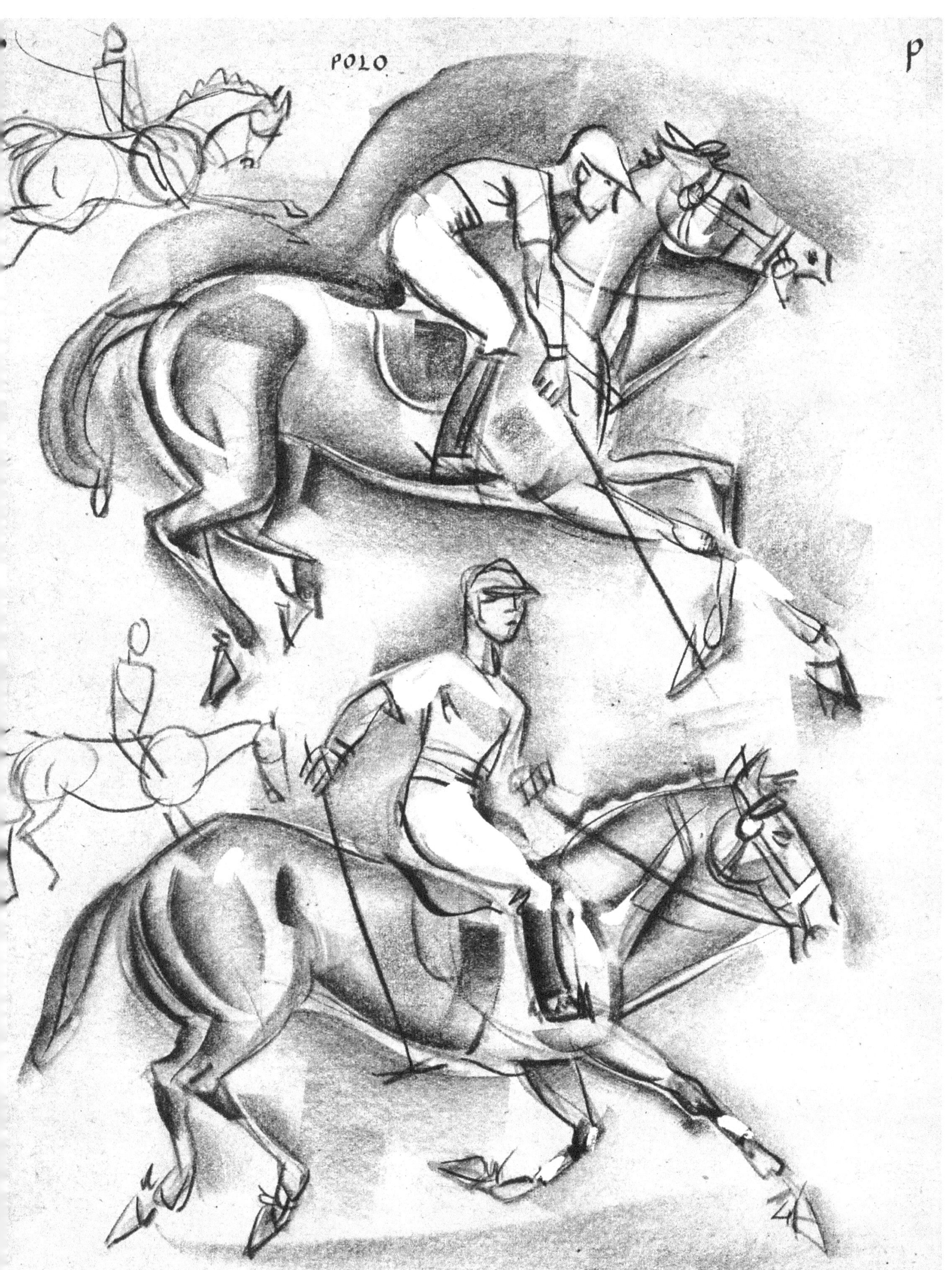
POLO
P

PREHISTORIC ANIMALS*

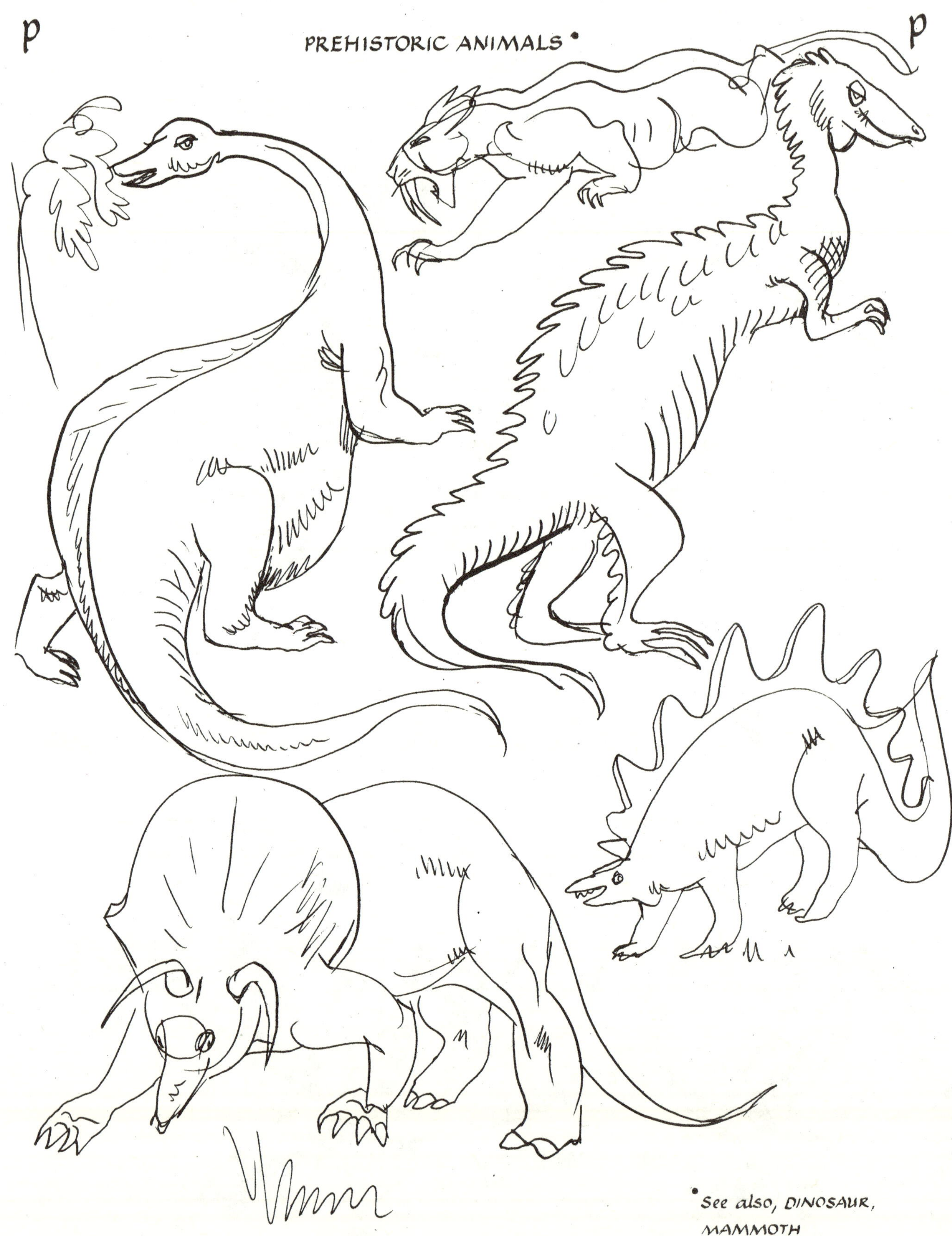

*See also, DINOSAUR, MAMMOTH

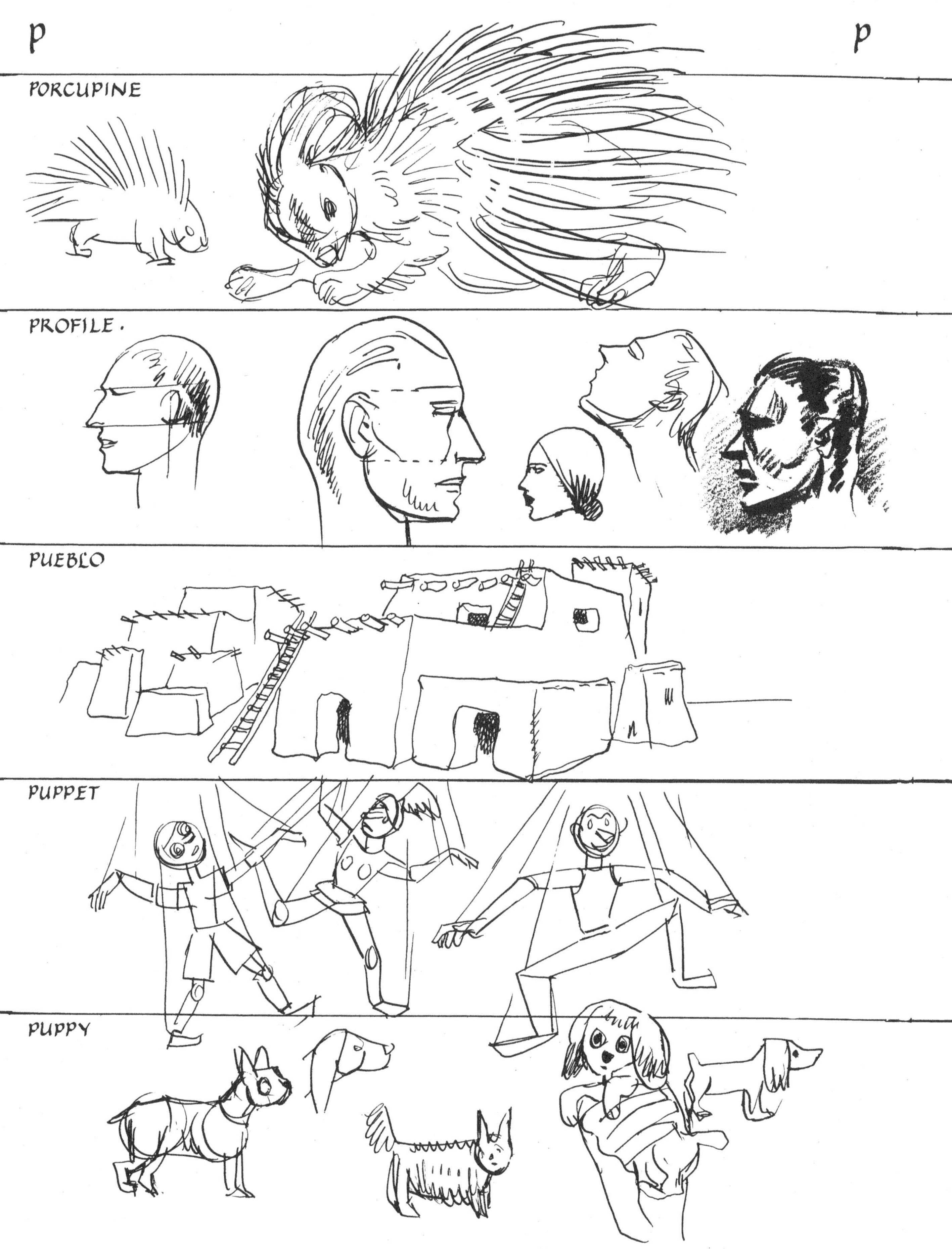
PORCUPINE
PROFILE.
PUEBLO
PUPPET
PUPPY

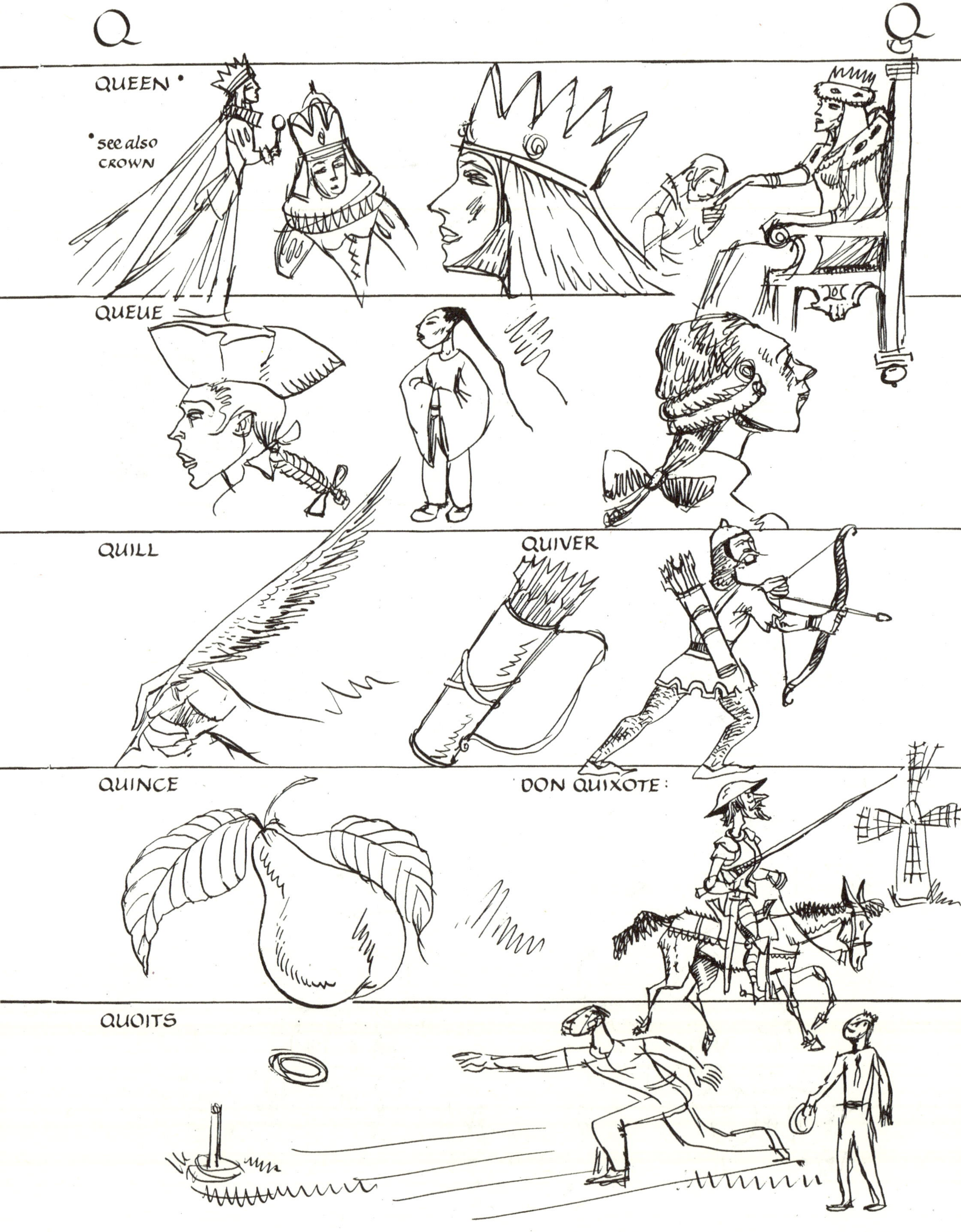
Q
Q
QUEEN •
• see also CROWN
QUEUE
QUILL
QUIVER
QUINCE
DON QUIXOTE
QUOITS

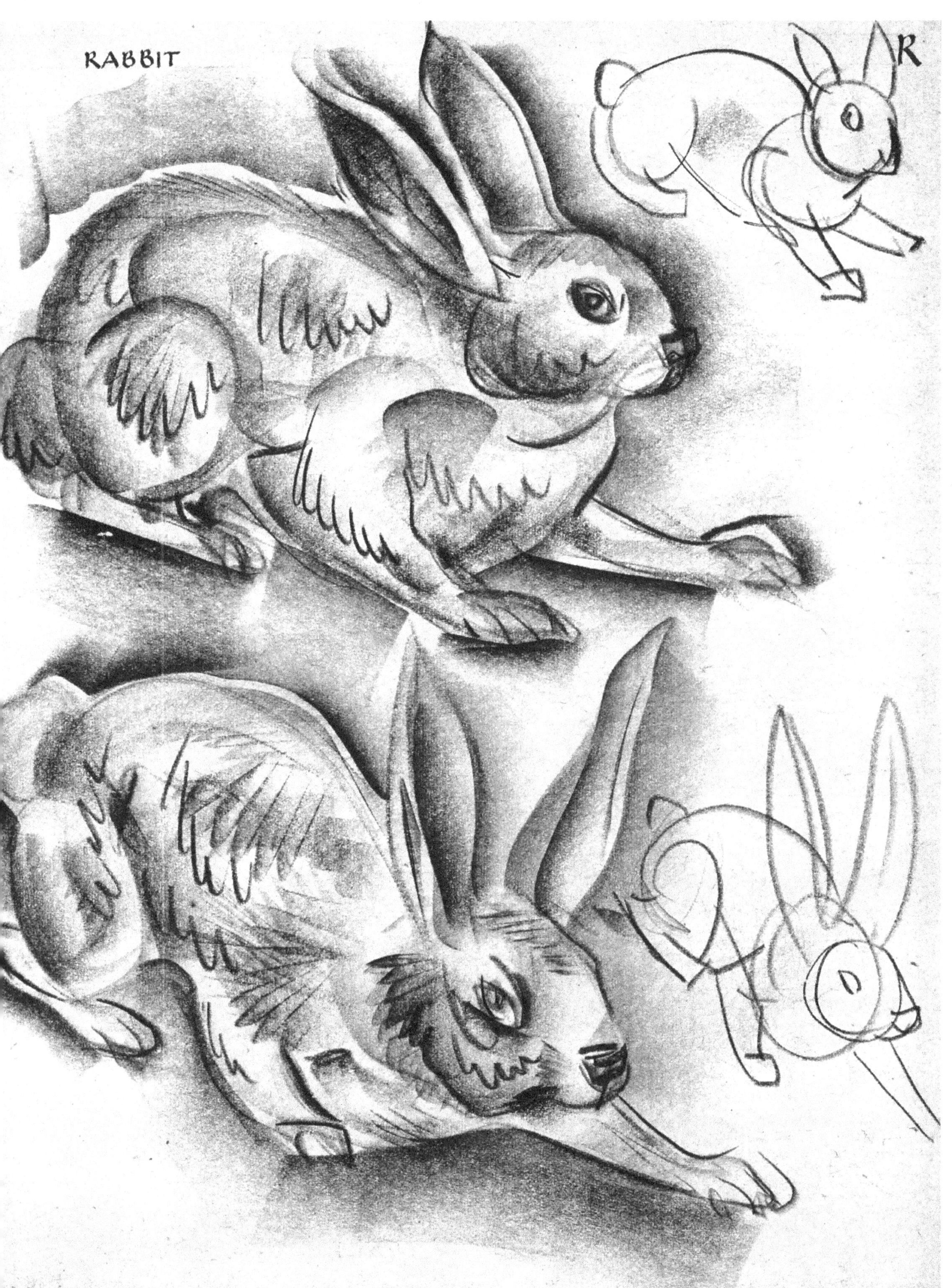
RABBIT
R

RABBIT

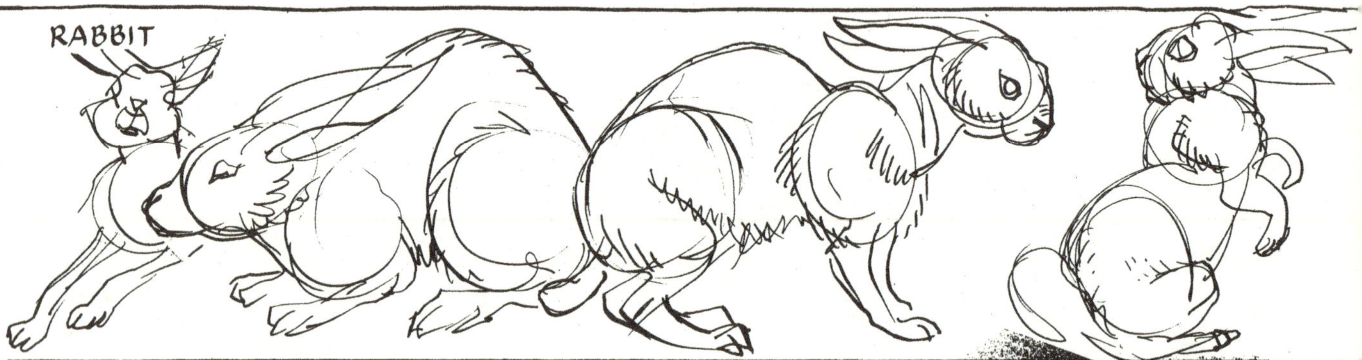

RACCOON

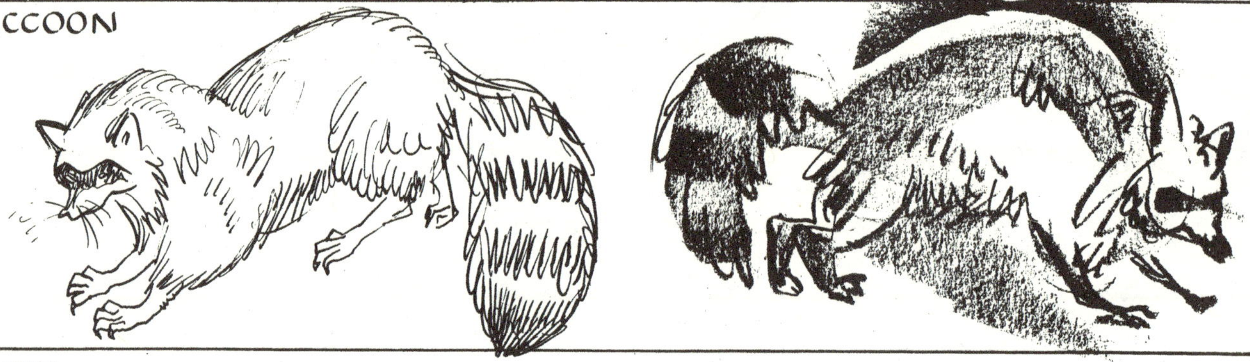

RACER

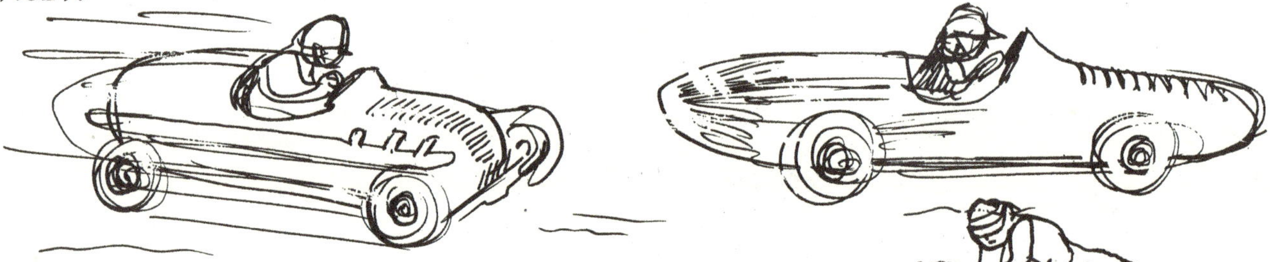

RACK

RAJAH

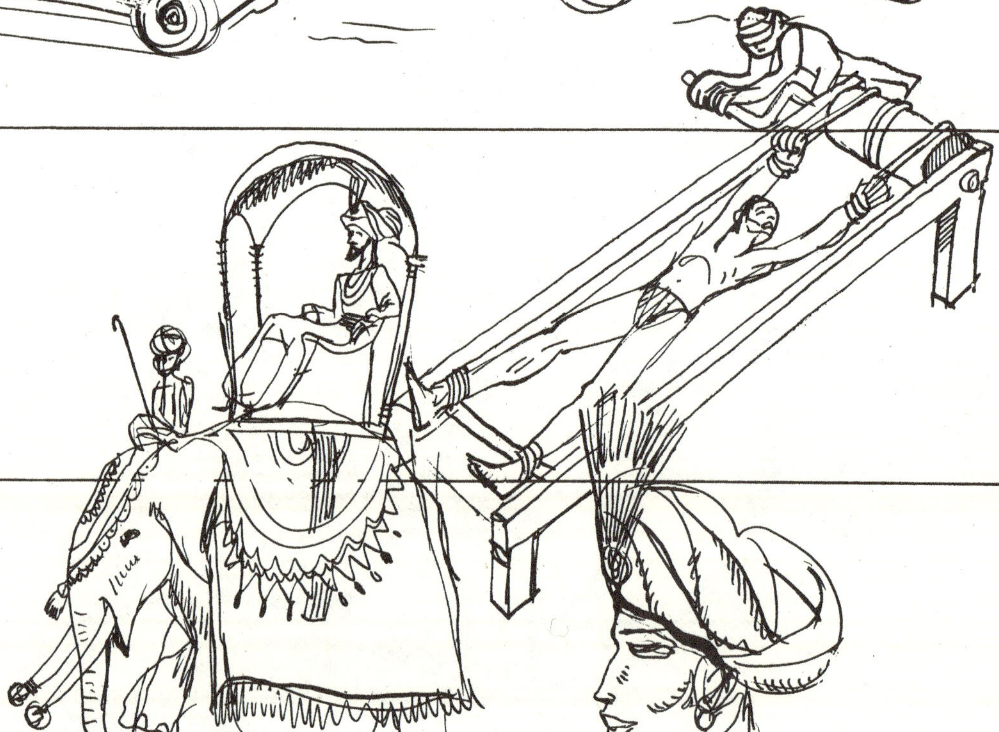

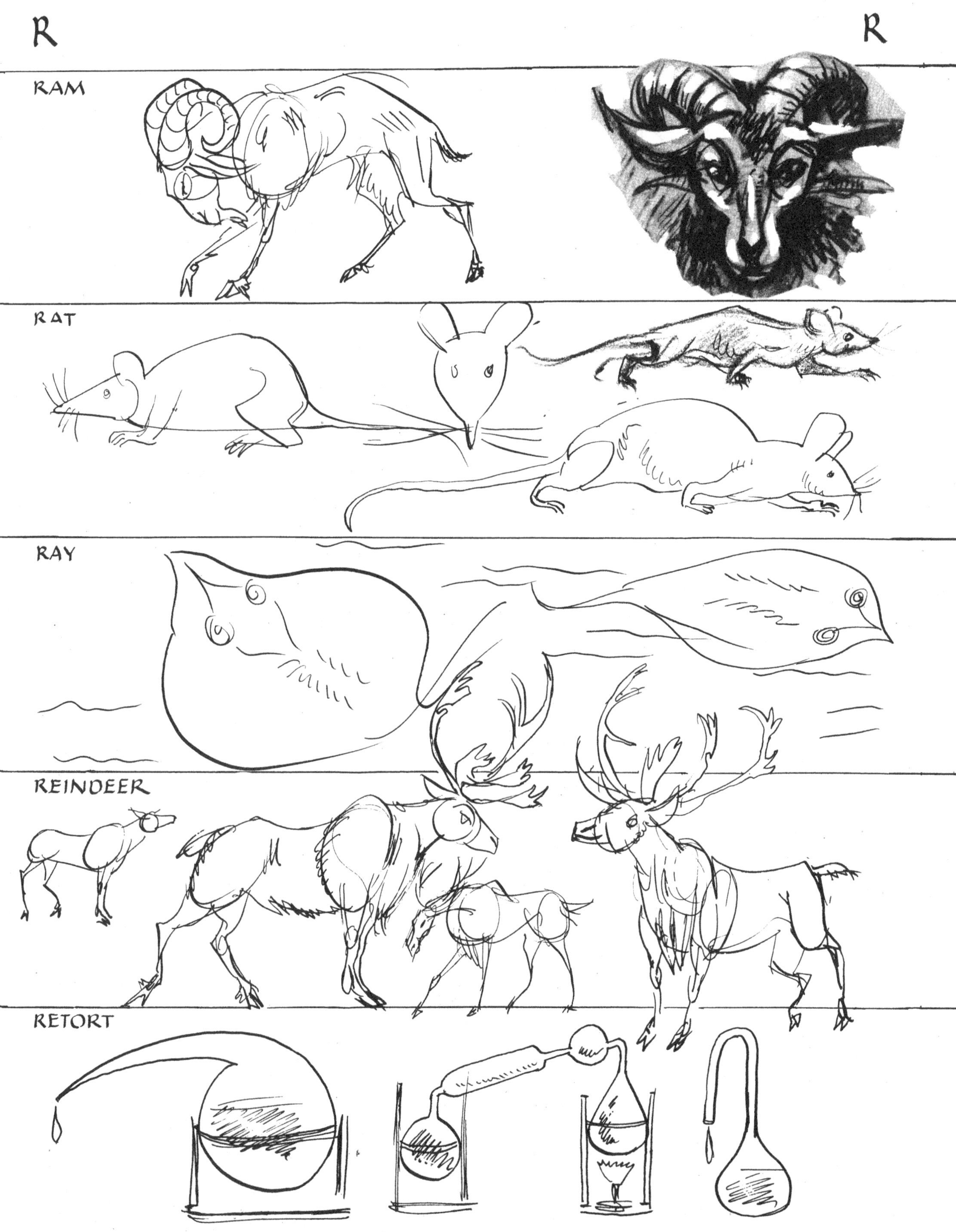
RAM
RAT
RAY
REINDEER
RETORT

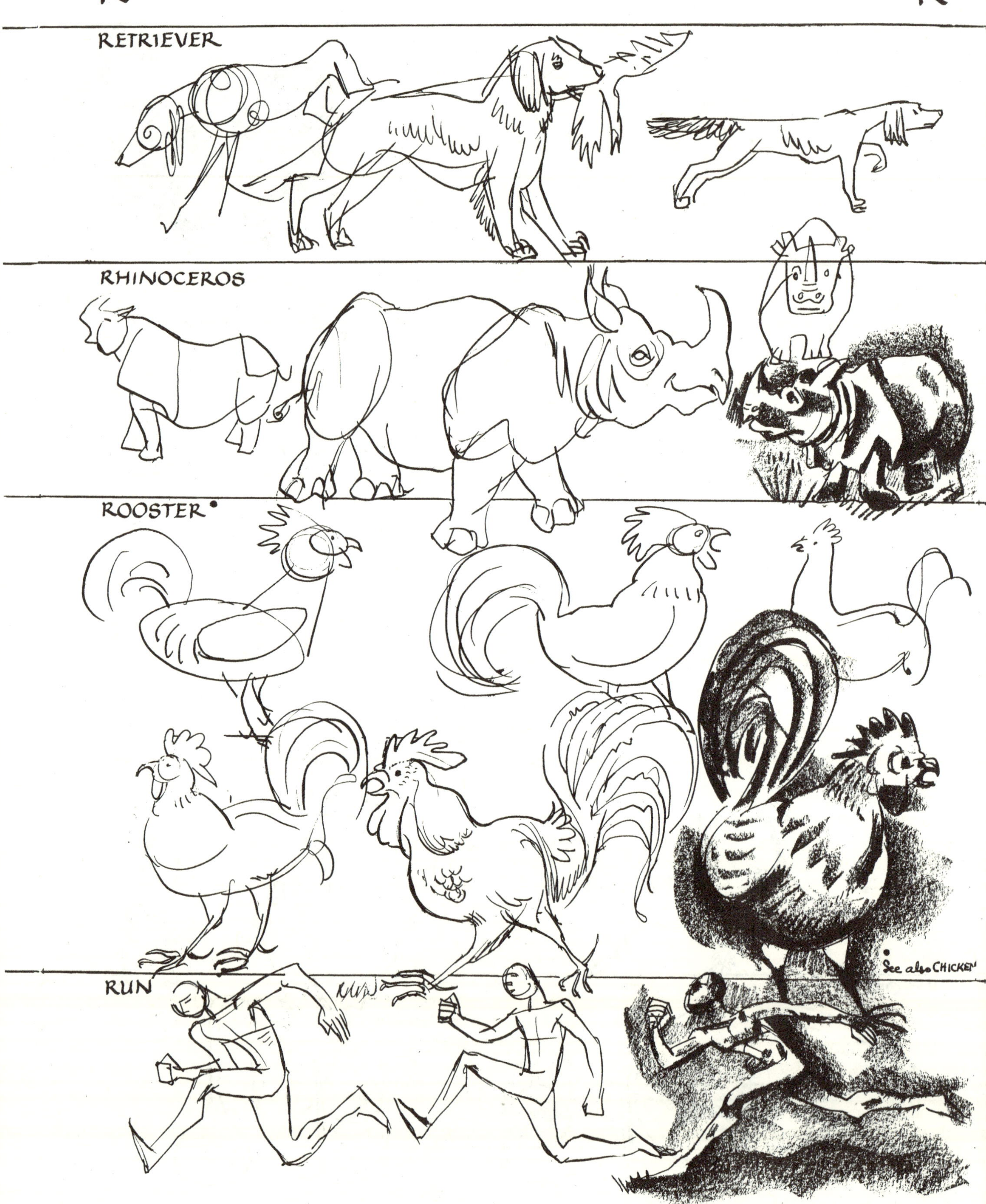
RETRIEVER
RHINOCEROS
ROOSTER •
RUN
• See also CHICKEN

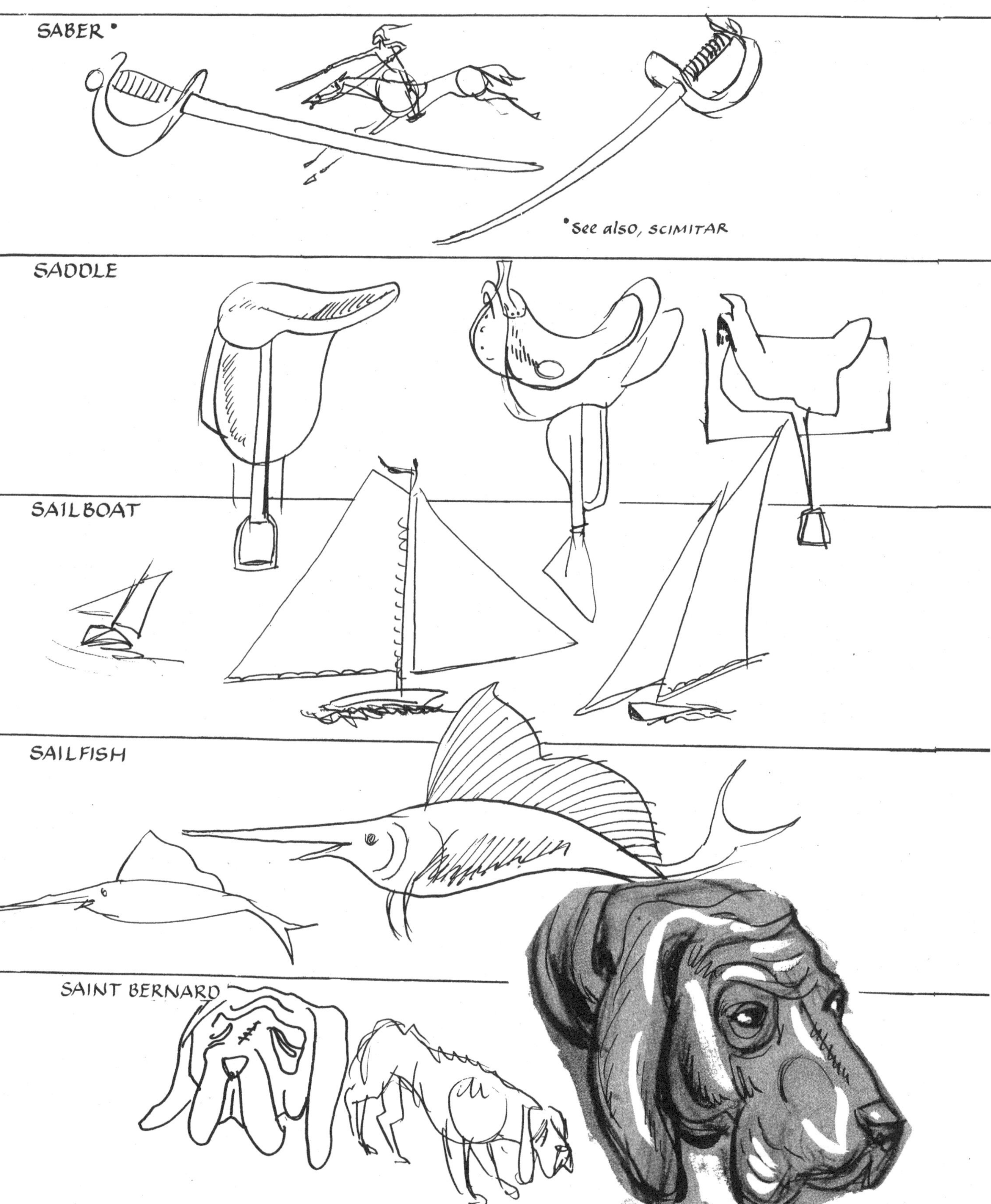
SABER*
*See also, SCIMITAR
SADDLE
SAILBOAT
SAILFISH
SAINT BERNARD

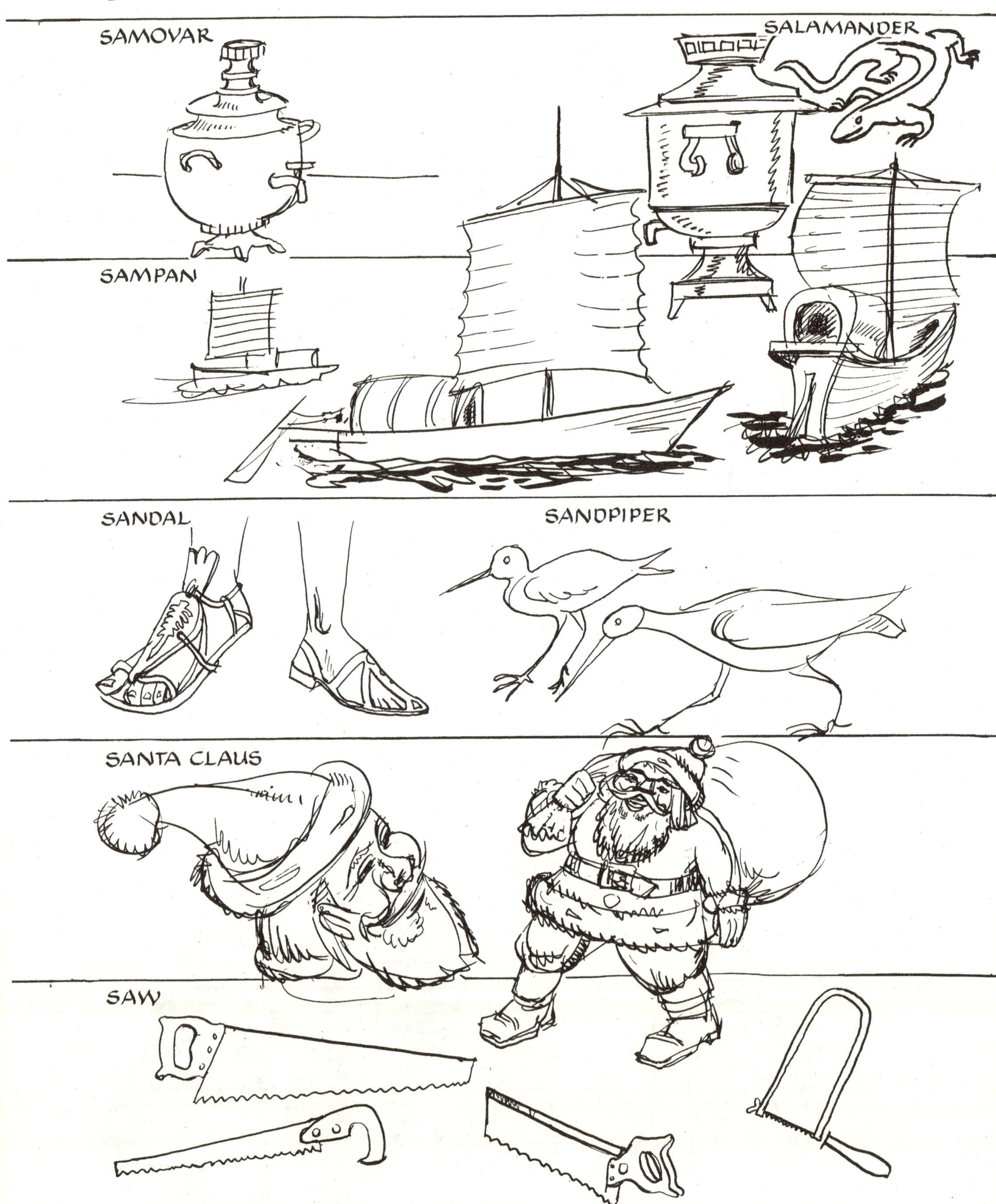
SAMOVAR
SALAMANDER
SAMPAN
SANDAL
SANDPIPER
SANTA CLAUS
SAW

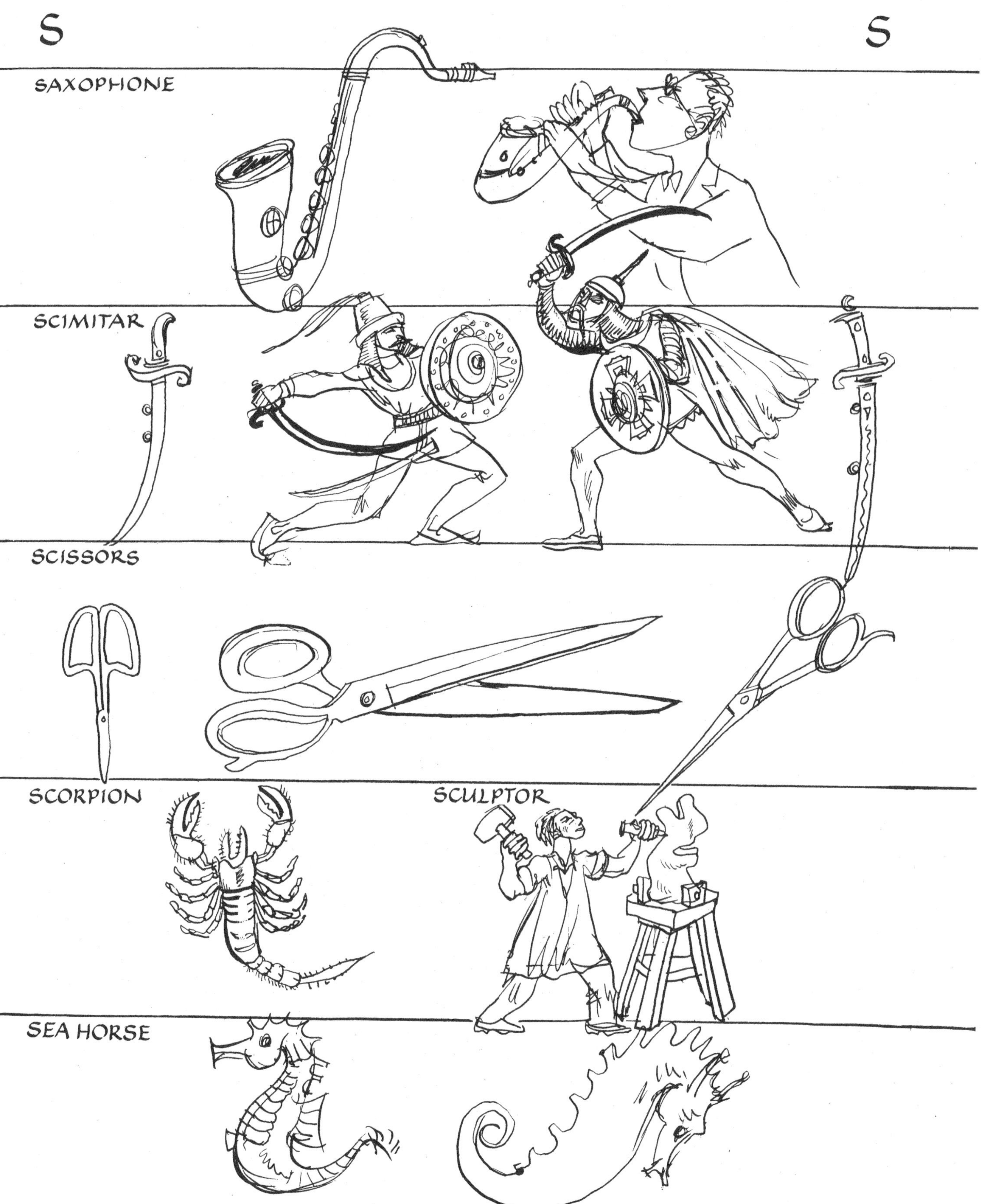
S
S
SAXOPHONE
SCIMITAR
SCISSORS
SCORPION
SCULPTOR
SEA HORSE

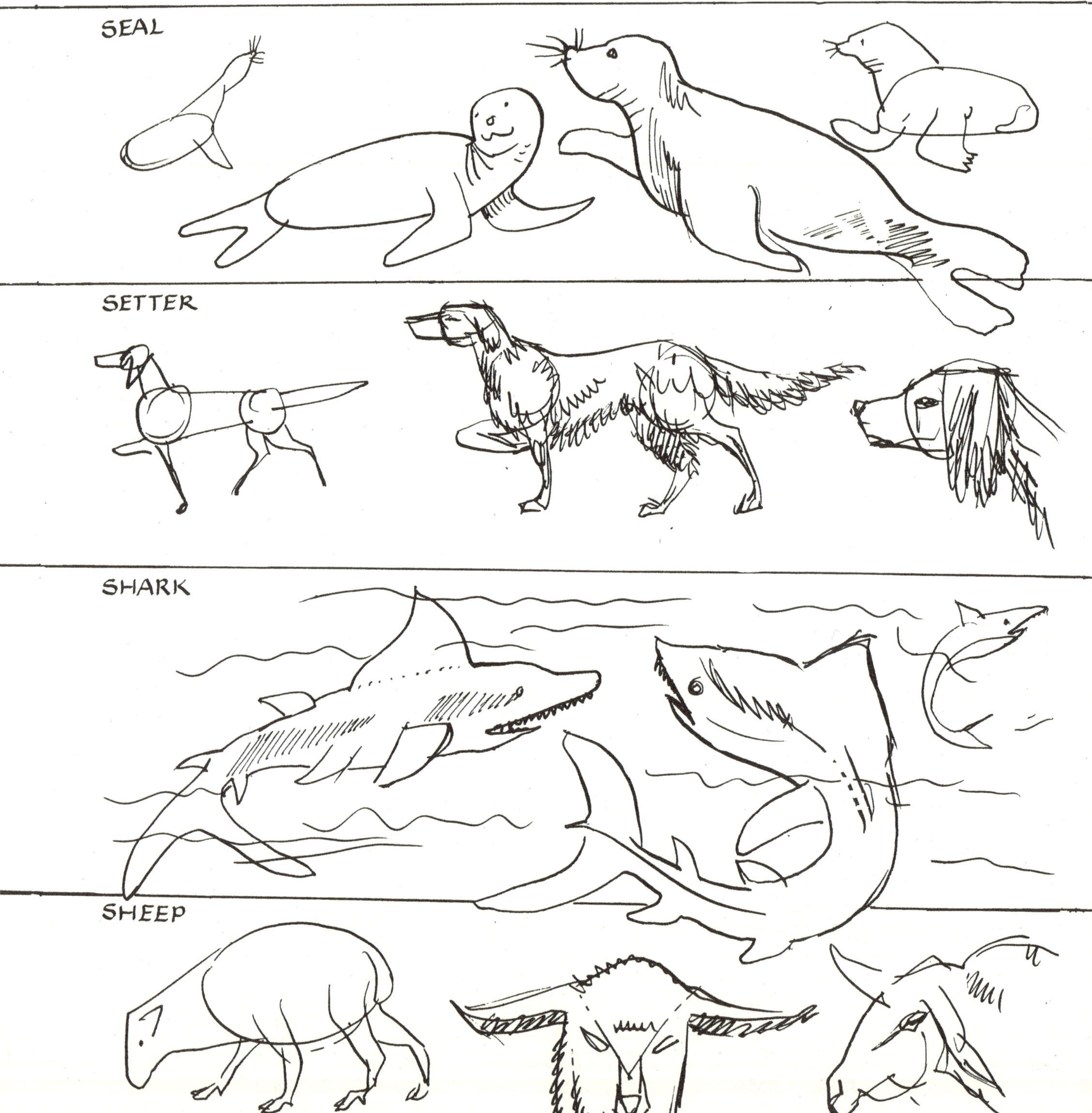
SEAL
SETTER
SHARK
SHEEP

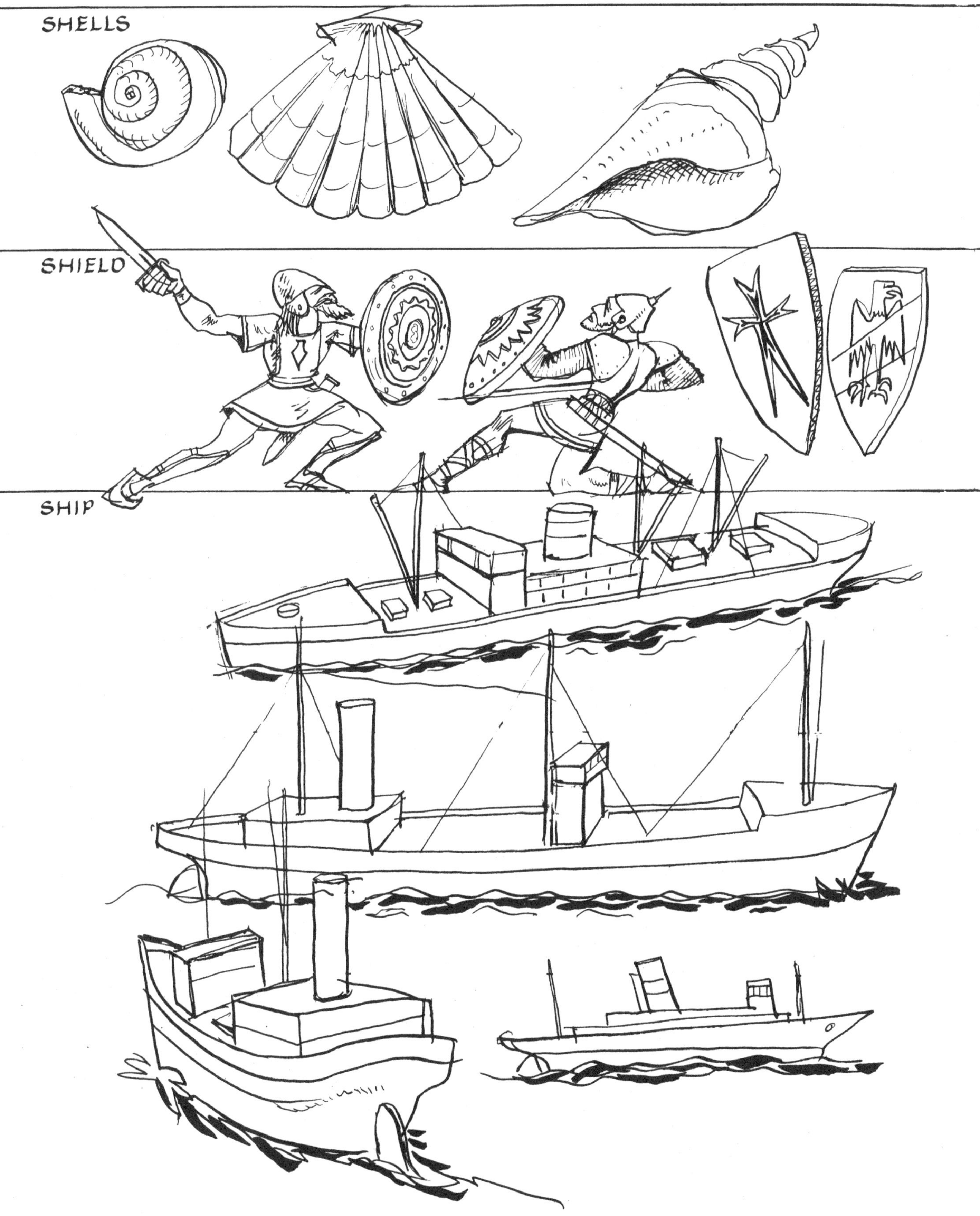
SHELLS
SHIELD
SHIP

SHIP*

S

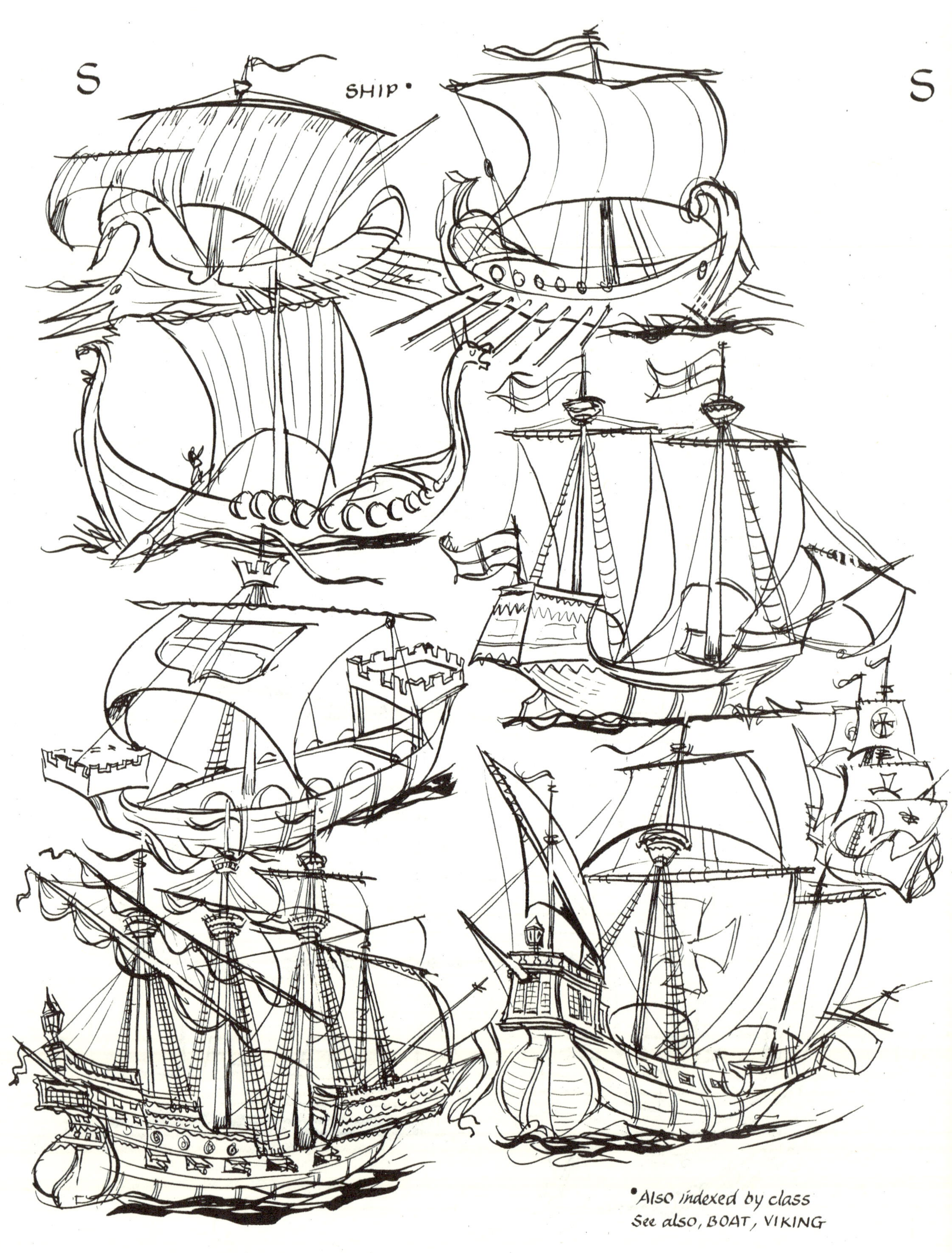

*Also indexed by class
See also, BOAT, VIKING

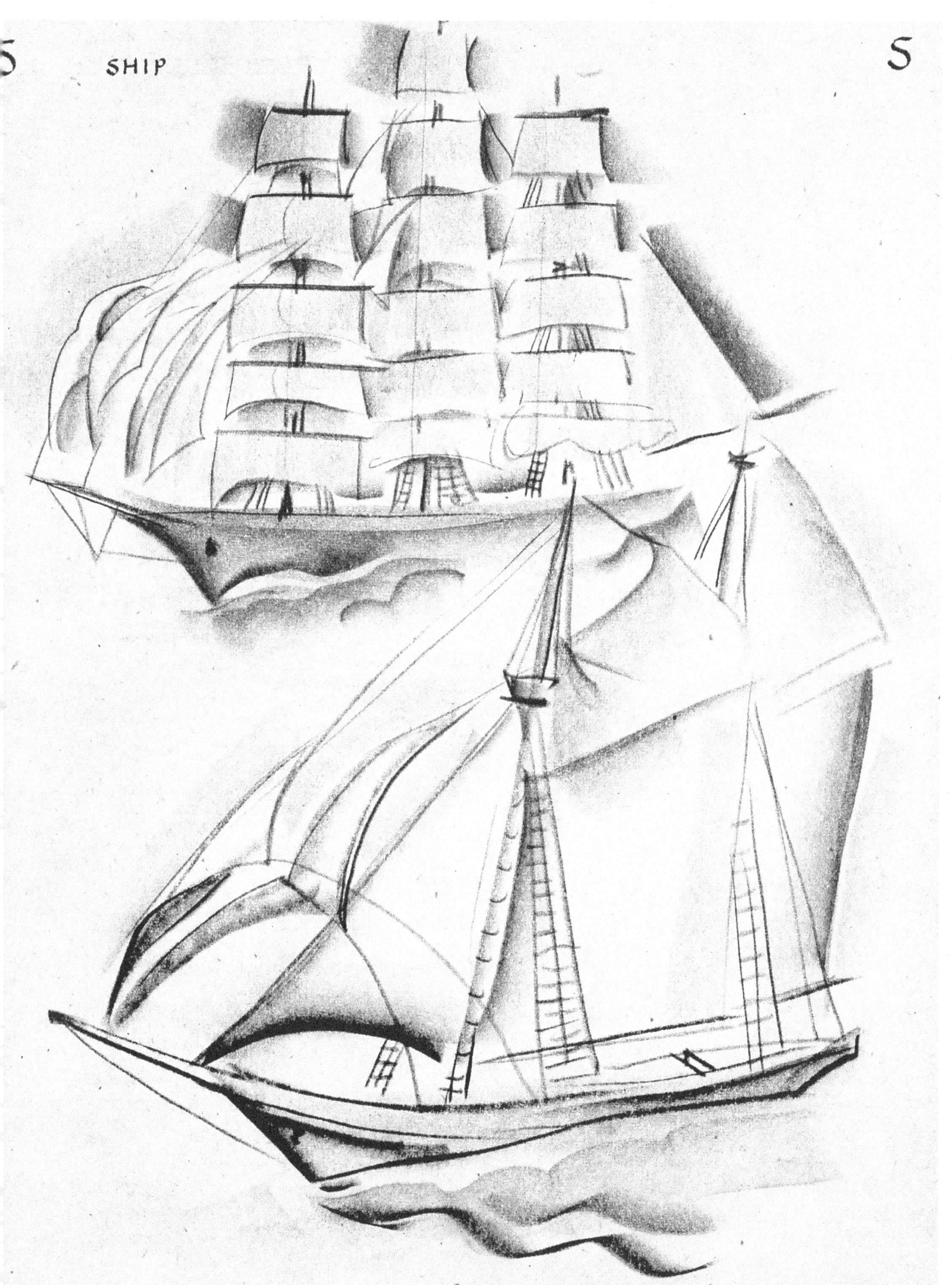
S
SHIP
S

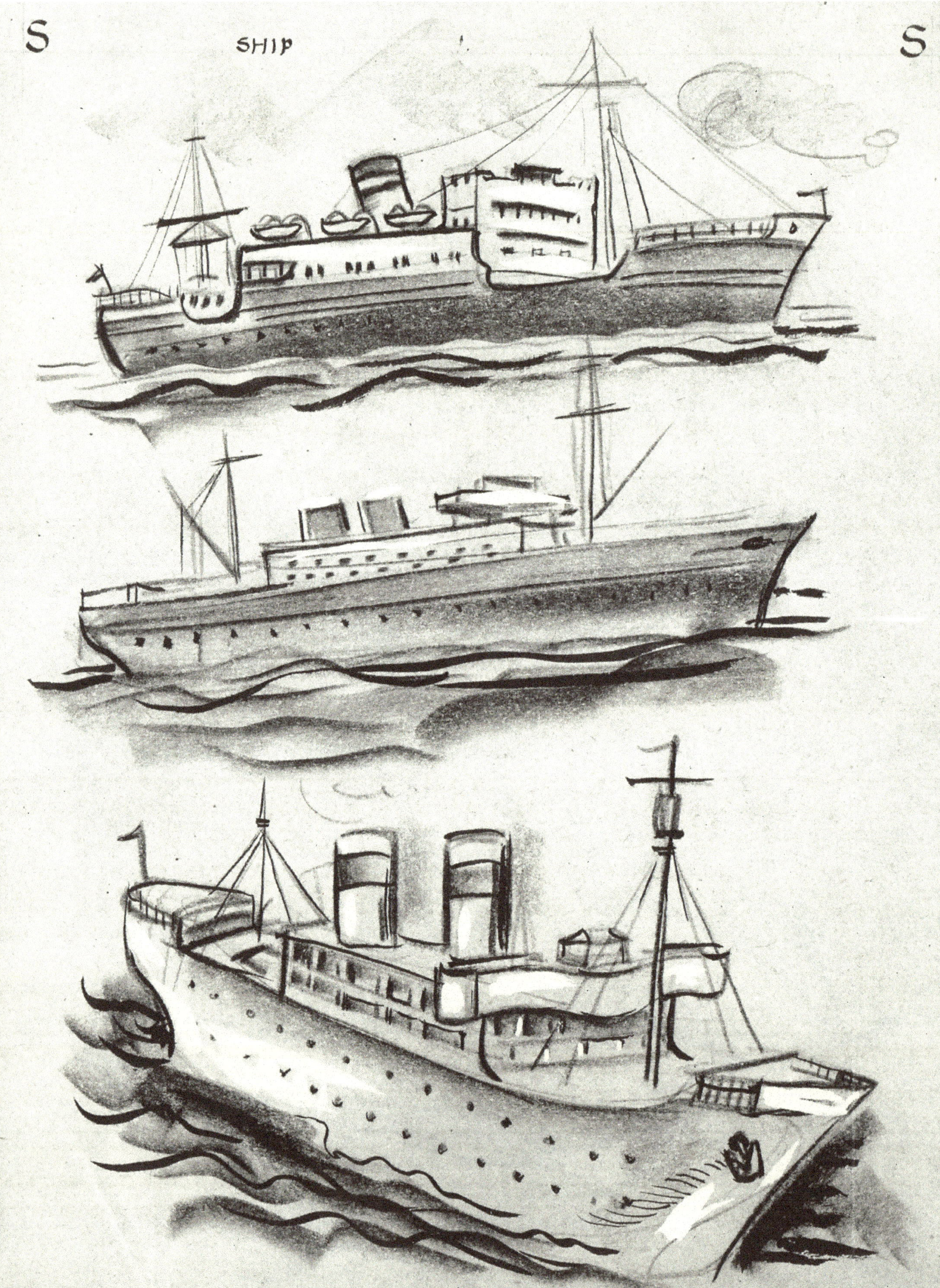
S
SHIP
S

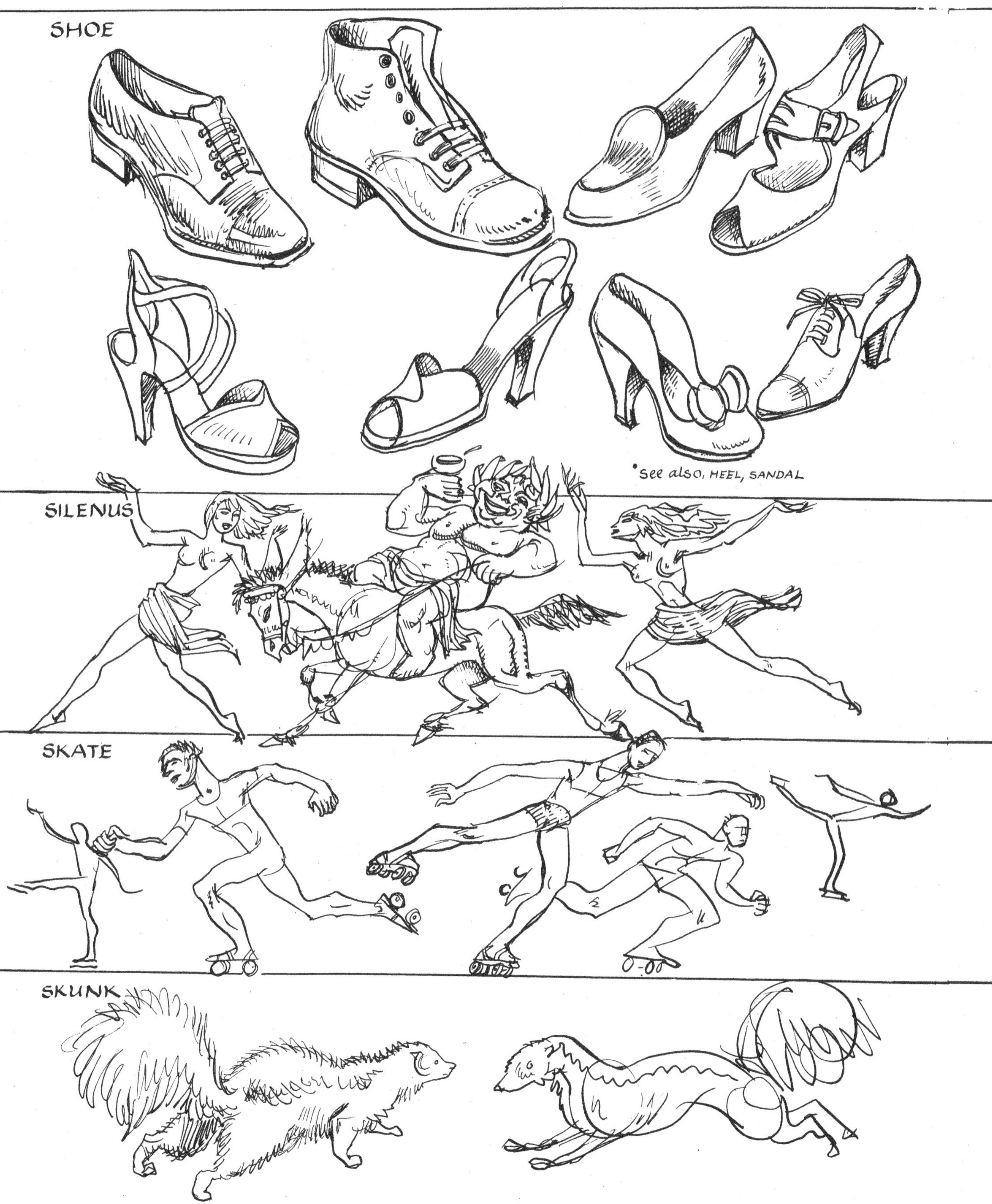
SHOE
*see also, HEEL, SANDAL
SILENUS
SKATE
SKUNK

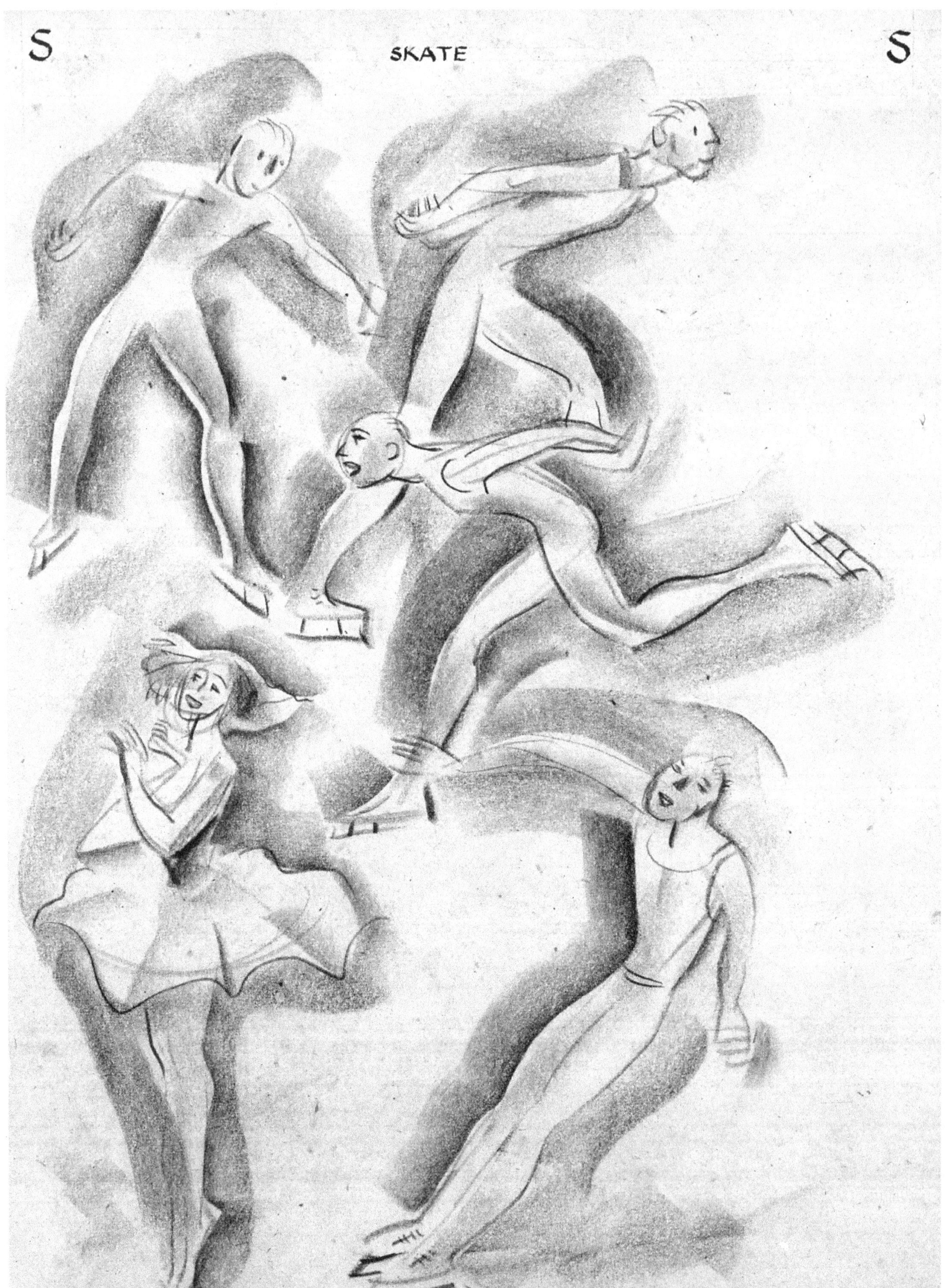
S
SKATE
S

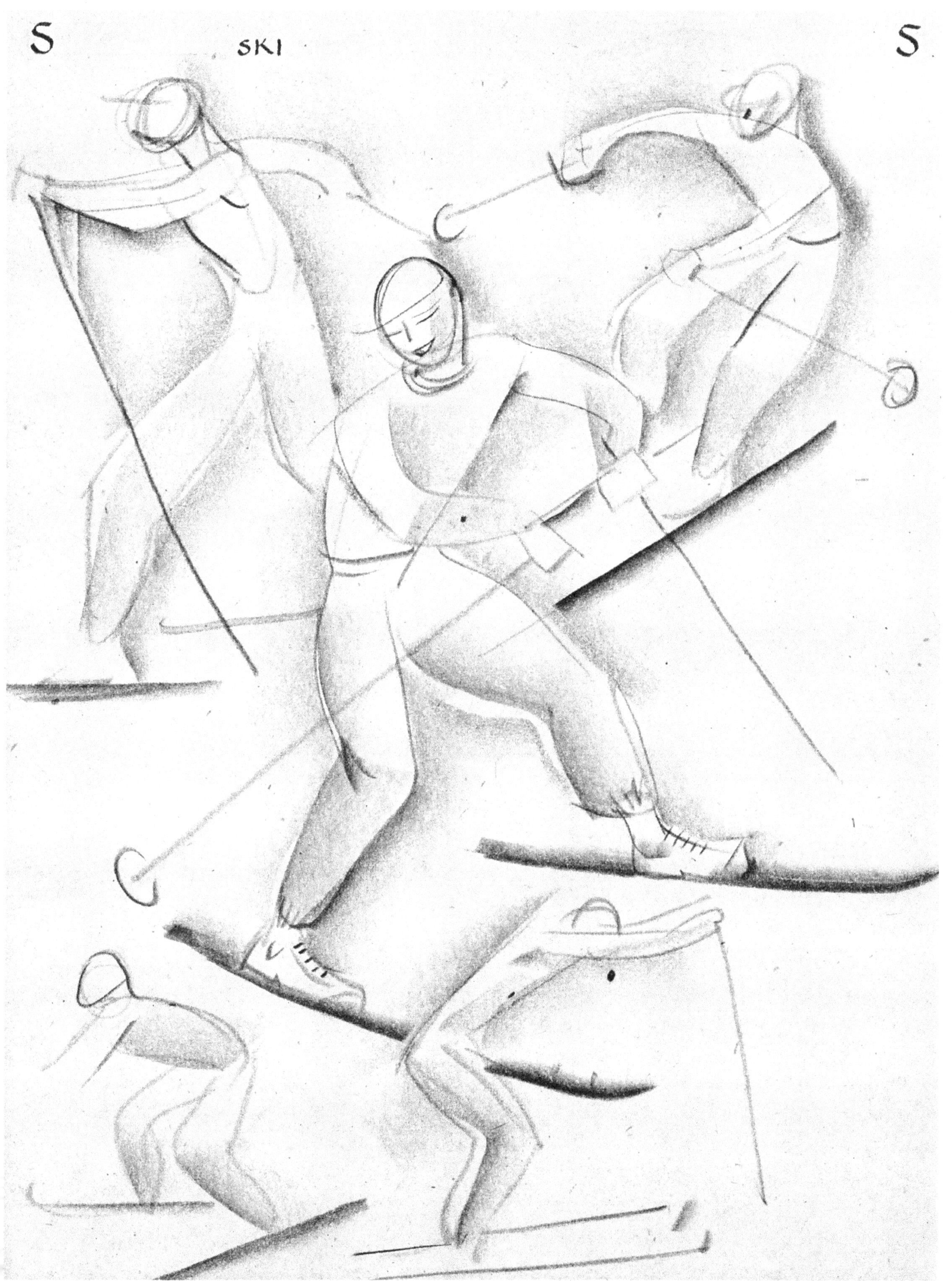
S
SKI
S

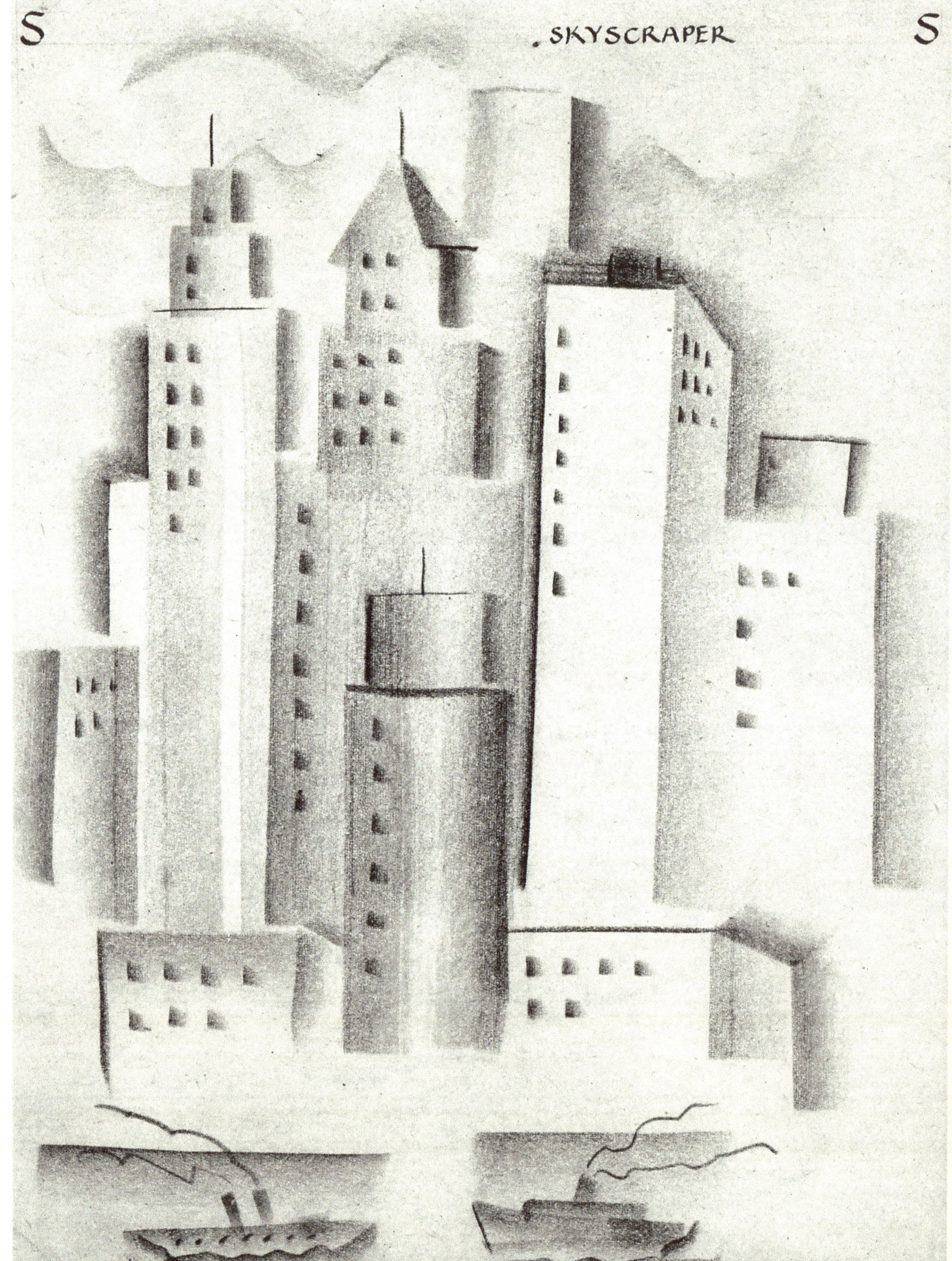
S
SKYSCRAPER
S

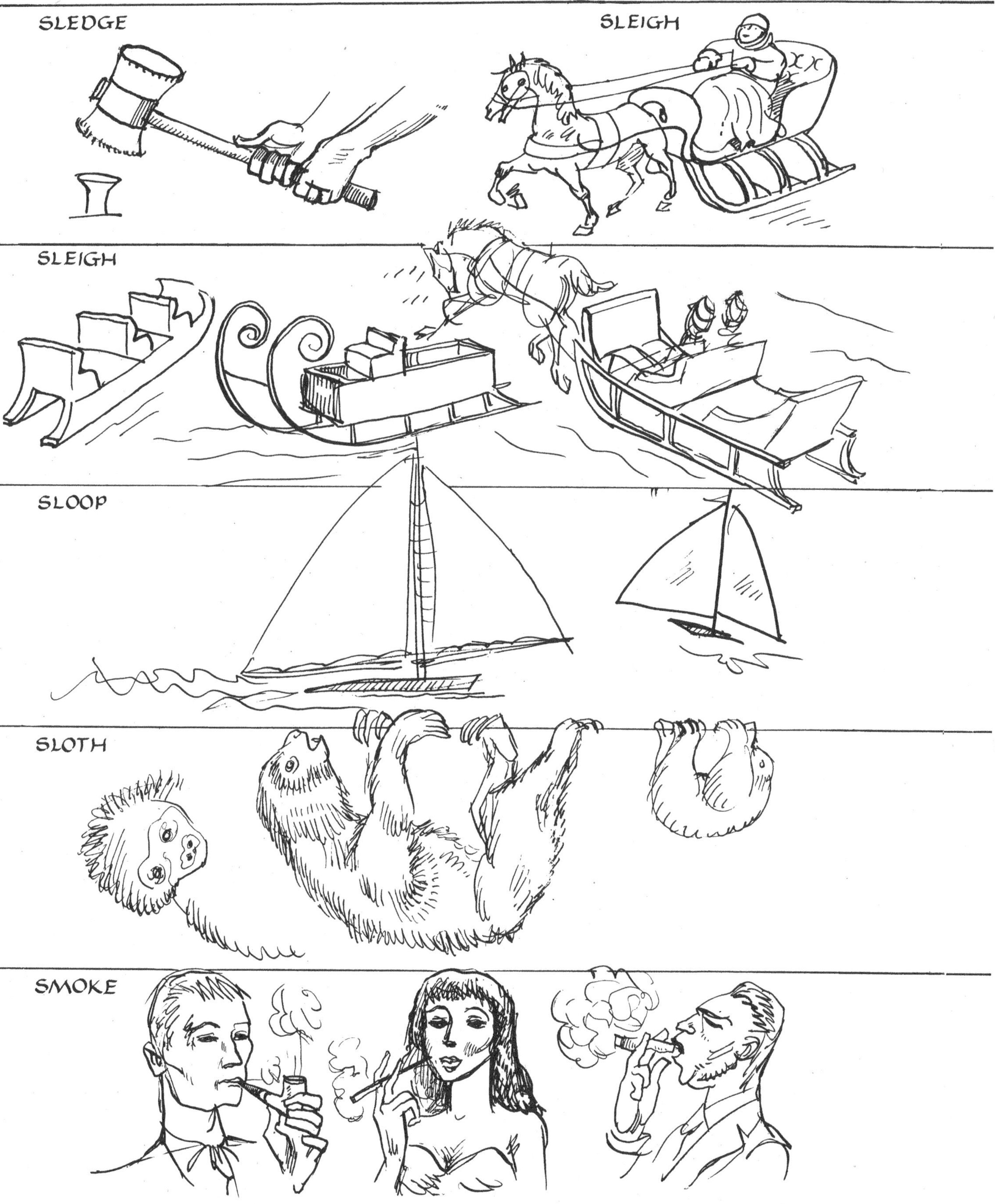
SLEDGE
SLEIGH
SLEIGH
SLOOP
SLOTH
SMOKE

SNAIL

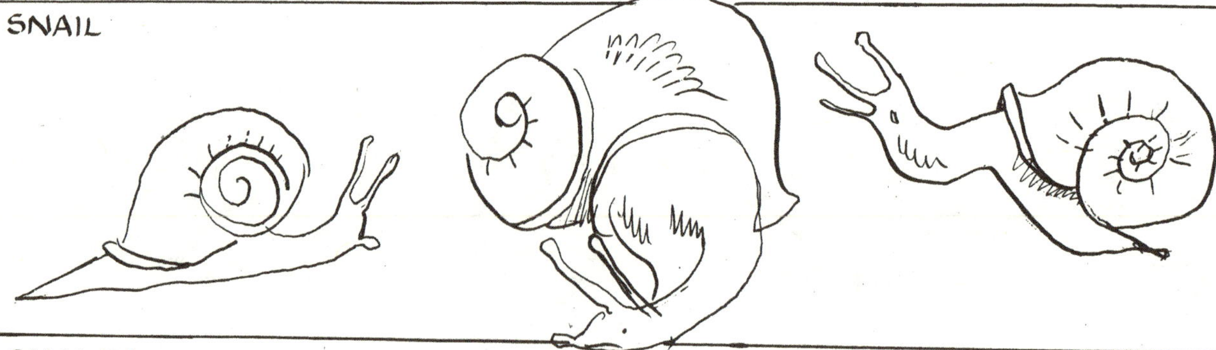

SNAKE•

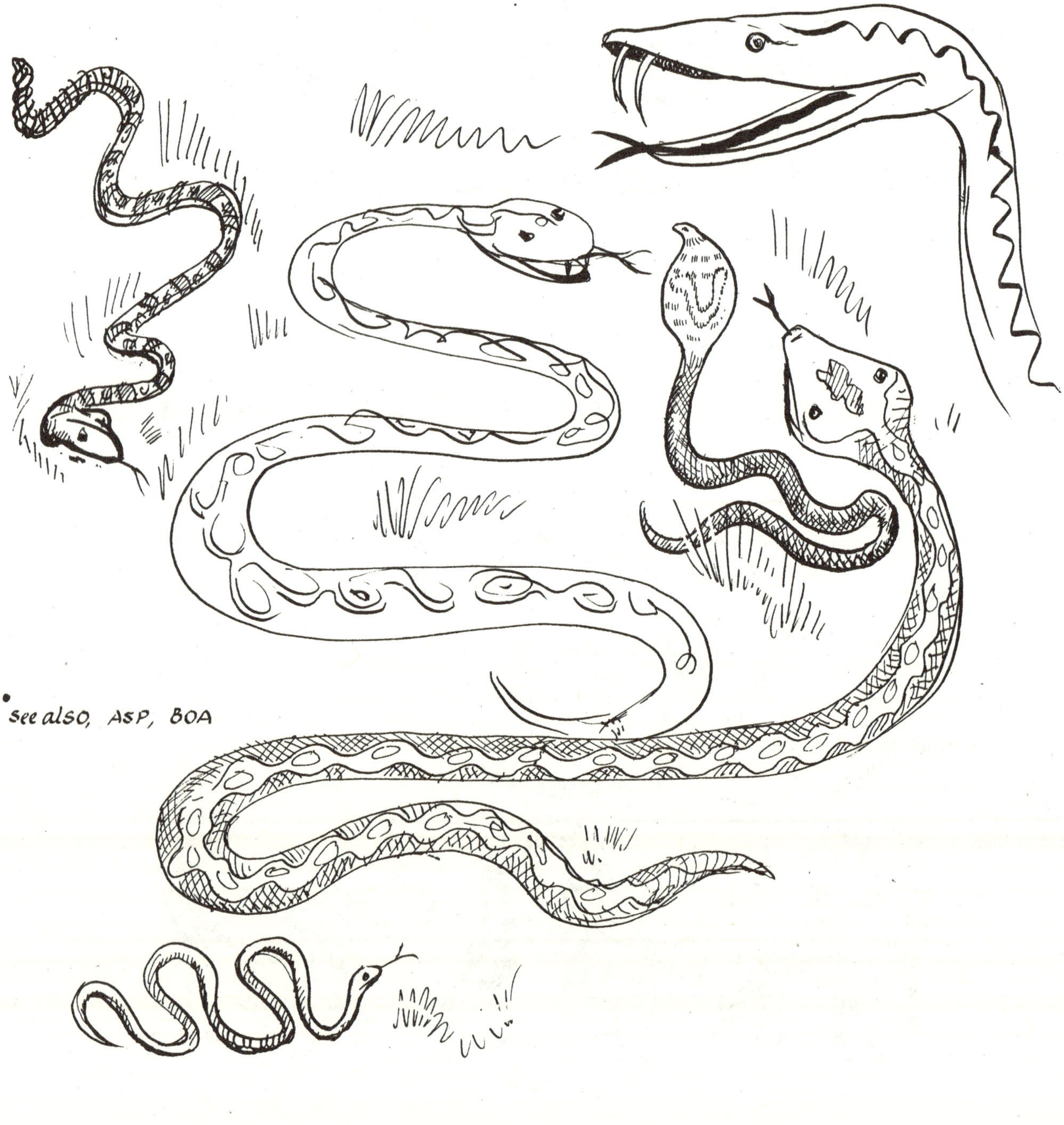

•see also, ASP, BOA

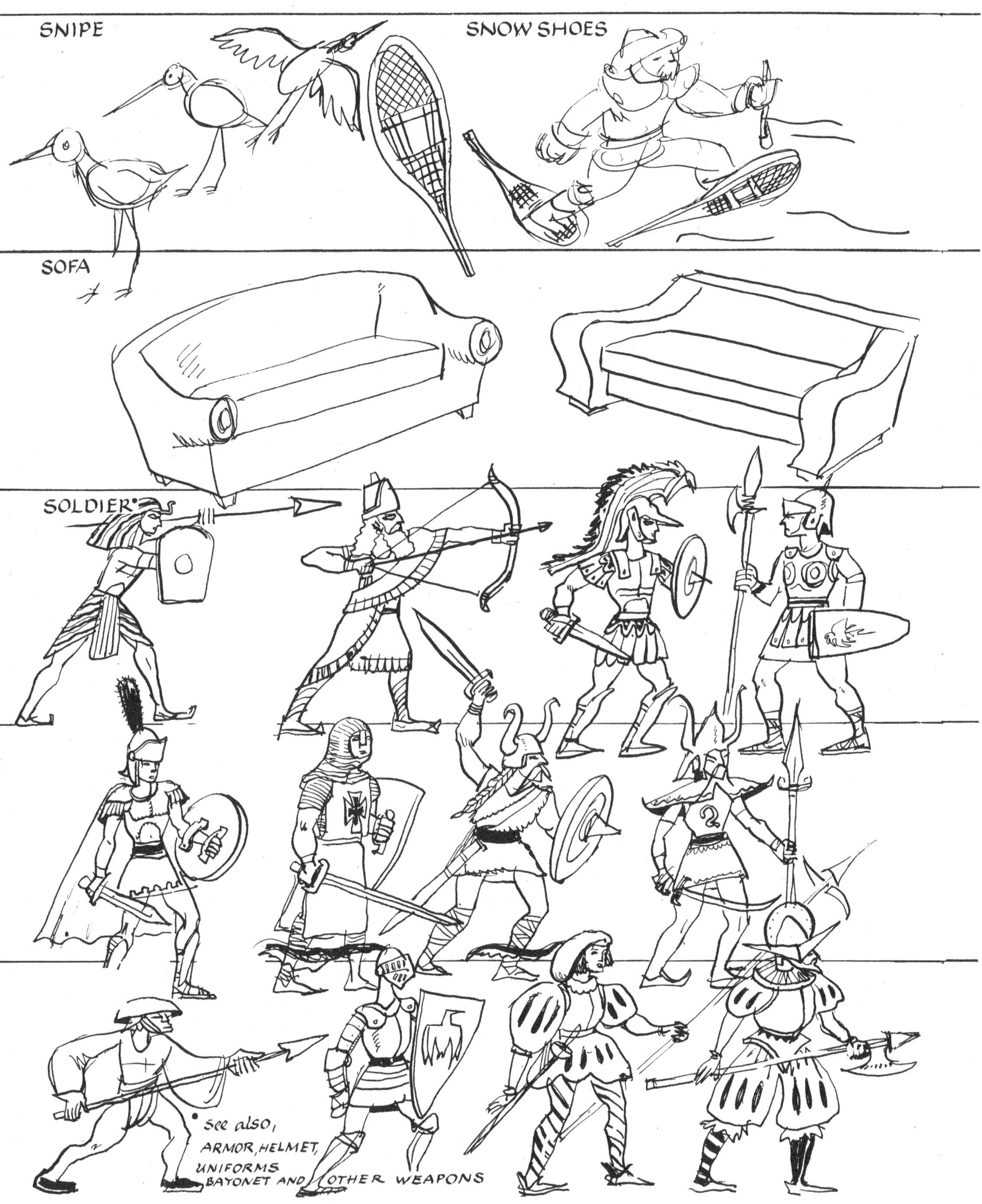
SNIPE
SNOW SHOES
SOFA
SOLDIER*
* see also,
ARMOR, HELMET,
UNIFORMS
BAYONET AND OTHER WEAPONS

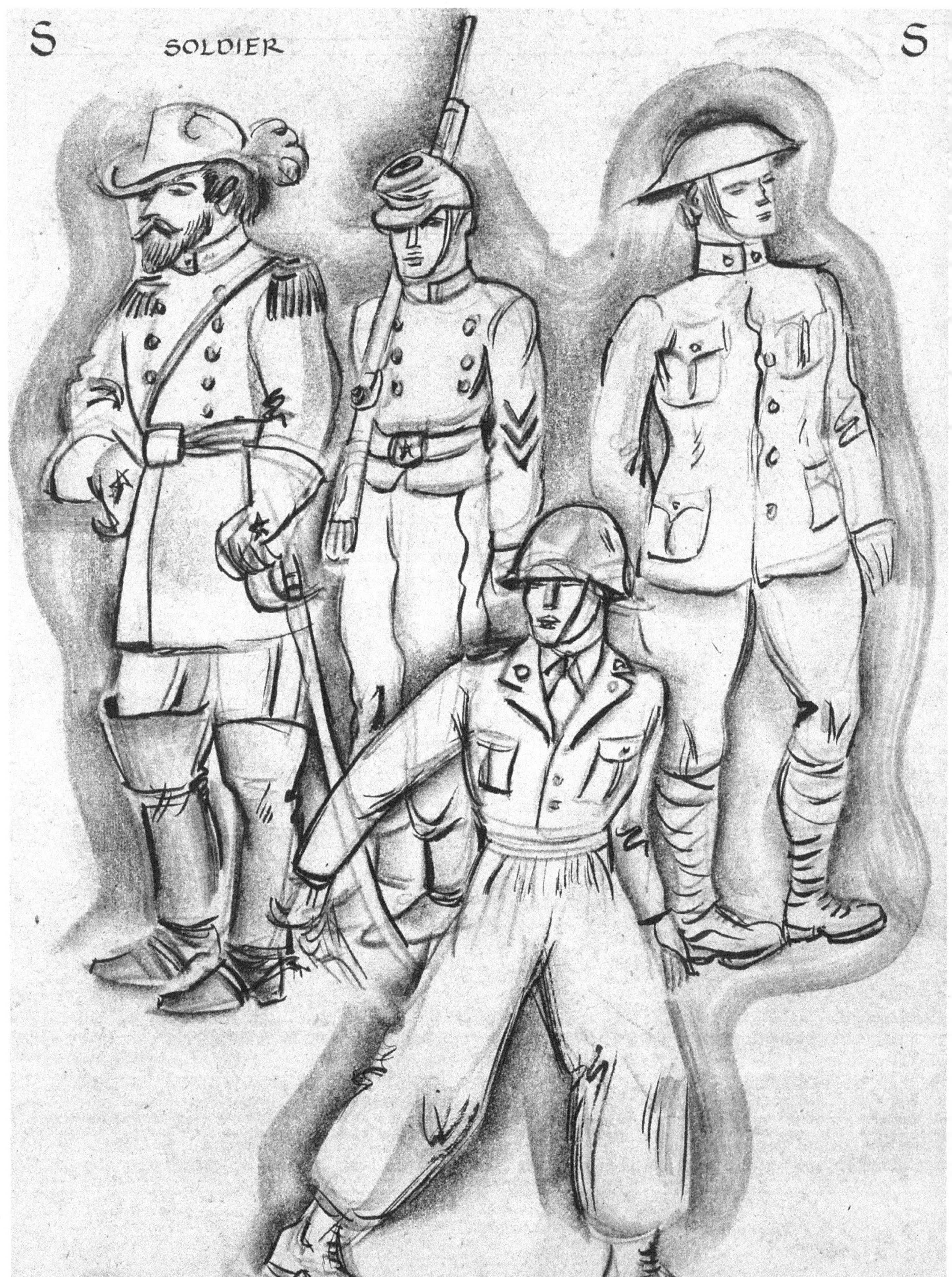
S
SOLDIER
S

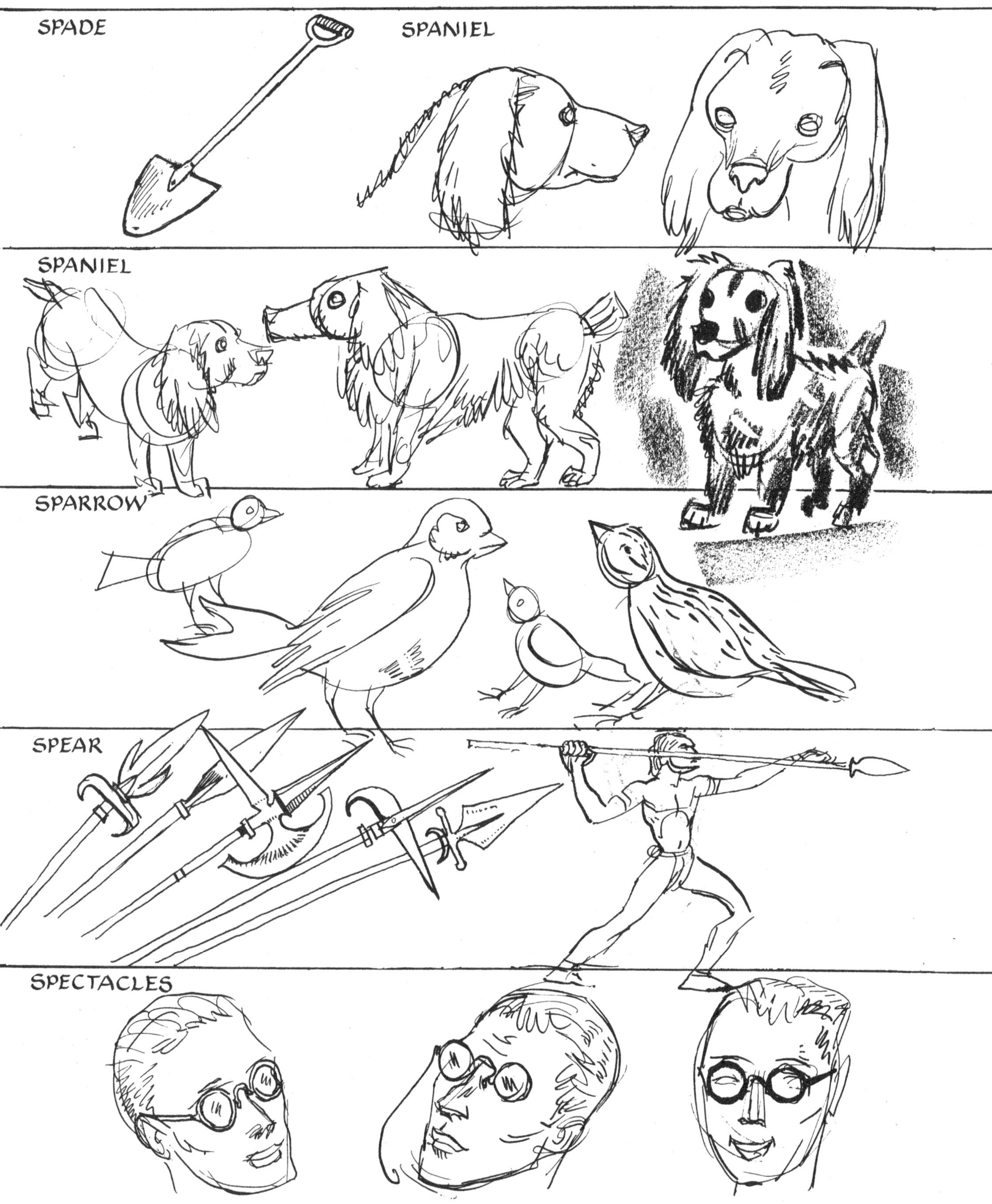
SPADE
SPANIEL
SPANIEL
SPARROW
SPEAR
SPECTACLES

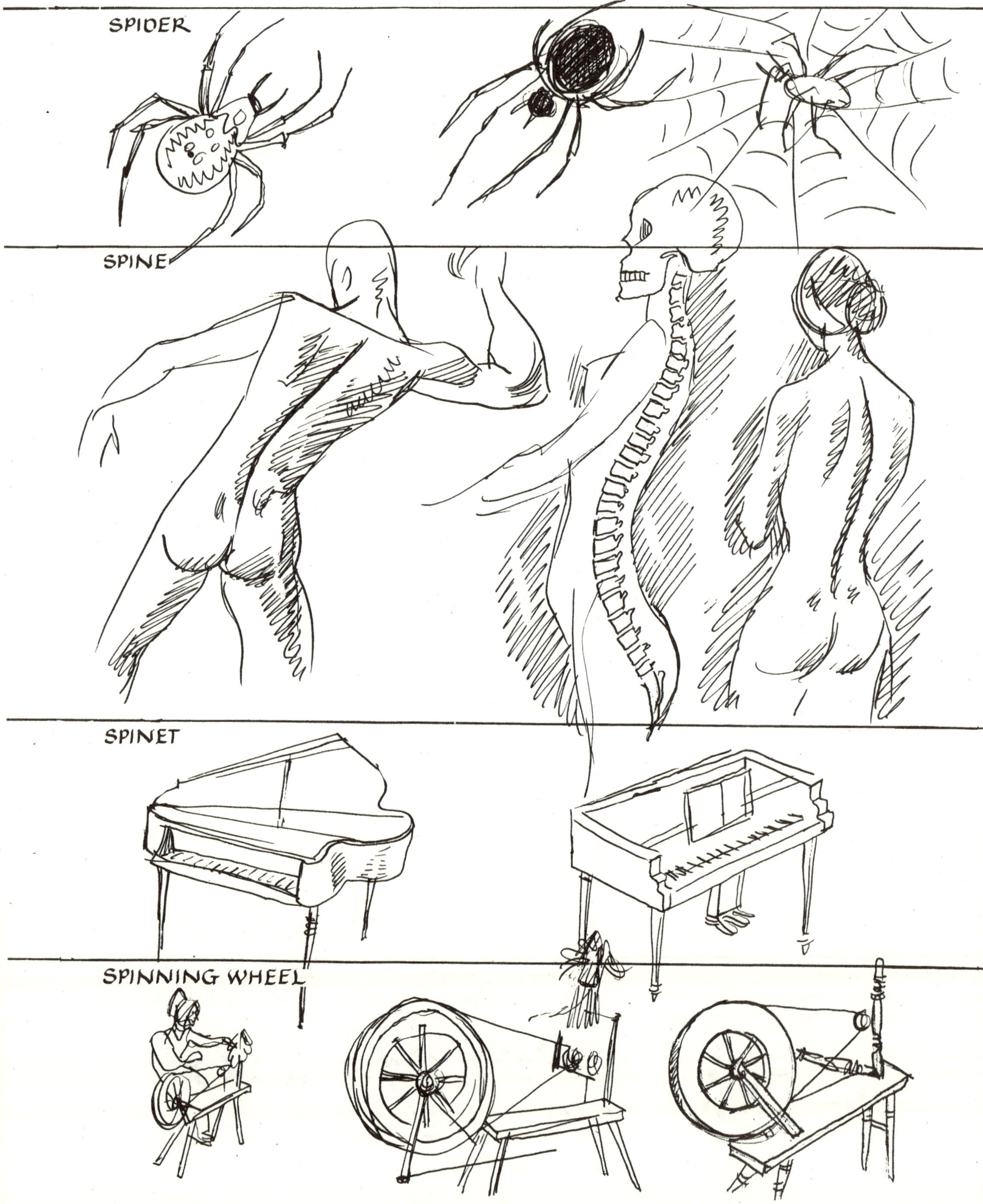
SPIDER
SPINE
SPINET
SPINNING WHEEL

S

SPITZ
SQUIRREL
SQUIRREL
SQUIRREL
SQUASH
STARFISH
STARLING

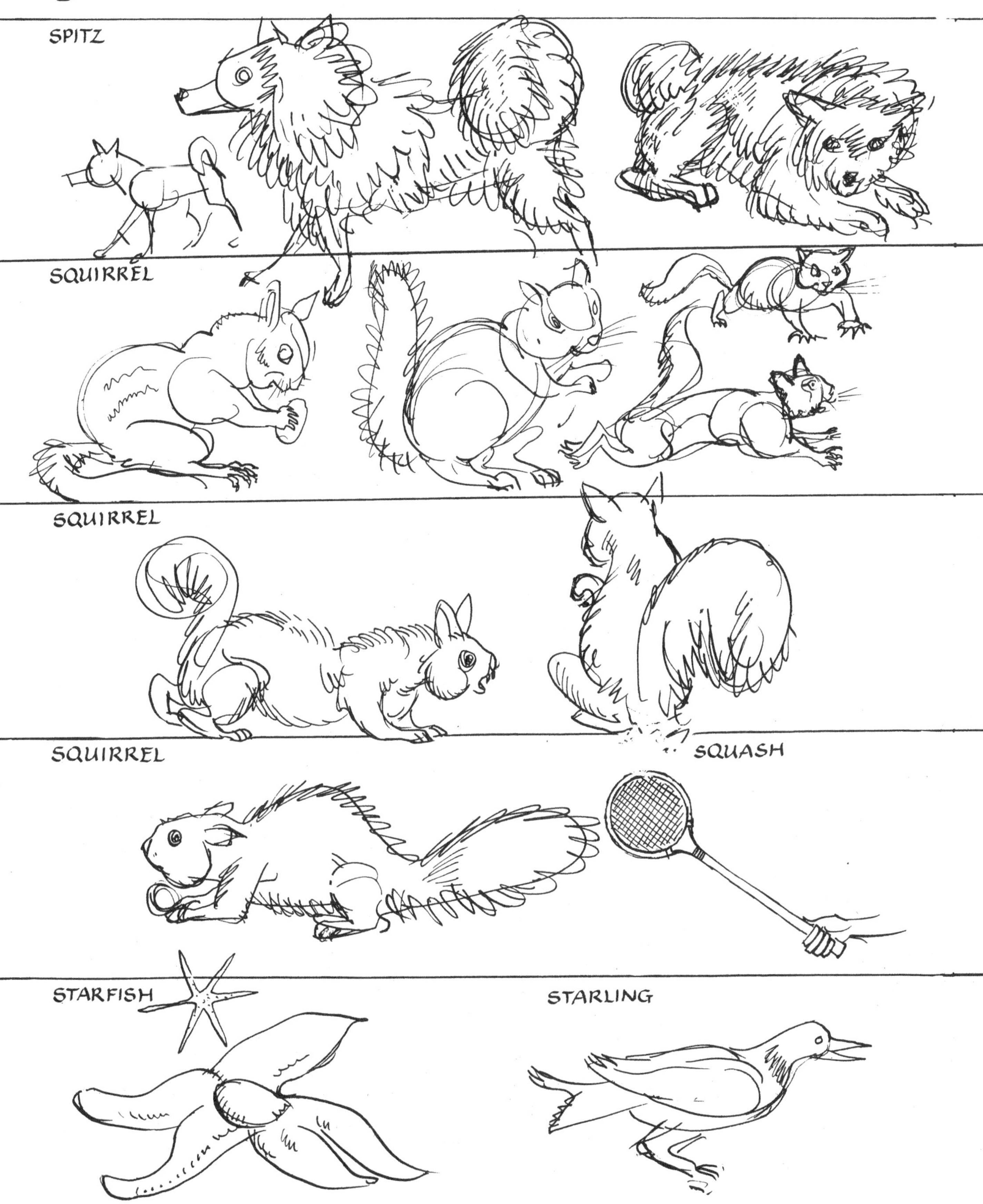

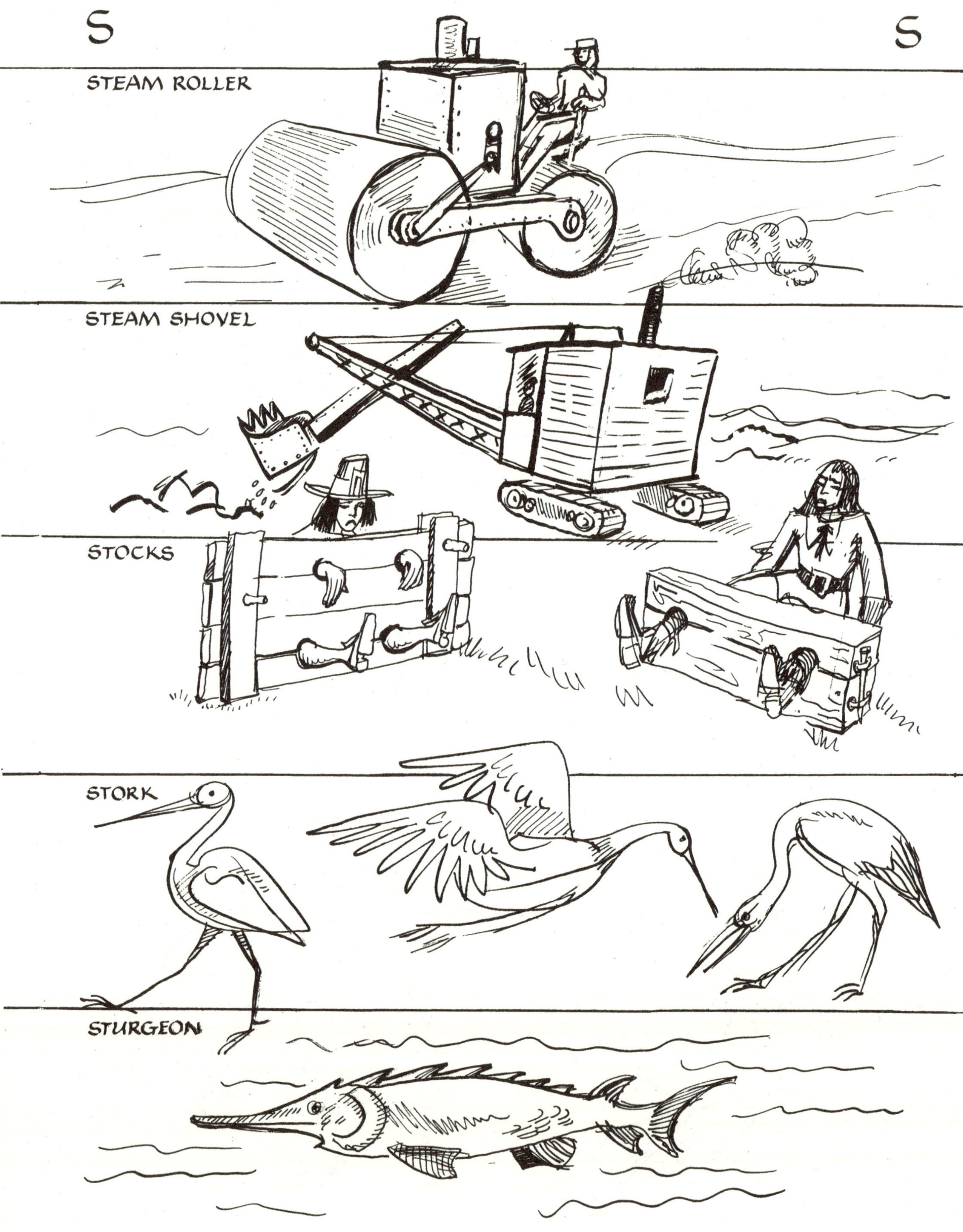
S
S
STEAM ROLLER
STEAM SHOVEL
STOCKS
STORK
STURGEON

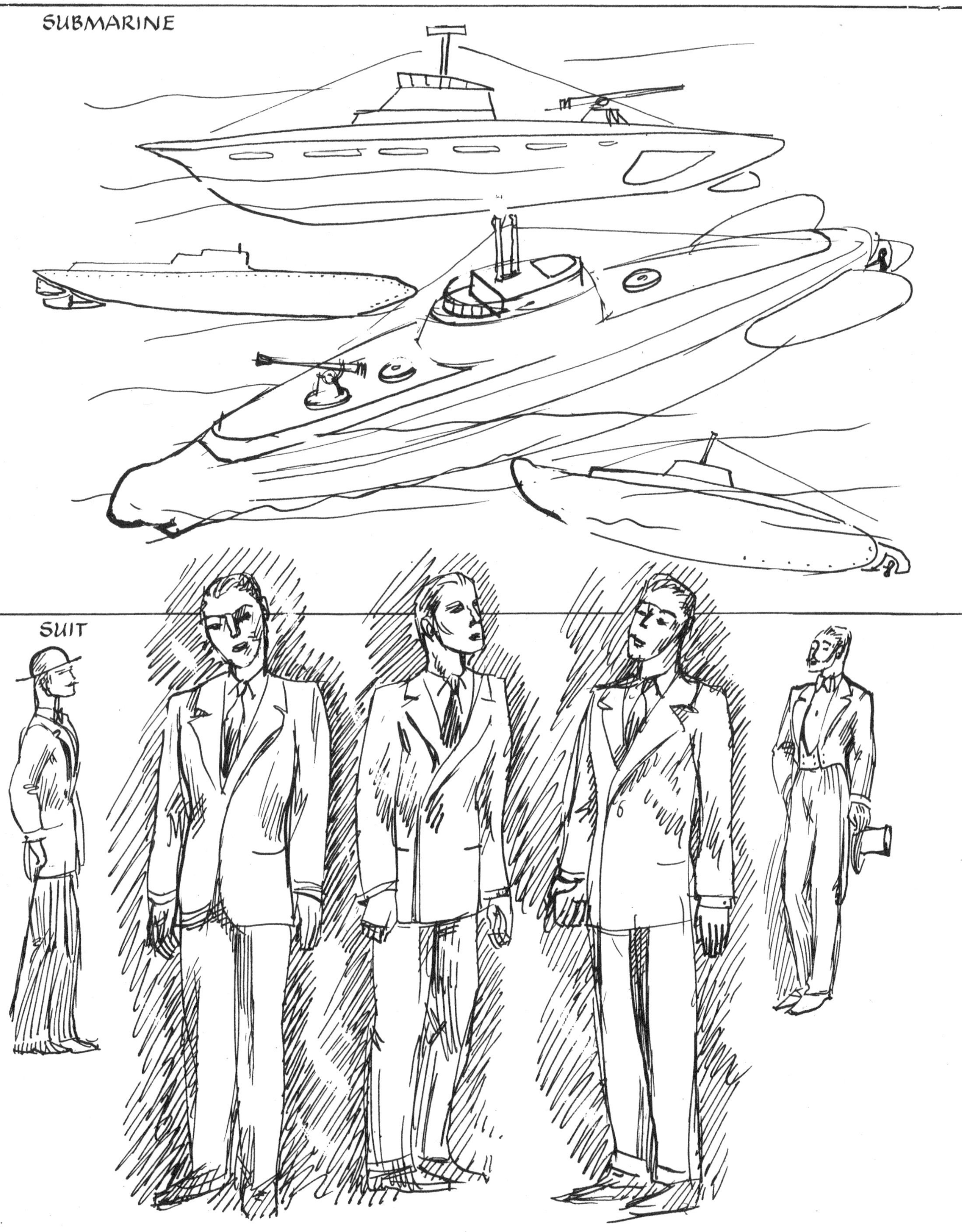
SUBMARINE
SUIT

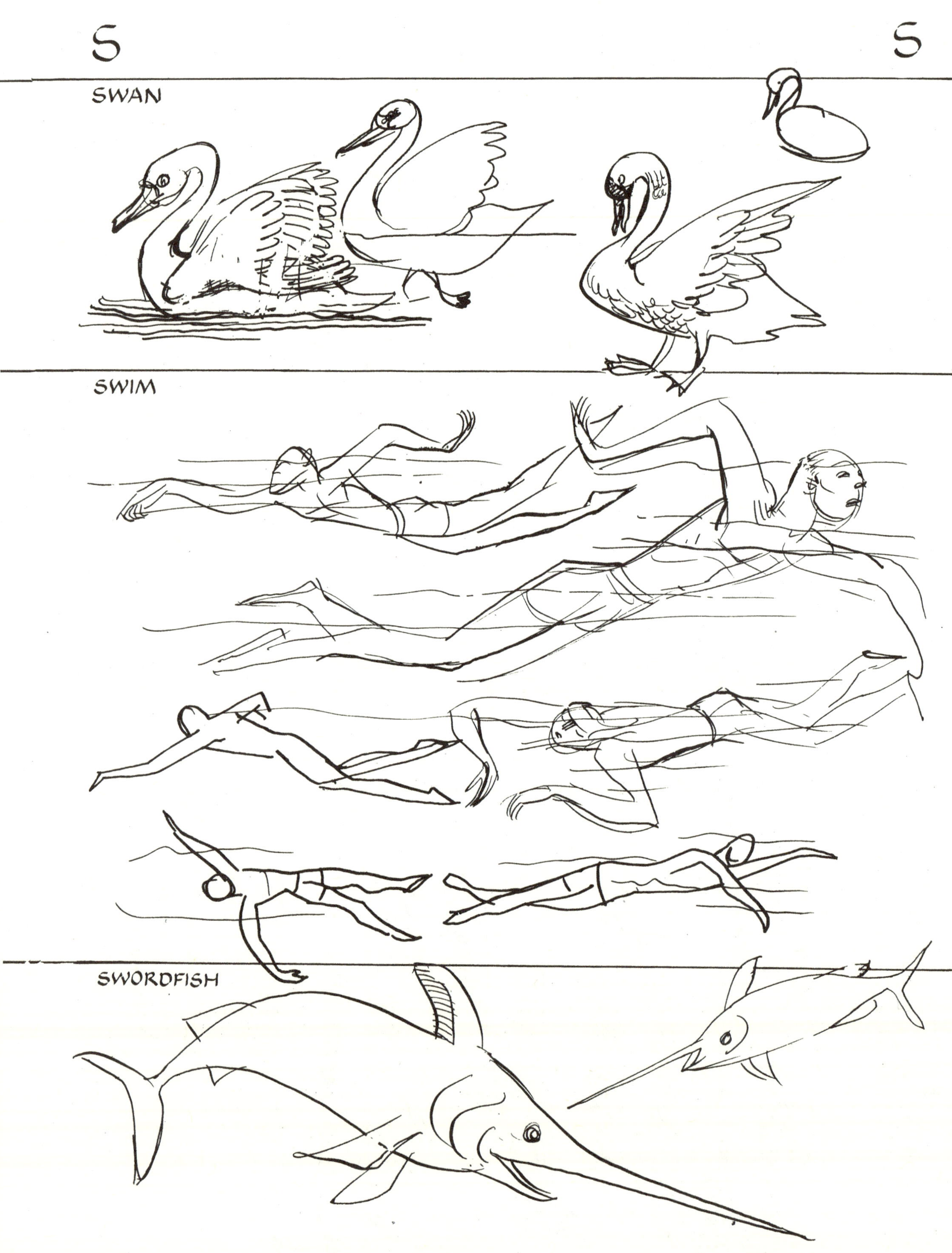
SWAN
SWIM
SWORDFISH

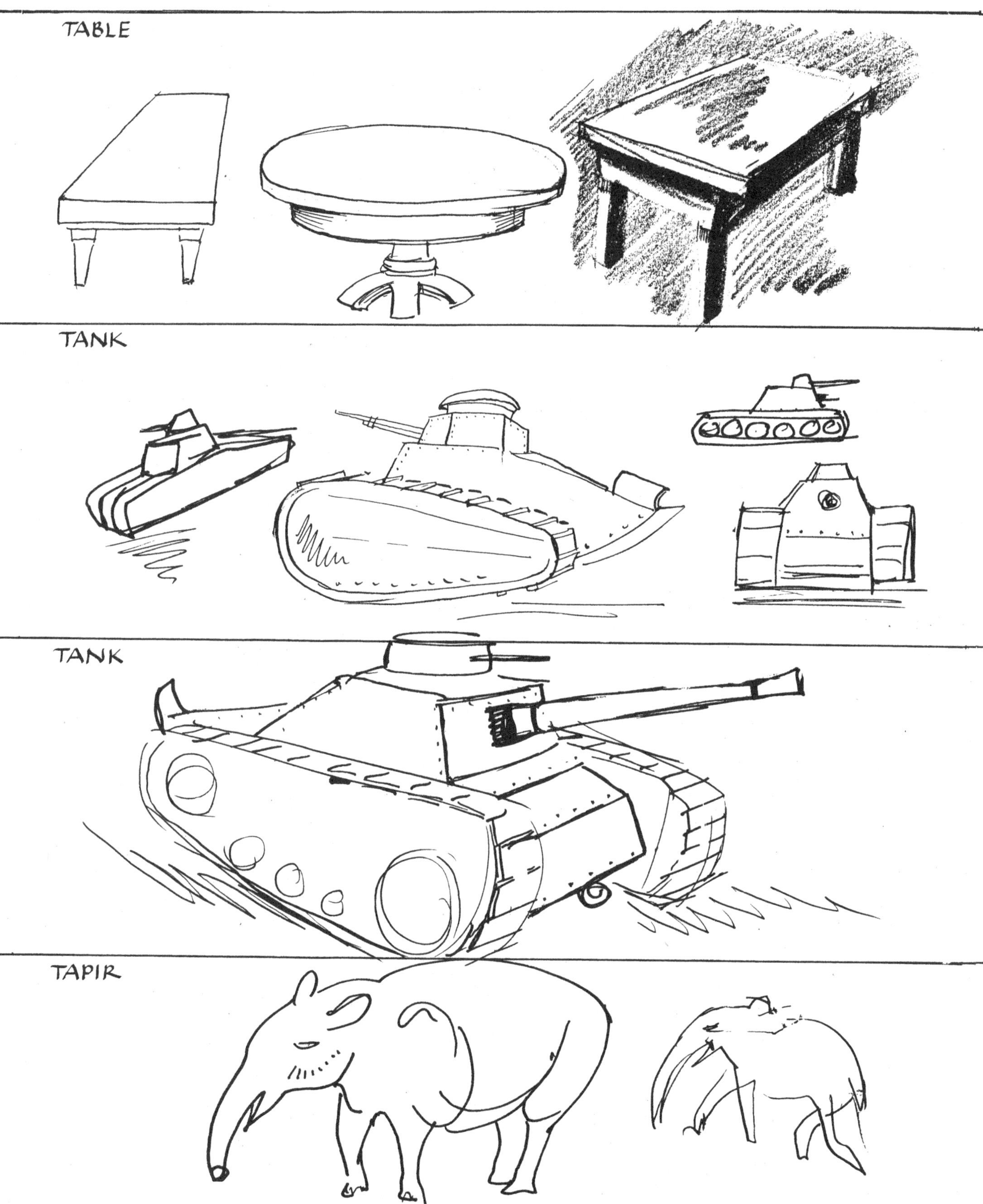
TABLE
TANK
TANK
TAPIR

TARPON

TEEPEE

TEETH

TELEPHONE

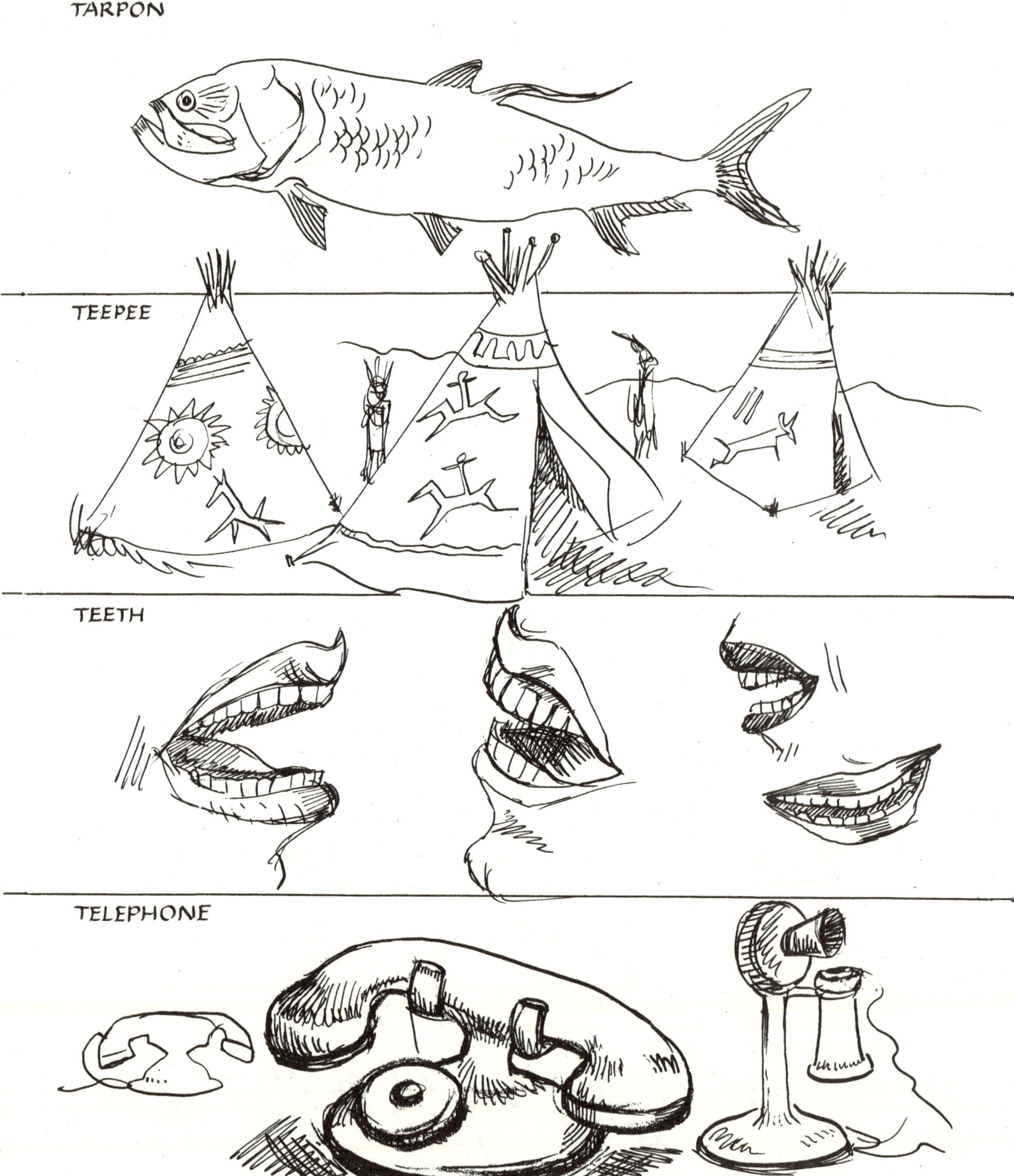

T

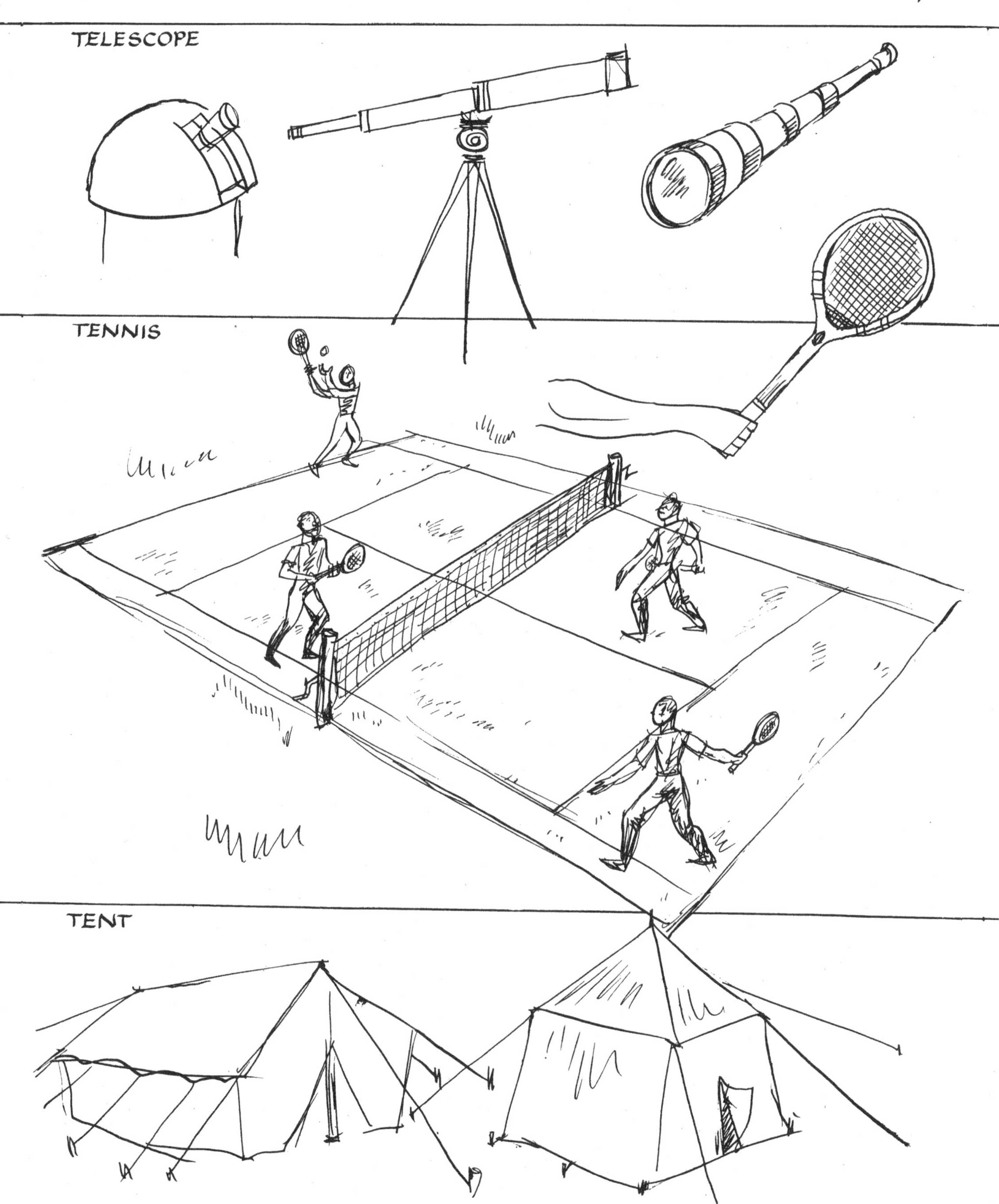

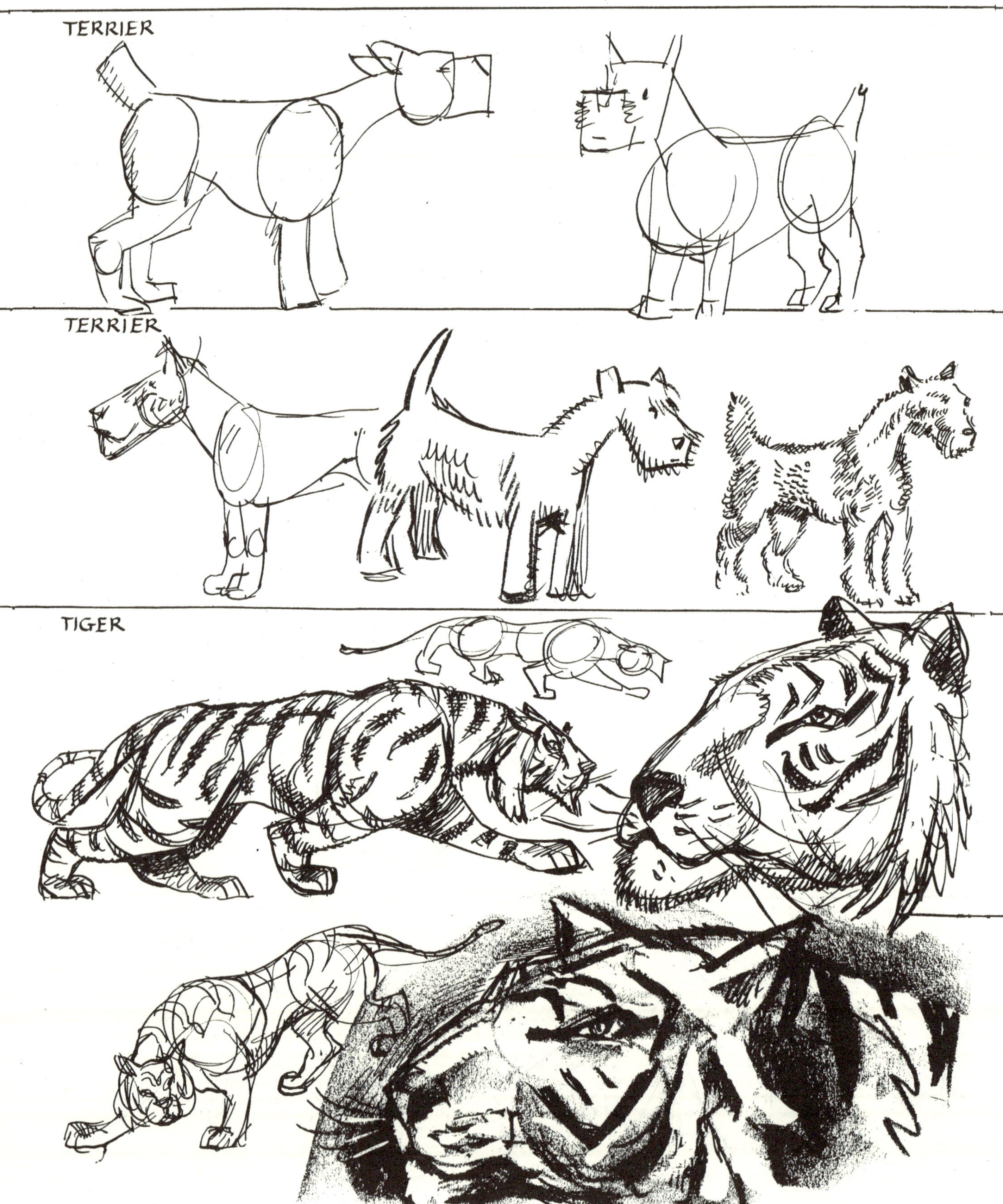
TERRIER
TERRIER
TIGER

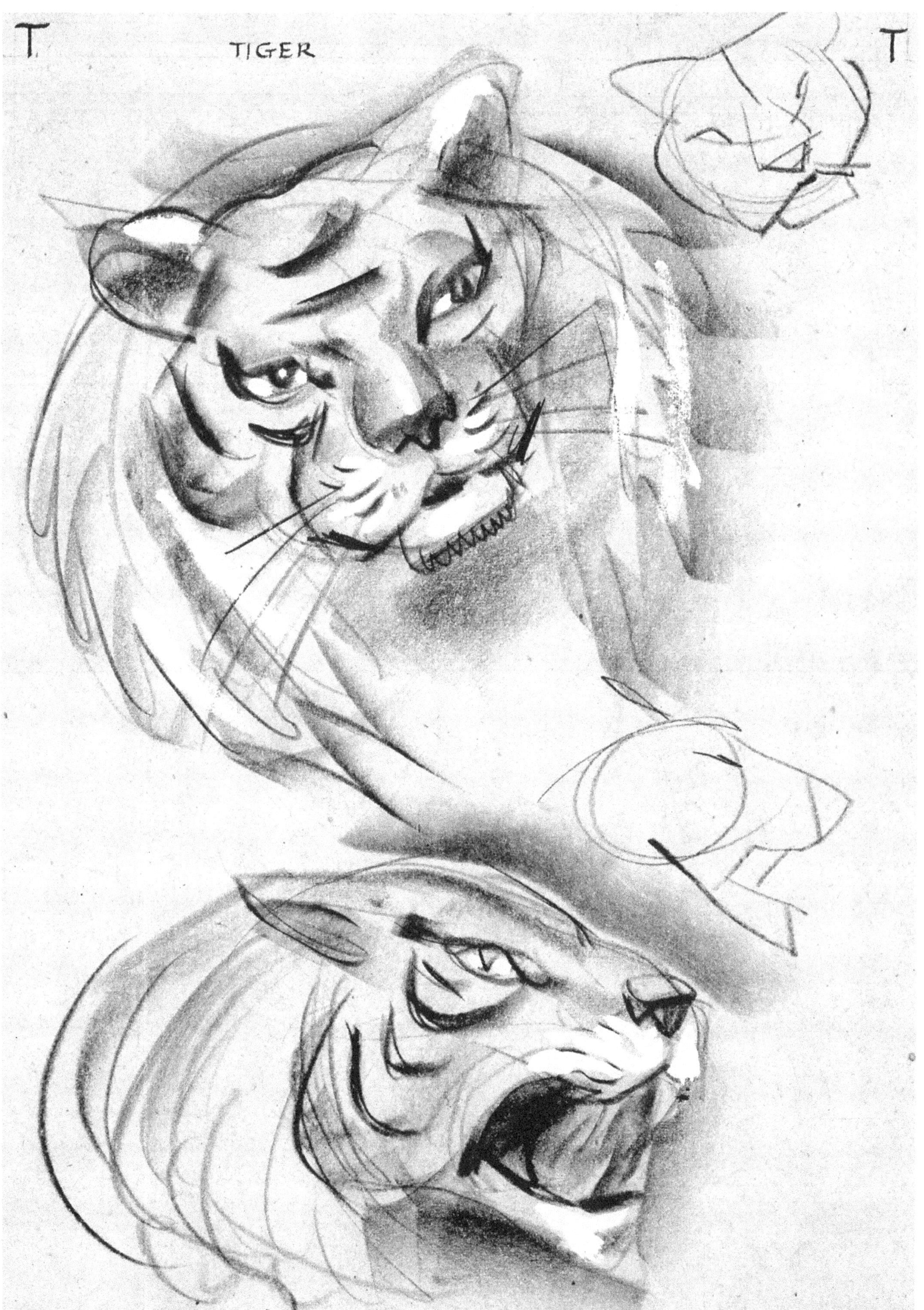
T
TIGER
T

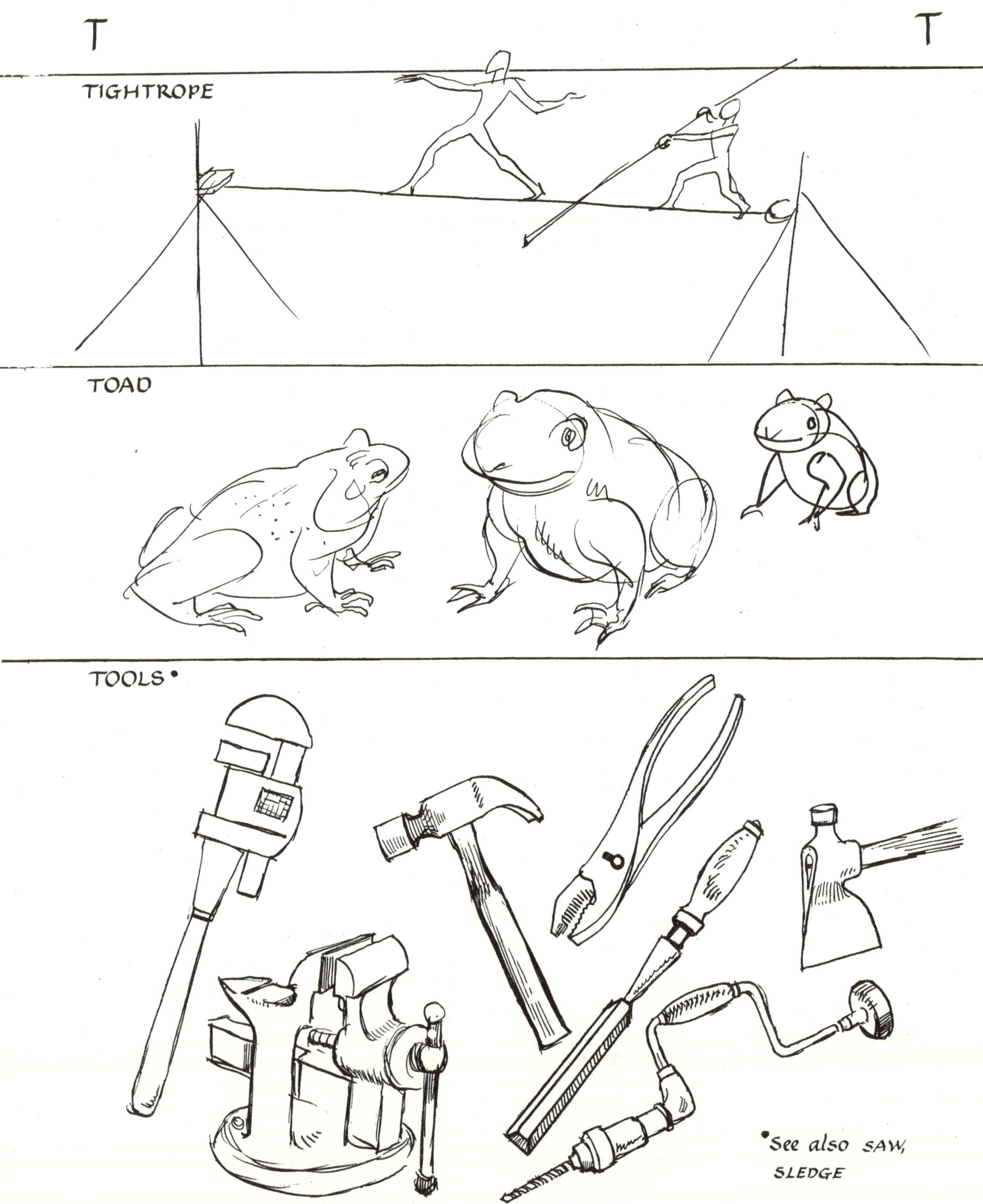
TIGHTROPE
TOAD
TOOLS•
•See also SAW, SLEDGE

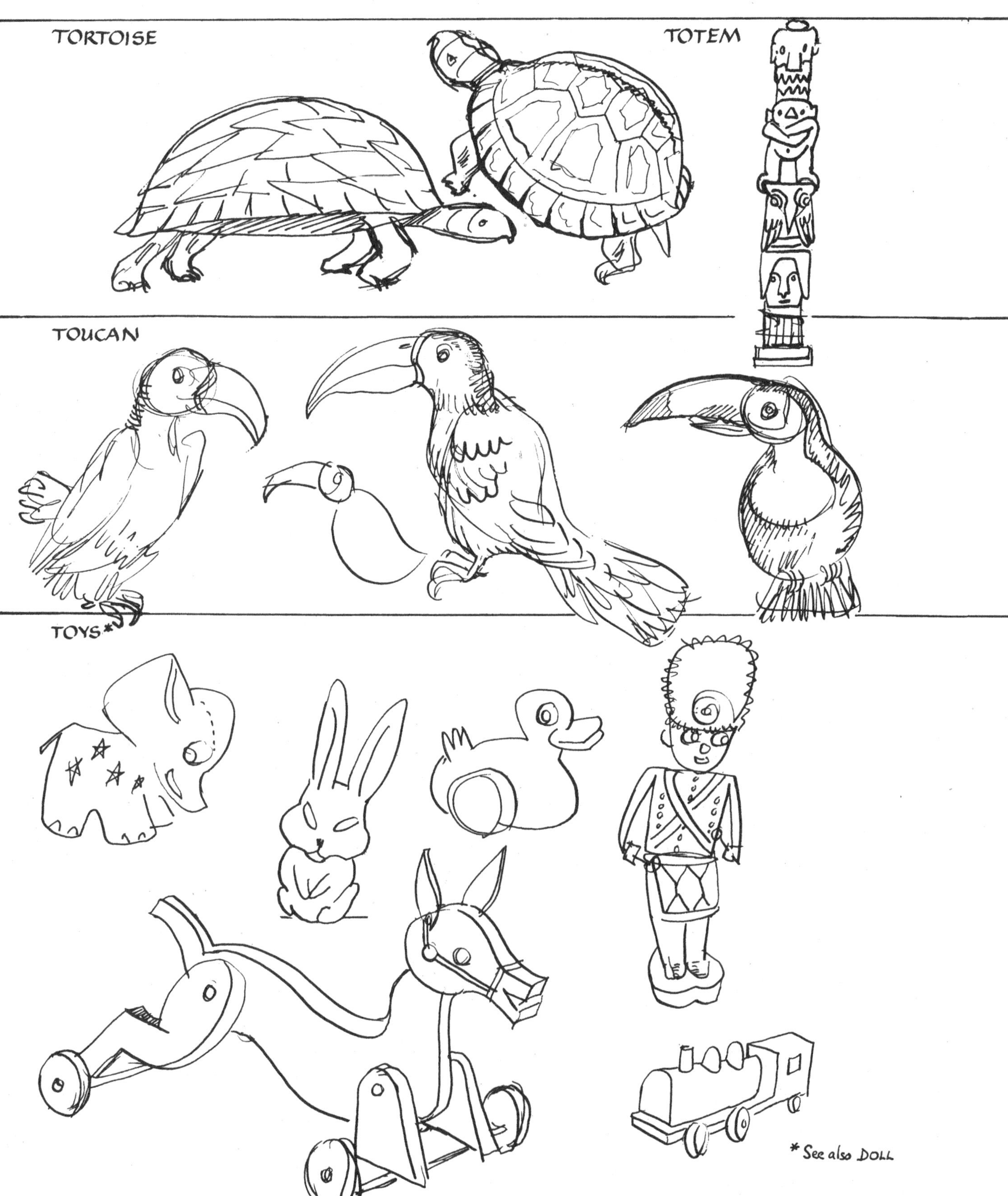
TORTOISE
TOTEM
TOUCAN
TOYS*
* See also DOLL

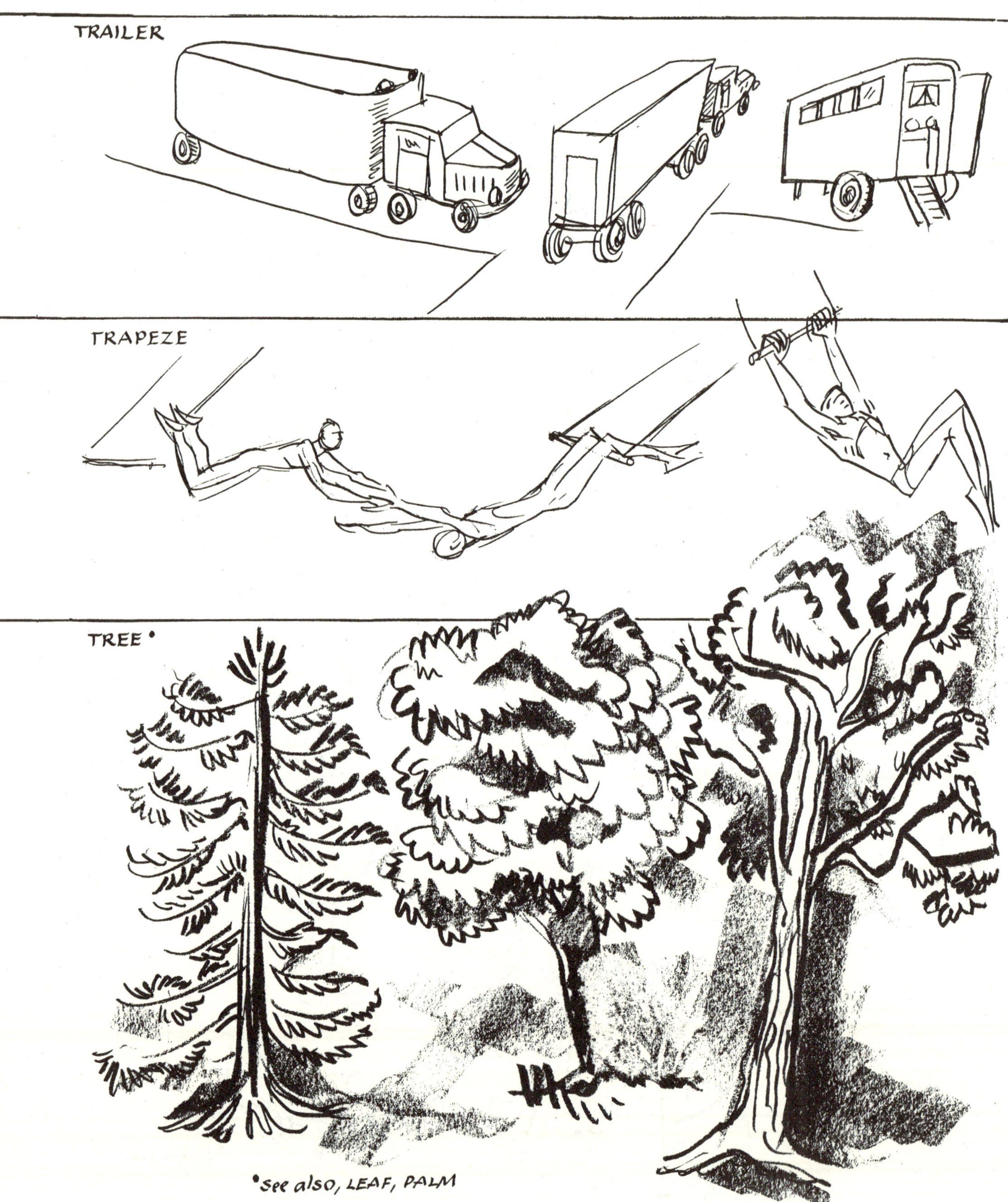
TRAILER
TRAPEZE
TREE*
*see also, LEAF, PALM

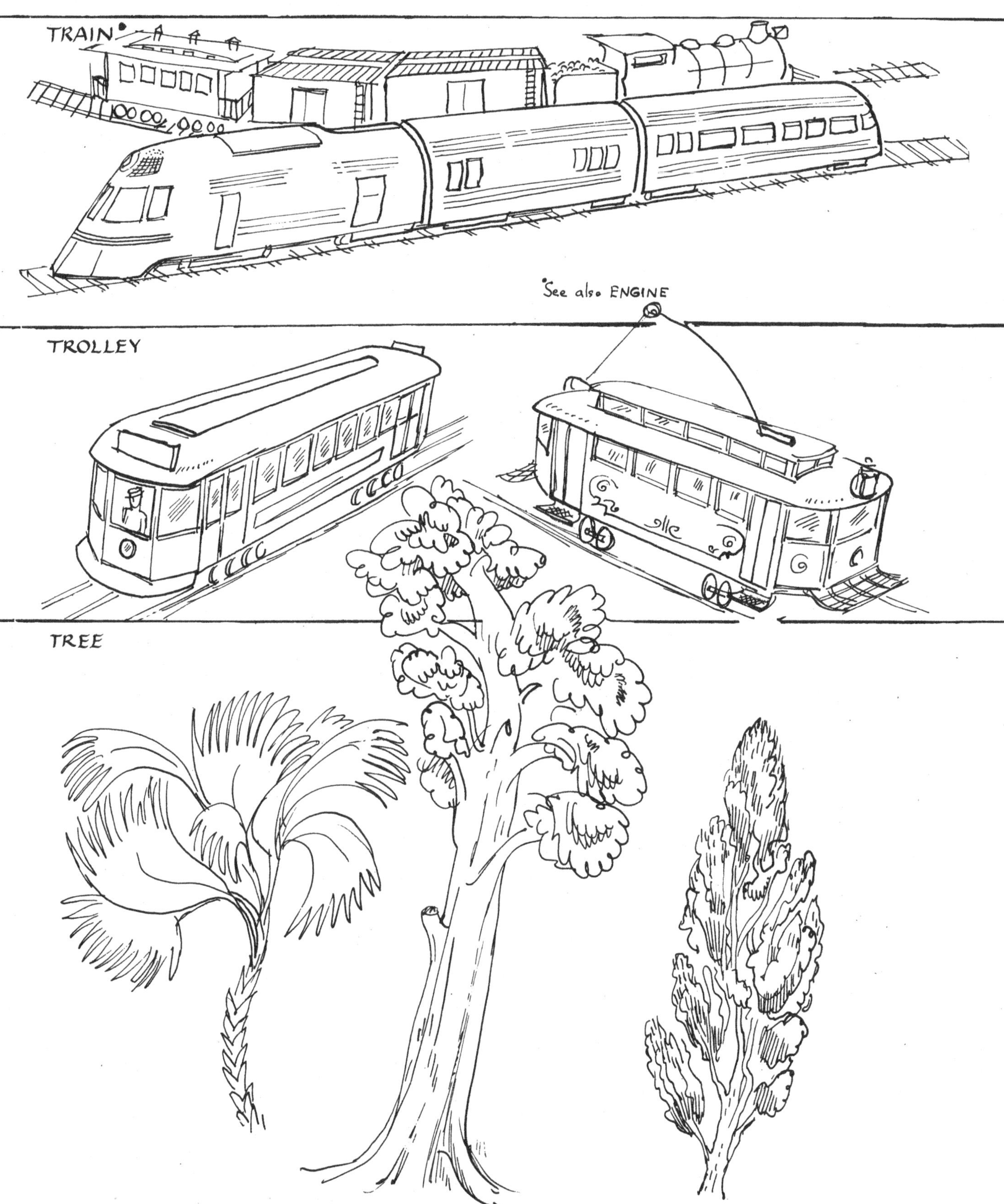
TRAIN*
*See also ENGINE
TROLLEY
TREE

TRICYCLE

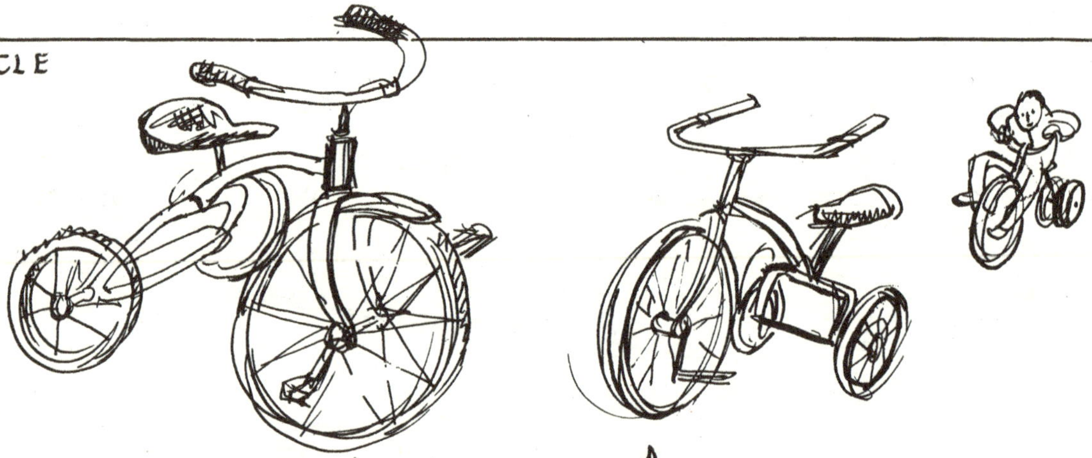

TROMBONE

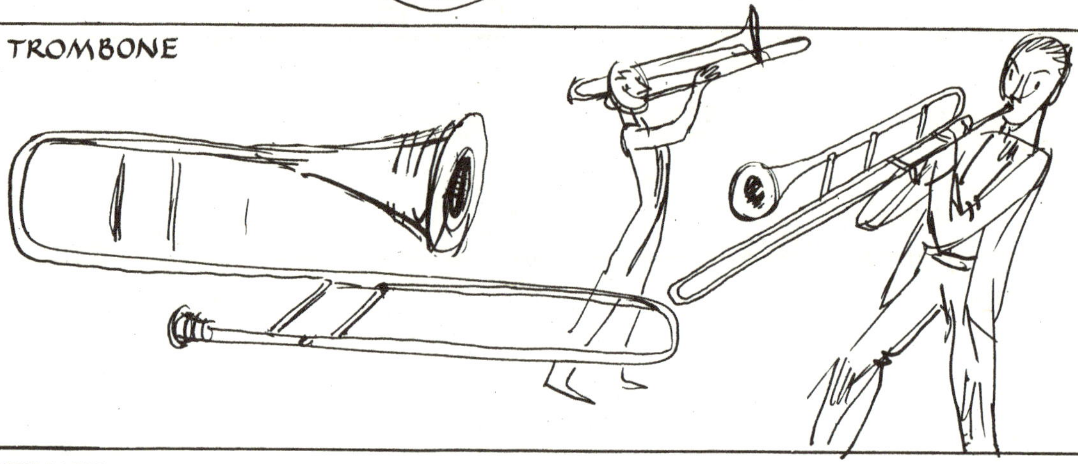

TRUCK

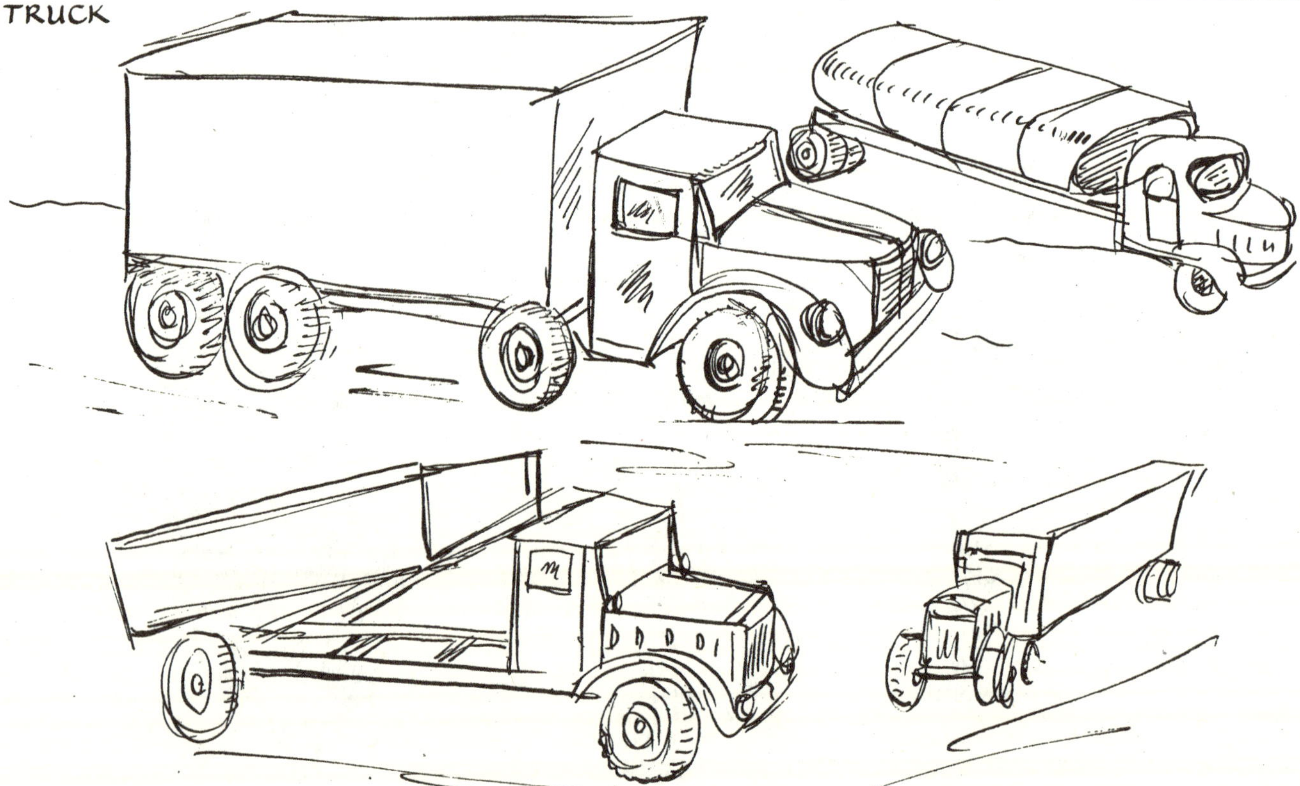

T T

TRUNK

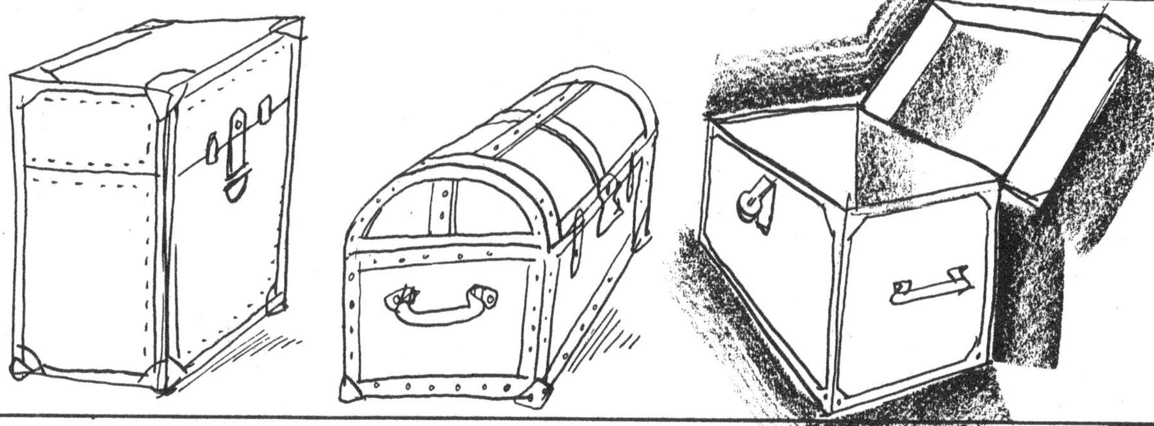

TURKEY

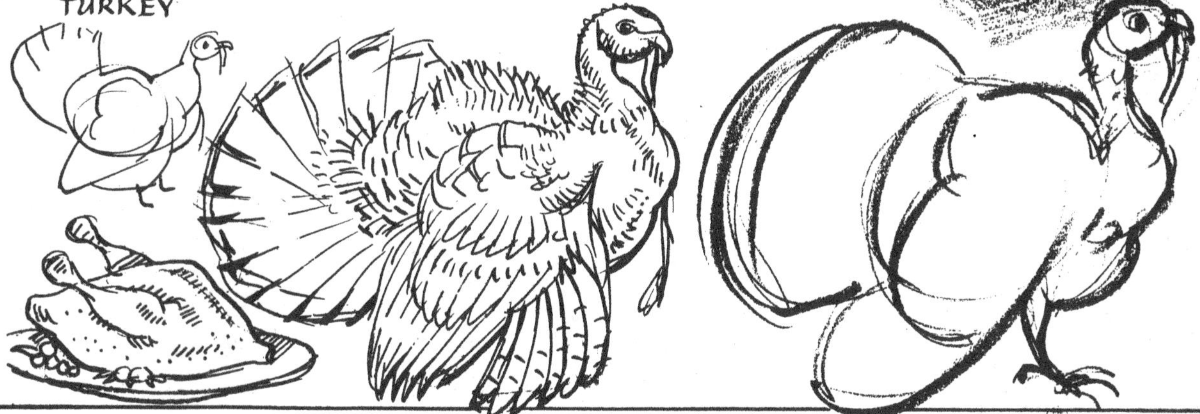

TURTLE

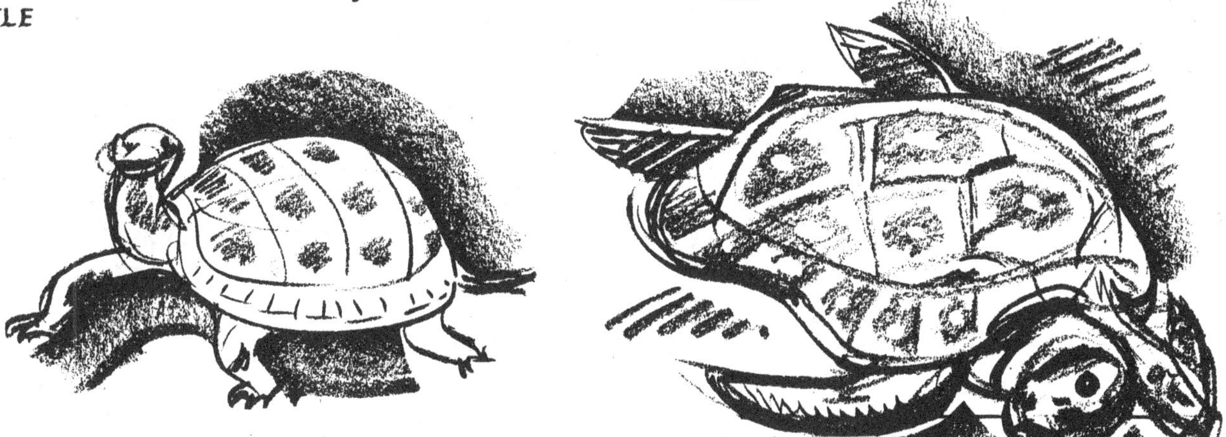

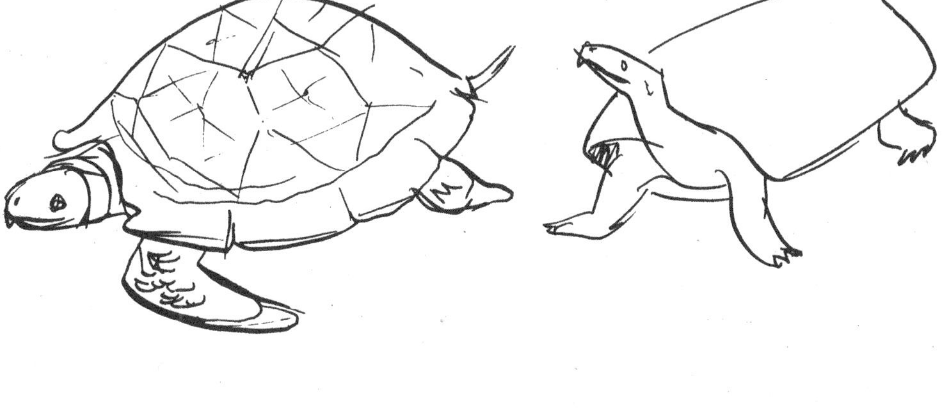

TYPEWRITER

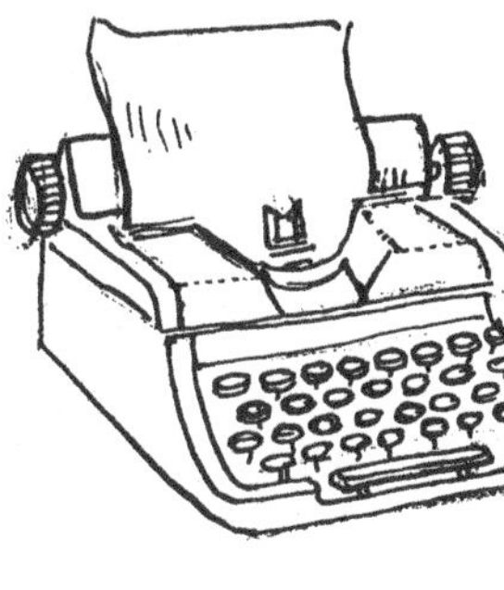

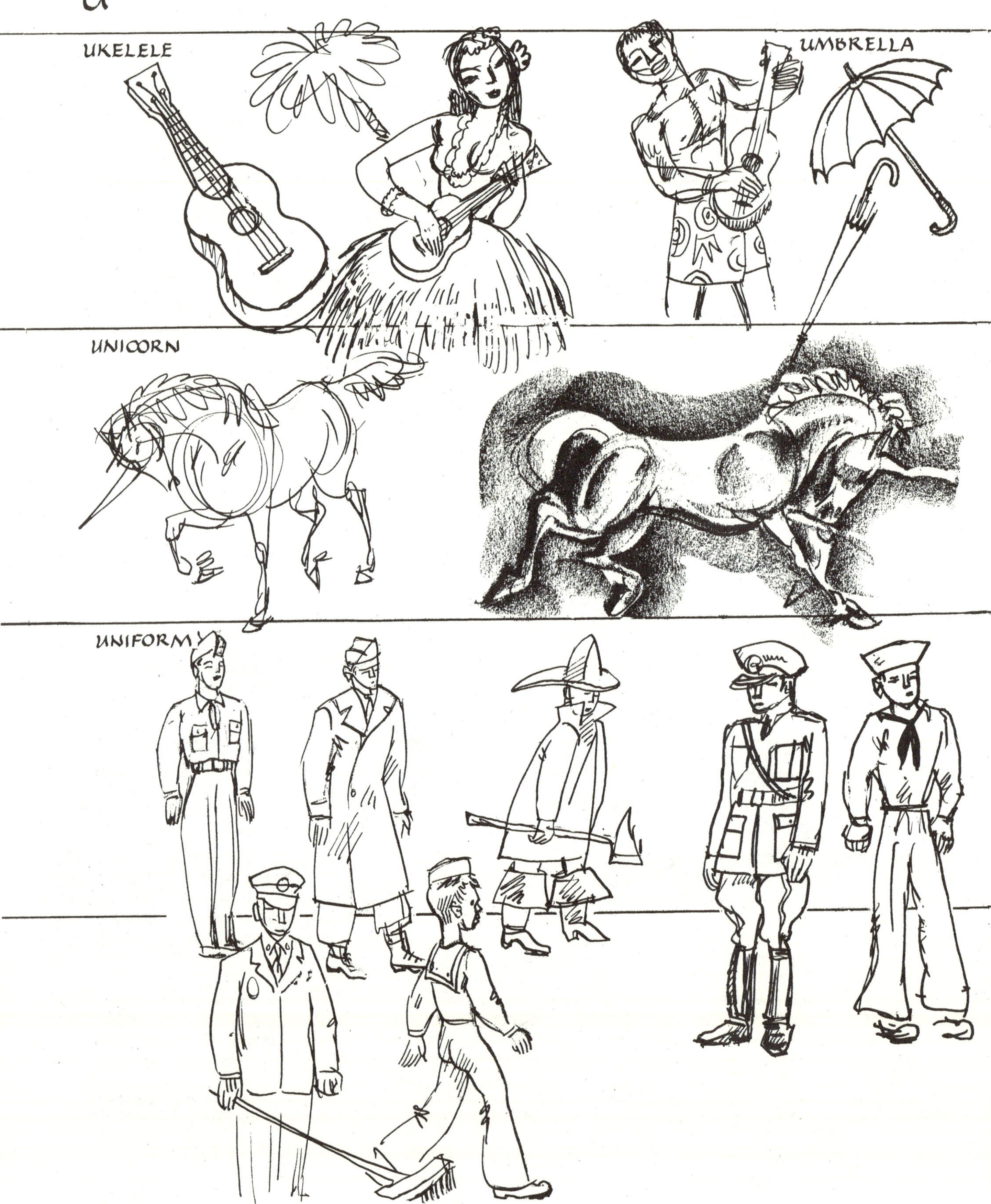
UKELELE
UMBRELLA
UNICORN
UNIFORM

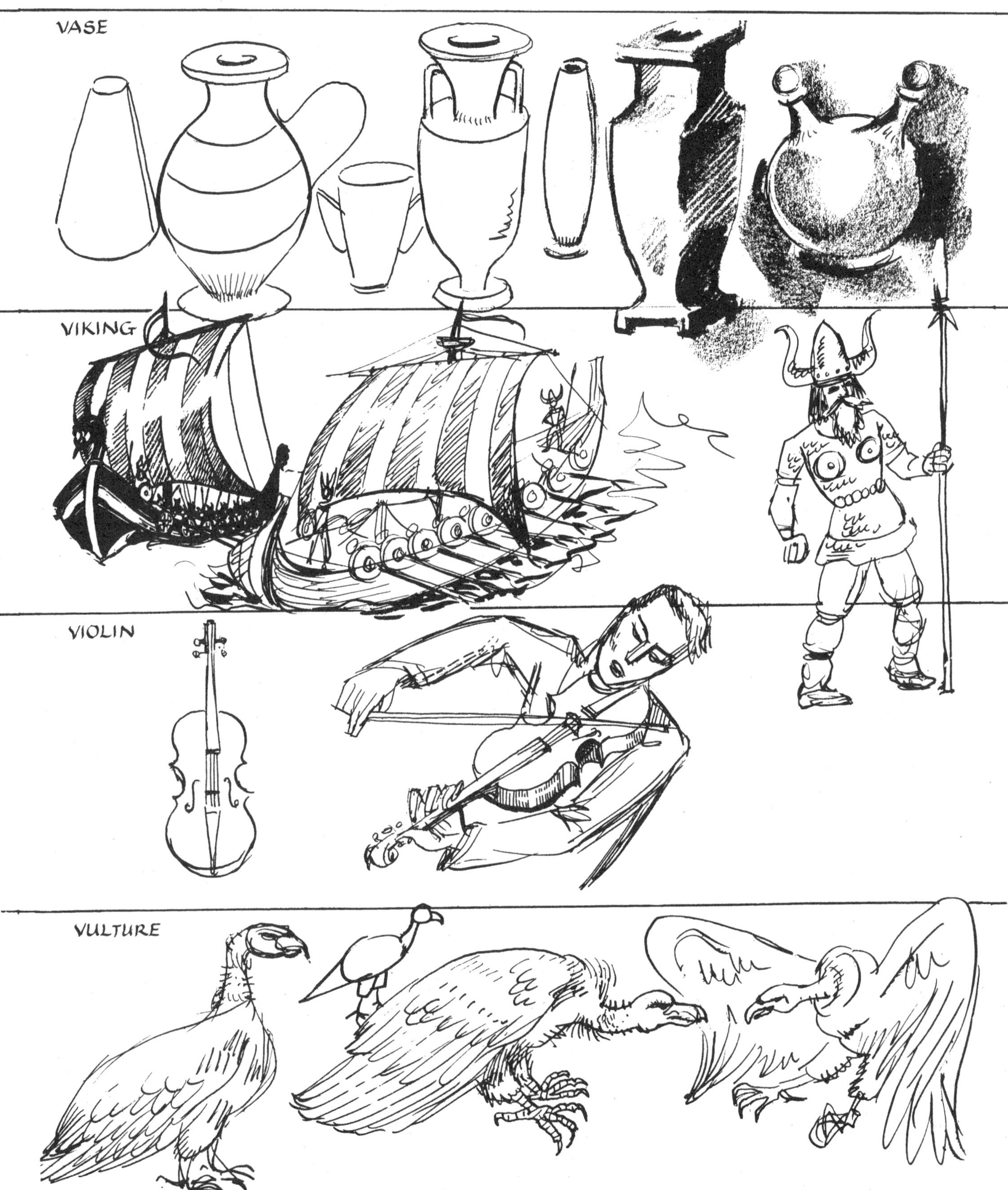
VASE
VIKING
VIOLIN
VULTURE

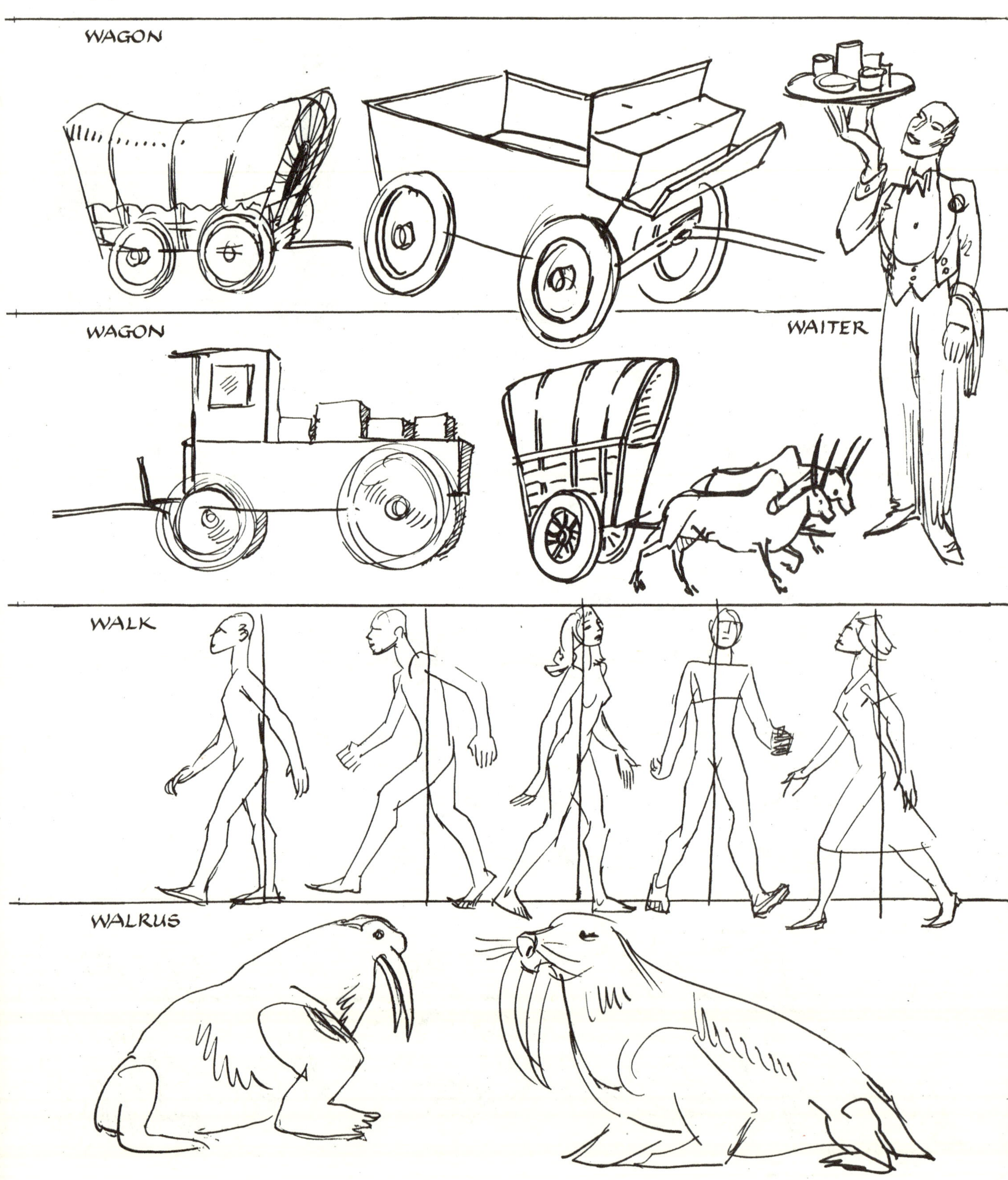
WAGON
WAGON
WAITER
WALK
WALRUS

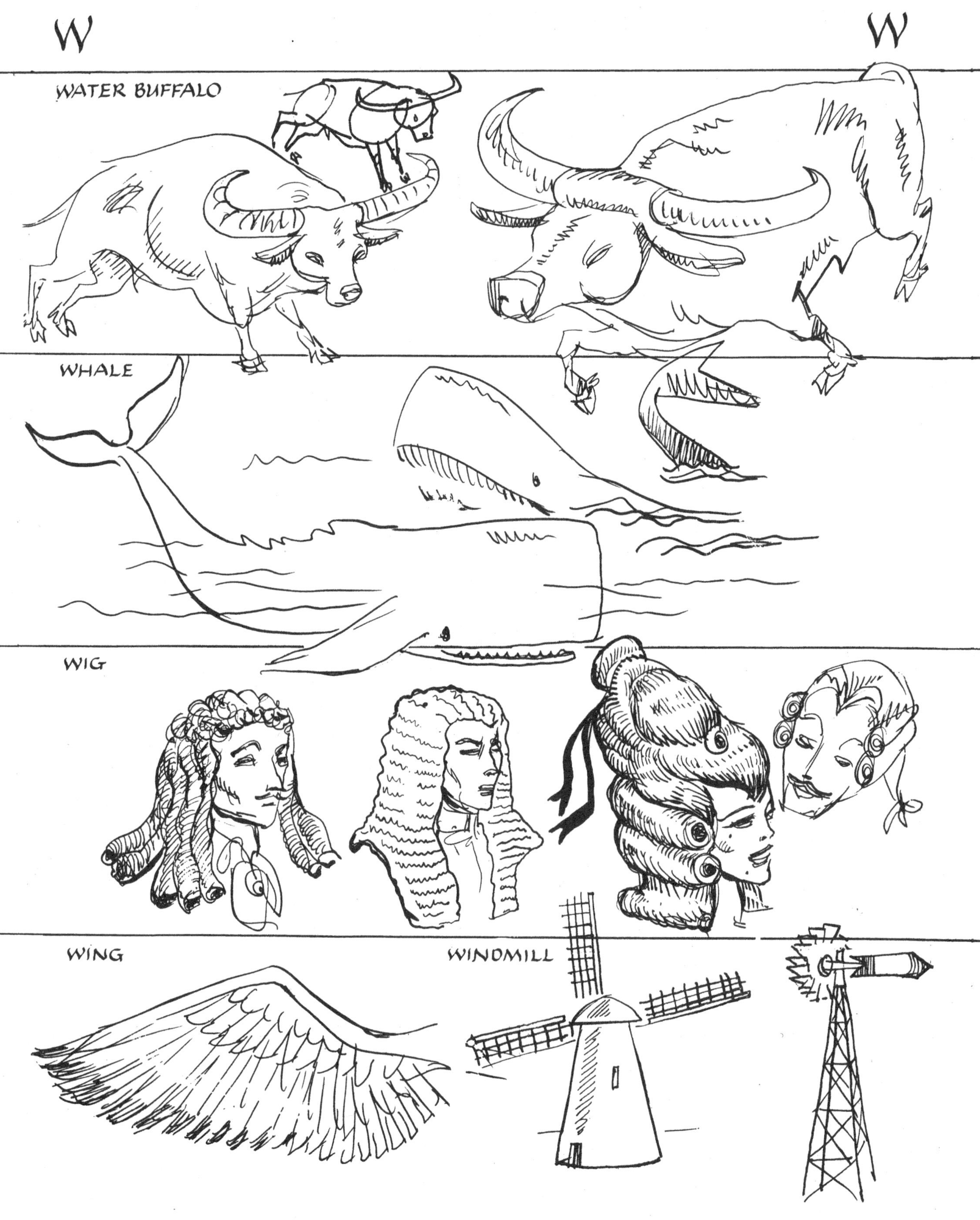
WATER BUFFALO
WHALE
WIG
WING
WINDMILL

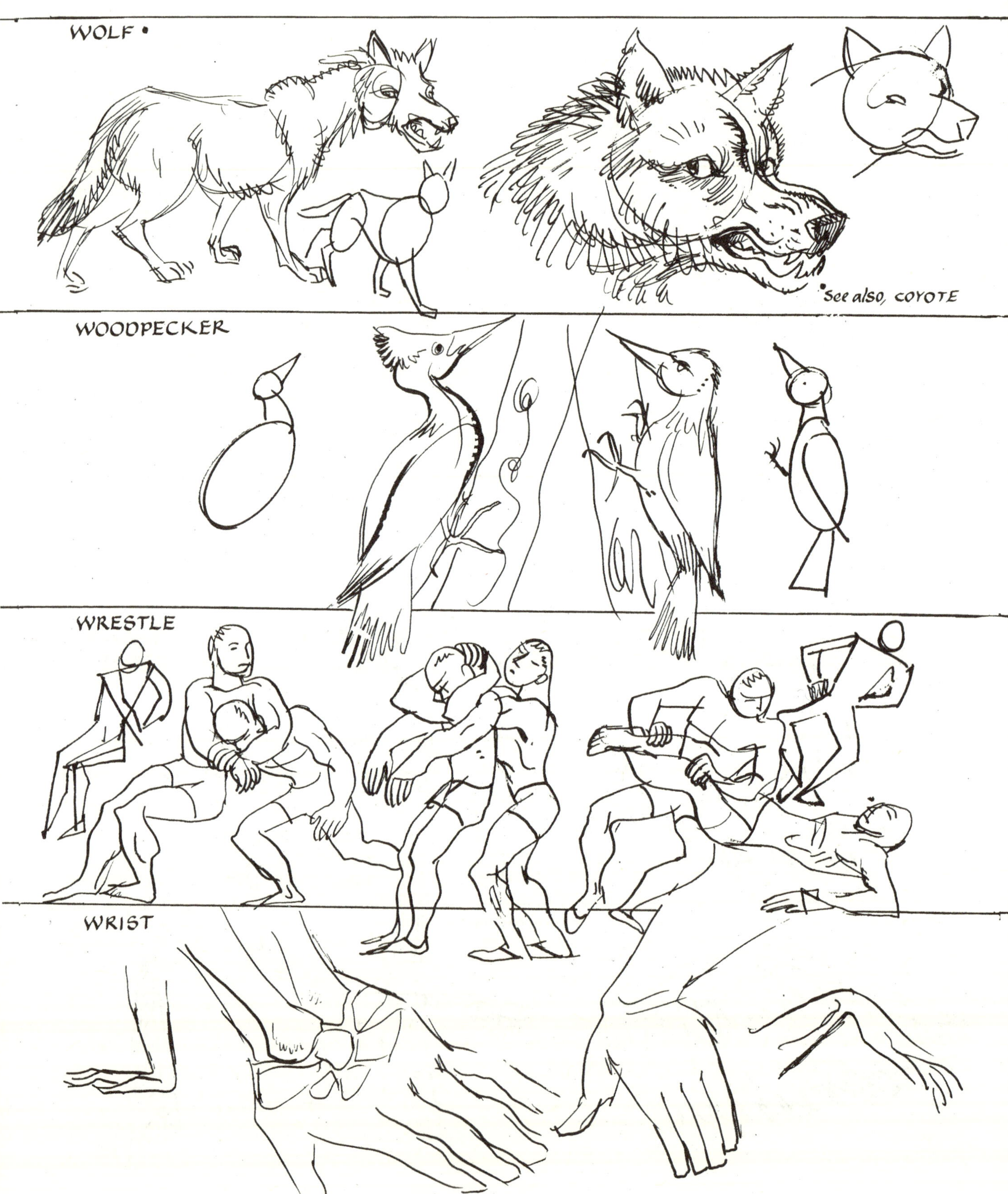
WOLF •
•See also, COYOTE
WOODPECKER
WRESTLE
WRIST

 Y-Z

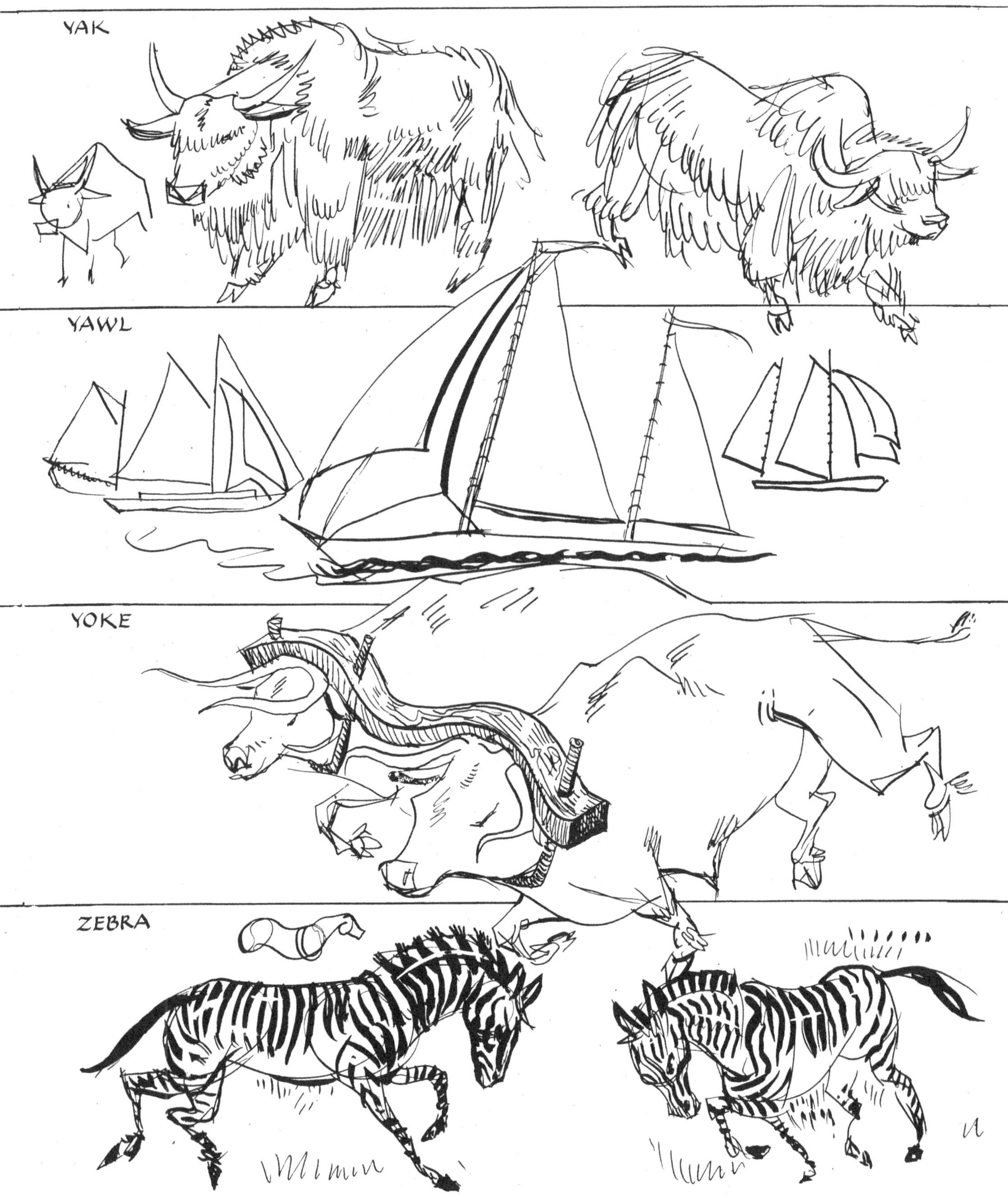

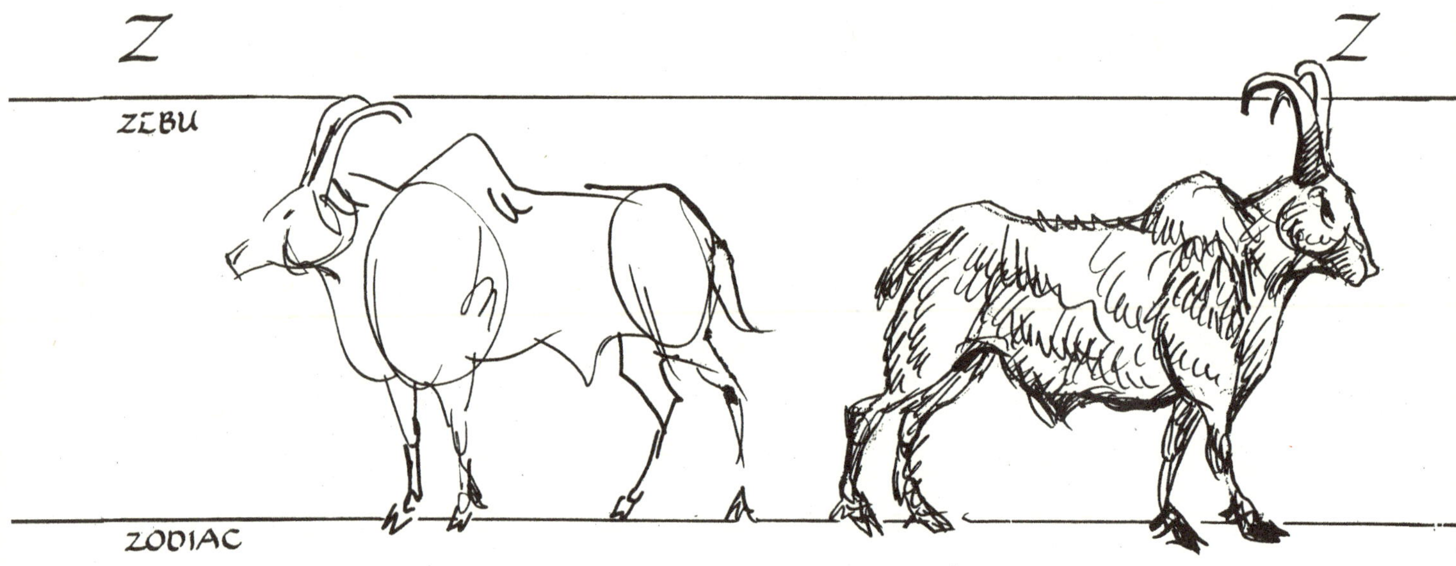
Z
Z
ZEBU
ZODIAC

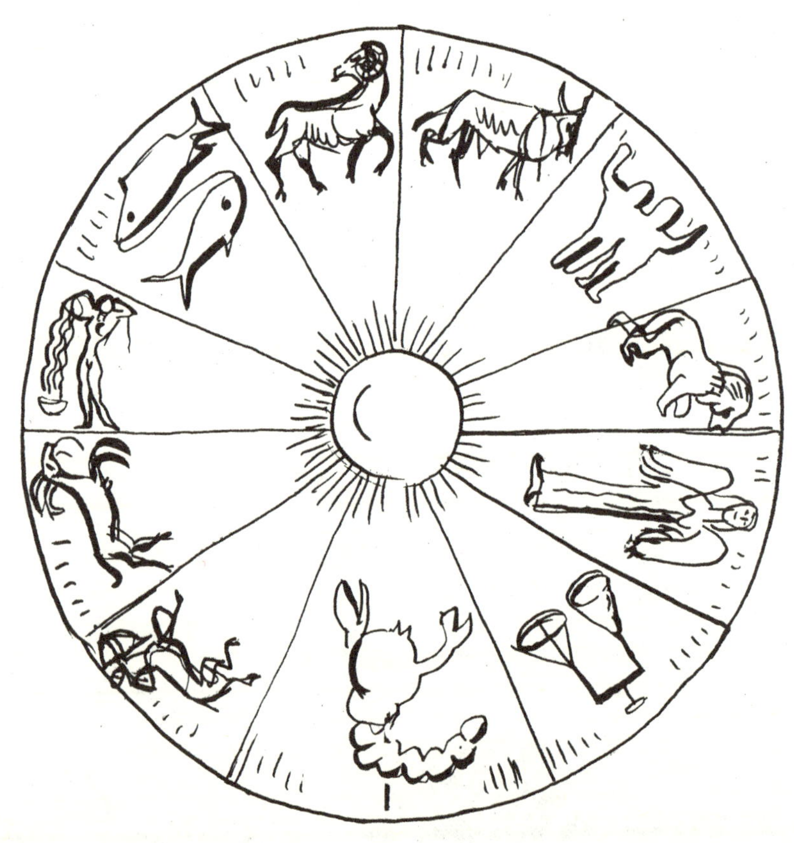